French Feminism in the Nineteenth Century

SUNY Series in European Social History
Leo A. Loubère, Editor

Cover photo courtesy of Bibl. Nat. Paris, *Elections de 1849, Suffrage des femmes* (artist unknown).

An abridged version of chapters 3 and 4 appeared in the *Journal of Modern History* 54 (June 1982) under the title "Saint Simonian Men/Saint-Simonian Women: The Transformation of Feminist Thought in 1830s' France."

Published by
State University of New York Press, Albany

For information, address State University of New York
Press, State University Plaza, Albany, N.Y., 12246

Library of Congress Cataloging in Publication Data

Moses, Claire Goldberg, 1941–
    French feminism in the nineteenth century.

    (SUNY series in European social history)
    Bibliography: p. 281
    1. Feminism—France—History—19th century.
I. Title. II. Title: French feminism in the 19th century.
III. Series: SUNY series on European social history.
HQ1615.M67   1984   305.4'2'0944   83–18040
ISBN 0–87395–859–4
ISBN 0–87395–860–8 (pbk.)

10   9   8   7   6   5   4   3   2   1

French Feminism
in the
Nineteenth Century

Claire Goldberg Moses

For Arnold, Lisa, and Leslie

Contents

Preface

This book is a study of the development of feminist thought in nineteenth-century France. Its focus is a body of ideas set into a social and political context, rather than a "pure" philosophical analysis. This approach derives from my belief that the questions feminists asked were based on their life experiences and that the remedies they proposed for their grievances were constructed with intellectual tools of analysis available to them in their time and place.

To place nineteenth-century French feminism in its historical context, I begin with a brief look at the pre-nineteenth-century history of the "woman question" in France, considering both the continued subordination of women and early feminist attempts to change that situation. The Revolutionary heritage was a particularly important influence on nineteenth-century feminism, both directly and indirectly. Nineteenth-century feminists were aware of the experience of earlier feminists and were inspired by their vision of emancipation; but nineteenth-century feminists' quite different ideology was also shaped by their knowledge of the violence of revolution and their fear of the Terror. While espousing Revolutionary egalitarian ideas, they conceptualized them in different ways and sought new methods to implement change, based on their concern for peace and social reconciliation.

The legacy of the French Revolution, briefly outlined in chapter 1, affected the evolution of feminism indirectly as well by shaping feminism's political context. Nineteenth-century French feminism existed in the shadow of repression. Governments, driven by their memory of the Revolution and the Terror, were slow to guarantee the right to free expression of new ideas. A continual shift from liberal to repressive to liberal to repressive government slowed the development of feminism; and it was often truly dangerous to espouse feminist views. Only as the Revolution receded into the more distant past and the fear of social unrest lessened somewhat was freedom of expression guaranteed by a secure and liberal republic, and only by the 1880s did feminism finally emerge from its start-and-stop cycles. This political context is crucial to our understanding of the distinctiveness of French feminism, particularly in contrast to American and English feminism.

In chapter 2, I examine the legal, social, and economic condition of nineteenth-century French women, a reality which also helps determine the nature of feminism of the time. Nineteenth-century French women were in some ways better off, in other ways worse off, than their eighteenth-century counterparts; however, their absolute level of well-being is less significant for understanding feminists' concerns than is the increasing divergence of women's lives from men's. Industrialism and urbanization were key factors here. Women increasingly worked—and sometimes even lived—in different settings from men. Sexual difference was enshrined in the new legal codes, which not only weakened women's position relative to men's but also, ironically, helped shape feminist consciousness by making unmistakably visible the significance of sex as a status category.

I have examined the lives of both bourgeois and working-class women who lived in urban centers. (Although the majority of nineteenth-century French women were still living in rural settings, feminism was an urban, indeed, primarily a Parisian, phenomenon.) I have focused especially on those aspects of their lives that were the main areas of feminist concern or that suggest the likelihood of feminist success or failure. Unfortunately, there exists no single, comprehensive scholarly study to simplify the task of presenting the general history of Parisian or urban French women. To describe the daily experience of working-class women, I used Suzanne Voilquin's autobiography *(Souvenirs d'une fille du peuple ou La Saint-simonienne en Egypte),* Pauline Roland's unpublished correspondence (housed at the Bibliothèque de l'Arsenal), and Julie Daubié's study of poor women *(La Femme pauvre au XIXe siècle),* along with numerous commission reports, considerable census data, and some studies by nineteenth-century moral reformers. I found it more difficult to reconstruct the lives of bourgeois women. Their "work" was not remunerated and, therefore, was not reported in census studies. Government officials were unconcerned about the condition of their work environment, and hence no commission reports were prepared to judge its quality. Moral reformers were satisfied with bourgeois women's behavior and habits and turned their attention and writings to more "dangerous" subjects. To draw the outline of the bourgeois woman's existence, I have combined statistics from official French sources with an overview of the values and laws that circumscribed her life options.

French feminists focused on that which was most new and therefore most unsettling for nineteenth-century women as well as on rights that had recently been granted to men but denied to women. Issues of sexuality were important, reflecting the impact of the demographic revolution. The birth rate declined earlier in France than in any other country: by the first decades of the 1800s family limitation was already widely practiced. The result was to split sexuality from reproduction and to transform the meaning of motherhood, which opened up a far-ranging debate on sexual behavior, family structure, and the nature of mothering. A kind of revolution—or evolution—in consciousness was under way in which feminists played a prominent role. Feminists were concerned, too, with winning political rights, civil rights, improved education (more important than ever to political and economic advancement), and access to jobs. The myth that had justified limiting these rights to an aristocratic caste had been destroyed by the Revolution; not surprisingly, feminists were now calling for a "Rights of Woman" to complete the Revolution.

Nineteenth-century French feminism reflected the increasing stratification of French society along class lines. Although feminists were both working class and bourgeois, the two groups did not always work together, their diverging class interests often leading them to set different priorities. The evolution of feminism over the century was influenced not only by the changing political or economic context but sometimes also by the changing class composition and interest of the movement's personnel.

Chapter 3 through 9 narrate the development of feminist thought and action in the nineteenth century. I have chosen to examine this history chronologically in order to clarify how the evolution in feminist ideology related to the changing political and economic context. Feminists chose carefully from among a variety of possible strategies and concerns to construct an ideology that appeared to offer the best chance for success in a given situation and at the same time to safeguard women's interests. Their decisions were shaped by events of a particular moment in history as well as by the success or failure of an earlier attack on the patriarchal fortress. Other scholarly histories of nineteenth-century French feminism have been limited to a shorter time period, discussing one or another moment of feminist action. By extending the scope of my study, I have been able to explain the logic of the progression of feminist thought and actions.

The first nineteenth-century feminists, Suzanne Voilquin, Reine Guindorf, Claire Démar, Pauline Roland, Prosper Enfantin, and Charles Fourier, among others, were utopian socialists. They called for a peaceful social transformation that would make possible, indeed inevitable, the full participation of women in the new world order.

This early alliance of feminists with utopian socialists foretold a pattern, which would be repeated throughout the century, of feminists linking with and emerging from Left groups committed to social transformation and/ or political equality. In the 1830s, most feminists were utopian socialists; in the 1840s, they were mainly republican socialists; in the second half of the century, they were likely to be liberal republicans or mutualist socialists. And always, they were connected to anticlericalism, which was a powerful political force unifying the Left during the concluding decades of the century. The evolution of nineteenth-century feminist thought will reflect the iedology of these allies; oftentimes, too, the fate of feminism will be linked to that of the Left.

Nineteenth-century French feminist began, then, with a utopian vision, and for sixty years they and the feminists who later continued their work— Frédéric Herbinot de Mauchamps, Flora Tristan, Jeanne Deroin, Désirée Gay, Juliette Adam, Jenny d'Héricourt, Léon Richer, Maria Deraismes, Hubertine Auclert, Léonie Rouzade, Eugénie Potonié-Pierre—sought to identify the best means to translate vision into reality. Their ideological explorations, their changing priorities, and the development of their program for action are the focus of this study.

Many of the sources for this study are published. The nineteenth-century French feminist movement was very literary: feminists published newspapers, wrote letters, kept diaries, wrote memoirs, and often published book-length statements. Most of this material is available on microfilm to American researchers. In recent years several significant nineteenth-century feminist works have been either reprinted or published for the first time. Lydia Elhadad has edited a new edition of Suzanne Voilquin's memoirs. Valentin Pelosse has published several texts written by Claire Démar, including her correspondence with other feminists. Michel Collinet has published Flora Tristan's diary, which she kept during her final speaking tour through France; prior to this publication, the diary was unavailable even to French researchers. (Jules Puech had found the original diary and made a typescript of it which Collinet—Puech's cousin—used for this 1973 publication. In 1980, Stéphane Michaud located and published the original manuscript.) Michaud has published a collection of Tristan's letters; the third edition of her *Union ouvrière* has also been reprinted. Most recently, Louise Michel's memoirs have appeared in an English translation.

Other materials, particularly personal correspondence, are unpublished and must be read in France. The Saint-Simonians were particularly zealous in their collecting of letters, and I spent several happy months reading hundreds of wonderful letters written by Saint-Simonian women. Their correspondence reveals their intellectual development and their reactions to their Saint-Simonian experience. The Bibliothèque Marguerite Durand has an excellent collection of source materials that are useful for the later decades.

I began this study of nineteenth-century French feminism more than ten years ago. Over the years, many people have facilitated this research and writing, reading my work at one or another stage or sharing their own work, often in its early, unpublished form. Their suggestions and encouragement have been invaluable. I would especially like to thank Roderic Davison, who guided me through the earliest stages of this research, Patrick Bidelman, Rachel Blau DuPlessis, Karen Graber, Sally Hall, Charles Herbert, Judith Jeffrey Howard, Caren Kaplan, Emmet Kennedy, Karen Offen, Phyllis Palmer, Elizabeth Phillips, Barbara Corrado Pope, Lois Schwoerer, Joan Scott, Theda Shapiro, Laura Strumingher, Alden Waitt, Judy Walkowitz, Sandy Weinbaum, and Elisabeth Weston. Part of the research for this book was funded by a grant from the General Research Board of the Graduate School, the University of Maryland. I am grateful for this assistance.

The research and writing of this book has been intertwined always with my own experience as a feminist. I believe that my ongoing analysis of feminist thought in the present has illuminated for me the slow process by which feminist thought unfolded in the past. I identify with the nineteenth-century French feminists and have drawn inspiration from their search for understanding.

CHAPTER 1

The Legacy of the Past:
Patriarchy and Resistance

Throughout the nineteenth century, the majority of French men and women accepted the centuries-old patriarchal system that regulated sexual roles and rights. This system, with roots extending into the distant past, had survived centuries of social, economic, and religious change. The seemingly constant nature of the subjugation of the female sex was the most powerful argument that nineteenth-century patriarchalists could muster in its defense.

Nineteenth-century feminists, however, believed that the unchanging patriarchal system was simply background to a drama rich with historical change. They were inspired by their belief that civilization had progressed to a point where further change would transform the patriarchal system itself. They were strengthened by their awareness that the challenge to patriarchy was not their invention. Feminism had a prior history, much of which was familiar to nineteenth-century French feminists and shaped their efforts to fashion an ideology suitable to the particular needs of their time and place. The dual legacy of patriarchy and resistance sets the stage for the development of nineteenth-century French feminism.

The Roots of Patriarchy

Historically, French social patterns are a fusion of three main traditions: the Greco-Latin, the Judaic, and the Germanic. Patriarchal family life is common to all three traditions.[1] The major characteristics of the patriarchal family in Western cultures are the insistence on legitimacy, since descent

1

is through the male line and paternity must be certain; the requirement that the wife be economically dependent on the male head of the family; and the exclusion of women from civil or political participation. Adultery— if committed by the wife—was seen as a threat to the male-centered social structure, as evidenced by harsh punishments meted out for female adultery: in Judaic society the adulterous wife was stoned; in Greek society she was forced to dress in such a manner that others would not fail to recognize her transgression; and in the old Germanic tribes, the adulterous wife was either put to death or mutilated.[2]

In traditional patriarchal societies, women were prohibited from either ownership or disposition of property.[3] Moreover, women were generally considered legal nonpersons, or, as stated in Roman law, *infirmus imbecillus sexus*. In Greece they had no more public rights than slaves, minors, or foreigners. Although they were permitted to defend themselves in court and serve as witnesses in trials, in Rome these rights were withdrawn by Justinian. In Jewish law, this deprivation of civic rights extended to the majority of religious observances, from which women were also excluded.

The Christian social revolution did not alter the ancient patterns of patriarchy. In church, women were forbidden to preach and were ordered to keep silent.[4] In their homes, they were instructed to obey their husbands: "Wives, submit yourselves unto your own husbands, as unto the Lord. For the husband is the head of the wife, even as Christ is the head of the church."[5] While there was "neither Jew nor Greek," neither "bond nor free," neither "male nor female" in the Kingdom of God,[6] "man was the image and glory of God! [Woman, however, was] the glory of man. For the man is not of the woman: but the woman of the man. Neither was the man created for the woman; but woman for the man."[7]

During the Middle Ages, the position of woman was somewhat ambiguous as a result of the confusion of sovereignty with personal property (the fief). When in control of a fief, women could—and often did— exercise power by administering justice, signing treaties, and decreeing laws. Women sometimes even played a military role, Joan of Arc being a notable example.[8] In some European countries, women ruled as queens, with the kingdom still viewed as a patrimony. In France, however, and also within the Holy Roman Empire, the Salic Law prohibited women or descendants through the female line from ruling. Nevertheless, some upper-class women wielded considerable political power as regents, abbesses of convents with extensive lands,[9] or through their personal influence over ruling males. And the cult of the Virgin Mary, with its secular parallel, the chivalric idealization of women, likely affected the position of ruling-class women in a positive way.[10] Most women, though, remained restricted to their homes and dependent upon their fathers, who either sent them into convents or put them under the control of other males, their husbands.

Historians have generally assumed that the more enlightened image of womanhood in the Renaissance signifies the beginning of a period of improving conditions for women, at least of the upper class.[11] Such was not the case, however.[12] Among the peasantry, to be sure, inequalities based on sex were less important: a blanket of poverty spread itself equally over both men and women, and a lack of property made the idea of protection of the patrimony meaningless. But from the time of the Renaissance, among the aristrocracy and the emerging middle class (both of whom had political and economic rights to preserve), inequality weighed heavily on women.

First, by defining sovereignty in public rather than personal terms, the codification of laws during the fifteenth, sixteenth, and seventeenth centuries increasingly excluded women from power. With the simultaneous growth of the modern bureaucratic state and the capitalist economy came the need for well-trained secular personnel. Education came to be highly valued, and the centuries-old exclusion of women from the universities took on a new, more powerful significance.[13] Family life was similarly undergoing a transformation, which further widened the gulf between boys and girls and men and women of the nobility and *haute bourgeoisie*. An increased number of years was deemed necessary to prepare boys for the expanded responsibilities of male adulthood. The same, however, was not true of girls.[14]

This new emphasis on "boyhood"[15] contributed to a new domestic role for adult women. Again, this role was limited to the more well-to-do. Among the popular classes, according to Olwen Hufton, the "married woman . . . was not in any modern sense a homemaker. Cleaning, washing . . . cooking and childrearing were fairly marginal aspects of her existence in the demands they made upon her time."[16] But among the upper classes, especially in the cities, the chasm separating female from male roles widened, with female accomplishments being subordinated to the needs of preparing the next generation of the male elite.

That changing definitions of manhood and womanhood were straining the relationship between the sexes is evident in the outpouring of writings over the fifteenth, sixteenth, and seventeenth centuries that were collectively labeled "la querelle des femmes." These were usually constructed as pro or con positions, defenses of or attacks upon the moral worth of women. Some of women's defenders also asked for increased opportunities for women to participate in some of the new activities, particularly the intellectual activities, that were engaging Renaissance men.

During the seventeenth century, the writings on the woman question focused especially on women's visible role in the new salons that had proliferated in Paris and some of the other major cities of France. The salons were one institution that seemed to bridge the gap increasingly separating the lives of upper-class men and women. According to historian Carolyn Lougee, "The distinguishing feature of the salons, which set them apart from other cultural institutions such as the all-male literary circles and the society of the cabarets and coffee houses, was the dominance of women in them. Salons were always run by a woman." Because of their dominant role in the institution that became responsible for integrating the new nobility with the old, some women, Lougee contends, achieved a new and higher level of social influence and political power.[17] Evelyn Bodek notes that during the eighteenth century, when salons "served as newspaper, journal, literary society, and university" for the intelligentsia, they became an ingenious way for women to obtain learning at a time when higher education was denied to them.[18]

Yet, the salonière learned to provide a comfortable environment in which others, not she, would display their talents. She was the *chef d'orchestre*, perhaps, but never the star of the show. Further, she was isolated by competitiveness from other salonières and thus lacking the encouragement which bluestockings across the channel received from their close-knit *female* circles; here the salonière feared to step out from the background. As Bodek explains, "She wrote, but rarely for [publication] . . . ; she spoke, but carefully modulated her voice; she questioned, but hardly ever pursued the unquestionable." [19]

In spite of the limitations of the power of the salonière, Jean-Jacques Rousseau thought her a threat to the "natural" dominance of men. Rousseau saw salons as "prisons" that subjugated men to the rule of women. He preferred the sexual segregation of Genevan social life, where men were "exempted from having to lower their ideas to the range of women." [20] During the seventeenth century, those who had opposed an increased public role for women were the same individuals who had objected to enlarging the ruling elite.[21] A century later, however, Rousseau coupled his attack on women's public role with arguments favoring democracy among men. The consequence was a theoretical widening of the chasm separating the sexes.

One is struck by the juxtaposition of new and old elements in Rousseau's writings about women. Unlike writers of the earlier *querelle des femmes*, Rousseau was depiciting a middle-class rather than an upper-class existence, specifically, a middle-class life that was unknown in earlier centuries when workplace and home had overlapped. He glorified the separation of private and public spheres and exalted bourgeois women's newly time-consuming maternal preoccupations as well as their role as men's companions. Women were indispensable to men's happiness and, in recognition, Rousseau's men loved and respected them. Women's innate aptitude for love and selfless devotion thus assured them dignity, respect, and happiness. In some ways, Rousseau reads more like women's defenders in the earlier *querelle des femmes* than their detractors.

But Rousseau's appreciation of women's familial role was central to arguments that actually strengthened older patriarchal values by reformulating them in terms that were relevant to eighteenth-century society. Women's maternal responsibilities now required their exclusion from the civil, political, and economic activities that Rousseau championed for all men and even demanded their exclusion from the intellectual activities that several centuries of practice had seemingly legitimated:

> What makes you think more highly of [a woman] . . . —to see her busy with feminine occupations, with her household duties, with her children's clothes about her, or to find her writing verses at her dressing table surrounded with pamphlets of every kind . . . ?
> The genuine mother of a family is no woman of the world; she is almost as much of a recluse as the nun in her convent.[22]

The ancient fear of uncertain paternity now threatened property rights: "[Pity] the poor father who, when he clasps his child to his breast, is haunted by the suspicion that this is the child of another, the badge of his dishonor, a thief who is robbing his own children of their inheritance." Therefore, adultery—if committed by the wife—threatened the entire bourgeois social structure:

> No doubt every breach of faith is wrong and every faithless husband, who robs his wife of the sole reward of the stern duties of her sex, is cruel and unjust; but the faithless wife is worse; she destroys the family and breaks the bonds of nature; when she gives her husband children who are not his own, she is false both to him and them; her crime is not infidelity but treason. To my mind, it is the source of dissension and of crime of every kind.

However appreciative, even respectful of his ideal woman—Julie, for example—Rousseau nonetheless reaffirmed the inequality of the sexes and men's dominion over women: "Woman is made . . . to be in subjection to a man. . . . [A] man should be strong and active; [a] woman should be weak and passive; the one must have both the power and the will; it is enough that the other should offer little resistance." [23]

That France was severed into two ideological camps by the French Revolution, a Right and a Left, is hardly true in the case of the ideology of womanhood. [24] In 1793, the republican Left, inspired by Rousseauist ideas, blamed the public role of women for the current internal disorders and recommended the closing of all political clubs that had female members. A report of the Committee of General Security posed the question, "Should women meet in political associations?" and responded: "No, because they would be required to sacrifice to them [the associations] the more important cares to which Nature calls them. Private functions to which women are destined by Nature are necessary to the general order of society; social order results from the difference between men and women." The most radical phase of the Revolution could offer only the following advice to women: "Women! Do you want to be republicans? Love, follow, and teach the laws which recall your husbands and sons to the exercise of their rights." Women were further enjoined to dress simply, work hard in their homes, go to meetings, not to speak out themselves, but perhaps to encourage their male children to do so. [25]

The royalist Right, restored to power in 1815, would not disagree with this particular republican dictum. Although Rousseau's attack on women's role in the salons had been one aspect of a thoroughgoing attack on aristocratic France, the aristocracy had come to accept his judgment—on women, at least. Their major thinkers, Louis de Bonald and Joseph de Maistre, insisted that aristocrats had only themselves to blame for their defeats during the revolutionary years of 1789–1815. Their sinful ways, exemplified by the visible role of women in aristocratic institutions, had undermined their virtue, sapped their strength, and caused their downfall. The subjugation of wives to husbands and the confinement of wives to the domestic sphere were deemed to be as necessary to the restoration of the primacy of royalty and church as Rousseau had earlier considered patriarchy necessary to the Republic. The strength of the aristocratic state depended on "the authority of the husband, the subordination of the wife, and the dependency of the children," according to Bonald. Maistre argued against the need to educate girls in publicly funded schools since they were destined for "a life of retreat and shall be solely concerned with familial needs." [26]

Across the full spectrum of otherwise varying political beliefs there was widespread agreement on women's place in society. Nineteenth-century French feminists thus faced an uncommonly unified opposition.

The First Feminists Challenge the System

Feminism is an ideology shaped by historical phenomena. It varies, at least in detail, in different times and places. There is nonetheless a common unifying bond across time and place—a shared comprehension of the world and a shared impulse for change that define the core of feminism. It is necessary to define this common unifying bond in order to identify feminists, and, particularly, to distinguish them from the many other reformers who wrote about women with concern and sympathy, but who were not, in spite of their compassion, feminists. The feminist ideology is based on the recognition that women constitute a group that is wrongfully oppressed by male-defined values and male-controlled institutions of social, political, cultural, and familial power. The ultimate vision of feminists is revolutionary. It demands the end of patriarchy, that is, the end of a political relationship of the sexes characterized by masculine dominance and female subordinance.

Despite the strength of the patriarchal system, some had spoken out against it in earlier centuries. Traces of feminist thought have been pointed to in the legend, based on reality, of Sappho; in Aristophanes's *Lysistrata* and *The Assembly of Women;* and in Plato's *Republic.* In the Middle Ages, a few religious sects, particularly the Waldensians and the Catharists, espoused some feminist ideas. It is now assumed, too, that many of the millions of women burned as witches between the fourteenth and the eighteenth centuries were punished for their implicit or explicit challenge to the patriarchal order.[27]

It was, however, the Renaissance *querelle des femmes* that created a transmittable literature about women's place in society. The seeds of modern feminist criticism were planted at this time. Early in the fifteenth century, Christine de Pizan formulated what would be the primary demand of feminists for centuries to come: that women be permitted to obtain a serious education.[28] She defended her sex against the misogynist attacks of Jean de Meung *(Le Roman de la rose)* and set the precedent for an outpouring of writings, the net effect of which was to create an opinion in intellectual circles more favorable for women than the medieval view. It is ironic but certainly not unrelated that this increasingly more positive view of women emerged at a time when the disparities in male and female opportunities were increasing.

One must be careful, however, not to exaggerate the Renaissance defense of women. Although these writers had named a problem and thereby created a new social issue, few moved beyond the demand for increased opportunities. Most failed to question the patriarchal understanding that the "correct" relationship of the sexes required the dominance of men over women.

Marie le Jars de Gournay, who in 1622 wrote *Egalité des hommes et des femmes,* went further than most. The mental and intellectual abilities of women, she wrote, would equal the degree of excellence attained by men if only women could be freed from their handicapped status, which was the result of faulty instruction and social limitation.[29] And writing fifty years later, François Poullain de la Barre went even further.[30] Christine de Pizan had defended the female sex by compiling lists of the achievements of women, culled from history and mythology, to prove that women were at least equal, if not superior, to men. Marie de Gournay had based her arguments on the authority of God, the church fathers, and the great thinkers of all times. In contrast, Poullain applied the Cartesian method of rational examination—"to accept nothing as true which I do not evidently know to be such"[31]—to question sexual inequality. His method yielded a doctrine far more revolutionary in its implications than those of any of his predecessors: Poullain became the first writer in the French language to link women's oppression to patriarchy.

Poullain argued that no field of intellectual endeavor, nor any profession, should be closed to women. He specifically mentioned teaching, the ministry, law, and monarchy or state governance. Acknowledging that it might at first seem surprising, even shocking, to see a woman occupy a chair at a university, march at the head of a police force, argue a legal case, preside over a court, lead an army, or act as an ambassador, he held that it would be strange merely because of the novelty. If women had from the beginning been admitted to the various professions, it would not cause any more astonishment to see them in government positions than in shops. The insistence that women's education be considered in relation to their needs as individuals, not just in respect to their duties as wives or mothers, places Poullain's work in an entirely different category from that of his predecessors or his illustrious contemporaries, Fénelon and Madame de Maintenon.[32] He was not only the first writer in the French language to link women's handicaps to patriarchy but also the first to state approvingly that the purpose of an improved education for women was to overturn male domination.

During the eighteenth century, interest in women's issues continued unabated,[33] although no Enlightenment writer developed as far-reaching a feminist position as had Poullain or even the less daring Marie de Gournay.[34] Nonetheless, the basic liberalism of the writers of that era guaranteed that women's plight would be treated with some sympathy. Furthermore, the willingness of the Enlightenment philosophers to question the basic immutability of apparently natural characteristics had revolutionary implications for the status of women. Voltaire wrote that women's inferiority was contingent upon circumstance, not upon natural necessity.[35] Montesquieu symbolized human tyranny in the person of a young Persian girl falsely presumed to be happy in her place in the king's harem.[36] In *De l'esprit des lois,* he advocated equality of treatment of men and women in divorce.[37] In the *Encyclopédie,* women were judged equal to men in intellectual capacity; their limited education was the reason they had not realized their full potential.[38] Diderot, in his treatise on public education, pointed out that improved education for boys would be in vain if effective reforms were not also carried out for the training of girls.[39] D'Alembert defended women's right to an education equal to men's in a direct challenge to Rousseau, *Réponse à la lettre de Jean-Jacques Rousseau sur les spectacles.*[40]

education

It is not surprising, then, that a feminist perspective on the women's issue reemerged with the Revolution. The years immediately preceding the storming of the Bastille witnessed a stepped-up circulation of pamphlets and brochures on a host of social and political issues. The woman question was not neglected among them. Madame de Coicy published *Les Femmes comme il convient de les voir* (1787); Madame Gaçon-Dufour issued her *Mémoire pour le sexe féminin contre le sexe masculin* (1787). Historian Evelyne Sullerot has discovered other brochures in a Bibliothèque Nationale collection: *La Très humble remontrance des femmes françaises* (1788); *La Requête des femmes à Messieurs composants l'Assemblée des Notables pour leur admission aux Etats-Généraux* (undated but probably 1788); and the *Lettre au peuple* of Olympe de Gouges.[41] A document of January 1, 1789, addressed to the king—*Pétition des femmes du Tiers Etat au roi*—demanded improved educational opportunities for women and insisted that certain occupations be reserved for them "so that we can be able to live, protected from misfortune."[42] The *Cahier des doléances et réclamation des femmes,* signed Madame B——B——, went further, to demand political rights for those who had fiscal responsibilities: "We believe that it is equally just to collect their grievances, at the foot of the throne; that it is equally just to collect their votes, since they are required, like men, to pay royal taxes and to pay commercial fees." She demanded not only a better education ("do not raise us as if we were destined for the pleasures of the harem"), but also that the Estates General recognize women's right to marry according to their individual desires.[43]

ie. not at mercy of their husbands

According to the French historian Paule-Marie Duhet, there is clear evidence that these brochures circulated throughout France, passed along by friends and relatives gathering in provincial salons. She notes that their ideas were frequently reproduced.[44] The *cahiers de doléances,* prepared in

1789 by the primary electoral assemblies to inform their representatives to the Estates General of their concerns, reveal that the demand for improved female education was widespread. According to one study of the several hundred edited *cahiers,* thirty-three recommended a program for girls, although the particular structure and content of this training was not specified.[45] Further, the third estate of Chatellerault sought equality for both sexes.[46] Clearly some women were beginning to protest their imposed silence in public affairs, and their voices were being heard. In the 1789 primary election for the third estate representative from Chevanceaux, women voted, and no one dared prevent them.[47]

The most important feminist publicists of the early years of the Revolution were Condorcet, Olympe de Gouges, Etta Palm d'Aëlders, and Théroigne de Méricourt. Condorcet's "Essai sur l'admission des femmes au droit de cité" appeared in July 1790 and demanded full political equality of the sexes. He did not propose universal suffrage, however, contenting himself with an electorate based on property ownership.

In September 1791, Olympe de Gouges presented her *Déclaration des droits de la femme et de la citoyenne,* which she dedicated to the queen. The formulation of both the preamble and the seventeen articles was based on the *Declaration of the Rights of Man,* to which she demanded the inclusion of the word "woman."

> All women are born free and equal to men in rights. Social distinctions must be based solely on the common good ["l'utilité commune"]. . . . The principle of sovereignty resides essentially in the nation, which is the union of women and men. . . . Laws must be the expression of the general will. All female citizens, like all male citizens, must participate personally or through their representatives in their formulation. . . . All female citizens and all male citizens, being equal in the law, must be equally eligible for all dignities, positions, and public offices, according to their abilities, and without any other distinction than that of their virtue and their talents.[48]

To the demands for equal political rights and freedom of opinion and expression, Olympe de Gouges added the demand for greater sexual freedom. She called for a "social contract between a man and a women" to replace the then-current marriage laws. And she was the first to propose a law to permit the establishment of paternity in the case of illegitimate births. "Women have the right to mount the scaffold: they must have the same right to mount the tribune," she concluded. Unfortunately, Olympe de Gouges was to have only the first "right."

Also in 1791, Madame Etta Palm d'Aëlders issued an "Appel aux Françaises," which proposed the establishment of a cohesive federation of women's clubs, one to be located in each of the eighty-three departments. These clubs would take charge of many public welfare concerns, including charity schools, public assistance, and nursing. The following year, Palm and a number of her followers presented a petition to the National Assembly calling for public education for girls, legal majority for girls at age twenty-one, the legalization of divorce, and political and legal equality for the two sexes.

Théroigne de Méricourt had been the first to grasp the significance of female participation in club activities. She had founded the Club des Amis de la Loi in 1790, but, this group was short-lived. Next she attempted to organize women to ferret out suspected counterrevolutionaries. She also demanded the right of women to bear arms.

An air of theatricality surrounded these three women feminists. Their social origins were far less lofty than those of the aristocratic Condorcet, and all three created legends to hide their ordinary pasts, just as they all fabricated their noble surnames. Olympe de Gouges was born in Montauban in 1748. Her father was a butcher, although she claimed to be the illegitimate daughter of the poet Le Franc de Pompignan. She married young and was soon widowed. Gouges then moved to Paris and began to write plays, one of which, *Zomar et Mirza ou l'heureux naufrage,* was performed at the Comédie Française in 1789. Etta Palm was originally from Holland; her life before coming to Paris is unknown, although assuredly not noble. Théroigne de Méricourt was born in Luxembourg and came to Paris as a professional singer. Perhaps partly because of differences of class and style, such luminaries of the "Paris establishment" as Madame Roland and Madame de Staël kept their distance from these outspoken feminists.

At the same time that women like Gouges, Palm, and Méricourt were publicizing feminist demands, a collective female consciousness was developing as a result of women's participation in the Revolution. A few women took part in the disturbances of July 14 and August 4, 1789, but they were notable for their singularity. The "October Days" of that same year, however, were a women's affair, and women participated in important numbers in the Champs de Mars demonstration of 1791. In 1789 the women of the Halles were singing:

A Versail' comme des fanfarons,
N'avions amené nos canons: (bis)

Falloit voir, quoiqu'n'étions qu'des femmes
Un courage qui n'faut pas qu'l'on blâme.[49]

The feminist newspaper *Etrennes nationales des dames* exhibited a similar inspiration, prefacing its demand for representation to the National Assembly with the reminder that "last October 5, Parisian women proved that they were as brave and enterprising as men."[50] A sense of the collective power of women was emerging.

Relatively few women attended the meetings of the predominantly male political clubs which had spread throughout France after 1789. Only the Cordeliers permitted women a public role; but here, too, their participation was limited. When Théroigne de Méricourt asked to be admitted with voting rights, she was refused. The other clubs, including the Jacobins, denied women even the freedom to speak.

Women did participate in politics through the "mixed fraternal societies" which had been created to inform and instruct "passive" citizens—including women—about the actions of the revolutionary government. These societies quickly spread through Paris; in May 1791, they were organized into a single organization under the presidency of François Robert.

In the provinces, however, clubs of entirely female membership were formed, initially to organize the festivals celebrating the federation of formerly autonomous provinces into the new, unified France in the spring of 1790.[51] For the most part, the women in these provincial clubs seemed to have understood their role to be that of auxiliary supporters to the male makers of the Revolution. They organized local festivals and revolutionary celebrations. They instructed themselves and young people—whom they organized into allied youth groups—in civic virtues, for example, by presenting recitations of such important documents as Rousseau's *Social Contract*. Many of the clubs attempted to take charge of education and public assistance, to fill the void left by the dissolution of the convents and monasteries. Following the outbreak of war in 1792, many of the clubs took on the function of workshops, knitting and sewing for the army. Some women in the clubs demanded the right to fight with the armies, and according to Duhet, about thirty women actually did so before this was expressly forbidden in 1793.[52]

The two elements of female activism of this period—feminist and revolutionary—were joined in the Société des Républicaines-Révolutionnaires, a Parisian women's club founded in the spring of 1793 by Pauline Léon and Claire Lacombe. At that time, the Republic, still young, was at war and further weakened by internal dissension. The more conservative of the republican legislative parties, the Girondins, were attempting to slow the pace of revolutionary reform in order to pay fuller attention to the war. Jacobins were pushing for controls on prices and supplies of the major commodities and a stepped-up prosecution of the so-called enemies of the Republic. The women of the Société des Républicaines-Révolution-naires had ties to several groups to the left even of the Jacobins—Enragés in the legislature, Hébertists in the Cordeliers Club, and *sans-culottes* in the Paris *Sections*. They supported the Jacobins in the coup ousting the Girondins from power and then kept up a steady pressure on the new government to implement their promises. They pressed for women's rights, too: on June 2, 1793, *Le Moniteur* reported that a deputation from the Société des Républicaines-Révolutionnaires demanded the right to deliberate with the Revolutionary Committee; after the Constitution of 1793, which granted universal male suffrage, was passed, the Société protested the exclusion of women.[53]

By the fall of 1793, however, all the feminist activists found themselves among the political opposition. Théroigne de Méricourt, who had ties to the Girondins, was publicly whipped, and her breakdown following this painful humiliation resulted in her incarceration in an insane asylum. Olympe de Gouges, critical of the Terror, was tried and found guilty of treason for publishing a pamphlet calling for a popular referendum on the form of government; she was guillotined on November 1. Finally, the government moved to silence the Société des Républicaines-Révolutionnaires, whose protests against continuing inflation and hoarding had come to appear to be as great a threat from the Left as the Girondins had once seemed to be from the Right.

The prosecution quickly moved from attacking the specific politics of the Société to condemning all women who dared to participate in politics. According to Duhet, the Société "provided a pretext" for the Jacobins: their real aim was to dissolve all women's organizations.[54] Jane Abray agrees: "By expanding its target to include all women, of whatever political or apolitical stripe, the Committee of General Security and the Convention made it clear that political questions were merely a pretext. What they wanted to do was to exclude women as a group from public life."[55] On October 20, 1793, the Société des Républicaines-Révolutionnaires was shut down, along with all other clubs of female membership. According to the French feminist historian and theorist Françoise d'Eaubonne, "If the members of the Convention were worried by the women's clubs, it was not only because of their affiliation with the *Enragés;* it was also because women were the most efficient agitators during mass movements due to the inflation in foodstuffs or famine; women, by their position within the family, were always in the middle of economic problems; housewives could either serve or destroy a revolution." [56]

Claire Lacombe and Pauline Léon were arrested in the spring of 1794. In May of 1795, when women joined men in the streets to protest the price of bread, the National Assembly responded by excluding women from all aspects of public life: "Be it decreed that all women should retire as formerly it was ordained, into their respective homes; those who, one hour after this decree is promulgated, are found in the streets, gathered in groups of more than five, will be dispersed by armed forces and arrested until public calm is restored in Paris." [57] The violent reaction against feminism, frequently believed to have been inspired by Napoleon, was in fact already in motion by 1793.

With the silencing of the women, feminism ceased to have a significant public outlet. Some isolated instances of feminist writings have been discovered, however. Evelyne Sullerot has found two issues of a feminist journal—*L'Athénée des femmes*—bearing publication dates of January and February 1806 in the Department of Manuscripts of the Bibliothèque Nationale. The contents indicate that the editor, Sophie de Senneterre, Madame de Renville, was well aware of a feminist heritage. She wrote, in the centuries-old tradition, that women's inferior education alone condemned them to intellectual inequality. Her express goal was to publish the writings of women and thus provide role models to other women. We do not know, however, whether these two issues were widely circulated. [58] Feminist aspirations were kept alive to a certain extent in the novels of Madame de Staël. Especially in *Delphine* (1802) and *Corinne* (1809), de Staël insisted that women, represented by the characters Delphine and Corinne, deserve our sympathy and have a right to seek personal fulfillment. Their plight, according to de Staël, resulted from social restrictions which punish women for manifesting independence—and punish them, what is more, for indiscretions that would be disregarded in a man. But despite these literary expressions of feminist-inspired sentiments, there was no further political expression of feminism nor any organized female collective action for nearly three decades.

Nonetheless, for the long-term development of feminism, these Revolutionary years proved extremely important. Before 1789, advocacy of the emancipation of women—or at the least, for greater opportunities for women—had been restricted to the upper classes, and support was usually in the form of approving women's desire for a better education. With the revolutionary upheaval came the rise of a feminism more sweeping in its scope and more inclusive in its following. Feminists not only added new demands to their "program"—the rights of full citizen participation in politics and government; the right to work; the right to equality in marriage; and even the right to share the burdens of a nation at war— but they also adopted new methods to obtain their goals. They comprehended that political action was more than a "demand"; it was a means to achieve their demands. They had grasped the potential strength of collective female action. This was an invaluable legacy to the nineteenth century.

CHAPTER 2

Roots of Nineteenth-Century French Feminism: The Image and Reality of Womanhood

Nineteenth-century French women's lives were quite different from women's lives in earlier centuries. Although the underlying patriarchal structure had survived the French Revolution, its form in the nineteenth century had changed in ways that explain the emergence of feminism at that time as well as the demands that feminists articulated over the course of the century and the means they would contemplate to achieve their purposes.

The very concept of womanhood had changed. Women were now idealized and, at the same time, sharply differentiated from men. This had not been so in earlier centuries, when women had been considered not unlike men but had been denigrated for their supposed lesser moral worth. As we shall see, the emergence of feminism in the nineteenth century related to this new conceptualization of womanhood.

Romantic Womanhood in Literature and the Law

In literature, the idealization of women was one aspect of Romanticism which, in reaction to eighteenth-century cynicism, rediscovered sentiment, passion, and love. Novelists and poets surrounded the female with fervent adoration. Woman was the Angel, the Saint, the Madonna. This is the language of Rodolphe, the seducer of Emma Bovary (Flaubert), of Dumas for Marie de Flavigny (later Marie d'Agoûlt), of Béranger for Delphine de Girardin (Delphine Gay). Balzac said of his mistress, Laura de Berny, "She is from heaven." [1]

The Romantic woman appeared in a variety of roles. She could be an ingenue—spontaneous, fresh, innocent, and in need of protection. She could be consoling, a tender-hearted confidante. Sometimes she was a mother, sometimes a sister—one thinks of *Atala and René* (Chateaubriand), with its suggestion of incest, or of Madame Chardon and her daughter Eve sacrificing themselves for Lucien's career (*Illusions perdues,* Balzac). She could also be the Muse, intermediary between Nature and the Poet—his intuition, his inspiration. This is the role of Madame de Mortsauf for Félix in *Lys dans la vallée* (Balzac). In *Nélida,* Marie d'Agoult says that the artist is nothing without the woman he loves: "His genius or his madness come from you [the woman], it's you who is responsible for him before God." [2]

In all roles, the Romantic woman was the ideal good. Feminists would build on this image, although they were ambivalent about it. Some women may have been encouraged to question the continuing limitations placed on their activities precisely because of women's positive depiction in popular literature. And certainly nineteenth-century feminists frequently employed Romantic language, idealizing women to further their cause. But they recognized, too, that the ideal Romantic woman was no equal to man: she was childlike, dependent on men's power for her very survival; she was also self-sacrificing, subordinating herself to men's interests.

The subordination of women to men, as well as the rigid differentiation of women from men, was enshrined in the uniform body of laws codified under Napoleon during the first decade of the century. The Civil Code recognized the equal rights of all citizens but excluded women from the definition of citizenship. Women had been reduced to the status of a legal caste at the same time that the *ancien régime* legal class system was abolished for men. Women's status had worsened, if not in absolute, then in relative terms. The code would serve as a rallying point for feminist protest not only because it discriminated against women but also because it intensified women's sense of sex identification. By proclaiming the political significance of sex, the code helped shape a feminist consciousness.

The Civil Code was drawn up between 1800 and 1804. Few of its provisions affecting women were truly new. Some of the early Revolutionary laws that had benefited women were incorporated into it. The new inheritance laws which prohibited primogeniture and required that the estate be divided among all children, daughters included, were retained. Women also retained the right to be guardians of children, although this right would be limited now to their own children, and even in this case was not as unrestricted as the right of paternal guardianship. Divorce was retained, too, although the liberal 1792 law was amended to preclude divorce on demand, and the terms of divorce were changed to favor husbands over wives. (In 1816, divorce was prohibited and the unequal terms of the 1804 divorce law became the unequal terms of a legal separation.)

Most of the provisions of the Civil Code affecting family life or women's rights reached back to the hodgepodge of laws issued from the regional royal courts and the feudal, military, and ecclesiastic courts of the *ancien régime.* Those who drew up the uniform civil law melded concepts from two differing traditions, the *pays de droit écrit,* which, based on Roman law, considered the woman a minor and, therefore, unable to exercise the "public" rights of citizenship, whatever her marital status; and the *pays de coûtume,* based on the Germanic tradition, which required a single authority in a marriage and, therefore, justified the wife's legal nonexistence ("couverture"). Roman law was the source of the proscriptions that refused to all women—regardless of marital status—the right to witness state documents, to be notary publics,[3] and to act as guardians to children other than their own.[4] Married women were even more restricted. They were totally interdicted from participating in the activities of jointly held property or from disposing of their own property without their husbands' sanction.[5] The wife, moreover, had to take on the husband's nationality[6] and was not permitted a separate domicile.[7] If she left home, the husband could cut off support, and the wife could be legally forced to pay an indemnity. What is more, the husband's authorization was required for the wife to operate a business or exercise a profession.[8]

The code assured men significant authority over children. Only the father was permitted to administer the financial affairs of minor children.[9] The father could withhold consent to a child's marriage,[10] and he retained the exclusive right to employ the ancient "right of correction" to imprison his children for six months (one month, if they were younger than sixteen years).[11] This legal authority vis-à-vis his children belonged to the father even when he no longer lived with the family.

The code permitted the husband the right to separation in the event of the wife's commission of adultery;[12] not unexpectedly, the wife did not have equal recourse. She could win separation only if she could prove that the concubine was resident in their home.[13] The criminal penalties for adultery were also inequitable: the wife could be imprisoned,[14] but the husband could merely be fined—if, that is, it could be shown that the mistress was living in their home.[15]

The essence of the Civil Code was the idea that a husband owes protection to his wife and the wife obedience to her husband.[16] As later feminists were often to claim, the position of the nineteenth-century French woman was more rigid in some ways than that of a slave in classical times because, while a master could free his slave, a husband was formally forbidden by the code[17] from abandoning any of his rights over his wife. The promise in the code that all French men would possess civil rights[18] meant exactly that and no more.

The feminist protest against women's legal inequality would be an uphill battle. Throughout the nineteenth century, French men viewed the code with deep reverence. They believed it to be the expression of the genius of French rationalism and would not easily agree to alter it.[19] Feminists alone sensed that women's status had worsened. Although they certainly knew that patriarchy had not been invented by the Napoleonic Code, they often pointed out that when many sets of laws had applied differently to French people from various orders, or geographic areas, opportunities had existed for some women, especially noble women, to escape the full harshness of patriarchal laws by slipping through loopholes created by differing and overlapping legal systems. Those opportunities had now been erased. This was the meaning, for women, of the new civil equality.

The Demographic Revolution

Not only had the concept of womanhood in literature and the law changed, but women's daily existence was changing too. Some of these changes are evident in the statistics that historical demographers have carefully reconstructed. Legitimate and illegitimate birth rates, mortality rates, and nuptiality rates were all changing, although unevenly. These changes help to explain the new concern with family structure and sexual issues that characterized much of the debate over women's role in the nineteenth century.

Traditionally, a married French woman had expected to spend the major portion of her adult life bearing or nursing children. The research on populations of seventeenth-century French villages indicates a pattern of very high fertility (as well as very high mortality). Louis Henry's research in Crulai indicates that the mean number of children per complete family was approximately eight, six, and four for women who married at twenty, twenty-five, and thirty, respectively. The model number, that is, the number to be found more frequently, was higher: eight, nine, or ten for women married at twenty; six or seven for women married at twenty-five, and four or five for women married at thirty.[20] Children were born at regular intervals of from twenty-five to thirty months.[21] Since "complete" families were exceptional—one or the other partner commonly died before the woman reached menopause—the average number of births per family was four to five, according to both Henry and Pierre Goubert.

Demographers date a "revolution" in European population characteristics at mid-eighteenth century. During the first stage of this "revolution," mortality rates, including infant mortality rates, declined. Because fertility rates continued to be high, births outnumbered deaths and the population increased rapidly.[22] In most European countries, fertility did not diminish until after 1880. France, however, was unique. There the decline in fertility rates began before the end of the eighteenth century.[23] By the mid-nineteenth century, the two-child household was commonplace throughout France.[24] This may have been the most important change in the lives of women of the nineteenth century compared with those of the *ancien régime*.

To indicate the long-term movement in French fertility, historical demographer Jean Bourgeois-Pichat uses the gross reproduction rate—the mean number of girls born per woman, without taking account of mortality—which he could establish with certainty for the years after 1851 and which he has reconstituted from data available for the years 1771 through 1851.[25] He shows a decline from 2.50 girls born per woman in the 1700 to 1770 period, to 2.39 during 1771 to 1775, to 2.01 in 1801 to 1805, to 1.69 in 1851 to 1855. The decline in the gross reproduction rate extended from about 1770 to 1935. From 1851 to 1871, during the period of the Second Empire, the decline slowed, but from 1881 onward—the time when fertility rates began to fall in other European countries—the decline in French fertility rates accelerated.[26]

Studies have definitively established that the fertility drop was not accidental.[27] By the end of the seventeenth century, some women were openly expressing the desire to limit the number of children they bore and indicating an awareness that this was indeed possible. Letters of Madame de Sévigné to her daughter, Madame de Grignan, clearly show a knowledge of birth control. Madame de Grignan's health had been ruined by six births in the six years following her marriage at the age of twenty-two. Her mother was concerned: "I beg you my love, . . . take pity on yourself, on your health and on mine. . . . Continue the nice custom of sleeping separately, and restore yourself, so that I may find you beautiful. . . . I kiss your Count. I like him even better in his apartment than in yours." [28]

Interpretations of the attitudinal change that explains family planning are still largely conjectural. In the seventeenth and eighteenth centuries, the desire to limit family size became an aspect of French married life, beginning first among the wealthiest classes and gradually spreading downward. People came to believe that they could improve the quality of their lives by limiting the size of their families. Inheritance patterns may have also played a role, for although the decline in fertility preceded the provisions in the Napoleonic Code that property be equally divided among children, there is evidence that primogeniture was already limited to the nobility one hundred years before Napoleon.[29] Philippe Ariès connects the phenomenon of family planning to the cultural revolution that made childhood a distinct and important phase of life. As each child became a more important individual to the parents, remained at home for a longer number of years, and represented a more severe financial burden, the desire to limit the number of children also increased. Ariès also mentions the impact of medical improvements, which made it possible to contravene fate by saving lives in cases that had previously been considered hopeless. This led, Ariès suggests, to a willingness to contravene fate by controlling births.[30]

These various explanations should have applied to a European-wide phenomenon, since the attitudinal and medical changes Ariès has described occurred throughout Europe. Yet widespread family limitation was unique to France before the last quarter of the nineteenth century. Alfred Sauvy theorizes that the collapse of the power and influence of religion—also unique to France at this time—explains the special French experience. The Catholic and Protestant churches alike were opposed to contraceptive practices within marriage. But only in France did the Catholic church lose control over individual behavior without being replaced by another church as it was, for example, in England, Germany, Holland, and Scandinavia.[31]

Much more needs to be known, particularly about the attitude of French women themselves, before the fertility drop can be understood. Ariès makes clear that women were the first to express approval of limiting births and that mention of the "new" practices was always accompanied by disapproval by male writers.[32] And not only do we lack information on why or how birth control practices became common within families, we also are uncertain which methods were commonly used by marriage partners. Abstinence was likely the most widespread "method" for limiting family size in the seventeenth and eighteenth centuries, although during the nineteenth century, *coitus interruptus* is assumed to have become more popular. Angus McLaren has hypothesized that induced abortion, as a backup measure, also became popular in the nineteenth century. Artificial devices such as the pessary were expensive, and their use, particularly among the poor, was uncommon.[33]

Marriage patterns also played a role in controlling overall fertility. French women of the nineteenth century fitted the general category of marriage statistics which demographers have labeled "the European pattern of marriage." [34] The "European" pattern was marked by a high age at marriage and a high proportion of people who never married. This pattern pervaded the whole of Europe, west of a line drawn from Saint Petersburg to Trieste, but seemed to be unknown in the histories of non-European civilizations. Probably the pattern emerged around 1600, although lack of statistical evidence makes any theory about precise dates highly speculative.[35] It was well-established, however, by the nineteenth century. Census figures for 1881 indicate that 60 percent of French women were still single by age twenty-five, 32 percent by age thirty, and 13 percent by age fifty; those still single at fifty can be presumed never to have married.[36]

Among the sixteen European countries that have been studied and that followed this basic marriage pattern, France had the lowest mean age at first marriage, and only Germany, Italy, and Spain had a smaller percentage of women who never married.[37] But the statistical variations among European countries are less important than their similarities when compared with figures for non-European civilizations. In these cultures, 0 to 2 percent of women never married, and most women were already married by age twenty.[38]

Contemporary observers often compared France with England, claiming that all French women eventually married, whereas a large number of English women remained single. Ghénia Avril de Sainte-Croix, an early twentieth-century French feminist, was only one of many who ascribed the greater strength of feminism in England to the existence of a large number of single women there, compared with France.[39] But contemporary observers overestimated the differences between English and French marital patterns which, we now know, were not great enough to explain the difference in the strength of feminism in the two countries. However, the statistics do indicate some interesting variations. The mean age for women at the time of first marriage was higher in England, where 66 percent of women were still single at age twenty-five in 1871, compared to 60 percent in France in 1881. In France, moreover, the percentage who never married was declining at the end of the century, from 13 percent in 1881 to 12 percent in 1900. In England, that same figure rose from 13 percent in 1871 to 15 percent in 1900.[40] In addition, it was commonly said that marriage was nonexistent among the poor in France. Although this cannot have been so, given the statistics, it does perhaps provide a clue to the discrepancy between belief and fact. Perhaps a much larger percentage of middle-class French women married than middle-class English women, leading middle-class observers to believe that "all" French women married.

The census figures contain no breakdown of marriage statistics by class. And yet contemporary observers were certain that the demographic statistics applied unevenly to women of different classes. If they were correct that nearly all middle-class women married, the number who never married among the poor would have been much higher than "average" and would explain feminists' concern with what they would have viewed as a breakdown of familial support systems for poor women. Their concern was exacerbated by the dramatic increase in the percentage of "illegitimate" births to total births, beginning about mid-eighteenth century. Until 1750, illegitimacy had been essentially unknown in *ancien régime* France; by the mid-eighteenth century it accounted for between 5 and 10 percent of all births in France, and in certain areas—especially Paris, Lyons, and Bordeaux—illegitimacy accounted for between 30 and 50 percent of all births.[41] These were the cities where the greatest feminist activism occurred; it is not surprising, therefore, that a concern for the consequences of illegitimacy on poor women's lives would affect nineteenth-century feminists' attitudes toward marriage and sexuality. Even "legitimate" fertility rates were higher among the urban poor, in part because of their higher infant mortality rates and their continuing custom of sending infants to a wet nurse in the countryside. Lactating bourgeois women, in contrast to working-class women who were not nursing, remained infertile for longer intervals.[42]

Looking beyond the aggregate demographic statistics, we can begin to glimpse the reality of life experiences that differed by class. Examining these differences is essential for understanding the nature of nineteenth-century French feminism and the obstacles placed in the way of building a cross-class women's movement. The bond between bourgeois and working-class feminists that was created by their uniform treatment under the law was fragile and was often shattered by divergent experiences that hampered women's understanding of their sisters or, worse, pitted the interests of one class against the other.

Working-Class Women's Experience

Poor women's lives were changed dramatically by the Industrial Revolution. At first, industrialization had consisted of the taking over of certain occupations by men in urban workshops of customarily cottage-style trades, which had been almost exclusively the province of women. By the end of the eighteenth century, men were acquiring such skills as salting pork, candlemaking, or weaving that were formerly considered women's work. At the same time, men began leaving their wives in the countryside to seek employment in the city. The "classes dangereuses," the subject of Louis Chevalier's study on Paris during the first half of the nineteenth century, were new immigrants to Paris—men who had left their wives behind to watch over the children and the land by themselves.[43] These changes sundered the traditional structure of rural society.

Soon women's work opportunities expanded, too. Throughout the nineteenth century, the largest number of French working women continued to labor in the agricultural sector of the economy, but they were increasingly able to supplement their families' incomes by taking in piecework. The domestic manufacturing sector was the second largest employer of nineteenth-century French women, and the continuing strength of the putting-out system of manufacturing throughout the century likely explains the high rates of French women's—particularly married women's—participation in the paid labor force.[44] Piecework was paid poorly, however. An 1860 article in the *Journal des desmoiselles* described the situation of one "domestic" lace worker: "Without raising her head from her work, thirteen hours of work a day permitted her . . . to obtain bread and charcoal for herself and her child. That was all. For the rest, it was necessary, being widowed, to depend on public charity." [45]

Not surprisingly, many women who could, began to migrate to cities, where they hoped to find better-paid jobs in workshops and the new factories. By 1866, almost one and a half million women were working in industry, comprising 30 percent of the total industrial work force. More than 70 percent of these women were employed in the textile industries, where they represented 45 percent of the total work force. Women were 23 percent of the work force in the food packaging and processing industries, 13 percent in chemicals.[46]

Although female factory workers were usually young and single, in the textile factories in the Nord the demand for women workers was so great that even married women were employed in significant numbers.[47] In Paris, where garmentmaking was the largest employer of women, women who worked in the *ateliers* (workshops) were typically young and single, but the expansion of ready-made clothing production, beginning in the 1830s, meant more work, too, for married women who assembled already cut pieces at home.[48]

Conditions in the cities were extremely harsh, and contemporary observers expressed amazement that women would leave the rural areas to come there:

In Saint Quentin, the poorest of the women live together, several to a room, where they sleep on miserable straw beds. In Amiens, for twenty sous a week, several of them live with poor families. In the Rhône valley, they can be seen coming down the mountains of the Drome, of Vivarais, of Cevennes, of the Ardèche. Those who don't live too far away return each Saturday evening to their villages, and go back again in the early hours of each Monday morning, clutching under their arms the small bit of bread which must last them all week long. The millers or the owners of the workshops provide lodgings for the others, those who live too far away. They are given one bed for two, or some straw.[49]

But pay in the factories or urban workshops was generally twice that in the rural domestic manufacturing industries. In Lyons and in the Nord, women working in factories earned the highest wages: 3.5 francs a day for a weaver, 3 to 4 francs for a warper (5F = $1). In Paris in the needlework trades, the highest paid workers could earn 4 to 6 francs. Average wages were much lower, however: for seamstresses, 1.70 francs; embroiderers, 1.71 francs; dressmakers, 1.98 francs. A deluxe linen-draper might get 5 to 6 francs, but most received barely 2 to 2.50 francs for an eleven-hour working day.[50]

Wherever women worked, they consistently received lower wages than men. Women in factories in Amiens were paid between 1.25 and 2 francs a day while men doing the same work in the same factories received 2.50 to 3.50 francs. At Fournies, female weavers earned 1 franc a day for labor that earned male workers 4 francs. For the city of Paris, 1850 official statistics showed women receiving from 50 centimes to 10 francs a day; male wages reached 20 francs. The average female wage was 2.41 francs, while the average for men was 4.75 francs.[51]

Employers, of course, benefited from paying lower salaries to women to do the same work as men and, therefore, often replaced men with women. This is the root cause of the male hostility toward female wage earners that was expressed over and over again in the *Rapport des délégations ouvriers à l'Exposition de 1867*. The harnessmakers blamed the employment of women for the generally low level of their wages. The report of the metal workers complained: "One of the biggest factories in Paris, the one that is mechanically best equipped, employs many women who do work which should be done by men." [52]

The pay differential was only partially explained by less pay for equal work; it was also the result of women being restricted to all the lower-status occupations by outright discrimination or lack of training.[53] In Paris at mid-century, more than fourteen thousand boys were enrolled in apprenticeship programs, compared to only fifty-five hundred girls. And fewer than one-half of these girls were in three-to-four-year programs with contractual protection. Professional schools financed and directed by the national or municipal governments were closed to young girls, and no scholarships were available for private schooling. Julie Daubié, a mid-century working-class feminist, reported that there was "no equivalent for them the schools of Chalons, of Aix, of Saint-Etienne, etc.; no equivalent of the Colbert and Turgot schools, which have trained so many superior men among the sons of the people." This, according to Daubié, explained why industrial statistics failed to uncover "one single girl knowing how to read and write in the match industry." [54]

The crisis of nineteenth-century working-class poverty was particularly acute for young and single women. Many left their families in the countryside and migrated alone to the cities, hoping to profit from the higher-paying jobs in the workshops and factories. They discovered instead that economic independence was virtually impossible for them to achieve.

Jules Simon, writing in 1860, estimated the budget of a working woman living alone in Paris. He assumed an average daily wage of 2 francs.[55] Not counting Sundays and holidays, the earnings would add up to about 500 francs a year, provided the worker was not sick a single day. The working woman would not have an easy time finding adequate affordable housing. Although inexpensive rental housing had been available earlier in the century, by 1860 much of it had been destroyed to construct Baron Haussmann's wide avenues. Simon reported that for a tiny seventh-floor garret, one would have to allow 100 to 200 francs a year on the Left Bank, 150 francs on the Right Bank; for an actual room, 20 to 30 francs more. In 1851, inspectors found a woman "buried rather than living in a hole five feet deep and three feet wide," and another who, in order to breathe, had to break a pane of her attic window. Simon's budget figured 115.50 francs per annum for clothing. For heat, a coal man could fill a foot warmer with charcoal and ashes for 5 centimes. Light was a wick steeped in oil; 10 centimes worth of oil would last for about three hours. Simon allowed 36 francs for light and heat. Assuming the rent to be the minimum (100 francs), necessities, excluding food, already totaled 287.50 francs. That left 212.50 francs—or 60 centimes a day—for food, enough not to die of hunger, Simon stated. Many working women ate only bread and milk. If one became ill, there was no way to pay for a doctor and medicine.[56]

Of course, many workers did not earn even 500 francs a year. Unemployment for certain periods of the year—"la morte saison"—was the rule rather than the exception. Employers imposed fines for a multitude of "sins": opening a window, being dirty, washing during work times, being sick and not sending a replacement.[57] In 1860, 500 francs per annum was a "good" salary, indeed.

Nor does this situation seem to have improved over the course of the century. The wages of women workers, particularly those in the traditional crafts, could not keep up with the increased cost of living. Marilyn Boxer has studied flowermakers over the fifty-year period 1860–1910. At the beginning of this period, when the usual wage for women in Paris was 2 francs per day, more than one-half of flowermakers were earning 3 or more francs. But fifty years later, when 3 francs per day was considered a subsistence wage, only 27 percent were earning that amount.[58]

Imagine, then, the young woman on her own who was suddenly faced with the prospect of an "illegitimate" birth. The French Civil Code did not permit paternity suits, nor did it punish seduction. Men were in no way legally responsible for the support of their illegitimate offspring. The courts refused to recognize the financial arrangements of unmarried partners—even long-term cohabiting partners—as contracts. Almost one hundred thousand illegitimate children were born in Paris during the years 1837 to 1846, accounting for about one-third of the total births.[59] Of these, it is estimated that fewer than 10 percent were recognized by their fathers.[60] The rest were either abandoned or became the charge of women who were hardly able to support themselves alone.

Some parents who hoped to protect their sexually vulnerable daughters placed them in work convents, where, working for minimal or no remuneration under the supervision of nuns, they could obtain food, some education, and most important, assurance of their chastity. According to Daubié, "The industrial convents alone would suffice to attest the difficult and often impossible position of the daughters of the people; they offer a wretched nourishment in return for hard work; nevertheless young girls rush to them to the point where, for the past fifteen years, the State has been authorizing eighty to one hundred communities of women annually." [61] The first of the industrial convents was set up in the 1840s at Jujurieux, in southeastern France, for the manufacture of taffeta. Girls as young as thirteen were signed up for three-year contracts. They worked from 5:15 in the morning to 8:15 in the evening. Rest hours and Sundays were reserved for prayers and catechism.[62] The industrial convents became so popular that, by 1860, forty thousand women were working in them in the Midi alone.[63]

But the development of the industrial convent system offered little improvement for most working-class women. Many work convents accepted only those who could buy their way in; none accepted women with children or those whose health was poor.[64] To women working in factories or at home, the convents were merely harsh competition, driving their wages down still further.

Many more parents chose for their daughters the relative security of domestic service. Domestic employment expanded throughout the nineteenth century, coinciding with the increased affluence of the employing classes. In 1851, almost one-third of single girls were employed as domestics; by 1881 that number had risen to nearly one-half. According to Theresa McBride, earnings were usually supplemented by room and board and such perquisites as the annual bonus, cast-off clothes, and kickbacks paid by shopkeepers. The total of the base wage plus these extras was often higher than manufacturing wages, and mere survival was always assured, provided the work did not come to an abrupt end by "layoff" or "firing" either because of the employer's misfortune or the employee's misdemeanor.[65] A fortunate servant in a "good" position could expect to ensure her respectability by living under the watchful eyes of a bourgeois family; she could even hope to accumulate a significant dowry and marry into a higher station in life.[66] But these hopes could be realized only at the cost of fifteen- to eighteen-hour work days, limited vacations, miserable housing, frequent mistreatment, and a total lack of independence. For many servants, of course, the hope would never be realized: dismissal, illness, aging, and illegitimate births led to immediate downward mobility, even to criminality.

How did women who could not earn sufficient wages to support themselves, or themselves and their children, manage to survive? What happened to the young servant girl who was dismissed from her job after giving birth to an "illegitimate" child? What happened to young and single garment workers during the *morte saison?* Some women tried to resolve their misery by going to prison: "A well-known philanthropist mentions one of these poor female workers who, working night and day, couldn't get her clothes out of Mont-de-Piété [the public pawnshop], and inquired if it would be possible for her to be imprisoned without having committed a crime." Some turned to begging or stealing. "Theft and other crimes became the ordinary methods of survival, and it should be no surprise that, since 1830, the number of female beggars imprisoned has more than tripled. . . . They get themselves imprisoned in order to find subsistence. The police, out of pity, open the prisons to these prostitutes who have nowhere but the streets to sleep during the winter." [67]

For unemployed young women an even more common solution to the problem of survival was prostitution. During the nineteenth century, a system of legal prostitution, involving registration and police regulation, existed, but clandestine prostitutes accounted for two-thirds of the total estimated number—a number which, for the city of Paris, is said to have

tripled in the first three decades of the century.[68] The lowest class of
prostitutes was usually recruited among women leaving prison or the
maternity hospitals. According to Daubié, "They send clothes to the half-
naked working-woman or domestic servant on their leaving the hospital
or the prison, to get them into their power through debt." Courtesans
("avowed kept women") were but a step up the ladder in the commerce
in sex. These "kept" women "are lodged in rooms which the respectable
woman could not pay for with the fruits of her industry nor of her talent,
however exceptional that might be. My personal inquiries have shown me
in Paris a number of kept women whose rent ranges from eight hundred
to four thousand, five thousand, and ten thousand francs yearly." [69]

The dramatic increase in the numbers of prostitutes in the first decades
of the nineteenth century was a result of the abject conditions in which
poor women lived and worked. Exploitative relationships that characterized
the workplace carried over to sexual relationships. Sexual relationships
outside of marriage frequently involved a woman from the lower classes
and her employer of the upper classes; almost one-half of the illegitimate
children born in Paris in the 1880s were born to servant mothers. But
employers were protected against their servants' claims, as the following
news story, which appeared in *Le Rappel,* August 1869, illustrates:

Félicie R. . . . daughter of honest peasants, worked at the home of M.C.
. . . notary, when it appeared that she was pregnant. She denied this
energetically, and, indeed, one day, after a momentary indisposition, she
reappeared, svelte, and only a little pale.

Now, some people doubt everything. Félicie's indisposition came under
suspicion, and was denounced; the police commissioner came with a doctor
who declared that there had been a delivery. They searched for the child,
and discovered it—where they are always discovered—in the privy.

Paternity suits being forbidden by the Law made by fathers, inquiry
concerning the identity of the father was made only to know if Félicie
had an accomplice in the infanticide. She took it all on herself and
courageously refused to name anyone.

She was arrested, tried, and condemned to death. . . .

Now, among the jurors was the notary in whose service Félicie was
working.

In the room to which the jury had retired for deliberation, after the
evidence had been presented, the notary began by suggesting that there
had been "extenuating circumstances." But another juror, who had some
kind of grudge against the notary, suggested, while smiling, that it was
perhaps he who was the father. The notary blushed, and hastened to retract
his first opinion and to cast his vote in favor of the death sentence.

The other votes were cast. A moment later the bell rang to announce
to the public that the defendant's fate was determined. . . . The defendant

was brought in, then the judges, then the jurors; all eyes turned anxiously to the jury foreman. The notary's enemy was the only one who noticed that Félicie's employer lowered his head and became horribly pale.

The jury foreman read the indictment.

To this question: "Is the defendant guilty?" the answer was: "Yes, unanimously."

Félicie uttered a cry: "Unanimously?" she questioned. And she stared at the notary.

The jury foreman repeated: "Unanimously."

"Well!" she said, "when I was asked if I had an accomplice, I said no; I lied! I did more than lie, for it was not I who killed the child, it was the father. And that wasn't good enough for him, now he is going to kill the mother!" . . .

The prosecutor, greedy to have another victim, signaled to let her continue speaking.

"So, you bourgeois! It's not enough that you get us pregnant, that you then kill our children out of fear that they would shame you at home and in the community! You must, in addition, be our judges and sentence us. And then you will go back home, all virtuous, and preach morality to your daughters! Unanimously, you said? In that case, I'll be following the baby to its death—but you will follow me! Mr. Foreman, I was only an accomplice: there is the assassin!"

And she pointed to the notary.

The notary was arrested and sentenced to death in his turn.

But the judges took into consideration the fact that he was a father, a friend of Order, and went regularly to church on Sundays, and pardoned him due to "extenuating circumstances." [70]

Working-class women were victimized by capitalism and by sexism. Not surprisingly, the first working-class feminists would blend a critique of economic oppression with a critique of sexual oppression. Sometimes, but not always, their interests would be supported by bourgeois feminists.

Bourgeois Women's Experience

The concerns of bourgeois feminists often differed from those of working-class feminists. The economic circumstances of their lives were never so miserable as those of working-class women, and they were generally protected from sexual abuse. They harbored feelings of deprivation, but their feelings were relative to men of their own class rather than to poorer women. The Romantic image of womanhood that sharply differentiated women from men reflected the reality of the bourgeois woman's life, even her physical reality. Particularly for those feminists who were raised in the cultural milieu of the political Left, where equality of opportunity and a reward system based on merit were highly valued, women's exclusion from new political and economic opportunities and from education no longer appeared justifiable. An examination of the lives of bourgeois women highlights their limited educational opportunities and their confinement to a sex-segregated sphere of activity, both of which served to buttress patriarchy in nineteenth-century bourgeois society.

For nineteenth-century French women, education was mediocre, if it existed at all. Daughters of the wealthy could attend private schools, some of which were more than one hundred years old and had been originally established at the end of the seventeenth century through the efforts of Madame de Maintenon and Bishop Fénélon to encourage female education. The expansion of learning opportunities for the majority of girls—and boys—was made possible, however, only when the government undertook the responsibility to provide free schools. The creation of girls' schools always lagged behind the creation of boys' schools, however, partly because of the continued belief that, ideally, girls should be taught at home by their mothers.

In 1807, the first government-funded school for young girls was created: the Institution Nationale d'Education des Jeunes Filles. Directed by Madame Campan, its purpose was to educate the close relatives of members of the Legion of Honor. Six hundred pensionnaires adhered to an austere regime designed to form "virtuous women." Frugally fed and clothed, these daughters, sisters, or cousins of the rich and powerful spent more time cleaning their surroundings than learning. Their "education" included religion, reading, spelling, some history and geography, some botany, but especially *des arts d'agrément*.

Although some attempts to create schools for girls were made in 1819 and 1836, only in 1850 was the creation of girls' schools finally ordered in every commune with a population of over eight hundred. But even this law was not always implemented. Of 48,496 public schools that existed in 1860, only 11,836 were for girls.[71] Secondary-level courses for young women were established in 1867 in forty towns and cities throughout France. The courses thrived from 1867 to 1869, but after Victor Duruy, the liberal minister of public education, was dismissed from office, they declined. By 1878, the courses were still offered at only ten locations.[72] *Lycées* and *collèges* for young women were authorized only by the Camille Sée law, December 21, 1880. Although their program of instruction was infinitely more rigorous than any available to young women before that time, it still differed significantly from the program offered by the young men's *lycées*.[73] These schools did not prepare women for the *baccalauréat* examination required for entrance to the university and hence the professions.

Throughout the century, most upper-middle-class or upper-class women were taught in privately run boarding schools. The teachers were sometimes laywomen but usually nuns. Ursuline, Benedictine, and Visitandine schools were considered the best because these nuns were trained to teach. Girls entered the boarding schools at the age of eight and stayed for five or six years. As at the Legion of Honor schools,[74] *les arts d'agrément* were the most important elements of the education. Some superior boarding schools, however, hired *lycée* professors to teach one or two secondary-level courses a week.[75]

Normally, a mother or grandmother completed the young woman's education after the age of thirteen, when she left either the boarding school or the public school. Some families of means, however, hired private tutors.

Girls' education was considered to be adequate to the need: bourgeois women were being prepared for marriage. The curricular emphasis on the "accomplishments" or *les arts d'agrément* was therefore consistent with the purpose of education: "The way to be married was to be displayed." [76] Family gatherings, parties, balls, and salons all served to permit an unmarried young woman to exhibit her talent for singing, piano playing, dancing, and conversation to the young man eager to find a wife who approximated as much as possible his Romantic ideal.

Her "education" completed, the unmarried young woman of the bourgeoisie was kept under constant guard, so great was the fear that her virtue might be corrupted. French Romantic literature makes clear that the French, unlike the English or Americans of the same period, continued to recognize women's innate sexuality and to fear its potential for social disruption.[77] Careful watchfulness was, of course, necessary. The young woman was not even allowed to mingle freely with other women her own age. She could leave home only if escorted by her mother or grandmother. Juliette Adam, the nineteenth-century feminist, described the guarded innocence of French girls in 1892:

> In social circles . . . our [French] girls rather exaggerated their reserve. . . . [They] never looked their partner in the face while dancing, and would blush at each word that seemed to them unfit for their womanly ears. . . . Indeed, our young girls had a respect for their own innocence that made them reject all knowledge, all comprehension of anything that might disturb their purity or make them lose in the least what they guarded with so much jealousy. They would have suffered, if they had guessed anything their parents hid from them, and would have considered that they were guilty in understanding it. . . . Our young women, whether

of the higher or lower nobility, of the peasantry or the tradespeople, lived in a complete and ethereal innocence.[78]

For young women of the bourgeoisie the traditional patriarchal family retained its capability for social control. For these women, sexuality and marriage went hand in hand. In traditional patriarchal fashion, as described by historian Edward Shorter, it was believed that "intercourse before marriage would harm the family by (1) sullying the daughter and ruining her prospects of an advantageous marriage, and (2) threatening the continuation of the family name and property from generation to generation." [79]

The young woman of the nineteenth century was still considered a chattel, and a valuable one at that. Marriages in middle-class and upper-class families were almost always arranged. According to Daubié, one commonly heard bridegrooms use such language as, "I've married a dowry of 300,000 francs." [80] Marie d'Agoûlt defined a marriage as "the uniting of two fortunes to create a larger fortune." [81] Historian Barbara Corrado Pope contends that "few families . . . really forced their daughters to marry someone against their will. Rather, most young women had already internalized a system of values that shaped their wills. . . . Young women tended to agree with their families that one did not hold out for an ideal relationship or a romantic attachment." [82] According to Juliette Adam, "A young girl who opposed her family in a reasonable marriage with no other pretext than that the aspirant did not please her was unanimously censured. 'Mlle. wishes to choose, herself, to marry,' they would repeat with severity. 'How could such a thing be permitted! Do not her parents know better than she what will suit her? She is a girl who will come to no good.' " [83]

The primary occupation of the married woman of the bourgeoisie was to manage the household. And as a young mother, she was responsible for the care and education of the boys up to school age, and the girls, ideally, until adulthood. This responsibility appears to have been taken more seriously and to have been more time-consuming in France than in England, partly because the French middle classes had fewer servants than the English.[84] Live-in "nannies" or governesses, in particular, were less common.[85] The practice of sending infants to the countryside for wet nursing—widespread among the upper classes in the eighteenth century— became less prevalent in the nineteenth century. In many cases a wet nurse was brought into the home, but an increasing number of bourgeois mothers, influenced by nearly unified medical opinion and the teachings of Rousseau, nursed their infants themselves.[86] Further, according to Barbara Corrado Pope, French women were required to fill in two gaps in the French educational system and to provide not only education of girls but also moral education of boys. Unlike the situation in England, the ideological divisions in nineteenth-century French society required French mothers to counter the teachings of schools when these teachings were at variance with the family's beliefs. Anticlerical families expected mothers to counter the Catholicism taught in French schools before the schools were secularized; after 1881, this situation was reversed, and Catholic families expected mothers to counter secular teaching.[87]

If marriage was the ultimate goal of the young bourgeois woman, what happened to the woman who did not marry? According to the nineteenth-century republican theorist Jules Michelet, "The worst fate for a woman was to live alone. . . . So many difficulties . . . she could hardly go out in the evening; she would be taken for a prostitute. There are thousands of places where only men go, and if some business should take the woman there, one would be astonished. . . . For example, if she were late, far from home, and became hungry, she would not dare enter a restaurant. . . . She would make a spectacle of herself." [88] And the historian Adeline Daumard concurs: "The old maid was a burden, useless and disdained. In truth, the older spinster woman, almost always with very limited resources, lived so completely on the edge of society that she hardly even belonged to the bourgeoisie.[89] Balzac's Cousine Bette reveals the bitterness and shame hiding in the heart of one spinster, who had seemed devoted to her family. Aunt Lison of Maupassant's *Une Vie* is a similar character. The lack of a dowry usually explained the existence of a spinster, and thus her condition was shameful for a family's honor.

The unmarried middle-class woman who did not have a brother or cousin who would charitably take on her support had few options. She might be a teacher in a public primary school for girls or a girls' *pension* or a private instructor of music, art, or foreign languages. In any of these professions, her existence was marginal.[90] Elementary school teachers were described by Edith Thomas as "a decently dressed proletariat." [91] More than four thousand schoolteachers each earned less than four hundred francs annually; almost two thousand earned one to two hundred francs. Many instructors in the private boarding schools earned only room and board. Individual private instruction was the least remunerative of all. (According to Daubié, in Paris in 1860, more than three thousand female piano teachers were competing with each other.) And the life of a governess was hardly different from the lives of other servants.[92]

Did women, married or unmarried, not recognize the injustice of their dependency? Daumard concluded that the majority of women accepted the status quo:

The situation of women seemed hard to some of them, but it was accepted as an inevitable fact of the human condition. The influence of Christianity, as it was then understood, only reinforced this belief. Brought up to be married, locked within the confines of the family, not being permitted the collective responsibilities of civic life or even professional life, most women could have had only limited horizons.[93]

But some signs of dissatisfaction were recorded. An administrative report concerning the commune schools explained that "the instructor [male] uses his wife as an associate. This helps her, giving her an interest both domestic and social and . . . liberates her from that emptiness, that boredom, that need for distraction which torments so many women, even in the most humble ranks of society." [94] Beginning about mid-century, literature took up the theme of the emptiness of the bourgeois woman's life, as, for example, Emma Bovary's repeated attempts and failure to achieve happiness as defined by the Romantic ideal. There were probably many women who rebelled against patriarchal restrictions, although we know only about the famous personalities, the writers, artists, and actors.

The most renowned example is George Sand, born Aurore Dupin, in 1804, to a family of means. Well-educated, well-connected, and independently wealthy after the separation agreement with her husband in 1836, she felt herself free to live beyond the standards of society, which she nonetheless accepted for others.[95] The same was true of Marie d'Agoûlt, whose father, le comte de Flavigny, was a royalist in exile, and whose mother was a rich German banker's daughter. She married the very wealthy and prominent Comte d'Agoûlt in 1827, but left him to run off with Franz Liszt. Like George Sand, Marie d'Agoûlt adopted a male pseudonym (Daniel Stern) for her literary career, but unlike Sand and the equally renowned artist Rosa Bonheur, she never adopted masculine mannerisms, such as smoking, or wore men's clothes.

Other bourgeois women expanded the scope of their activities in different ways. Wives of merchants were closely involved in their husbands' work, and wealthy widows often exerted a powerful influence on the property left to them by their husbands.[96] For some women, charitable activity, which expanded during the last half of the century, offered purposeful work. French charitable organizations founded thousands of schools for infants and preschool children of working mothers over the course of the century.[97]

Some women wrote important works designed to help women achieve usefulness and dignity. Claire de Rémusat, Pauline Guizot, Albertine Necker de Saussure, and Nathalie Lajolais are the most famous of the female writers who devoted themselves to teaching women how to be better homemakers and mothers. The expansion of the feminine press after 1830 offered another forum for women writers. Although these magazines were most often fashion magazines which gave beauty advice, they also offered useful information for running a home: menus and recipes, hygiene, and childrearing information.[98]

In nineteenth-century France, the continuing spread of humanistic values and a more enlightened view toward women resulted in a widespread willingness to question some of the worst abuses of sexual oppression. Many social reformers were appalled by the conditions in which poor women lived and asked that bourgeois women be permitted, even encouraged, to develop their talents. But some few went further and created a revolutionary ideology—feminism—which related the wrongs women were experiencing to the underlying patriarchal social structure.

Nineteenth-century feminists were both bourgeois and working class. Unity among them was most successfully achieved at the level of theory building. In theory, women's shared subordination was illuminated. For working-class and bourgeois women alike, the cardinal elements of patriarchy remained intact: the subordination of women to men assured by the insistence on legitimacy (and, consequently, severe punishment for illegitimacy), on economic dependency, and on the exclusion of women from political and civil participation. At the level of program building, unity was more difficult yet could be achieved by focusing on areas in which even class privilege did not protect women from oppression because of their sex. This explains the feminists' focus on legal oppression and on the difficulties that single women of both classes had earning their own way.

Although privileged women were sometimes leaders of the nineteenth-century French feminist movement, particularly late in the century, the greatest number of adherents were poor women, whether from working-class or bourgeois families. Suzanne Voilquin once characterized her friends as a group of modest bourgeois and honest workers, an accurate description of the largest number of feminists throughout the century. They were, typically, of the upper levels of the working class or the lower levels of the bourgeoisie, among whom mobility, both upward and downward, was commonplace, and the line separating the two groups was fluid. For these women, upward mobility was possible only through marriage to an upwardly mobile man. Among feminists, only Maria Deraismes was independently wealthy. A substantial inheritance enabled her to support herself well, even though she was unmarried. But many other feminists worked in the garment trades or, in the case of bourgeois feminists, struggled to support themselves by writing, speaking, and, especially toward the end of the century, by teaching.

The development of feminism would proceed slowly in nineteenth-century France. The legacy of the French Revolution included a fear of revolutionary violence that resulted in the government periodically repressing those who espoused new ideas. This repression significantly hindered the growth of feminism until the last decades of the century. And the dominant value system that buttressed patriarchy had ideological support from both the Left and the Right.

Most frequently, those who challenged the entrenched system were brought to their revolutionary perception by special circumstances—either involvement with other radical political activities or atypical opportunities for intellectual and political growth. Their numbers were small. Women's access to institutions that encouraged intellectual growth was also severely limited. For most of the century, few women had access to schooling. Schools were not, of course, the only institutions in which intellectual growth or political awareness might be cultivated. Among working-class men, labor organizations often served that purpose, but for most of the century, working-class women were excluded from these groups. Women were also denied access to revolutionary political groups by male revolu-tionaries, who thoroughly accepted patriarchy. And meeting places where bourgeois women could gather together, discuss their common experiences, and develop organizing skills were not common in France, unlike in America and England. In America, especially, the origins of a mass feminist movement owe as much to the socially acceptable activities of Protestant church women organizing for moral reform as they do to the less acceptable activities of women within the abolition movement. The transition of Susan B. Anthony from temperance organizer to feminist revolutionary is the most famous example. In England, too, the female control over charity created opportunities for the development of new skills and perceptions that led ultimately to a challenge to patriarchy. The careers of Florence Nightingale and Josephine Butler are proof that efforts that began within the confines of traditionally acceptable women's work could culminate in a challenge to tradition. But the charitable activities of middle- and upper-class French women were subordinated to the male leadership of the Catholic church and the state, neither of which ever relinquished respon-sibility for such work to the extent that their counterparts in the more individualistic Protestant countries did. In France, where education for women was limited, where women had few opportunities to control charitable work, where Left and labor groups excluded women, where greater isolation was imposed on young girls and married women—and perhaps most important, where the fear of the Terror led to harsh repression—a mass feminist movement would develop only slowly.

CHAPTER 3

The Saint-Simonian Vision: Creating a New World Order

Feminism reemerged as a force in French public life beginning about 1830 among some of the groups labeled utopian socialists. Thirty-five years had passed since the Jacobins had silenced the Revolutionary feminists, and nineteenth-century feminists needed to begin again as if they were the first. Such discontinuity in the development of feminism was a pattern for most of the century: a burst of feminist activity captured the attention of the public at large; a fearful government perceived this movement either as intrinsically threatening to "order" or as dangerous by association because of feminists' alliances with the political Left; the government retaliated fiercely enough to silence feminists for decades. When feminism reemerged—normally in a moment of more liberal government when censorship and assembly laws were relaxed—it had new leaders, new goals, and new reasoning. Although historians can see the connecting links from one generation to the next, the nineteenth-century public reacted to each new wave of feminist arguments as if they were brand new. Thus did government repression effectively slow the development of French feminism in the nineteenth century.

The utopian socialist feminists were very different from their Revolutionary predecessors. In the first place, they opposed revolution because of its association with violence and terror. Second, they were Romantics rather than Enlightenment rationalists. They were spiritual, mystical, and visionary. Concerned with morality, sentiment, and the emotions, they were determinedly nonpolitical or even antipolitical. They called themselves socialists to indicate that they wished to create new ways for individuals and classes to relate to each other. The form of the political regime—whether it be

41

a monarchy or a republic, for example, was of little concern. Third, they were internationalists and pacifists, opposed not only to war but even to national boundaries. Their propaganda knew no boundaries either. Particularly because the issues they addressed and the solutions they proposed were not limited by the strictures that a narrower national politics imposed on other reformers, their teachings appealed to an audience throughout the Western world. As a result, their feminist message gained widespread, international exposure.

Saint-Simonism in Theory: The Gospel According to Enfantin

The followers of Claude Henri, comte de Saint-Simon, under the leadership of Barthélemy Prosper Enfantin, were the first among the French socialist groups to propagandize the emancipation of women.[1] Although Saint-Simon had said little about women, the group that organized to popularize his theories, following his death in 1825, increasingly focused on the women's issue. By 1831, it had become their central concern.[2]

During the years 1825–34, Saint-Simonians created first a "school," then a "society," and finally a "religion."[3] Initially, they were only a small group of men, many of whom were young engineers—graduates of the Ecole Polytechnique—who had been attracted to Saint-Simon's idea of progress and the special leadership role he had envisioned for "industrial producers" such as they imagined they would be.[4] Prosper Enfantin was twenty-nine when he joined them in 1825. Historians of Saint-Simonism consistently comment on his good looks and attractive bearing, which they credit for his rise in the Saint-Simonian ranks. He was the son of a banker and had attended the Ecole Polytechnique but was forced to withdraw after his father's bankruptcy in 1814. In the early 1820s, while working in the Saint Petersburg branch of a French investment banking house, he began to read and discuss social and economic theory with a group of former polytechnicians. Back in Paris at mid-decade, he was introduced to the ideas of Saint-Simon by his former teacher, Olinde Rodrigues. Saint-Simon's writings, distinguished more for their prophetic acumen than their scientific precision, appealed to the mystic in Enfantin. Perhaps, too, he sensed that their ambiguity would permit ample opportunity for the expression of his own ideas, although he would, at first, present them only as interpretations of Saint-Simon's.

The Saint-Simonians publicized their doctrines in the journals *Le Producteur* (1825–26), *L'Organisateur* (1829–31), *Le Globe* (1831–32), and

Prosper Enfantin. Courtesy Bibl. Nat. Paris

Les Feuilles populaires (1831–32).[5] In 1829 and 1830 they presented a series of public lectures, later published in a two-volume work, *Exposition of the Doctrine of Saint-Simon,* which was the most coherent statement of their philosophy and particularly of their socialism. Their message was that a new, peaceful relationship between the classes should replace social conflict; that the work of the industrialist and the proletariat should be equally valued, even if not equally remunerated; and that inheritance of wealth, although not the private ownership of property, should be abolished. They indicted laissez-faire liberalism and called instead for a central planning authority and state control over investments. They held that property was a public trust rather than an individual right and that owners must place the means of production at the disposal of workers. Failure to do so should be punished by confiscation of their property.

By this time, the group had reorganized into a religion, building on the final and never-completed work of Saint-Simon, *Le Nouveau Christianisme* (1825). For this former Enlightenment philosopher, religion had come to represent an essential social bond, and a clerical elite was deemed necessary to lead the masses. Thus in December 1829, Saint-Simon's followers constituted themselves as a church under the priestly authority of Saint-Amand Bazard and Enfantin. Their "new Christianity" was organizationally not unlike the "old"; it was both hierarchical and dogmatic. But its metaphysics denounced the "old Christian" split of matter and spirit and conceptualized an androgynous God, "Father and Mother." This religious aspect of Saint-Simonism gave the movement its fantastical quality and alienated more rationalist or "scientific" socialists. But among young women and men of the late 1820s and early 1830s, the religious structure, symbolism, and language had a wide appeal. Saint-Simonians preached to audiences that were tired of Enlightenment rationalism, seemingly dull when contrasted to Romantic emotionalism, but tired also of the conservative Romanticism of Chateaubriand, Bonald, or Maistre that looked backward to some golden age of the past. Saint-Simonism, in contrast, offered hope for the future, a belief in progress, and the promise of human or social regeneration.

The Revolution of 1830 seems to have caught the Saint-Simonians by surprise.[6] Although some of them were also republicans, as a group they were uninterested in the constitutional issues—the best form of government, the appropriate size and basis for the electorate, or the proper relationship of legislature to ruler—that figured in the political debates of the Bourbon Restoration years and eventuated in revolution. Nonetheless, the Saint-Simonians' popularity rose sharply after the July Days. Artisans and skilled workers, energized by the knowledge that it was their role on the barricades that had forced Charles X's abdication, were frustrated by the Orleanists' political compromises that ignored workers' economic interests. They flocked to hear the Saint-Simonians prophesy that the "new Christianity" would emancipate them. During this time, the Saint-Simonians were particularly active in Paris and Lyons, where they presented lectures several times a week to audiences that commonly numbered in the hundreds.[7] They also experimented with new and peaceful methods to achieve social change. To reach the Paris working class, for example, they organized, by arrondissement, a special teaching program and two cooperative workshops, one for tailors and one for seamstresses.[8] And to sustain their "faithful," emotionally as well as physically, they established *maisons de famille* (communal living arrangements), where meals could be served to the workers who were inscribed as Saint-Simonian adherents.

The feminism of Saint-Simonism was shaped by the Romantic sensibility of the period and by the movement's other concerns—pacifism and socialism. Saint-Simon's followers took as their starting point their master's project to reorganize the globe by replacing the rule of "brute force" with the rule of "spiritual powers." They perceived that sexual equality would be a natural consequence of this utopia. Women as well as industrial workers, both of whom had been sacrificed by the "military age," would be emancipated in the "new age." This idea was first put forth in 1829 in the "Exposition of the Doctrine, Sixth Session":

> [We must show] how woman, who at first was a slave, or at least in a condition bordering on slavery, was associated little by little with man, and acquired each day a greater influence in the social order, and how the causes which to this day have determined her *subordination* have been successively weakened and shall at last disappear and carry away with them that domination, tutelage, and perpetual minority which even now are imposed on women, and which would be incompatible with the social state of the future which we foresee.[9]

Later, the Saint-Simonians strengthened their position on sexual equality; in the new age, it would be the deserved reward for women whose character had served as an example for a peaceful and therefore superior way of life. This theme became the leitmotif of the weekly *prédications* (sermons):

> We are here to proclaim the reign of peace and love. You are surprised that here they [women] are placed in possession of the religious and social life from which they were excluded under the reign of war and brute

force! But who else throughout the common ages, stained with blood, rust and tears, has won man over to peace and love, if it is not woman.[10]

Lengthy ideological debates to define the exact meaning of sexual equality were held from 1829 to the end of 1831. All agreed that women's inequality was twofold: they were excluded from public life and were subordinated to men in private life. But the Saint-Simonians disagreed over proposed solutions, and each issue that was debated caused some to defect, leaving Enfantin more completely in control of the remaining "faithful."

First, the Saint-Simonians debated the form that women's public role should take. Enfantin argued for recognition of distinctly different functions based on sex, paralleling his conception of God as Father and Mother.[11] The new world order would be ruled by a "couple-pope," the male to represent "reflection," the female "sentiment." Although Enfantin had accepted the prevailing prejudice of his era that men and women were innately different and that women were emotional rather than rational, his innovation was to construct a system that prized emotion (the female quality) over reason (the male quality). Saint-Simonians preached that only a sentiment—the universal sympathy of humans for humans termed "love"—and not reason could provide a strong and solid bond for a peaceful society. The future direction of the new age could be entrusted only to those who were especially endowed with sentiment: women and also priests and artists. Unlike the definition of womanhood advanced by Romantic patriarchalists, which stressed women's innate "piety, purity, submissiveness, and domesticity" and was intended to justify their restriction to a domestic role,[12] Enfantin's definition sought to justify women's full participation in all public functions. Indeed, when Enfantin proposed that the new world order be created immediately within the Saint-Simonian group, he established two hierarchies, one male and one female.

Enfantin's definition of a sexual equality based on gender distinction was not accepted by all Saint-Simonians. The doctor Philippe-Joseph-Benjamin Buchez opposed it, and his arguments clarify the significant philosophical differences separating him and earlier feminists from Enfantin. Buchez's feminism derived from the radicalism of the French Revolution and its politics of individual rights. Like feminists of that earlier period, Buchez believed that individuals of both sexes were born similar in capacity and character, and he ascribed male/female differences to socialization. Thus, he argued for one pope:

I know of no being who has deep feelings, [whose feelings are] not accompanied and served by the greatest rational strength. . . . Then, why have two individuals compete in order to obtain an integration of that which each possesses integrally without competition? . . . Your division of the papal unity into two beings will serve no useful purpose.[13]

Enfantin's feminism, in contrast, derived from the new socialism, which rejected radical individualism in favor of a harmonious association of differentiated classes and now sexes. Just as Jacobin or radical republican politics had led ultimately to war and terror, so, too, according to Enfantin, did the French Revolution's espousal of individual rights mask a policy of rapacity, greed, and entrenched inequality. Enfantin equated a politics of individualism, like "politics" itself, with conflict and therefore "brute force." It was necessary, he believed, to recognize the differences between the sexes and among classes. Only through the association of these differentiated groups, would women and workers be able to attain full equality. The debate over how the sexes were alike or different extended from August to December 1829, culminating in a victory for Enfantin and the resignation of Buchez from the group.

An even more serious schism occurred when the Saint-Simonians examined the form that women's equality should take in private life. According to Enfantin, the new world order of sexual equality necessitated a new sexual morality. Building on the principle that woman's nature was defined by "love," Enfantin arrived at the daring conclusion that the emancipation of women required the "rehabilitation of the flesh." [14] On this point, too, Enfantin appeared to accept the widespread view of his era of woman as quintessential temptress, responsible for carnal sin. But again, he turned partiarchal doctrine upside down—"carnal sin," would be "regulated" and then elevated to a virtue:

Until now coquettishness, frivolity, fickleness, beauty, and gracefulness have given rise only to guile, trickery, hypocrisy, wantonness, adultery, etc., because society has not been able to regulate, or satisfy, or use [these] human qualities. They therefore have become sources of disorder, instead of being as they should be, sources of joy and happiness. People who are *inconstant, fickle, volatile,* are therefore damned by the law of Christ (and notice well that woman, more so than man, possesses these qualities) and must use their power . . . to corrupt rather than construct. This explains very well the anathema pronounced against *physical* pleasures and against *woman.*[15]

On November 19, 1831, in a "lesson" to the Saint-Simonian "family," Enfantin presented his complex system to "regulate" love. The realities of human affections, he declared, require three different but equally valid moral codes: (1) that of the "constants"; (2) that of the "mobiles"; and (3) the synthesizing love of the couple-pope charged with harmonizing all social relations by "rekindling the numbed feelings" of the first and moderating the "unruly appetites" of the second. The papal priest and priestess would combine unity and variety ("limited to a single one but belonging to all").[16]

Although Enfantin reassured the family that his system was not an invitation to unregulated license, he met stiff opposition from many Saint-Simonians, who considered his ideas immoral. His most formidable opponent had been Saint-Amand Bazard, who, with Enfantin, was head of the Saint-Simonian family. Bazard, however, was not present at the November 19 meeting. He had already been outmaneuvered by Enfantin, and, having suffered a cerebral hemorrhage the previous August, he was weakened for the struggle. Others, less powerful than Bazard, had to represent his position: Pierre Leroux, joined by Hippolyte Carnot (future minister of public instruction), Jules Lechevalier (who next joined the Fourierists), and Jean Reynaud all protested. But seeing their words fail, they resigned. Two months after the meeting, in January, Bazard attempted to win over Saint-Simonians to his position. He published a pamphlet in which he explained his side of the debate: "Twenty months ago an important debate broke out between Enfantin and myself on one of the great questions of morality. . . . From the first moment that this question of promiscuity was introduced I opposed it vigorously. . . . The distinction between individuals as mobile or immobile corresponds to the notion of antagonism." Bazard went on to argue that Enfantin's complex system that recognized three sets of moral laws would ultimately lead to a single moral law of promiscuity, which would hurt the people the Saint-Simonians were to serve:

> It is to misunderstand the needs of the people . . . to come to them with such a doctrine, when it is promiscuity itself, in its diverse forms, that has been the state to which the people have been particularly condemned, as slave, as serf, or wage-earner, either because of the tribute that violence or poverty have obliged them to pay to their masters, or because of a more personal motive acting strongly on their own relations, namely the lack of cultivation of their moral faculties . . . consequence of their social abasement. What the people are asking for is to leave this confusion . . . and to be at last elevated to the dignity of marriage, which has been until now only a . . . [future] promise.[17]

But Bazard, in poor health, was no match for Enfantin. He died in July. Thenceforth Enfantin became the sole leader ("chef unique") of Saint-Simonism. Declaring himself the "Father of Humanity," he challenged anyone who protested his authority to leave.[18]

Yet Enfantin purchased his supremacy at the price of ideological retreat. To avoid further challenge, he backed away from his radical position on sexual morals and announced instead a temporizing and face-saving strategy, proclaiming a new policy under the banner of "l'attente de la Femme." The new morality, Enfantin confessed, could not be divined by a man alone, whose vision was necessarily incomplete. The work of the Saint-Simonians would have to "wait for the Woman," the Woman Messiah, to complete the doctrine.[19] The period of doctrinal development was halted, but, it was hoped, only temporarily. Actually, it was halted for good.

During the next two years, Saint-Simonian activism gave way to Saint-Simonian mysticism. Enfantin proclaimed, "Up to now . . . we have been teachers. . . . Now we are going to carry out [our teachings]. We are going to found a religion. . . . We are therefore apostles." [20] This period of the "apostolic mission" saw the full flowering of what may be termed mystical feminism. Missionaries ventured out of Paris into the provinces in search of "the Woman." Others went to England, Germany, or the United States. Apostles preached that their search must take precedence over all other efforts at social regeneration. In a letter to Paul-Mathieu Laurent, who protested the neglect of workers' concerns, Enfantin wrote that although he felt all the suffering of the people, he remained "calm enough" to wait for "the real savior of the people, woman." [21] The mystical vision was translated into numerous *prédications* exhorting the faithful to extend their compassion and faith to even the most oppressed of women: prostitutes.[22]

The "apostolic mission" was as much a response to a change in Saint-Simonian material fortunes as it was to the theoretical shift engineered by Enfantin. The ranks of the Saint-Simonian leadership—including many of the *fonctionnaires* who had administered the practical enterprises—were decimated by the power struggle between Enfantin and Bazard, which dragged on until Bazard's second cerebral hemorrhage in April. Enfantin took over the "exposition of the doctrine" and presented five lengthy *enseignements,* all of which were reprinted immediately in the *Globe* and later as separate brochures and distributed widely. And Bazard, in addition to publishing the brochure that explained his position on morality, hosted frequent meetings and carried on a vigorous correspondence with potential sympathizers. The public, once supportive, was now thoroughly confused by the fathers' charges and countercharges of immorality and wrongdoing and became less generous with donations to Saint-Simonian coffers.

Then, on January 22, the police shut down the Saint-Simonian lecture hall and residence in Paris on the rue Taitbout and began a grand jury inquest into charges of "corruption of public morals" against Enfantin and Michel Chevalier.[23] In April, the *Globe* ceased publication, and the last communal dining hall that was still in operation, at the rue Monsigny, shut down. Forty male "apostles" joined Enfantin in a further retreat from public life, going to Menilmontant, Enfantin's country home, to prepare themselves for the coming of the Messiah by an exemplary life devoted to celibacy, labor, and acts of symbolic communalism (such as wearing clothing that buttoned down the back, thus necessitating assistance from a "brother"). They sang; they prophesied; they prayed; but they would not, perhaps could not, act.

The most "faithful" were led to deny even Enfantin. In November 1832, Gustave d'Eichtal and Charles Duveyrier left Menilmontant. Eichtal explained to Enfantan: "We must impassion the world today, not for YOU, but for her who is to come; it is for HER and not for YOU that we shall have a nation; but SHE will bring it to you. . . . Do not hope to keep the group of men who are gathered around you today; the power of *women* will take them all from you in succession."[24]

When Chevalier and Enfantin were imprisoned in December 1832, their followers (now calling themselves Le Compagnonnage [or Les Compagnons] de la Femme) turned their "search" for "the Woman" to the East. They went first to Constantinople, then to Egypt. And there, under the Egyptian sun, mystical feminism burned itself out.

Saint-Simonism thus led to an impasse. As apostolic mission, the religion precluded action. "The Wait" and "the Search" replaced criticism, experiment, and social action. Ultimately, the apostles of "the Woman" lost their zeal and turned to other projects. Enfantin joined Le Compagnonnage in Egypt in 1834, after serving his prison term. From there he wrote to Henri Fournel, "I ask you to regard my participation in the building of the dam [on the Nile] as an *ordinary* industrial act, in which there is only a distant relationship to the human regeneration that we have been announcing since . . . Saint-Simon."[25] And indeed the concrete results of Saint-Simonism finally remained "*ordinary* industrial act[s]": the Suez Canal, the Crédit Mobilier and Crédit Lyonnais, the Paris-Lyons-Marseilles Railroad, the Cobden-Chevalier Trade Treaty. The Saint-Simonian struggle for "human regeneration" was over.

Saint-Simonism in Practice: The Female Experience

Although Saint-Simonian theory had led to an impasse that precluded action, women in the movement struggled to break that impasse and ultimately transformed Saint-Simonian ideology. Many later nineteenth-century feminist ideas can be traced to Saint-Simonism, but it was the feminism of the women, not of Enfantin, that was transmitted to later generations.

In its original formulation, Saint-Simonian feminism was an ideology of masculine invention. In 1829 and 1830, Eugene Rodrigues, Charles Duveyrier, Pierre-Joseph Buchez, and Prosper Enfantin—all middle-class men—determined the public role of women in the new age. In 1831, Bazard and Enfantin alone debated the new sexual morality, and finally, Enfantin alone was largely responsible for the definition of Saint-Simonian feminism. But after 1831, women, responding to Enfantin's "call" that they, rather than men, should define the appropriate relationship of the sexes for the new world order, spoke out on a full range of issues that affected their lives. They began with Enfantin's vision but soon changed its content dramatically. Recognizing that Saint-Simonian feminism was imbued with a masculine perspective, they struggled to link a feminist vision to the reality of women's experience and to define a feminism that, unlike Enfantin's, would lead to action.

Most of the women first recruited to Saint-Simonism were close relatives or family friends of important Saint-Simonian men. Among them were Bazard's wife, daughter, and sister; the wives of Olinde Rodrigues and Henri Fournel; the sisters of the Rodrigues brothers (Mesdames Sarchi and Pereire, whose husbands were also Saint-Simonians); and Enfantin's cousin Thérèse Nugues and close family friend Aglaé Saint-Hilaire. They held meetings, separate from the men's, to study Saint-Simonian issues, and they created a female hierarchy based on the male model.[26]

The most prominent of the Saint-Simonian women from 1829 to 1831 was Claire Bazard; the "mother" to the "daughters" of Saint-Simon, she was in charge of their indoctrination. Bazard was reserved by temperament, and her personality poorly suited her for the prominent role into which her husband's position had thrust her. Her letters to Enfantin complain of her difficulty in obtaining the same respect from the "daughters" that Saint-Amand Bazard and Enfantin could expect from their "sons."[27] But she had a superior intelligence, was well versed in the doctrine, and was both ambitious and proud. On October 26, 1830, she became the first woman to officiate at a Saint-Simonian ceremony, presiding over the "reception" to the second degree of the hierarchy. And when, in October 1830, the weekly "expositions of the doctrine" were moved from the Salle Taranne to a larger hall on the rue Taitbout, she was seated on the dais with the male "apostles," so her position as an equal in the otherwise masculine hierarchy would be visible to the public.[28]

Aglaé Saint-Hilaire and Cécile Fournel were next in importance after Bazard. Saint-Hilaire had been Enfantin's friend since childhood and was among the Saint-Simonians who took up residence together, early in the spring of 1830, on the rue Monsigny. She directed their salon on Tuesday, Thursday, and Saturday evenings, and after Claire Bazard resigned from the church, took over the indoctrination of new female adherents. Fournel was the best liked of the prominent Saint-Simonian women.[29] Her special influence was partially the result of her personal popularity but also of her husband's role as financial administrator of Saint-Simonian affairs. (In 1831, Henri resigned his position as director of the Creusot mines, turned over a personal fortune of more than 150,000 francs to the Saint-Simonian "church," and took on full-time direction of the group's activities.[30])

By early 1830, the numbers of women associated with Saint-Simonism had expanded beyond the original circle of close friends and relatives of prominent Saint-Simonian men; about one hundred women were attending the weekly "expositions of the doctrine."[31] That number at least doubled after the July Revolution, when the Saint-Simonians began to present their lectures almost daily. Enfantin estimated that two hundred women regularly attended these lectures, which would mean they constituted between one-third and one-half of the estimated total audience.[32] Religious questions were discussed by Charles Lambert on Saturdays, and on Wednesdays, the Pereire brothers discussed financial questions in one hall while Paul-Mathieu Laurent and Léon Simon were developing social theory in another. Of Laurent and Simon, Suzanne Voilquin wrote: "When they recounted the abuses that weighed heavily on the people and on women, everyone clapped enthusiastically." Sunday was the day that the entire hierarchy assembled. Seeing women on the dais, among the leaders, must have been a dazzling spectacle for many woman as, Voilquin wrote, it was for her.[33] Women—many single and some married—often came to these Saint-Simonian lectures alone. Eugénie Niboyet, who was active in the Société de la Morale Chrétienne, a group which in 1830 shared its lecture halls with the Saint-Simonians, stayed one day to hear the Saint-Simonians speak and was won over to their cause; in turn, she "converted" her husband and son to the new group.[34] Missionaries were active outside of Paris, too; in Lyons, about one hundred women were reportedly adherents in 1833.[35] Elisa Lemonnier became active in the Montauban "church."

Although the women who were prominent in the Saint-Simonian hierarchy, like the men with whom they were closely associated, were bourgeois, working-class women were also attracted to Saint-Simonism. In late 1831, following the creation of the workers' "degrees," 110 working-class women were inscribed as "faithful adherents." [36] Some had heard about Saint-Simonism from their husbands' male friends who worked in *ateliers* where Saint-Simonism was much discussed, especially in the months following the July Revolution. Suzanne Voilquin became a Saint-Simonian late in 1830. She and her husband were then living with her sister Adrienne and Adrienne's husband, Charles Mallard. This brother-in-law, a typographer, first heard of the Saint-Simonians from his fellow workers at the printing house of Firmin Didot. Together, the four attended the lectures at the Salle d'Athénée (Place de la Sorbonne) and at the Grand-Centre, rue Taitbout, and were won over "instantly." [37] Jeanne Deroin was brought to these same lectures by her friend, the engineer Desroches. Other working-class women were introduced to Saint-Simonism by the bourgeois missionary women, who in late 1830 and 1831 were proselytizing the new "religion" in the working-class quarters of Paris. Some of their projects—such as a medical and pharmaceutical service, a free vaccination program for children, and a cooperative workshop for seamstresses—reached out directly to women. [38]

Many women were recruited to Saint-Simonism through the pages of the *Globe,* the Saint-Simonian newspaper, which was distributed free from September 1831 to April 1832. At the Bibliothèque de l'Arsenal, where the Fonds Enfantin (the official archives of Saint-Simonism) are housed, there is a carton holding 112 letters from women to the *Globe.* [39] This separate file is evidence of the special concern of the *Globe* propagandists that their message reach women as well as men. [40] And apparently they were successful. Although almost one-half of the letters are from Paris, others show that women from all parts of France read the *Globe.* Two letters—one from a woman who directed a reading room in Toul and the other asking for the journal for a reading circle in Montauban—suggest that the *Globe*'s actual readership was much larger than the twenty-five hundred copies printed. Although most of the letters are addressed to "the director of the *Globe,*" some are to Aglaé Saint-Hilaire, who was at the time responsible for the indoctrination of new female adherents. Pauline Roland, who had been introduced to Saint-Simonian ideas by her tutor and had obtained the *Globe* from him, began a lengthy correspondence with Saint-Hilaire in January 1832, which continued even after she left Falaise, more than a year later, to live among the Saint-Simonians in Paris. [41]

Marguerite Thibert postulates that Saint-Simonism's mystical religious direction appealed readily to many women, perhaps even more so than to men, who had probably been educated in a rationalist tradition.[42] Certainly this view is reflected in the words of Suzanne Voilquin: "At the time that I understood the notion of infinite and eternal progress, I appreciated the fundamental idea of our freedom and the religious future in these words of Father Enfantin: "God, Father and Mother of all men and all women." . . . I experienced a sort of dazzlement. . . . God had spoken to me and truly brought me back to life." [43] Of course, some men were attracted to Saint-Simonism's religiosity: Hippolyte Carnot remembered of that time in his life that "we were drawn to all of the philosophies that had a religious tendency." [44] And some women, Jeanne Deroin, for example, were put off by Saint-Simonism's "religious tendency": "Still shaking from the bloody battles that were required to escape from feudal and religious domination, must we not recoil at the thought of confiding our future or of putting our freedom into the hands of a new pontiff or at the feet of new altars? " [45] Even Suzanne Voilquin was wary of Saint-Simonism's religious structure, if not its sentiments. She wrote that she had to overcome her fear that Saint-Simonians would be "jesuitical" before agreeing to attend her first lecture.[46]

Of the many letters to the *Globe,* only a few suggest that female converts were won over to Saint-Simonism by an a priori concern for women's emancipation. Jeanne Deroin was one of these few. She had been a republican activist but became disaffected because republicans "ignored the slavery of women and workers." [47] In contrast, however, most of the letters from women readers to the *Globe* suggest a greater interest in workers' emancipation than in their own condition as women. Nor did the women— even working women—consider themselves to be workers. Apparently the feminism of many Saint-Simonian women grew only with their experience in the movement.

But that experience was fraught with contradictions. Although Saint-Simonian theory encouraged women to believe themselves equal to men, the reality did not uphold the ideology. The story of the Saint-Simonian women parallels, in ways that are thought-provoking, the experience of American women in the nineteenth-century abolition movement and in the New Left of the 1960s. Out of the contradiction of their subordinate role within a male-dominated social change movement that touted egalitarianism, women became feminists and ultimately built a separate and autonomous movement.

Initially, Enfantin wrote letters indicating that he did not consider women to be the true equals to men. The distinction he conceptualized between the "natures" of men and women would empower men with rights that women would not share. In August 1829 he wrote to Charles Duveyrier: "Would woman be more powerful than man? Yes, religiously; no, politically. Yes, when it comes to reminding us of our goals; no, when it comes to conceptualizing or administering the means of attaining our goal. Yes, as prophet revealing the future; no, when we must administer the social movement which will bring that future into being." [48] These words, of course, were an expression of patriarchal Romanticism, seeing woman as inspiration, man as historical agent.

By 1831, however, Saint-Simonian theory was clearer that women and men should share power and all public functions including governance of the "church": "All law that has been made by man alone is bad, for it is oppressive to woman. All law should be made by man and by woman." [49] Perhaps Claire Bazard had forced this shift in Saint-Simonian theory. In October 1830, Enfantin and Bazard proposed to her, as head of the then-separate female hierarchy, a special seat in the new meeting hall that would honor her position. She demanded instead thaat she be integrated into the all-male hierarchy and seated among them on the dais:

> Enough of these passing elevations from which we have always fallen so painfully; enough of these false distinctions that have never brought us nearer to you and have always separated us from our sisters. . . . I would still see my brothers all assembled, all at your side. . . . It is there [at your side] that I should be: proof of the truth of your words to the unbelieving eyes of men. By my presence, you should accustom women to seeing me with the Apostles, to make them want to come join me.[50]

She apparently made her point: not only did she gain the place for herself that she had demanded, but she won a victory for other Saint-Simonian women as well. In early 1831, the previously sex-segregated hierarchies were combined. Three women (Claire Bazard, Cécile Fournel, and Aglaé Saint-Hilaire) were named to the Collège, the "superior degree" of the hierarchy; four women were named to the second degree and five to the third. Cécile Fournel, along with Charles Duveyrier and Jules Lechevalier, "directed" the second degree. Claire Bazard was appointed to the Conseil Privé, sharing responsibility with Olinde Rodrigues and Charles Hippolyte Margerin to advise the two fathers (Enfantin and Bazard) and to represent them in their absence.[51]

All the new institutional structures of the "church" were designed to put theory into practice. Women were not only admitted to the hierarchy but were given joint responsibility for the practical enterprises established by the Saint-Simonians. Each enterprise was directed by a "couple": the *maisons de famille* by a "brother" and a "sister"; the *degré des ouvriers* (later renamed *degré des industriels*) of each arrondissement by a director and a directress. Claire Bazard and Henri Fournel together oversaw the general administration of the Saint-Simonians. And two women, Aglaé Saint-Hilaire and Cécile Fournel, were chosen by Enfantin to represent him at his trials in August 1832 and April 1833 as a gesture of protest against the exclusive masculinity of the jury and the denial of public rights to women.

But still the hierarchy remained a male-dominated sphere, composed of twelve women and sixty-seven men. And in Paris, at least, no woman ever became a "priest" (*prédicateur*) with responsibility for the exposition of the doctrine to the public.[52] Although a letter from Claire Bazard to Resseguier suggests that Eugénie Niboyet was being groomed for that office,[53] Niboyet instead became codirector of the fourth arrondissement, *degré des industriels*. Finally, no woman ever attained the "supreme degree," although after Bazard's resignation, the seat next to Enfantin remained vacant, waiting to be filled by the longed-for Woman Messiah.

In fact, as the theoretical power of women was rising to its commanding position in Saint-Simonism, their actual power was declining. Ironically, this contradiction was made most explicit the very day Enfantin announced the "attente de la Femme." Having proclaimed that a female must create a new moral doctrine, Enfantin concluded by dismissing women from the hierarchy:

> Man and woman, this is the social individual, but woman is still a slave; we must set her free. Before teaching a state of equality with man, she [first] must be free. We must then create for Saint-Simonian women a condition of freedom by destroying the hierarchy . . . and have them participate in the law of equality among themselves. THERE ARE NO LONGER ANY WOMEN IN THE DEGREES OF THE HIERARCHY. Our apostolate which is *l'appel de la Femme* is an apostolate of men.

Women, he specified, would no longer sit on the dais with the hierarchy nor would they even be considered part of the "family." An empty chair next to Enfantin's would be a symbol of the "appel" (call).[54] Thus the retreat to Menilmontant was exclusively masculine, even to the point of disrupting marriages (the Fournels' and the Rogés', for example).

During the months that followed Enfantin's pronouncement, Saint-Simonian women, particularly those who had formerly been a part of the hierarchy, flailed about searching for a new role for themselves as part of a group that now denied them participation. Could no one of them have assumed the papal mantle? It is likely that Claire Bazard had hoped to do so before she and her husband withdrew from the movement. Now Aglaé Saint-Hilaire aspired to the position, but, like Claire Bazard, generated only hostility for her pretensions. Suzanne Voilquin remembers that

> Mlle de Saint-Hilaire, for whom I have always professed the greatest regard, gathered us together in the Monsigny salon, in order to agree among ourselves and to act as one. It was good. Proletarians, as well as bourgeois, we were prepared to unite our activities and our devotion. But this lady, who could lead a discussion without challenge from anyone, had the unfortunate idea to place herself in the middle of us like some supreme agent, demanding the name of *Mother,* and wanting to establish us into a hierarchy before really knowing us; it was inconsistent. My independent heart and spirit rejected both of these pretensions.[55]

The Lyonnais women apparently reacted similarly to Clorinde Rogé's attempted domination there. Louise Crouzat explained in a letter to Claire Démar that she had at first been impressed by Rogé's closeness to Enfantin and urged the Lyonnais women to acknowledge her as their leader. But then, "I realized that Mlle Rogé was only telling us that which I had known for a long time and was not helping us to progress at all. I announced that I no longer acknowledged her as a leader because I felt in myself the strength and the power to go forward and that I did not want to regress." [56] As Suzanne Voilquin concluded, the competitiveness engendered by hierarchical ranking "was regrettable; much energy was lost by divisiveness." Those with little hope of ever attaining high positions in the hierarchy probably accepted Enfantin's self-serving strategy for it liberated them from a rigid structure against which they had chafed. Voilquin recalls, "Had Father Enfantin not broken . . . the female hierarchy, I would have remained forever in the preparatory degree. . . . In my opinion, one cannot think of hierarchically ranking women before they have acted on their own free will. . . . Happily, the Father put us all in a state of equality." [57] A symbolic and future "mother" was apparently far preferable to a present authority.

Nevertheless, it was clearly easier to reject old authority figures than it was to create a new structure based on equality and sisterhood. The very essence of Saint-Simonism constituted as a church had precluded the development of such a structure. First, there had been the obstacle presented by the church's rigidly hierarchical organizing principle, as exemplified by the following 1830 "instruction" from "Bazard-Enfantin, father of the human family," to Claire Bazard, "*mother* of all my daughters": "You have treated the women as equals even though I have told you that you were their superior. . . . The tumult, disorder, chaos of your first meetings is now understood: they all feel the lack of a mother." [58]

Nor had Saint-Simonism encouraged sororal affiliations. If at the center of the Saint-Simonian doctrine was a woman, the Woman Messiah, at the center of its church was a man, Enfantin. Women such as Voilquin who were unwilling to accept female authority figures found it difficult to reject Enfantin. He was a truly charismatic leader. As Frank Manuel has written, "The fascination Enfantin exerted upon men and women alike remains something of a mystery, hard to explain in terms of his beauty and his charm." [59] One disciple, Michel Chevalier, called him "one of the greatest hypnotists who exists and who has ever existed." [60] Valentin Pelosse argues that Enfantin's hypnotic effect on Saint-Simonian women and men was self-conscious. He bases his interpretation on the recent studies of Léon Chertok and Raymond de Saussaure tracing the origins of psycho-analysis to Mesmer, who, one hundred years before Freud, worked out the theory of transference of the patient to the therapist and determined that it was by this process that a "cure" was achieved. These ideas of Mesmer, Pelosse makes clear, were widespread in Paris in the 1820s and 1830s, and Enfantin knew the value of "transference" for energizing the Saint-Simonian group's cohesiveness. Among the documents that Pelosse cites to prove his point is the following letter that Enfantin wrote to one adherent's doubting parents:

> I tire her head, you add, and I do not touch her heart. I believe that you are mistaken; you should have said: the *doctrine* tired her head but she has some affection for *you* [Enfantin]. And it is indeed because of her affection for me that I can count on her understanding the doctrine, which is to say that she cannot yet elevate herself to *general* affections except through individual affections, that she will not love religion until after she has felt some love for the priest, that she will be a Saint-Simonian because she will have started to become my daughter. It is inevitable; she has been too little taught to understand general or generous feelings for it to happen otherwise. It is certain that she will never want to love, to learn, to practice that which I love, that which I teach, that which I do, namely the doctrine, if she has no love for me.[61]

Other of Enfantin's letters abound with similar pronouncements. He continually described himself as the source of all power and the inspiration for all action. He wrote to Claire Bazard: "Your voice would be without force; it would tremble; but today it is me who will speak through your mouth and your voice will tremble no more." [62] And to his mother: "I am in a state of giving birth. . . . Now it is I who give birth to woman." [63]

The result of Enfantin's insistence that all energy and enlightenment flowed from him was to discourage women's individual or collective autonomy. The ties binding Saint-Simonian women were vertical ties from each of them to Enfantin, rather than lateral ties from each to the other. In practice, the experience of women in Saint-Simonism before the summer of 1832 was characterized by competitiveness and jealousy among themselves and submission to the authority of "the father." Yet even those who accepted Enfantin's authority were sometimes able to recognize the contradiction between Saint-Simonian theory and practice regarding sexual equality. As Suzanne Voilquin complained, "They believe they see a tendency toward usurpation on our part whenever we dare to express our own will. In general, men, even in the context of the [Saint-Simonian] family are to women as governments are to the people; they are afraid of us and do not yet love us." [64] The seeds of distrust planted in the early years would bear fruit in 1832–34, following the dismissal of the women from the hierarchy and coinciding with the imprisonment of Enfantin.

1er NUMERO. *

On souscrit, rue du
Caire, n. 17, à
l'entresol.

PRIX : 15 C.

Chaque exemplaire.

Pour les renseigne-
mens tous les jours
de midi à 4 heures.

LA
FEMME LIBRE.

APOSTOLAT DES FEMMES.

APPEL AUX FEMMES.

Lorsque tous les peuples s'agitent au nom de *Liberté*, et
que le prolétaire réclame son affranchissement, nous, femmes, resterons-nous passives devant ce grand mouvement
d'émancipation sociale qui s'opère sous nos yeux.

Notre sort est-il tellement heureux, que nous n'ayons
rien aussi à réclamer? La femme, jusqu'à présent, a été
exploitée, tyrannisée. Cette tyrannie, cette exploitation,
doit cesser. Nous naissons libres comme l'homme, et la
moitié du genre humain ne peut être, sans injustice, asser-
vie à l'autre.

Comprenons donc nos droits; comprenons notre puissance; nous avons la puissance attractive, pouvoir des
charmes, arme irrésistible, sachons l'employer.

* Le second numéro paraîtra le 25 août.

CHAPTER 4

The Birth of an Autonomous Women's Movement

The year 1832 did not begin auspiciously for the Saint-Simonian women. Their loyalties to each other and to Saint-Simonism were shaken by their disagreements over the sexual question. Cécile Fournel, the best-liked of all the women in the former hierarchy, had joined the dissidents. At the November 19, 1831, meeting of the family at which Enfantin had presented his ideas on sexuality, she had declared,

> My voice will sound weak after all those that you have heard, [but I] must declare before you that I reject the important-sounding theory that has been exposed here, no matter what you say. I reject it, and in rejecting it, I reject him [Enfantin] who teaches it, him who would spread it. . . . I think that all the women who hear me, who know me, understand that to reject this theory . . . I must have felt something profoundly immoral in it, and I hope to share my fears, and make the women, over whom I may still have some influence, aware of the danger they are running.[1]

She tried to remain neutral vis-à-vis the two "fathers" and was able to do so as long as her husband Henri stood by her. But Henri soon joined Enfantin, and Cécile was alone. Elisa Lemonnier found herself in a similar situation, separated from her husband Charles by her disagreement with him over the new morality and her unwillingness to submit to Enfantin's authority. For Cécile Fournel, the separation was especially hard because she and her husband had donated their entire fortune to the Saint-Simonian community. She and one daughter scraped by for six months, until her loneliness, rather than economic hardship, caused her to return to the rue Monsigny.[2]

There Cécile discovered that the other Saint-Simonian women were also demoralized.[3] Their husbands, like her Henri, were with Enfantin at Menilmontant. Earlier that spring, Aglaé Saint-Hilaire had tried to organize the women for independent activity but had failed. The Saint-Simonian funds that were supporting them were low: "We will have to work *materially*," Cécile wrote to her friend Elisa Lemmonier, "for several of us whose husbands have taken on the apostolic costume are without resources." Yet she welcomed the challenge, declaring, "Truly this will be our first step toward independence and liberty." [4]

Cécile Fournel was still angry at Enfantin but seemed to experience her anger as potentially liberating. She wrote him that she continued to find his position on the moral issue "false"; that his all-male retreat infuriated her ("You have broken our union, a union so tender, the most complete that I have known"); and that her return to the family must not be interpreted as submission to his authority, that she returned only because of her love for Henri.[5] She was thereby making a declaration of independence. She explained to Lemmonier, "We are about to begin the true emancipation of women which until now has been among us more an expression of desire than a reality. . . . As long as our activity remained tied to the men's, we could only follow along behind them. . . . Perhaps this separation is necessary." [6] And to her husband she wrote, "Woman will emancipate herself *by herself,* marching *alone,* without that support from men which was for her the measure of her continuing enslavement." In June 1832 she was confident of success: "I shall unite with the women; I shall help them; I shall support them; I shall call them: together we will know how to find our way toward independence. . . . I have too much desire to do this to fail." [7]

But Cécile Fournel did fail, and the historian searches for some understanding of why. Was it because the other women among whom she lived did not share her intense desire for independence? Was it because her health was too frail to sustain an effort to galvanize them into action? [8] Did she suffer too much from her separation from Henri? [9] During the next eighteen months she undertook two activities: she published *La Parole de la père,* which explained the Saint-Simonian beliefs Enfantin presented in his defense at his August and December trials; and, beginning in January 1833, she published the monthly *La Foi nouvelle: Livre des actes,* which recounted the activities of the male apostles as they traveled eastward in search of "the Woman." She fought hard to obtain from Enfantin the right to undertake both activities; she clearly doubted her capacities and would rather have entrusted Henri or Beranger with the task.[10] But even though she won her right for "some work to do," that work went no further than "to praise the acts of men." [11]

The Emancipation of Saint-Simonian Women

A different group of Saint-Simonian women, who had played no significant role in the former hierarchy, finally broke the impasse into which Enfantin's "apostolic mission" had led feminists. In August 1832, a small group of former "industrielles" founded a newspaper that would "publish articles only by women." [12] This was likely the first female collective venture in history whose purpose was specifically and exclusively feminist. [13] It was certainly the first consciously *separatist* feminist venture.

The first issue, undated, was entitled *La Femme libre* (The free woman), an unfortunate choice that exposed the fledgling enterprise to public ridicule. The second took the title *Apostolat des femmes* (The apostolate of women) and used the words "La Femme libre" in smaller type above the title. The third issue removed the words "La Femme libre" and substituted for them "La Femme de l'avenir" (The woman of the future). The fourth issue used "La Femme nouvelle" (The new woman) in small type above *Apostolat des femmes;* later issues placed "La Femme nouvelle" above *Affranchissement des femmes"* (The emancipation of women). Finally, *La Tribune des femmes* (The tribune of women) was settled on. [14] Issues number three and four of the newspaper carried the slogan:

> With the emancipation of woman
> Will come the emancipation of the worker.

Later issues declared:

> Liberty for women, liberty for the people through
> a new organization of the household and industry. [15]

And eventually the slogan became:

> Equality among us, of rights and duties;
> Since our banner is to pain,
> It is just that it be to honor (Jeanne d'Arc). [16]

La Femme Nouvelle.

TRIBUNE
DES FEMMES.

VÉRITÉ.   **UNION.**

Notre bannière étant à la peine, il est juste
qu'elle soit à l'honneur.   Jeanne-d'Arc.

Egalité entre tous de droits et de devoirs.

APPEL AUX FEMMES.

Plusieurs dames ayant refusé d'écrire dans ce journal,
parce que ce titre d'*Apostolat*, qu'il portait, était une
solidarité qu'elles ne pouvaient accepter; et ne voulant en

In publication, the editors used only first names, a symbolic gesture of female emancipation from masculine control: "We who bear men must give them our name and take our name from our mothers and from God. . . . If we continue to take men's names . . . we shall [continue to] be slaves." [17] The first issue named Jeanne-Désirée (Désirée Veret) the founder, and Marie-Reine (Reine Guindorf) the director. Both were young seamstresses, ages twenty-two and twenty, respectively. In September Suzanne (Suzanne Voilquin) joined Marie-Reine as codirector. Some months later, Marie-Reine gave up her administrative responsibilities to devote more time to teaching in a night school for poor women, but she continued to write articles for the journal.[18] Suzanne Voilquin continued to direct the publication, sometimes alone, sometimes with a codirector (Isabelle, Céléstine, or Angélique).

Among the other regular contributors were Marie-Pauline (Pauline Roland), Jeanne-Victoire (Jeanne Deroin), Isabelle (Isabelle Gobert), Céléstine (Céléstine Montagny), and several who cannot be identified beyond their first names—Sophy-Caroline, Amanda, Nancy, Angélique, Joséphine-Félicité, Christine-Sophie—destined to be known only as they designated themselves, *femmes prolétaires.*[19] Other writers, clearly sympathizers, nonetheless distanced themselves from the regular contributors by signing two names—Caroline Beranger, Angeline Pignot, Adèle Miguet, Louise Dauriat, and Adèle de Saint-Amand.

Specific biographical information is available for only a few of the regular contributors to the *Tribune des femmes,* but, from the little that can be pieced together about them, it appears that they were either of the lower levels of the urban middle class or the upper levels of the working class. Suzanne Voilquin labels them all *femmes prolétaires,* as does Pauline Roland in an 1834 letter to Charles Lambert.[20] Voilquin had been an embroiderer before her association with Saint-Simonism.[21] Roland was an instructor *(sous-maîtresse sans appointment)* in a girls' boarding school in 1832; she began her always uncertain career as a free-lance journalist in 1834.[22] Reine Guindorf and Désirée Veret were seamstresses.[23] None of the women were from the former Saint-Simonian hierarchy, which in contrast, consisted entirely of bourgeois women.

The women of the *Tribune des femmes* also differed from those of the former hierarchy by their greater distance from the men of the hierarchy. Most were either unmarried or, if living with a man in either marriage of "free union," were with men who held no power within the Saint-Simonian establishment and had played no role in the development of its ideology.[24] Unlike Cécile Fournel's *Foi nouvelle: Livre des actes,* the *Tribune des femmes* was entirely the inspiration of the women rather than of Enfantin or other male leaders.[25] The journal also did not receive any direct financial support from the Saint-Simonian group.[26] Nonetheless, there can be no doubt that its success—however short-lived—resulted in part, from the popularity of Saint-Simonism in 1832. The movement had extensive communications networks, including bookstores and reading rooms, that secured readers, subscribers, and authors for the *Tribune des femmes*. Its initial print run was one thousand,[27] and because costs were limited to printing and mailing (there was no remuneration to authors or editors), it appears that sales were adequate to cover costs, for a while at least.

But the stability of the journal was always precarious. Marie-Reine wrote that she had "no financial resources other than the product of [her] needlework,"[28] thus suggesting that her work for the journal was in addition to a full work day elsewhere. It was easier for Suzanne Voilquin to direct the journal. For the first six months of her association with the *Tribune des femmes,* she was still married and supported directly by her husband and indirectly by more well-to-do Saint-Simonians. The Voilquins lived in a comfortable two-room apartment rented to them by a Saint-Simonian sympathizer who also assumed responsibility for finding enough clients for Voilquin's husband, an architect, to assure that they could always make their rent payments.

In May 1833 the Voilquins separated, but Suzanne's means of support were uncertain for only a month or two. Then a wealthy Saint-Simonian, Alexandre de Berny, at the urging of his mother who had befriended Suzanne, began to provide support for the journal. And "to satisfy [her] personal needs," Suzanne worked as a housekeeper for still another Saint-Simonian, Madame Prud'homme, three days a week, receiving room and board for those days plus 3F75—enough, she wrote, to support her in her own apartment the other four days of the week. These four days were for the journal, her correspondence, and to prepare for the meeting that she hosted once a week.[29]

Freed to write, think, and act, "each according to [her] own inspiration,"[30] the *femmes prolétaires* of the *Tribune des femmes* developed a feminist perspective and strategy quite unlike that of Enfantin. Probably their differing class perspective as much as their sex accounted for their originality. The journal certainly gave ample evidence of the nascent "class consciousness" which we associate with pre-1848 socialism. "We who come from the ranks of the proletariat . . . will devote ourselves to the women of the lower classes *[du peuple],*" the editors wrote. Praising the Lyons workers whose protests proved "the morality of the people and the progress that they have made in the past several years," they proclaimed that everywhere, "the people begin to understand their own dignity."[31]

But feminist as well as socialist, they gave birth to a new consciousness: that of sex.

In a bold proclamation of emancipation, the editors wrote in the first issue: "What we want most of all is that women rid themselves of the state of uneasiness and restraint that society has put them in, and that they dare to say in all sincerity what they perceive [and] what they want for the future." [32] All women were welcome to contribute to the newspaper: "We call on all women, whatever their rank, their religion, [or] their opinion, provided that they feel the oppression of women and the people and that they wish to join with us, to associate themselves to our work and share our efforts." [33] Suzanne Voilquin explained that the ultimate choice of the title *Tribune des femmes* was to encourage even non-Saint-Simonian women to write for them: "Several women have refused to write in our journal because the title *Apostolat* suggested an affiliation that they could not accept. Not wanting to frustrate the development of social ideas, we have decided that this journal should be entitled the *Tribune des femmes*. A place shall be granted to all opinions, to all women's thoughts. Among us, there shall be no censure." [34] Lest there remain any misunderstanding, the *Tribune des femmes* announced (November 4, 1832) that "the cause of women is universal and not only Saint-Simonian." [35]

The editors maintained that divisions among women masked their shared subordination to men. Rich women, too, must recognize their oppression: "Your reign lasts but a short time; it ends with the ball. [Then] back home you become slaves again, finding there a master who makes you feel his power." [36] Surely, then, they would join the common struggle: "I strongly believe that one day all women will feel their solidarity and that those who are most favored by their birth and fortune, touched by the fate of our less fortunate clients, will join with us proletarian women." [37] The very first article of the first issue of the *Tribune des femmes* included a plea to "privileged" women: "Let us no longer belong to two camps, that of the women of the people and that of privileged women; let our common interests bind us together." [38]

Class division was only one of the barriers artificially separating women. The contemporary sexual morality was seen as another masculine invention that created two "camps" of women and further subjugated both, "one group by fear of erring and being rejected," the other by the thick barrier that their "depravity" established between them and society. "Thus, standing between these two such opposite camps, of which one is as exclusive by its regularity as the other is by its disorder, we shall use all our conciliatory powers to end the antagonism between them and to make each camp appreciate the other's virtues and values." [39]

The *Tribune des femmes* writers' originality lay in the way they blended an analysis of class and sex oppression: "Our fate [as women] is always improved with that of the people," wrote Marie-Reine.[40] And "the woman question is fundamentally connected to that of women workers." [41] Fusing a sex and class analysis also allowed the women of the *Tribune des femmes* to uncover the causes and examine the meaning of prostitution. One writer argued that although poverty forced "poor daughters of the people" into prostitution, women of all classes were vulnerable. "A stock market reversal, a fire, a bankruptcy . . . could . . . throw [rich women] rudely onto the streets." [42] Another writer argued that prostitution was both sex and class subordination of poor women to rich men. She wrote, again addressing "rich women": "Oh, how you must suffer when you think that these wretchedly unhappy [prostitutes] have been lost by your *husbands,* your *brothers,* your *sons.*" [43] A third writer, Christine-Sophie, recognized that prostitution was "everywhere," including rich women, "whose fathers would sell them." (She was referring, here, to dower practices.) [44]

The issues of the *Tribune des femmes* numbered 6, 7, and 8 carried the heading, *Union, liberté pour les femmes.* Union or association were, of course, often-used Saint-Simonian words. According to male Saint-Simonians, the emancipation of women would result from an association of the couple, male and female; they termed this association "universal." What emerges from the pages of the *Tribune des femmes,* however, is a call for a different union—that of women acting in concert as a group opposed to men: "We cannot change their minds until we can present ourselves to them with accomplished deeds, until we can present a unified body, *all* having the *same wish,* the same goal. . . . It is by *association* that we shall be able to reach this goal." [45] The *Tribune des femmes* editors were expressing an awareness that women constituted a "class" whose interests conflicted with those of men and that political and social change required that women join together—across male-constructed barriers—to emancipate themselves, by themselves:

WOMEN ALONE SHALL SAY WHAT KIND OF LIBERTY THEY WANT

Whoever else desires our liberty, I desire it: that is what matters the most. I wanted it before I knew the Saint-Simonians; I wanted it in spite of those who deny our rights; and I shall work for it independent of those who support our rights. I am free. We have had enough of men's advice, direction, and domination; it is up to us now to march in the direction of progress without a tutor. It is up to us to work for our liberty by ourselves.[46]

The "emancipation of female thought" had begun to transform Enfantinian feminism. Universal association gave way to sororal association, and liberation through the couple (male and female) gave way to liberation of women by women.

Although the editors had not initially meant to break with the male-dominated Saint-Simonian group, a rupture was in fact occurring, at least on the level of theory. In October 1832, Désirée Veret had written to Enfantin to explain to him the rationale for the journal's separatism and, at the same time, to reassure him of its writers' continued loyalty:

> My goal is to form an association of women of all opinions. . . . I want those women who would work with us to rid themselves of the overly great preoccupation with Saint-Simonism which prevents them from having their own ideas. It is in the interest even of Saint-Simon that I do this; women must add to [his work] and for that they must search elsewhere, within themselves. . . . Moreover, that which they have to say is as different as the natures of man and woman are different.[47]

In November, however, she took a further step, announcing to a Saint-Simonian gathering that she would no longer use for herself "the name of Saint-Simonian." She did this, she explained, not out of anger at, nor even in opposition to, Saint-Simonians: "Better than anyone, they have sensed the future of humanity. . . . If I were to identify myself by name, it would certainly be theirs that I would take. But I have a different work to accomplish. For me, all social questions depend on the liberty of women; they will resolve them all. . . . It is under the banner of the new women that I shall do work for our emancipation."[48] It was for Désirée Veret an individual act of emancipation not unlike the collective emancipation that the journal had theorized for women as a group.

Tensions were also growing between Saint-Simonian women and men that may have been either cause or effect—or both—of the theoretical rupture. Evidently the women's growing insistence that they be recognized as agents of change met with bewilderment, if not outright hostility. From the fall of 1832 through the spring of 1833, Cécile Fournel's request to edit the *Foi nouvelle: Livre des actes* met no response. To Enfantin, who had reportedly sounded out Beranger's willingness to do this work instead, Fournel wrote: "Father, have a little confidence in us 'poor women' that you have just emancipated. . . . Your distrust discourages [us], wipes [us] out, kills [us]." And to Aglaé Saint-Hilaire she expressed her exasperation: "Again, it's the men who will act, the men, always the men! " [49]

Also in the fall of 1832, Emile Barrault conceptualized his project for a mission to the East to locate the Woman Messiah. Some Saint-Simonian women questioned the value of this "Search." Clorinde Rogé wrote: "Ever since Barrault breathed the wind from the Orient . . . they cry 'orient' like sailors . . . cry 'land! land!!!' . . . [and] all our sorrows are forgotten. . . . Poor women of the west! We are still treated like children." [50] Louise Crouzat, a Lyonnaise, wrote to Claire Démar, in Paris, that a female mission, not a male one, should seek the Messiah: "I feel strongly that it is up to women to search for the Mother, to tell her what they want. . . . It is in America that I want to search, and [I hope] that I, a woman, shall find her." Claire Démar showed herself ecstatically receptive to this plan: "Never had I risen to the thought that it is up to women to call the Mother, to discover her. To you go the honor and glory of this revelation, for which I honor you and accept a new way for progress." Démar also endorsed the idea of turning the search toward "this young America" but added regretfully that "Paris is as lacking as Lyons in the two indispensable elements for the realization of your enterprise: women and money." She named herself as the only woman she knew of who might be interested in such a venture. [51]

It was the Saint-Simonian women's examination of the theory and practice of Enfantin's new morality, however, that caused the greatest conflict among the women and between the women and the men. Here, too, the women, "acting on their own inspiration," ultimately transformed Enfantinian ideology.

The Women Speak to the Sexual Question

From the time he articulated it, Enfantin's proposal to alter radically the rules of sexual experience wrought disagreement among the Saint-Simonian women. Some, such as Eugénie Niboyet and Elisa Lemmonier, had left the movement in protest; those who continued their association with Saint-Simonism divided on this question. They spelled out their disagreements privately, in their correspondence, and publicly, in the *Tribune des femmes* and in separately printed brochures. Doubtless, many of the remaining faithful followed Cécile Fournel, who remained a "model of conjugal love":[52] "I reject these so-called novelties that are in truth only a pale copy of society seen from its sad side." [53] But some women clearly interpreted Enfantin's "call" as encouragement to *"act out the practice of the new life."* [54] We can piece together the experiences of at least three *dévôtes*—Suzanne Voilquin, Pauline Roland, and Claire Démar—who attempted to live, in somewhat different ways, the new theology.

For Suzanne Voilquin, the "new morality" provided an opportunity to turn a potentially humiliating experience into an act of religious transcendence. In 1833, she discovered that her husband was having an affair with a new Saint-Simonian recruit and determined that

> if this passion was the whim of my husband's excited imagination . . . I would warn [her] and never receive [her] again in my home. If, on the other hand, it was a *true love* between them, a *deep love,* as he had tried without success to find in me, then with *my new ideas* about future unions, it would be up to me to show my devotion, to give an example to women by giving him back his freedom before God and as much as possible before other men, without condition or afterthought. [55]

Apparently she concluded that the latter was the case, and the Voilquins ended their marriage. (A legal divorce was obtained six years later in the United States, where M. Voilquin went with his new "wife.") [56] The *dénouement* was publicized through the pages of the *Tribune des femmes.* [57] Never hesitating to expose the most intimate details of the circumstances of the separation, Voilquin explained to the readers that she and her husband had had a passionless relationship and therefore she had "resolved to be only a sister to him, since more intimate relations demanded constant pretending on his part." [58]

The frankness of her public avowal, coupled with the dignity with which she expressed herself, was to serve as a model of the "publicité" or public confession practiced (but with much ambivalence) by faithful Saint-Simonians. For Voilquin, at least, this "publicité" clearly had a therapeutic effect. "I am alone now," she wrote to Enfantin, but, "I have put a man into the world, leaving my rights on the altar of humanity, making him free. Forevermore, free of my past, it is my turn to *think, love, act freely.* I want to live at last!" [59]

Pauline Roland had a similar propensity for turning the choices in her personal life into examples of Saint-Simonian teachings. She had been introduced to Saint-Simonism by a tutor, named Desprez, with whom she was in love, but hopelessly, because he was married. In her early 1832 correspondence with Aglaé Saint-Hilaire in Paris, Roland, who was living in Falaise, emphatically rejected the new morality as proclaimed by Enfantin, even though this doctrine held out some hope for her own self-fulfillment:

"I found myself by nature inclined to reject with honor a doctrine that could make me happy, or that could justify the feelings that I had until then regarded as sinful." [60]

In the fall of 1832, she left Falaise to join the Saint-Simonians in Paris, leaving also Desprez. She vowed to embrace a life of celibacy: "I gave him my promise that never would another possess the one who could not give herself to him." Among the Saint-Simonians, she expressed her vow in more religious terms: "I have given myself a *mission* . . . for which I have imposed celibacy on myself." [61]

By 1834, however, her religious sentiments suggested a different "mission." She determined to take a lover (Adolphe Guéroult), seemingly more as a matter of religious principle than sexual desire: "I have committed an act of the future . . . sacrificing myself to a work that I believed good and great—to make of a *child* a *man*." [62] Guéroult, too, saw their relationship as a way of living the Saint-Simonian theology: "We loved each other without promises, without any vows. It was love in all its freedom and at the same time full of loyalty and confidence. . . . The Father's ideas were strongly at work here. For many people, they are still only ideas. For Pauline and for myself, they are a way of life." [63]

Claire Démar went further than Voilquin and Roland. In her brochure, *Ma loi d'avenir,* she attacked Enfantin for timidity. His tripartite system made no sense to Démar. "There are, you say, men who are constant and others . . . who are mobile—show me then the *separation* point between *constancy* and *mobility,* where *one ends* and the *other begins?* To tell the truth, my weak and near-sighted eyes cannot distinguish it." She demanded the logical extreme, "une liberté sans limite." "It is by the proclamation of the *law of inconstancy* that woman will be freed; it is the only way." She did not believe in "love at first sight."

> I have the misfortune of not believing in the spontaneity of [this] feeling, or in the law of irresistible attraction between two souls; I do not believe that from a first meeting, a single conversation, can result the certainty, the awareness of *shared* thoughts, *shared* feelings always, always in agreement on all points, and (I believe) it is not until after a long and mature self-examination, serious thought, that it is permissible to admit to oneself that at last one has met another soul that complements one's own, that will be able to live its life, think its thoughts, mingle with the other, and give and take strength, power, joy, and happiness. [64]

To Démar, therefore, love logically required "a physical trial of the flesh by the flesh." Even then, there could be no guarantee that love would last: "It happens often that, on the threshold of the bedroom, a devouring flame dies. For more than one great passion, the perfumed bed sheets have become a death shroud; perhaps more than one woman who will read these lines, came to the marriage-bed throbbing with feeling and desire only to get up in the morning frigid and icy." If such is the reality of love, can any constraint on freedom of action be justified? Démar believed not: "Fidelity has always been based on nothing more than fear or the inability to do better or otherwise." She specifically attacked the Saint-Simonian public confession as an unacceptable form of social control: "Association shall be founded one day on limitless freedom, surrounded by mystery. . . . Let women keep the secrets of the heart to themselves; let them confess to God alone." [65]

All of these three "new women"—Volquin, Roland, and Démar—had to consider how they would balance the possibility or the reality of motherhood with the freedom of the new morality. Here, too, the relative conservatism of Suzanne Voilquin is clear:

> If I had had children, I would not have believed it my right [referring to the "divorce"]. I would on the contrary have quarreled with any woman who tried to take him from me! For, even though in theory Saint-Simonism was well ahead of the actual world, the family group that I was a part of was not powerful enough, nor was it organized strongly enough, to replace paternal protection. But then I was alone.[66]

Once again Démar took a more radical position. "Le pouvoir monstrueux"—paternity—must be destroyed: "No more paternity, always in doubt and impossible to prove." [67] Free love requires the end to the concept of either "legitimacy" or "illegitimacy." "Any presumption of paternity is dashed to pieces by my theory of trial, of mystery. . . . A mother who has several lovers can suspect, but can never prove who the father of her child is." [68]

Having disposed of paternity, she next redefined maternity:

> No more motherhood. . . . Women must work, fulfill a function; and how can she, if she is always condemned to fill a more or less long part of her life by attending to the education of one or more children? Either the work will be neglected or poorly done, or the child will be poorly brought up, deprived of the care that his weakness and his lengthy period of growth demand.

The emancipation of women requires, then, not only the suppression of paternity but the end of mothering as a "career." The child, she explained, must be taken "from the breast of the natural mother, to the arms of a *social* mother, a publicly employed wet nurse." The ultimate logic and the unexpected modernity of her position are dazzling, but she did not develop her argument. Having stunned the reader by her radical proposition, she abruptly concludes: "Then, and only then, will man, woman, and child be freed of the law of bloodlines, of exploitation of humanity by humanity." [69]

Pauline Roland put into practice the new theories of sexual morality. She faced up to the possibility of conception from the beginning of her brief relationship with Guéroult and decided that the responsibility for children must be hers alone:

> I want to become a mother, but with paternity unknown. I have questioned myself severely on this subject. I asked myself whether, in the sick state that pregnancy always brings on, I would be strong enough not to ask a man to give a name to the child in the eyes of the world, to whom he would be father before God. I also asked myself whether I had the right to bring into the world a being who would be rejected because of his birth. I resolved both questions affirmatively: I will be proud of my maternity and my child will be proud of his birth.[70]

In fact, Pauline Roland had four children, one with Adolphe Guéroult and three (one of whom died in infancy) with Jean-François Aicard, with whom she was "associated" for twelve years. In true faithfulness to her doctrine, their name was hers, and Roland took full responsibility for them: "I alone was the *family* of the children." [71] Her son Jean never knew that his father was Adolphe Guéroult until after Pauline's death.

Biographical information about other Saint-Simonian women is scanty, so it is hard to know how many others lived their own variations of the new morality. It is certain, though, that Voilquin, Roland, and Démar were not alone. One editor of the *Tribune des femmes,* Isabelle Gobert, wrote that, "faithful to the laws of nature, we shall love without pretense and laugh at prejudice." Another Saint-Simonian *dévôte,* Angélique (surname unknown) lived with Ernest Javary in a "free union." Voilquin wrote of them: "Each of them, free to accept the laws of this world, refused to do so, being inspired by the new life." [72] Clorinde Rogé and her husband were similarly inspired: "I asked [Rogé] for my liberty in order to be able to act without lies, without remorse. . . . No woman ever searched for the secret of the liberty of women with as much zeal! " [73] Enfantin himself had a son out of wedlock. He legitimized the son in public ceremonies but explained his refusal to marry the mother, Adèle Morlane, as the result of his religious principles.

Josephine-Félicité (surname unknown) tried to unite the most radical of the Saint-Simonian women in 1832. Writing in the *Tribune des femmes,* she avowed that she never had believed in "Christian" morality: "To me who yearned for love, it [Christianity] only said not to love. To me who yearned for pleasure, it only commanded suffering. To me who believes as much in the flesh as the spirit, it exalted the latter but condemned the former." She called on women who would "love without marriage" to wear a flame-colored ribbon *(le ruban ponceau)* as a "sign of communion of ideas among us." [74] But Suzanne Voilquin disagreed: "Whatever secret desires, whatever our dreams for the future, we remain obedient to the law of society until we have, over us, the couple who will have the right to bind us and unbind us." She proposed a deep violet-colored ribbon *(le ruban dahlia)* for those who would "wait" and in the meantime "obey the Christian morality." [75] Less than a year later Voilquin would "disobey" at least one tenet of traditional morality by disavowing her marriage.

The *Tribune des femmes* had promised to continue to print all opinions concerning the sexual issue, stating that "the new woman does not consider herself a judge of her friends; it is not for us to praise or blame." [76] Nevertheless, the more radical opinion that favored free love disappeared from that journal. One wonders if Voilquin reneged on her promise to print all opinions or if, perhaps, the range of opinions narrowed partly as an unfortunate, possibly undesired, consequence of the decline in the number of authors contributing articles to the journal in the final months of its publication. But there are other explanations as well. Some radicals, such as Reine Guindorf, continued to write for the *Tribune des femmes* but changed their opinions on the sexual issue. Others, such as Roland, changed their minds in subsequent years. In fact, the radical position on sexuality that vanished from the pages of the *Tribune des femmes* in 1833–34 disappeared from French feminism for most of the nineteenth century. I contend that its demise was not because radicals either quit the movement or were forced out but rather because they, too, came to doubt the liberating potential for women of Enfantin's new morality. This evolution in their feminist theory related to their lived experiences, to women's social and economic reality in nineteenth-century France.

First, the "new women" were threatened by the hardship of social isolation. Following her "divorce," Suzanne Voilquin experienced this isolation:

[Enfantin to Voilquin]: Well, dear daughter, I received your letter; are you free now? [Voilquin]:—Independent, yes Father, but free, in the accepted meaning of that word, on no, less than ever. I am prepared to accept responsibility for my actions, but in the face of the world, I remain isolated, outside of the law, under constant suspicion.[77]

Could not the Saint-Simonian family shield such women as Voilquin from "the world"? The increasingly intimate ties that bound the inner circle who lived, or at least took meals, together were for this purpose as much as for pooling financial resources. Nonetheless, the family failed to support "new women," as was already evident during the months of doctrinal discussion in 1831. Enfantin was then extracting "confessions" of either nonmarital or extramarital sexual relationships among family members in order to prove his case that a new morality was necessary. If "honesty" was the victor, some individual women were the losers.

Both Claire Bazard and Euphrasie Rodrigues, having privately confided "indiscretions" to Enfantin, were humiliated by having their secrets divulged to the Collège. Family life became burdensome. Claire Bazard wrote, "Among us, we are obliged to reveal all the secrets of the heart; . . . we lose, little by little, our spontaneity; we withdraw into ourselves . . . we write no more letters which became like bulletins of the Grand Army. This farce that we can love everyone in the same way results in loving no one." [78] Although the Bazards did not withdraw from the group at this time, it is apparent that the rupture had begun with this experience: "Yes, Father, you said it, I was used by Margerin [her lover]. But also have the courage to look into your heart and see if I have not been used, though probably in a very different way, by you." [79] A worker named Haspott criticized the "public confession":

> Women who confess their past lives will certainly find absolution among us, but we will not be able to rehabilitate them in the eyes of the world. . . . And let me add that they will not even be understood by those sisters who do not have similar confessions to make, because of the powerful prejudices that will live with us for a long time to come.[80]

And indeed, "powerful prejudices" were operating, even among the Saint-Simonians, exemplified by Claire Bazard's warning against welcoming someone of "loose morals" into the Saint-Simonian family. (The occasion was Jules Lechevalier's engagement to an actress.) Thérèse Nugues was concerned that Enfantin expressed unwarranted compassion for prostitutes.[81] Even Enfantin proved himself susceptible to the "powerful prejudices" of civilization's double standard, Voilquin informs us. The occasion was her "confession" to her husband, in Enfantin's presence, of a premarital affair. As she told her story, sobbing, her husband suddenly burst into tears, too. He threw himself into Enfantin's arms, "but neither man held out a comforting hand to [her]! . . . . [What] an unfair meting out of male justice." [82]

The even more radical words and actions of Pauline Roland scandalized the Saint-Simonian family: "It seems that Pauline, in Guéroult's absence, has started to love one of his friends. . . . And now he has returned. . . . I do not know to whom she will belong, for they do not care to share, but they understand full well that while going with one or the other of them, she is probably looking for a third one who need only be passing through." [83] Thus wrote Aglaé Saint-Hilaire, uncharitably, to Enfantin. Cécile Fournel was disapproving, too: "What I have learned about Pauline causes me great sorrow." [84] Roland had just broken off with Guéroult and begun her long-term involvement with Aicard. She shocked the Saint-Simonians even more when they realized that she was pregnant with Guéroult's child at the time.

For Claire Démar, lack of social support led, tragically, to suicide. She had dared to speak the unspeakable, to venture where "so many hardy innovators [feared to go], afraid of the outcry, the uproar, and the odious allegations that would arise from the reverberation of their courageous and incisive words." She had claimed to fear not: "Let slander come, with its retinue of stinging jest, bitter words, treacherous insinuations. . . . Let excommunication and persecution come; I am ready." [85] And in fact, she was "excommunicated": "On Thursday evening, I spent six hours in discussion at Voilquin's. There were about fifty men and women there. I found opposition on all sides. All the women disowned me and the men were just about as bad." [86]

More than one factor may explain Démar's extreme isolation. She was a recent convert to Saint-Simonism and perhaps could not break into the tight circle. In 1832, right after arriving in Paris, Pauline Roland had complained of Saint-Simonian cliquishness. [87] The Saint-Simonian women were also scandalized by her relationship, in 1833, with Perret Desessarts, who was ten years younger than she. Certainly, they disapproved strongly of her radical ideas. Démar's radical stance alone would have been sufficient to isolate her from the other women. They refused to publish her pamphlet, *Ma loi d'avenir*. Voilquin finally published Démar's work posthumously in 1834 but used a preface to dissociate herself from the author's radical views: "Even though I am an independent and liberated woman, I feel the need for a general bond that would hold all individuals together. . . .

We must regulate [morals] if we want to live without anarchy, for absolute liberty cannot exist alone." [88] And, in Voilquin's *Souvenirs,* she refers to Claire Démar only to dissociate herself from the other's radical views. She compares a woman she met in Narbonne to Démar: "What they really want is the right to use and abuse our independence without limits . . . without rules, and without control. Permit me to tell you that in any system, to push too far is to will failure." [89]

Despite Démar's earlier declaration to fear not "excommunication and persecution," it is clear that she found the relentless disapproval excruciating. Early in 1833, she wrote to Enfantin:

> "Father, I suffer, physically, morally. . . . Father, to tell the truth, this world is killing me, and every time I close my eyes, I always see a pistol; and already I can feel the bullet entering my skull. It will be the end of me, yes, I am sure of it." [90]

In August, she and her lover shot each other through the skull. She was thirty-three years old.

Claire Démar was not the only Saint-Simonian woman to decide to end her life. In 1837, Reine Guindorf-Flichy committed suicide, throwing herself off the Pont de Grenelle into the Seine. She was married by then and had a fifteen-month-old child when she fell in love with a Fourierist "papillon." [91] Eugénie Soudet wrote a lengthy eulogy, "Une Parole de femme!" interpreting this suicide as Claire Démar would have:

> Her husband had been jealous with no cause *before* this unfortunate feeling had overtaken her whole being. . . . To continue to live with him now, she would have had to accept a life . . . of hypocrisy. For an honest heart, what a frightening situation. . . . We speak in vain of duty; THERE ARE NO LAWS IN THE HEART. . . . Reformers, make it so that feelings which we can not master no longer bring on blame. [92]

One young Saint-Simonian, Adrienne Baissac, captured the essence of these tragedies. Soon after Claire Démar's death she attended a meeting called by the women to discuss a plan to colonize in Australia. Baissac came away enraged, partly because the meeting had been dominated by men, but especially because of what she heard one of them say. In a letter to Enfantin she repeated his words: "The time has not yet come . . . when the women must be free; they must still suffer. And if two hundred, three hundred suicides are necessary, we must let them commit this so they may serve as example to other women. Only when they will have felt all of their sorrows will they arise with all of their force to break their chains." Adrienne Baissac was wise beyond her seventeen years: "Do you hear this, Mesdames? Two hundred, three hundred suicides, and the way he said this number he could have said two thousand, three thousand. Doesn't this thought make you sick? It repulses me and I firmly believe . . . that we must immediately find some ways to make these sorrows cease and not to put women into situations of self-destruction." [93]

Saint-Simonian women may have hoped to shield themselves from the world by creating ideal communities in far-off lands. The meeting about which Adrienne Baissac wrote was called for this purpose. Colonies were created in Louisiana and Egypt. Both Suzanne Voilquin's sister and husband went to Louisiana with new partners whom they could not marry according to the laws of France. And in the Saint-Simonian archives are letters that have never been published and that are not easy to decipher, but which clearly indicate that the new morality reigned in Egypt.[94] Clorinde Rogé was there from September 1833 to May 1836 in search of "more noise, more excitement." [95] Caroline Carbonnel lived with Enfantin there, and a young proletarian woman, Judith (surname unknown), lived with Lambert. Suzanne Voilquin, who lived in Egypt from December 1834 to September 1836, had affairs with a Dr. Delong—father of her son who survived only two and one-half weeks—and also with Charles Lambert.[96]

Voilquin never mentions these affairs, however, in her otherwise candid *Souvenirs*. Perhaps she remembered her vow, taken the evening of her "confession" to Enfantin, "never to tell my thoughts, or the intimate acts of my apostolic life *to any man,* and to confess my sins only to my conscience, reserving the right, that should I meet some great woman who was loving enough to understand in her heart all actions, to explain to her what motivated my deeds." [97] Nor did she change her opinion, even in that far-off land, that had she had children, she would have been less free to live the new morality. A careful reading of her letters and of Lambert's diary indicate that had her child survived, she would have married Dr. Delong, although she had either ceased to love him or perhaps had never loved him.

The continuing double standard and the consequent threat of social ostracism only partially explain the feminists' ultimate rejection of Enfantinian morality. The evolution in their theory related in large measure to women's economic reality.

The short period of time during which some of these "new women" championed sexual activity for women outside marriage coincided with the brief period in which they had cause to view their economic future optimistically. The "new women" were, for the most part, young, unmarried, self-supporting, and living apart from their families of birth. They expected that their financial independence would continue.

This expectation is expressed clearly in the letters Pauline Roland wrote to Charles Lambert and Aglaé Saint-Hilaire during 1833 and 1834. For example, she wrote of her decision to have a lover: "I could become a mother. But . . . I did not want the world or him [Guéroult] to feel obliged to provide for the needs of a woman and a child." She insisted that her lover and the father of her child must "renounce any belief that he has the right to support [her]." And as long as Roland was able to find work, she got by. While pregnant with Jean, she worked twelve to fourteen hours a day, in spite of illness, to save for the time when work would be temporarily unfeasible. She arranged for a wet nurse so that her confinement would be as limited as possible.[98] Few details, emotional or financial, are known about her life with Aicard. She did continue to write, first for L'Encyclopédie nouvelle (edited by Pierre Leroux and Jean Reynaud), then for La Revue indépendante and La Revue sérial (both edited by Leroux), and it appears certain that her earnings plus a small inheritance (her sister Irma died during this time) contributed—perhaps more than equally—to her and Aicard's mutual expenses.

Suzanne Voilquin also insisted on being responsible for her own support. After separating from her husband, she wrote: "One of my friends who had remained faithful to me, in spite of our difference of opinion, blaming Voilquin for leaving, felt very sorry for me in spite of all my explanations of the subject. She wanted constantly to draw me to her home. To all this goodwill I always answered: let me work and I will accept the wages of a worker."[99] In April 1834, she gave up the direction of the Tribune des femmes "to think of the practical life."[100] She departed for Egypt, where she was supported at first by Saint-Simonian contributions but soon by her own earnings from her work as a midwife. In 1837, back in Paris, she passed the Faculty of Medicine examinations allowing her to practice midwifery in France, but she chose instead to take a position in Saint Petersburg, where her earnings enabled her to support not only herself but also an aging father and a young niece.

In 1832, Saint-Simonian women may have expected the success of their movement to sustain them economically, if work would not.[101] Only one year earlier, the Saint-Simonian group had been able to maintain housing for those who worked exclusively for the society. The Voilquins lived in one of these establishments, at rue Taitbout, where Suzanne was in charge of meals. Reine Guindorf and Désirée Veret had taken their meals at rue Monsigny, the other such establishment. But these communal houses had closed early in 1832, after government harassment of the movement slowed financial contributions to Saint-Simonian coffers. Still the Saint-Simonians remained hopeful: "Our apostolic life of poverty and deprivation was without discouragement or tears. In 1832, we had a deep faith and friends to love us and support us." [102] But in the years that followed, their hopes were dashed. Claire Démar wrote that she had trouble supporting herself: "I have not yet been able to begin working. I have borrowed money, and I am going to sell my last two pieces of furniture to pay my debts." [103] Even Voilquin and Roland, so resourceful during the 1830s, were overwhelmed by the decline in work opportunities for women that they confronted in the 1840s. And by then there was no movement to support them.

In 1847, Roland left Aicard. She wrote to his lawyer demanding "from the 35,000 francs that I brought into the union, in addition to my earnings, . . . the repayment of 17,500 francs, taking for myself, in this common union of nearly twelve years, half of the expenses and half of the debts." [104] But satisfaction was not immediately forthcoming from Aicard, and Roland's material situation became precarious: "I am moving heaven and earth to find what I need to depart [she wanted to join the Boussac community]. May God take pity upon my poor children and come to my rescue so that they will not perish." Since God did not come to her aid, she turned to her old Saint-Simonian mentor, Charles Lambert: "I am leaving with 500 francs in my pocket. . . . I no longer have the option to sit down at my table and dispatch articles as I used to do. In any case, the field of journalism is so overcrowded, book-selling at such a low point, that no matter what I did, I probably could not find a job. So, once again I must appeal to my friends. You are the first one to whom I am writing, Lambert." A detailed explanation of her financial needs followed; primarily she needed money to keep her eldest son in boarding school and pay off old debts; she expected to cover her expenses and those of the three children who would be with her from her work at Boussac: "I ask you, Lambert, if you can be of any help to me in this critical circumstance; I believe that my well-being and that of my orphan children depends on my prompt departure. And I ask of you: help me to save us, as I would help you if I were Lambert and you were Pauline." [105]

Unfortunately, her request fell on unhearing ears, and the proud and independent Pauline Roland was reduced from such dignified appeals to begging. In 1851 and 1852, the special circumstances of being a political prisoner (first in Paris, then exiled to Algeria) renewed her need to beg merely to assure the survival of her children. It was at this time that

Pauline finally, after seventeen years of fidelity to her vow, wrote to Adolphe Guéroult, Jean's father, to ask for his assistance. He did not respond to her letter.[106]

After her return from Russia, Suzanne Voilquin experienced similar difficulties. In 1847 and again in 1848, she sought Enfantin's assistance, first to sponsor her establishment for wet nurses, and when that project failed to materialize, to obtain for her a tobacco concession in one of the railway stations.[107] In the summer of 1848, she organized the Paris midwives to demand that the government pay them salaries. This campaign was unsuccessful, however; women had lost the battle between midwives and obstetricians a decade earlier, when men gained access to the Paris maternity hospitals for their training. Women who, like Reine Guindorf and Désirée Veret, had been employed in the needlework trades fared badly also. The restructuring of the garmentmaking industry from dressmaking and tailoring to ready-made production resulted in more jobs for women, but the new jobs were mostly unskilled and paid poorly. Garmentmaking was depressed in the 1840s, and although the industry later recovered, female wages never rose to a level that could support a woman on her own.[108]

This worsening of employment opportunities for all the "new women" differs from what happened to many men of their class. For upper working-class and lower middle-class men, the nineteenth century was a period of expanding opportunities that benefited at least some and likely raised expectations of success for most. In fact, the number who would not be disappointed was significant, for in spite of booms and busts, social and economic dislocations, and increasing proletarianization of many men, upward mobility was not uncommon for others.[109] The male leaders of Saint-Simonism, of a slightly higher class, were even better positioned to benefit from changes in the French economy. A disproportionate number of them were former students of the professional schools, especially the Haute Ecole Polytechnique. Some were trained in engineering and other practical sciences, and some came from banking families. Saint-Simonian ideology reflected their material reality: industrialists, scientists, economic planners, and credit managers would replace the aristocracy of birth and inheritance in the new age. This ideology did not reflect women's quite different reality.

The explanation already advanced by historians of nineteenth-century American women that links their unwillingness to favor sex outside of marriage to their economic dependency can be applied to nineteenth-century French women as well.[110] This explanation is buttressed, rather than refuted, by noting that in 1832–34, when some women could hope to sustain themselves independently, they also considered "love without marriage." In later years, after a worsening in their economic fortunes, they reconsidered.

At the meeting of November 19, 1831, Enfantin had declared to the family, "You must regard my ideas on woman as the opinion of a single man and not at all as law, as a doctrine, for there will be no law or moral doctrine until woman has spoken." [111] Indeed, the women spoke, and what they said, finally, was quite different from the words of Enfantin. First, they temporized. According to Suzanne Voilquin: "For the time being, the question of the relationship between the sexes must be a postponed question." She explained why: Women must realize that "before being morally free," they must be "materially self-sufficient." [112] She thus opened up discussion on a subject Enfantin had not so much rejected as ignored: economic independence. Other women contributed to the dialogue. Claire Démar wrote that "women [must be] released, freed from the yoke of guardianship, from the protection of men from whom they will receive neither food nor wages, from men who will no longer pay them the price of their body; women must owe their subsistence, their social position, only to their own ability and work. . . . To accomplish this, women must work, must fulfill a function." [113]

In an article for the *Tribune des femmes,* Reine Guindorf explained that "what we mean when we speak of *liberty,* of *equality* . . . is to be able to own possessions; for as long as we cannot, we shall always be the slaves of men. He who provides us our material needs can always require, in exchange, that we submit to his wishes. It is very difficult to speak freely when one does not have the means to live independently." In another article she wrote: "In industry, very few careers are offered to us. Agreeable work is all done by men; we are left only the jobs that hardly pay enough for survival. And as soon as it is noticed that we can do a job, the wages there are lowered because we must not earn as much as men. It's true, it is essential that our earnings be very modest to assure our dependence on men." [114]

Women understood that to be economically independent, they needed the educational opportunities still reserved for men alone. Guindorf implored: "There must be for women as for men, an equal chance for development. [Women must have an] education that develops in us our intellectual strengths; so that we shall be able to embrace a scientific career if such is our vocation." [115] The occasion for this article was the recent passage of the Guizot Law for reform of the national school system. The *Tribune des femmes* editors were angered that the law made no mention of female education except to say that "girls' schools can be founded if there is a need." They exclaimed, "If there is a need! What? Do not women everywhere need an education? " [116] The editors spoke here, as elsewhere, from personal experience. Suzanne Voilquin had no formal education: her brother taught her to read and she improved by reading newspapers to her father. Jeanne Deroin was entirely self-taught: in the 1840s she failed the primary school teaching certificate examination twice— because she could not write in cursive or do simple arithmetic—before finally passing. Pauline Roland was privately tutored by Desprez, a local *lycée* teacher.

We can trace through the *Tribune des femmes* the declining interest in free unions. Saint-Simonian women turned their attention instead to marriage reform. They generally agreed that divorce should be reestablished, "so that those of an ardent nature can change without dishonoring their families." [117] They agreed also that the subordination of women in marriage, sanctified by the Civil Code, had to be eliminated: "We no longer want this formula: woman, submit to your husband. We want a marriage based on equality. Better celibacy than slavery." [118] And they insisted that exclusive paternal authority, also sanctified by the code, had to be abolished: "The father has sole authority over his children. But in a family what is a mother? . . . Her influence is enormous; but her rights? Nil! " [119]

Saint-Simonian "free love" became the "freedom to love," the right to abstain from, as well as to participate in, sexual relationships. *Tribune des femmes* authors not only railed against "fathers who would sell their daughters" but also against Saint-Simonian men who would support women's freedom only when it resulted in "their pleasure and their glory: You like it fine that we are . . . freed from obeying our parents or religious law or worldly opinion, but slaves to your appetites." [120] Suzanne Voilquin, writing in the *Tribune des femmes,* described at some length one young woman's inability to protect herself from repeated rapes by a nearby neighbor. The story, well-written to elicit readers' sympathy, was interesting because, unlike other articles in which rape figured, it was not an explanation for a woman's "fall" into prostitution, which did not occur in this case. Its focus was on the man's overwhelming physical force and the absence of any legal protection for the woman: "What could this poor young girl do? She was 16. The courts recognize as criminal only the rape of those 15 years or younger." The clear moral was that French law left all women vulnerable to rape: "These deeds happen every day in our society." [121]

Voilquin knew of what she wrote. In her *Souvenirs,* she recalled her own vulnerability to forced sex. The late-night walks home from the embroidery workshop, where she and her sister had worked in the 1820s, had especially frightened her: "We could run into one of those horrid men who make a game of accosting young working women and frighten them with their ignoble propositions." They lived alone for awhile. One night two drunkards almost broke down their door. "With no protection . . . to guarantee our security we felt overwhelming terror." And Voilquin's first sexual relationship had been forced on her. She was unofficially engaged to a young medical student who implored her constantly to consummate their promised union. She held back, and he accused her of distrusting his intentions: "I did not know then that this was men's habitual tactic to arrive at their goal." But the "habitual tactic" failed; so one day "he became violent, carried away." The experience traumatized her. Years later she noted that it was the cause of her "distrust of men." [122]

"Vienne le Grand Concile de Femmes" [123]

The Saint-Simonian women responded to Enfantin's call to speak. But their words ultimately transformed Saint-Simonian feminism. Enfantin had declared that the emancipation of women required sexual liberation, or "rehabilitation of the flesh," to use his language. If woman is carnal love, and that love is sin, as in Christian thought, then woman is sin. If woman is love, and love—even carnal love— is virtue, as in Enfantinian thought, then woman is virtue.

Saint-Simonian women, however, were little interested in the "rehabilitation of the flesh." Their concern was to achieve autonomy. The common meeting ground between them and Enfantin was their shared rejection of the French marriage laws, which required indissoluble monogamy and the subjugation of wives to husbands. Seemingly more conservative than Enfantin, the women were in fact more radical. They had enlarged the feminist vision of sexual emancipation, for by linking it to economic, intellectual, and legal emancipation, they had placed the sexual question into the larger context of the political relationship of the sexes.

Enfantin had declared that the emancipation of women would be effected by religion. He created a churchlike structure, hierarchically organized, that would implement the spiritual vision of a couple-messiah. But the women, on their own, built political collectives. The most successful of these was the *Tribune des femmes*. Although it was published for less than two years and then slipped into oblivion, it was not without influence in its time. Letters to the editor indicate that it was read throughout France, in England, and in Louisiana. Some of its articles were translated into English by Anna Wheeler and reprinted in Robert Owen's *The Crisis* in 1833.[124]

Suzanne Voilquin was the journal's motivating force for most of its two-year existence. Her spirit of tolerance and her "republican nature" imbued the journal's pages. Voilquin also hosted the Wednesday night meetings for the "proletarian women" at which theoretical issues were first presented and developed. She was both insider and outsider within the Saint-Simonian movement, which may account for her special position within the autonomous women's movement. Because she had directed one of the communal houses, she had close ties to the men and women of the hierarchy. But Voilquin was not of them. Some of her letters suggest that her working-class origins separated her from the bourgeois elite;[125] others imply that it was her wariness of men, "sad companion of my youth which since 1823 weighed heavily on me," which explains her independence: "I approached the Saint-Simonian personnel with reserve. This tendency safeguarded me from being overcome by disillusionment later." [126]

The proletarian women of the *Tribune des femmes* had hopes of doing concrete work with poor and working-class women. They organized a Société d'Instruction Populaire to teach poor women, living their belief that, "that which men have not done it is up to us to do." [127] Reine Guindorf worked three to four nights a week on this activity, and the school, founded in 1832, was ongoing still, Voilquin informs us, in April 1834.[128] Other projects were proposed but not brought to fruition. In the *Tribune des femmes,* Angélique and Sophie-Caroline spelled out, in elaborate detail, their plan for a shelter for unmarried pregnant women and widows "by death or absence of their husbands." They itemized all of their estimated expenses, including the rental of a building in the neighborhood of the Luxembourg Gardens, and described the work each resident would do to minimize the shelter's expenses or to earn income for it.[129] In 1838, Voilquin tried to establish a "maternal society" for young unmarried mothers. Twenty-eight women agreed to support it with monthly payments, but evidently this funding was not adequate.[130]

All the proletarian women's projects were to be organized nonhierarchically. In 1832 the *grandes dames* of the former hierarchy had tried to rank the women in Saint-Simonian fashion, but the proletarian women had resisted. Voilquin contrasted herself to Aglaé Saint-Hilaire: "The lady, not wanting to preside over a republic, and I, for my part, not understanding the possibility of a hierarchy, considering our dispositions, were unable to reach agreement." [131]

The proletarian women's rejection of hierarchy extended beyond the organization of their projects. They challenged, too, Enfantin's concept of a Woman Messiah. In April 1834, the *Tribune des femmes* printed a tirade against the Compagnons de la Femme: "No! They will not find the Ideal that they are seeking, not so long as their narrow vision does not widen to see it in all women. . . . The *Mother* . . . is not one woman; she is all women." [132] When asked if she believed in the coming of the Woman Messiah, Voilquin responded:

> I only saw the "call" as a symbol. Every woman must make herself known, beyond the reach of masculine influence, by feelings or acts of her own free will. . . . These women will search each other out by the force of circumstances, to form among themselves an assembly where each one will bring her building block for the moral edifice of the future. It is this consciousness, totally feminine, that the Saint-Simonian men call the Mother. [133]

Women had replaced the Woman. Collective action had replaced revelation. Politics had replaced religion.

CHAPTER 5

Searching for Direction

S aint-Simonian feminist propaganda subsided after 1834. Suzanne Voilquin had given up the directorship of the *Tribune des femmes,* and although she may have hoped that someone else would take on the job, the journal ceased publishing.[1] Many of the feminist leaders had left Paris; some, including Voilquin, were in Egypt with Enfantin and Charles Lambert. The Saint-Simonians' "church" was dissolved, their newspapers and public lecturers silenced. The Saint-Simonian women had identified the value of constructing a women's movement at the very moment when the scattering of their members to distant places made such organizing most difficult. For the next decade and a half, feminism would be characterized by sporadic attempts to create the kind of cohesive movement dreamed of by the Saint-Simonian women.

At first, feminists who had become disenchanted with Saint-Simonism looked elsewhere for another group that would encourage their activities. The Fourierists appealed most to them and offered feminists many of the advantages that Saint-Simonism once had, especially a ready-made audience. But the Fourierists' other concerns soon eclipsed feminism. The apparent lesson was that feminism was better off on its own. The group of bourgeois liberals who supported the *Gazette des femmes* were not separatists, as were those of the all-female *Tribune des femmes,* but they did focus solely on feminism, unlike either the Saint-Simonian church or the Fourierists. The group's fate, however, was too closely linked to the fate of one person, the newspaper's editor. Government persecution did him in, and the paper collapsed. During this same period, Flora Tristan, a charismatic leader, initiated a project for a "workers' union." If successful, this effort would have strengthened feminism by linking it to the newly emerging working-class groups while, at the same time, retaining feminist control over the

89

union. But again, a solitary feminist could not make a movement, and her project died when she did.

Feminists were clearly flailing about. Their attempts to execute concrete projects failed for lack of capital. Their efforts to force legislative reform ran into a wall of patriarchal resistance. When they attached their cause to a well-organized movement with broad revolutionary goals, they reached larger audiences only to have their purpose subordinated to that movement's other concerns. Yet on their own, feminists were unable to influence large numbers of people.

However unsuccessful or short-lived feminist activities were before 1848, they were significant nonetheless. The strength of the feminist movement in 1848–51 is partly explained by the fact that its leadership would have had nearly two decades of political experience. They would be well known and respected, at least among revolutionary leftists, and would have broadened their ties to include among their friends bourgeois liberals and new organizers of the working class, as well as their older allies, the utopian socialists. In the 1830s and 1840s, feminists who would become important leaders during the years of the revolutionary upheaval (1848–51) accumulated new ideas and fresh approaches to solving old problems.

Fourierism

A political movement based on the ideas of Charles Fourier was organized during the 1830s, although his major works had been written during the preceding quarter century. And although the ideas of Fourier predated— even influenced—Enfantin's, political Fourierism was influenced as much by the history of Saint-Simonism as by the ideas of Fourier himself.

The feminisms of Fourier and Enfantin compare and contrast in subtle ways. For both Fourier and Enfantin, human progress required the emancipation of women. Enfantin had, however, accepted the nineteenth-century dichotomization of the human personality: human progress required the guidance of women's special and unique virtues. Fourier, on the other hand, believed that all individuals, male and female, were born equal and were basically similar in nature. Only "savagery" had denied women rights and opportunities equal to men's.

In the visions of both Fourier and Enfantin, liberation of women and sexual liberation were connected. Their increased interest in sexuality reflected the separation of procreation and sex that was encouraged by the demographic revolution of the time. For Fourier, however, sexual freedom was required because the liberation of both men and women depended on the freedom to express all the passions. Again, this view differed from Enfantin's line of reasoning, which suggested that the liberation of women required sexual liberation because women were equated with sexuality.[2]

Both Fourier and Enfantin believed that a new social order was necessary to achieve equality. But whereas Enfantin expected increased concentration of capital and industrial production to advance human progress, Fourier distrusted industry and cities and proposed self-sufficient agrarian communities in their stead. Both agreed that in the new society, "association" must replace the individualism or *égoïsme* that characterized nineteenth-century capitalism, but here, too, the application of their theory would differ. The associationist bonds of the Saint-Simonians were patterned after both the church and the family; emotional ties were emphasized and hierarchy was accepted. In contrast, the associationist bonds Fourier proposed emphasized economic cooperation, and although private ownership of property and inequality of wealth were not abolished, they would cease to have significance. An important step toward communistic equality had been taken. (more Owen-ish

Charles Fourier published his major work, *Théorie des quatre mouvements et des destinées générales: Prospectus et annonce de la découverte*, in 1808. Later works—*Traité de l'association domestique-agricole* (1822) and *Le Nouveau monde industriel et sociétaire, ou invention du procédé d'industrie attrayant et naturelle distribuée en séries passionnées* (1829)—merely elaborated, in the case of the earlier three-volume work, or pared down, in the later work, that which he had proposed during the first decade of Napoleon-imposed silence. Unlike Enfantin, who developed his theory in the midst of an energetic group, Fourier worked in isolation. There was no feminist movement, and he had no allies.

Fourier was poor, although he had been born to wealth. His relatives had been well-to-do cloth merchants from Besançon. His father died when he was young and left him a significant inheritance, which required that he take over the family business. He did so unwillingly. Then, during the Revolution, the family fortune was confiscated, leaving Fourier free to choose his work but desperately poor. He lived for a while in Lyons, then moved to Paris in 1826. He worked at a series of low-level jobs in commerce: as a cashier, a bookkeeper, a traveling salesman, and a correspondence clerk for the Paris branch of an American company. His hatred for the world of business pervaded his writings.

A man of little formal education, Fourier distrusted all previous thinkers, Newton alone excepted. He claimed that his ideas were based solely on personal observation. His anecdotal stories about corrupt business practices and unhappy family life were likely picked up during his travels, in restaurants and pensions. But the roots of his vision of harmonious relationships and unrepressed passion are more complex. Fourier's focus on human happiness as the rightful goal of society is in the tradition of eighteenth-century thought, as is his sense of history and faith in human progress. His ideas have been linked most specifically to Rousseau's because of their shared conviction that people are basically good and "civilization" is to blame for their corruption. Similarly, both favored agrarian societies and distrusted urban life and industrialization. Yet such links to earlier thinkers are impressionistic and vague; the originality of Fourier's thought—particularly as it pertains to male/female relationships—is far more striking.

where do his ideas come from?

Fourier was a most unlikely person to inspire a movement that put human relationships first. All his recorded childhood memories are unhappy. He lived alone for most of his adult life; he never married and may never have had a love relationship. His closest disciple, Just Muiron, was deaf, and they communicated only in writing. Until the 1830s he worked alone, with no following. Although he carefully regulated his schedule so he was always at home at noon to greet a wealthy patron who, Fourier hoped, would enable him to put his system into practice, no one came forth. Only in the last decade before his death did he achieve some popularity.

Fourier's writings remained so long unknown largely because they were unreadable. They are filled with bizarre details and flights into fantasy that create the inescapable impression that the author was insane. He invented a cosmology; he wrote of stars and planets that have sexual relations and of anti-lions and anti-whales; he cataloged 60 different kinds of adulterous relationships and 810 different personality types. Yet his writings did attract early attention from some writers, including Robert Owen and Prosper Enfantin. His influence on nineteenth-century French feminism was immeasurable.

Already, in 1808, Fourier had put the cornerstone of nineteenth-century—and even twentieth-century—feminist thought into place.

like Owen

> As a general thesis: *Social progress and changes from one era to the next are brought about in proportion to the progress of women toward freedom, and social decline is brought about in proportion to the decrease in women's freedom.*
>
> Other events influence political change; but there is no other cause that produces so rapid a social improvement or so rapid a social decline as the change in women's lot.[3]

In *Théorie des quartre mouvements,* Fourier placed women center stage in the drama of history. Not only did the position of women serve as an indicator, measuring and setting the standard for the degree of progress of a particular epoch, but, more significantly, a change in the position of women acted as a catalyst for other change, forcing a culture upward or downward in historical evolution. The emancipation of women would serve to liberate the entire human race. Conversely, human progress would forever be blocked if the talents and capacities of half the human race were not fully used. Human liberty remained a chimera if all humans, male and female, were not free: "Now, God only recognizes as freedom that which extends to both sexes, and not just to one; thus, he willed that all precepts of social men, in the stages of savagery, barbarity, and civilization, derive from the servitude of women; and that all precepts of social good, such as in the 6th, 7th, and 8th stages, derive from the emancipation of the fair sex."[4]

Fourier's complex cosmology viewed human progression through stages of developments. France had already passed through savagery, patriarchy, and barbarity and was then in the stage of civilization (nothing to boast about, in Fourier's vocabulary). Higher stages were the fifth, sixth, and seventh ones. In the final (eighth) utopian stage of human progress, which Fourier named Harmony, men and women would be equal, free, and productive. A unique educational system would scrupulously treat girls and boys alike. Fourier even demanded that the two sexes dress the same, in recognition of the variety of ways that socialization may affect equality. In Harmony, women would not be excluded from any social or economic function, "not even from medicine or teaching."[5] The corps of professors ("le corps Sybillin"), the most important in his social system, would include as many women as men. True, Fourier declared that men were more gifted in science, women in the arts,[6] and that many occupations would be better suited to one or the other sex. But no function would ever have fewer than one-eighth representation of one or the other sex.

Central to Fourier's thought was his law of passionate attraction—a "law" he stated to be as fundamental to understanding human nature as Newton's law of gravity was to physical nature. "Passionate attraction" was the one constant of evolving human interactions. The "passions," Fourier declared, can and have been subverted (today we would say sublimated) but not extinguished: "Even though these passions are completely smothered by our civilized habits, nevertheless their seed exists in our soul."[7] Fourier believed, without question, that human beings are innately good. If civilization was less than perfect, it was because innate human nature had been thwarted in its desire for spontaneous expression.[8] To restrain human passion was to "correct" the work of God, a sinful and heretical error. The passions, which God has created in us, are the elements of progress. They should be satisfied, not denied. The final utopian stage of humanity—Harmony—would be characterized by an absolute liberty to follow the law of passionate attraction.

In detailing the law of passionate attraction, Fourier identified twelve passions: five "luxurious" passions of the senses, four group passions (honor, love, friendship, and parenthood), and three "distributive" passions. The distributive passions—the cabalist, the composite, and the butterfly— practically unrecognized in civilization, would, in Harmony, operate in love, work, family, and friendship. In love relations the cabalist (competitive) passion[9] would stimulate interest in the opposite sex, the butterfly would kill boredom, and the "composite" would regulate extremes. Every individual had all of these passions, and all passions would be given free rein in love.

In Harmony, couples would no longer be bound in the marriage of "civilization," marriage based on dupery for men and servitude for women. Love alone would unite couples in Harmony, and the union would last only so long as the attraction that joined them.

With surprising modernity, Fourier insisted that both sexes have the same emotional and sexual needs, capacities, and rights. Like feminists of the 1970s and 1980s, he was concerned with women's right to experience sexual fulfillment. In comparison, Enfantin, and even the Saint-Simonian women, were concerned with the external arrangements regulating sexual relationships. Not that Fourier was unconcerned with these structures: he, too, condemned patriarchal marriage. Fourier expressed amazement that men could believe that they benefited from the then-current marital system:

> One says in political affairs, that the strong have made the law; it is not the same way in home affairs. The masculine sex, although the strongest, has not made the law to its advantage by establishing isolated households and that which follows, permanent marriages. . . . If one thinks about the innumerable inconveniences attached to conjugal life and permanent marriage, one will be surprised at the dupery of the masculine sex, which has never perceived the way to free itself of that kind of life.

Among the numerous inconveniences he specifies are expenses, vigilance, monotony (which Fourier says is worse for women), sterility, widowhood/ widowerhood, and cuckoldry. But, he warned, only in Harmony might the passions express themselves freely. In civilization marriage was still necessary: "One must remember that I admit the necessity of this bond [marriage] in civilization, and that where I criticize it is in comparison with the new social order, where different combinations of events will find use for the freedom of loves now inadmissible among us." [10] And even in Harmony, an enforced period of celibacy would be required to end venereal disease; only then could freedom exist.

Women's equality in Harmony was characterized not only by educational opportunities, sexual liberation, and freedom from a marriage of servitude, but also by freedom from the isolation and tedium of housework. Fourier notes that most women dislike housework. The 25 percent who by nature "make a game of domestic work" are all that are necessary to do this work for all persons living in Harmony. Fourier asserts, in fact, that nature intentionally denies three-quarters of women the inclination to do housework so as "to maintain the proportion suitable to the communal order which will use barely a quarter of them in its duties." [11] Fourier makes a similar example of men and their work maintaining the wine cellar. Further, domestic work—like all other productive labor—would be performed communally:

> Among the domestic nuisances one must place that of individual service. In contrast, [in Harmony] servants are not attached to an individual but to the group; each one of them attaching himself to the diverse members whose characters are in sympathy with his own, and this ability to choose renders the duty agreeable to the superiors as well as to the inferiors. It is friendship more than self-interest that brings them together, and this is still an unknown pleasure in societies with families, where servants are usually secret enemies of the masters.[12]

To create the final utopian stage of humanity, no revolution such as the one Fourier himself had witnessed (1789–93) would be necessary. "The little that I have said about progressive households is sufficient to demonstrate the extreme ease with which one can get out of the civilized labyrinth, without political upheaval, without scientific effort, but by a purely domestic transaction." [13] Merely by creating associationist communities ("phalansteries"), Harmony could be achieved. All would see the benefits. All would hurry to participate. And women had a special role to play in transforming society.

> It is upon women that civilization bears heavily; it is up to women to attack it. What are their lives like today? They live only lives of deprivation, even in industry, where man has invaded all, even down to the meticulous occupations of sewing, of feathering, whereas one sees women striving away at hard work in the country. Women should have produced not writers but liberators; political Spartacuses, geniuses who would devise a way to pull their sex out of degradation.[14]

French women were to remain unaware of Fourier's challenge for several decades. His obscure style condemned his writings to neglect until Victor Considérant made them intelligible to the general public in the 1830s. In 1832, Fourier, Considérant, and the Saint-Simonian apostate Jules Lechevalier founded a "school" and a publication, *La Réforme industrielle ou le Phalanstère.* They took care to avoid the errors of the Saint-Simonians but to imitate the successes even when, to do so, they departed from the teachings of Fourier. They called themselves "associationists" or members of the Ecole Sociétaire, rather than Fourierists, to emphasize that they were a political organization, not a religious grouping of devoted disciples. They sought to avoid the pitfalls of helplessly awaiting a utopian future by offering an immediate program to achieve their goals—the establishment of associations ("phalanxes") based on communal production and communal sharing of housekeeping functions. They stressed their economic program because of the failure of visionary, mystical appeals.[15] And they downplayed those aspects of Fourierism that threatened either the family or traditional sexual mores.

Some of the school's first recruits were Saint-Simonians who had left that movement after Enfantin's "pronouncements" on sexual morals. Eugénie Niboyet became an associationist early in 1832 and urged Lechevalier to impose a politics of sexual restraint on the new school.[16] Perhaps because they had the strong support of Clarisse Vigoureux, the *éminence grise* of the associationists' school,[17] the sexual "traditionalists" had their way. The associationists' moral position was carefully distinguished from the Saint-Simonian position as well as from Fourier's. They discarded "la politique galante" and family reorganization. Fourier himself was prevailed upon to write in *Le Phalanstère* that the transformation of morals which he envisioned in Harmony was "generations away." After his death in 1837, all discussion of a new morality ceased, to be replaced by less shocking statements that freedom to love could be achieved by reestablishing divorce. And even this limited measure would, according to associationists, rarely need to be exercised. Ultimately, the words "freedom to love" came to mean that which would be achieved when women were economically independent and could freely choose a marriage partner out of love rather than financial need. In 1841, the Fourierist Madame Gatti de Gamond wrote:

> Strange error one falls into on the subject of women. There are those who believe that to demand their emancipation, their increased freedom, that one must demand a greater enlargement of corruption and immorality. This is to mistake the nature of women. Corruption is forced upon them; they do not consent to it voluntarily; they do not stop detesting it, even

as they surrender to it. They struggle and fight against the fatality of circumstances and curse an unjust society that condemns them to degradation and offers them no road to salvation. To young women of the lower classes, it is poverty and brutishness that push them to the abyss. In women of the upper classes, it is boredom, disgust, emptiness of the soul that result from isolation or unhappy marriages that they enter because of need. Misconduct is almost always for women a result of their state of misery, servitude, and idleness. One must, therefore, understand by moral emancipation, for women, an independence of position that would allow them never to sell themselves, never to give themselves against their tendency, but to choose the man they love, to whom they may freely promise love and fidelity.

> The subjection of women, their close dependence on men in relation to poverty, due to their always precarious financial position, is the main cause of immorality.[18]

Marriages, freely chosen, would be permanent by choice.

There is no doubt that some of the *Tribune des femmes* women found associationism appealing. The new school espoused many of the ideas that the Saint-Simonian women had come to believe in, such as an increased focus on economic issues and a retrenchment on sexual freedom. It seems to have encouraged women such as Désirée Veret and Reine Guindorf in their growing independence from the former Saint-Simonian hierarchy. As early as October 1832, the *Tribune des femmes* reflected the influence of Fourierist ideas. In the October 8, 1832, issue, the slogan, "Liberty for women, liberty for the people through a new organization of the household and industry," appeared on the *Tribune des femmes* masthead. An article in that same issue, signed by Jeanne-Désirée (Désirée Veret), identified Fourier as the source of the proposal to reorganize the household. She went on to say that "his theories of associations are the most complete which have yet appeared on this subject" and promised to say more about him and to explain (*vulgariser*) his work: "The religion of the future [Saint-Simonian] must not, like those of the past, push away that which is not born within it." In a later issue, Marie-Reine (Reine Guindorf) wrote of Fourier: "We hear a lot about improvements that can be brought about in the fate of the people. . . . Everyone's intentions . . . are good; but the people suffer. We must have more active remedies. . . .We must have more than a distant future; we must have a theory that we can realize immediately. Monsieur Fourier has one." [19]

But the associationists' apparent promise to take feminism out of its mystical impasse and construct model communities foundered on lack of capital and personnel. The attempt made in 1832 to set up a trial phalanx at Condé-sur-Vosges never moved beyond the planning stage. Associationists' concern for respectability led first away from free love but soon away from feminism. In 1836, the associationists founded *La Phalange* and in 1834, *La Démocratie pacifique*. Both were more popular than the first associationist periodical; yet both downplayed feminist concerns and focused instead on class issues and pacifism (mostly in the form of Franco-German reconciliation).[20] Women like Eugénie Niboyet who may have hoped that the associationists would advance feminism beyond where the Saint-Simonians had left it soon knew that they were on their own.

La Gazette des femmes

The women of the *Tribune des femmes* had suggested another strategy to break through the impasse of utopianism: legal reform. This issue was pursued by a group quite unlike the *Tribune des femmes* women that clustered around the *Gazette des femmes* (1836–38). The *Gazette des femmes* group, calling itself "une société de femmes et d'hommes de lettres," [21] consisted mainly of bourgeois women and men. Most likely these members of the bourgeoisie were particularly sensitive to the law codes' double standard based on sex because of the way the codes favored the men— but only the men—of their class. They had an interest in governmental politics that distinguished them from both Saint-Simonians and associationists. They seemed personally to know the leading legislators and other influential political figures, such as the important journalists of their time.

France during the regime of Louis-Philippe was no political or economic democracy, even among men. Although the 1830 Charter had enlarged the franchise to include a greater number of the propertyowning bourgeoisie, a property tax payment of two hundred francs annually was still required in order to vote or to stand for office. Only about 2 to 3 percent of the adult male population met this criterion.[22] The *Gazette des femmes* constituency was the women of this elite group.

A Madame Poutret de Mauchamps was the journal's "propriétaire-gérante responsable." In the first issue—July 1836—she wrote that she had "at her disposal 220 acres of land in the Beauce, worth at least 180,000 francs." She had inherited this wealth from Madame Louise-Caroline Tridon Herbinot de Mauchamps. A notice bordered in black on the last page of the first issue read:

> During her lifetime, Madame Louise-Caroline Tridon Herbinot de Mauchamps involved herself deeply and industriously with the rights and duties

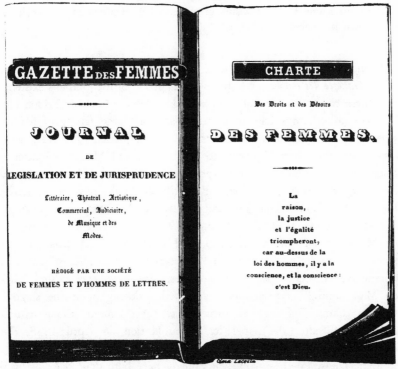

of women, and the improvement of their social position as daughters, wives, and widows. At her death, she charged her son and her adoptive daughter, Madame Poutret de Mauchamps, to gather together the numerous documents that she had collected and to publish them. It is this pious work, it is this testamentary wish, that we execute today. May the respectful accomplishment of the wishes of a beloved mother obtain the results for which her noble heart hoped! [23]

If one compiles a list, as I have, of all the authors who signed articles in the *Gazette des femmes* over the two-year period of the journal's existence, one might conclude—wrongly—that Madame Louise-Caroline Tridon Herbinot de Mauchamps had an extraordinary and large family of feminist writers. The Frédéric de Mauchamps who, in the journal's last year, signed articles as "the editor," appears to be the son, and Madame Poutret de Mauchamps, the journal's owner and "responsible director," the "adoptive daughter." And there were other authors who could also have been relatives: Louise T.H., Caroline Herbinot, and Tonibreh de Mauchamps, for example, as well as Louise T., C.F.H. *(jurisconsulte)*, De M., Frédéric de M., H. de M., Herbinot *(électeur éligible)*, and Herbinot de Mauchamps. The identity of this family has engaged the curiosity of historians, who have questioned whether, in fact, many of these individuals ever existed. These de Mauchampses and Herbinots appeared suddenly upon the stage of feminist drama. Before 1836 their names never figured among feminist activists, and after the paper ceased publication, in April 1838, they disappeared again.

Marie-Louise Puech and Evelyne Sullerot have both done detective work to identify each of the supposed family members, and both have concluded that all their writings are the work of one man, Charles Frédéric Herbinot de Mauchamps.[24] The copy of the *Gazette des femmes* that I have examined at the Bibliothèque de l'Arsenal, in the Fonds Enfantin, is autographed, "To Père Enfantin, head of the Saint-Simonian Religion, [from] His former comrade of the collège . . . Charles Frédéric Herbinot de Mauchamps." But this presents another mystery, for I have never found his name in any listing of prominent Saint-Simonians and certainly not in any listing of members of the Collège. Sullerot has discovered that Herbinot had a doctorate in law, that in 1830 he had been one of the publishers of *L'Opinion,* a republican newspaper that was silenced by the government of Louis-Philippe after the king had consolidated his power, and that from 1831 to 1833, Herbinot had written articles and music, theater, and book reviews for *Le Journal des femmes,* which he signed with a variety of different names and initials. He was evidently able to express his feminism

if she's articulate it doesn't necessarily mean that she's literate

even then. Announcing Madame Guizot's book on female education in
1835, for example, he wrote: "Monsieur Guizot's wife has won a prize
of 8,000 francs for her work on women's education; but this has not
prevented the Prime Minister from declaring that the moment has not yet
arrived to create primary schools for girls." [25]

Madame Poutret de Mauchamps was not Herbinot's adoptive sister; she
was his lover. In 1836, she was twenty-one years old, twenty years younger
than Herbinot. Both Puech and Sullerot are certain that she wrote none
of the articles or petitions that bore her signature. The original handwritten
petitions were clearly the work of a person other than the signer, according
to Sullerot, who has examined them in the Archives Nationales. [26] Puech
states that Poutret's signature had the uncertainty of an illiterate. [27] Yet
Poutret was probably an intelligent conversationalist; the group of feminists—those "femmes et hommes de lettres"—who clustered around the
Gazette des femmes and met with Herbinot and Poutret every Thursday
evening seem not to have questioned that Poutret was the author of all
she claimed to be.

Sullerot questions why Herbinot hid his identity behind Poutret. She
finds this particularly incomprehensible since he claimed that he wished
to publish the *Gazette des femmes* daily but could not because women
were not permitted to do so. In fact, the journal could, legally, have
published daily, if only the real *gérant responsable* had not hidden his
identity. For Sullerot, this compounds the mystery. [28] I, however, doubt
that Herbinot had the capital to publish more frequently than monthly.
Indeed, after only seven issues, the number of pages of the *Gazette des
femmes* decreased from thirty-two to sixteen. Even if money had not been
a problem, there would have been good reason for Herbinot to publish
under Poutret's name; it was a tactic designed to press his claim that
women should have the right then denied them to direct a political daily
newspaper.

women in history have taken pen-names of men to legitimize their writing, What's the diff?

The politics of the *Gazette des femmes* were moderately republican.
Although the memory of France's revolutionary past was warmly evoked,
the compromise that republicans had made with Louis-Philippe in 1830
that established the constitutional monarchy was apparently acceptable. A
mildly anticlerical deism was evident, and Enlightenment language—words
like "reason," "justice," and "equality"—runs through the text. The
feminism of the *Gazette des femmes* was limited by the possibilities of
liberal republicanism but was still extraordinarily advanced; the journal
reads like the feminist republican periodicals of the 1880s and 1890s.

The journal also shows the influence of Saint-Simonism, particularly in
its attention to the abuses of the double standard of sexual morality.

Although neither Herbinot's style of writing nor his legal reform strategy is Saint-Simonian, there are many Saint-Simonian references in the journal— more frequent in the last months of its existence. For example, the December 1837 issue invoked the trinity of the Saint-Simonian church: "Let us hand over the Chamber of Deputies to the *women, proletarians,* and *artists*." [29]

Herbinot set forth his publishing program in the first issue of the *Gazette des femmes* and faithfully adhered to it thereafter. It would be a "Journal of Legislation, Jurisprudence, Literature, Theater, Art, Commerce, Law, Music, and Fashion." [30] It would analyze those sections of the 1830 Charter and of the other French codes that pertained to the rights and duties of women and would "demand by legal petitions, addressed to the [legislative] Chambers, political and civil rights for women." [31] During the second volume year, the back cover carried the pronouncement that the "sole and unique goal [of the *Gazette des femmes*] is to obtain the exercise of POLITICAL AND CIVIL RIGHTS FOR WOMEN." The back cover statement went on to explain that each issue would feature a legal petition to the legislative chambers "to obtain the exercise of a right or the improvement of a law concerning women." In addition, each issue would include a theatrical review "conceptualized in the same way"; a critical examination of court judgments concerning women; a commercial or industrial article "of interest either to business women or to consumers of factory products"; and arts, music, fashion, and "confidences," that is, a section "to express hopes, good wishes, or regrets."

Meetings of subscribers and editors would take place every Thursday evening and assure that the journal expressed, as well as created, the opinion of a group, perhaps eventually a movement.[32] Eugénie Niboyet attended these meetings, and she interested Flora Tristan in going to them also.[33] Writers Elisabeth Celnart, Anaïs Ségalas, Clémence Robert, Caroline d'Huillet, Antoinette Dupin, Virginie de Sénancourt, and Hortense Allart all attended.[34] Hortense Allart was likely the most active among them. She had had frequent contact, earlier, with the Saint-Simonians and had written letters of encouragement to the editors of the *Tribune des femmes.* Her 1836 *La Femme et la démocratie de nos temps* showed this Saint-Simonian influence. She believed in hierarchy, she wrote, but disapproved of "ranking men by birth and women by chastity." Her language was religious in the way that Enfantin's was, rather than political.[35] Although her Romantic style was different from the more reasoned, classical style of the *Gazette des femmes,* the two evidently coexisted happily.

In the fall of 1836, Allart announced in the pages of the *Gazette des femmes* a project to form an Association for the Improvement of the Status of Woman: "Improvement will happen gradually. We will make nothing precise at first. We will study this serious question, but we demand the support of those who interest themselves in the moral [question]." She wrote that her project had been discussed and approved at a Thursday night meeting.[36] There is, however, no evidence that the association ever materialized.

The *Gazette des femmes* invited its readers to draw up their own petitions, which the journal would announce and keep on file for other women to sign. Several petitions to reestablish divorce were announced, and a petition for the abolition of the death penalty, written by the Société de la Morale Chrétienne,[37] was printed in the *Gazette des femmes* pages. One petition for divorce, initiated by a Madame Delpeschin, gathered more than five hundred signatures.

The petitions that the *Gazette des femmes* originated were all signed by "Madame Poutret de Mauchamps, propriétaire-gérante responsable."[38] They were usually addressed to the king and to the Chambers of Deputies and Peers. One was addressed simply to Louis-Phillippe.[39] Another was a request to the Institut de France to admit women as members. These petitions were all lengthy and written in a sophisticated style, obviously by someone familiar with French law. Usually they were "argued" like a case in a court of law: similar to lawyers' briefs, they were designed to prove that some right already existed. They referred often to articles 1 and 2 of the 1830 Charter, which proclaimed that "Frenchmen are equal before the law whatever their former title or rank" (art. 1) and that "they contribute similarly, in proportion to their wealth, to the expenses of the state" (art. 2). According to Herbinot, the reference to "Frenchmen" in article 1 was clearly meant to include women since both men and women were subject to the taxation called for in article 2.

The first petition that the *Gazette des femmes* printed related to the demand to publish the journal daily. The initial July 1836 issue carried "Madame Poutret de Mauchamps's" letter to the Interior Ministry requesting such permission, a negative response signed by Interior Minister Cave, and a petition to the Chambers to override that decision "in accordance with the 1830 Charter which guarantees freedom of the press."[40] How nineteenth-century French press laws were meant to apply to women is not clear from a simple reading of the laws, nor have legal or press historians clarified this point. Evidently the law evolved as successive ministries interpreted the code's provision that every newspaper have a "responsible director" (art. 980) who meets the qualifications for state witnesses (art. 37), including that they be male. Herbinot asked both that article 980 be separated from the article concerning witnesses and also that article 37 be changed. In the meantime, the *Gazette des femmes* would publish only monthly, and it stated that it would "not concern itself in any way with politics." [41] Yet women were not necessarily prohibited from publishing political journals. Neither the *Tribune des femmes* nor *Foi nouvelle: Livre des actes* had male "responsible directors," yet both paid the special stamp tax that applied only to political journals and were recognized as political by the government. And after its fifth issue, the *Gazette des femmes* was seized and forced to pay the stamp tax. [42] Evidently women were excluded only from directing *daily* political newspapers.

Other petitions printed in the *Gazette des femmes* demanded a range of rights for women. In August 1836, a petition called for the suppression "entirely and completely" of article 213 of the Civil Code, which read: "The husband owes protection to his wife; the wife obedience to her husband." [43] Four months later, the *Gazette des femmes* proposed "to suppress article 214 of the code which required that a woman live with her husband and that she follow him wherever he moves." [44] Among the subsequent petitions printed were ones to obtain for women the rights to sit on juries; to study at all of the royal colleges, law and medical schools, and to take the qualifying examinations required to practice law and medicine and teach at the university level; and to vote if they met the age and tax qualifications that pertained now only to men. [45] One petition demanded rights for mothers equal to those of fathers over minor children. [46] Another championed businesswomen's rights to be admitted to the Bourse and sit as jurors on the commercial tribunals. [47] The most sweeping petition of all was the one that argued that "it be recognized and declared by the king and the Chambers that IN VIRTUE OF THE 1830 CHARTER, WOMEN HAVE THE SAME CIVIL AND POLITICAL RIGHTS AS MEN." [48]

Some of the petitions are reminiscent of Herbinot's ties to the Saint-Simonians. One called for the decriminalization of adultery. [49] Another demanded the reestablishment of divorce, "not only as it was under the Empire of Napoleon but for INCOMPATABILITY OF HUMOR and for IMPOSSIBILITY OF LIVING TOGETHER IN THE STATE OF MARRIAGE declared by one or the other or both of the spouses." [50]

The petition was the *Gazette des femmes*'s strategy for feminist reform. It had never been tried before in France. Interestingly, it was in 1836 that the first petition for women's rights was circulated in the United States—for a married woman's property law in New York State. In America, petitions were a strategy that had been pioneered by the Abolition movement; women's right to circulate and sign petitions themselves had been eloquently defended by John Quincy Adams in Congress in 1834. [51] Although there is no mention in the *Gazette des femmes* of American antislavery or women's rights campaigns, French socialists and republicans were sympathetic to the American antislavery movement. Very likely Herbinot was aware of the tactics of the American—as well as the British— movements. In the spring of 1838, he reported that a petition circulated by a Female Anti-Slavery Association in England had gathered sixty-seven hundred signatures.[52]

The *Gazette des femmes* was informational as well as activist. Particular care was taken to include news that Herbinot considered favorable to women, and publications of "friends" were hearalded. For example, the *Gazette des femmes* praised Victor Considérant as "a man of talent and conviction" and noted that in his journal, *La Phalange,* "women are esteemed and considered the equals of men. His journal therefore merits our praise." [53] *Pérégrinations d'une paria* by Flora Tristan was recommended, as were the works of Eugénie Niboyet and Elisabeth Celnart. Jules Janin (the editor of the well-respected *Journal des débats*) reviewed the work of George Sand. News of Sand's legal separation was also covered in the *Gazette des femmes,* which expressed the hope that she would now begin to write under her own name.[54]

The journal also summarized the court judgments that pertained to women, particularly blatantly unfair rulings that could be exploited for their propagandistic value. One such example is of a woman whose husband forced her into prostitution. Her body was covered with scars from beatings, and she was able to get her spouse arrested, tried, convicted, and sentenced to fifteen days in prison. But once liberated he accused her of adultery for her prostitution work; the court found her guilty and sentenced her to three months' imprisonment. Other judgments exposed in the *Gazette des femmes* "proved" the necessity of reestablishing divorce:

> In Bredfort, in England, a husband, alleging as cause for a separation the attachment that his wife had for a worker, led her by a rope tied around her neck to the marketplace. There . . . the worker offered one piece of gold and . . . purchased the wife.

> In Soissons, the neighbors of M.*** heard frightening cries, broke down the door and found the unhappy Mme.*** tied up and half devoured by three starving cats that her husband had locked up with her, without food, for three days.[55]

Again the Saint-Simonian influence on Herbinot is evident. The decisions that caught his attention frequently concerned the double standard of sexual morality that had been written into the French civil and criminal codes.

The authorities were evidently not pleased by Herbinot's critiques of their judgments or by his petition campaign. He did succeed in forcing the French legislature to discuss feminist issues, but unfortunately to little avail. The transcription of the Chamber of Deputies' hearing on "Mme. Poutret de Mauchamps's" petition to abolish article 213 expressed the government's concern that she was speaking for a "new sect": "The petition is not the result of a caprice or a work of no reflection . . . it is the development of a cold, serious, and calculating system." Although the legislators responded to the commission report with "hilarity," "more hilarity," and "new laughter," the government would later decide that more than ridicule was required to silence "la femme libre." [56]

Herbinot may have moved beyond the limits of the government's forbearance only in 1838, after he stepped up Saint-Simonian references in the pages of the *Gazette des femmes*. After a seven-month publishing hiatus in 1837, the tone of the *Gazette des femmes* changed. For example, in 1836, the original voting rights petition had asked for this right only for unmarried women over twenty-five years old who paid two hundred francs in annual taxes. Not only had Herbinot not disputed the tax qualification that was the basis of political power in the constitutional monarchy, he had also seemingly endorsed it. In 1838, however, he was writing: "*Proletarians* and *women* are white slaves in relation to privileged men. . . . Let women . . . who fear not the laws of September [1834, against associations] form organized associations and let proletarians join them in order to present to the Chamber of Deputies petitions demanding rights for white slaves." [57] In 1838, too, "Mme. Poutret de Mauchamps" added "Magdaleine" to her signature, and the judicial cases reported in the *Gazette des femmes* had more explicitly sexual themes.[58]

Herbinot had overstepped the boundaries of acceptable protest. In the spring of 1838, he and Poutret were tried for "corruption of morals." The charges against them recall the charges that had sent Enfantin and Chevalier to prison for a year. The case against Poutret and Herbinot is shrouded in mystery. Both Puech and Sullerot have examined the court records as best they could—much of it was *huis clos*—as well as the press accounts of their trials. Herbinot was accused of seducing three young women who worked in his home as domestics. Two withdrew their accusations, but one of them insisted he was guilty. Herbinot was convicted and condemned to prison for ten years. Poutret was tried as an accomplice, acquitted, then tried again in a different court for "habitual incitement to debauchery." The prosecutor, declaring that in the publications she directed,

[handwritten margin notes: "association of women + workers - big threat (constant fear of replay of french revolution) any organization of workers looks threatening"]

"everything that is disgusting to good morals is exalted," this time got the guilty verdict he had sought. Poutret was sent to prison for eighteen months.

Both Sullerot and Puech suggest that the charges against Herbinot and Poutret were trumped up. The biographical information that both authors have uncovered does not suggest that Herbinot was given to "debauchery." According to Sullerot, the court record indicates that in 1830 Herbinot was found guilty of a similar crime, but Sullerot believes that the 1830 charges may also have been fabricated; his crime then most likely related to his role on the opposition newspaper *L'Opinion*. Even if he was guilty as charged in 1838, Herbinot's sentence was extremely severe. In France in the 1830s, it was extraordinary for a man of property to be found guilty of seducing a nineteen-year-old servant and be imprisoned for ten years for that crime. The case against Poutret was even more obviously unfair; she was found guilty of charges that related entirely to the *Gazette des femmes*.[59] The fate of Poutret and Herbinot was unexpectedly severe, reminding us that it was very dangerous to espouse even a moderate version of feminism in the 1830s.

Flora Tristan (1803–1844)

The politics of Flora Tristan would be no more acceptable to French authorities. In her last years she would be tracked by the police, and her meetings with workers would be infiltrated by the spies of the Interior Ministry. But government persecution, in this instance, failed to obliterate her name from history. In this way, at least, she succeeded where Herbinot and the Saint-Simonian women had failed.

Tristan is perhaps the most celebrated of all nineteenth-century French feminists. She had a special talent for attracting others' attention. Contemporaries remarked on her forceful personality, her daring, her beauty, and her indefatigable energy. Victor Considérant wrote in *La Phalange* that she was "the most gifted woman for the social cause." In 1848, four years after her death, Bordeaux workers erected a monument at her gravesite, and eight thousand people were there to honor her memory.[60] She had become a legend.

Tristan was born to a wealthy Peruvian father, who died when she was four, and a French mother. She was raised in poverty because the government, refusing to recognize the legality of her parents' marriage—a religious ceremony in Spain—confiscated her father's property as "alien property" after his death. Flora Tristan was declared "illegitimate."

At eighteen, Tristan went to work in a lithography workshop and soon after married her employer, André Chazal. In *L'Union ouvrière* she wrote about young, poor girls who jump at the chance to marry in order to escape the dreariness of their parents' homes, only to end up in even drearier circumstances, unhappily married. She was certainly writing from her own experience. Tristan and Chazal had three children, one of whom died in early childhood, before she left him in 1825. For the next nine years she traveled as a "ladies' companion," going several times to England. She also went alone to Peru to reestablish her ties to her father's family. Her experiences in Peru are described in her autobiography, *Pérégrinations d'une paria* (1838), and are the background for her novel, *Méphis,* published that same year.

Tristan returned to Paris from Peru in January 1835. She was soon embroiled with Chazal, who had custody of both children, Ernest and Aline. In 1837 he sexually attacked Aline. Tristan took him to court and won custody of her daughter. The next year Chazal shot Tristan. Only then could she finally win a legal separation from him and the right to take back the name Tristan.

It was during these years of domestic turmoil that Tristan began her intense involvement in feminist and socialist activities. By the summer of 1835, she was in contact with the Fourierists, and during 1836–37, she attended the Thursday night meetings of the *Gazette des femmes* group. She published several short pamphlets on topics that showed the influence of these groups (for example, *Nécessité de faire un bon accueil aux femmes étrangères* [On the necessity of welcoming foreign women]) and sent her own petitons to the Chamber of Deputies to reestablish divorce and abolish capital punishment.

In 1839 Tristan traveled again to England. Her recorded impressions of working-class poverty, *Promenades dan Londres,* won her acclaim, particularly in the republican and socialist press. In 1843, after her return from London, she published her most famous work, *L'Union ouvrière* (The workers' union), a proposal "to organize the working class by means of a compact union, solid and indissoluble": "Isolated you are weak and fall under the weight of all kinds of distress!—Well then, leave your isolation: Unite! *Union creates strength.*" [61] Five years before the *Communist Manifesto* was written, Tristan had called upon the working class to emancipate itself.

Tristan's feminism was now inextricably linked to her socialism. Although her earlier works, narrower in scope than *L'Union ouvrière,* had examined one or another area of concern to women, the focus of *L'Union ouvrière* shifted from feminism and women as a category of analysis to socialism and the working class. The result of her shift in focus is at first jarring to those who examine *L'Union ouvrière* in an attempt to trace Tristan's feminism. Although she sometimes self-consciously used both feminine and masculine gender forms to stress that when she spoke to the working class she spoke to *ouvrières* and *ouvriers,* more often she assumed that her working-class audience would be male. "*Brothers,* let us unite," [62] she wrote, in a style that was not uncharacteristic of the book as a whole. She devoted one entire chapter to "the necessity for women's emancipation" but addressed it to male workers, arguing that they must liberate women. Tristan had reversed Enfantin: whereas he waited for "the Woman" to emancipate workers, Tristan would have the organized working class (presumed male) emancipate women.

Her assumption that her working-class audience was male, not female, contrasts sharply with the assumptions of the Saint-Simonian women who, ten years earlier, were publishing the *Tribune des femmes.* Still, Tristan's purpose was not unlike theirs. She, too, groped for a strategy that would realize the utopian socialist feminist vision. What had changed since then was the political reality. By the early 1840s, an organized working class that was male had emerged as an independent force in leftist politics. Tristan proposed to harness that force for socialist and feminist revolution.

She called for a workers' union, which would be created by workers taxing themselves. The union would construct a series of "workers' palaces" (within thirty years there would, according to Tristan's plans, be one for each arrondissement) to educate their children, to aid "the wounded of work," and to care for the aged. Although Tristan was clearly indebted to both Fourier and Owen, especially for their ideas about education,[63] she stressed that the "palace" would not be a model utopian community, nor merely a mutual aid society. It alone would be a tangible expression of an organized working class asserting its newly acquired power[64] throughout all areas of the political economy. She borrowed freely from the Irish Daniel O'Connell, too, whom she had met in London in 1838. Like the power bloc that he had organized to represent the Irish in Parliament, the French working class should, Tristan declared, support a "defender of its rights."

This strategy would have been inconceivable ten years earlier. That Tristan proposed to organize the working class to implement the utopian socialist feminist vision was evidence of the strength, in 1843, of independent workers' groups. A transformation of the working-class movement had occurred since the days when bourgeois Saint-Simonians first began their "missionary" activity in workers' quarters. During the round of illegal strikes in 1833 and 1834, skilled workers—printers, tailors, glovemakers and hatters—had opened their own "national workshops" to employ striking workers and put competitive pressure on their capitalist employers. The working class soon came to believe that these producers' cooperatives would be their means to emancipation. By 1840, utopian socialists and most republicans supported this cooperative program. The idea of producer cooperatives gained popularity nationally throughout the working class, publicized through the older, traditional workers' organizations—*compagnonnages* and mutual aid societies. A "trade association" movement had been born. Its base of power was the traditional *compagnonnages,* which were now beginning to function more like modern trade unions. Workers had their own newspapers, the *Atelier,* the *Artisan,* and the *Union,* and their leaders, including Agricol Perdiquier and Pierre Moreau, were skilled craftsmen themselves.[65]

Although Tristan's strategies emerged from her understanding of the new strength of the French working-class movement, her thinking was heavily influenced by utopian socialist ideas. Like utopian socialists, she wanted to transform the social order to assure more equitable development of the individual human personality. She emphasized, as did all utopian socialists by 1840, the "right to work"[66] and the need to "reorganize" work. Similarly, she shared the utopian disinterest in purely political questions: the nature of the regime or even the question of popular sovereignty. She opposed class conflict and abhorred revolutionary violence. Finally, she shared their evangelical zeal, motivation, and language.

Like the utopian socialists, too, Tristan linked workers' freedom to women's position: "The emancipation of male workers is *impossible* so long as women remain in a degraded state." And her definition of women's role, like theirs, elevated women's importance:

> In the life of the workers, woman is everything. She is their providence. If she is missing, everything is missing. It is woman who makes or breaks a home. . . . As a mother, she influences man during his childhood; it is from her and only her that he draws his first notions of this science so important to acquire, the science of life. . . . As a sweetheart, she influences him during his entire youth. . . . As a wife, she influences him during three-fourths of his life.—Lastly, as a daughter, she influences him in his old age.[67]

Whereas Enfantin made woman central to human emancipation because of her special nature, Tristan exalted woman because of her unique role within the family.

Despite her emphasis on women's domestic influence, however, Tristan did not envision limiting women's role to the family. She attacked the subordination of women within marriage and called for two changes that would liberate women from marital bondage: the right to work at a remunerative wage equal to men's and the reinstitution of divorce, without which all women were condemned to one or another form of prostitution.

Tristan, again like the utopian socialists, frequently used this metaphor of the prostitute to symbolize the oppression of women. She wrote compassionately about prostitutes, recognizing the common bond between them and all other women, for all were required to sell themselves for money and all were unable to rehabilitate their fallen status:

> Aware of her powerful attractions, aware of her social weakness, woman is forced into using her charms in the conquest of life. . . . If one wants to criticize her, give her at least other means of defending herself, let her be taught to earn a living; let her be given an alternative other than selling herself as a young woman to a husband without benefit of love or later to prostitute herself before falling in any case into poverty.
>
> Look at the prostitutes on the street, that lamentable flock marked by shame; if only they had known enough to sell themselves at an earlier age, they would not have fallen to such a low mark, and they would be honorable women. Those unfortunate women, for the most part, have loved and let themselves be seduced; they did not have the courage of hypocrisy, because they had a heart.[68]

Tristan herself had "sold herself as a young woman to a husband without . . . love," and like any prostitute, she was ever after unable to rehabilitate herself. Although she later was granted a legal separation from Chazal, French law would not permit her to remarry.

In 1837, Tristan addressed a petition to *Messieurs les Députés,* requesting that the original divorce law of the Revolution, which was based on the principle of reciprocity "and not the odious law of Napoleon which worked to the advantage of the husband in a manner as immoral as it was arbitrary," be reinstated. She admitted that she herself was unhappily married but assured the deputies that her petition was not put forward simply out of self-interest but was for all who suffered as she did. She concluded with an appeal to the deputies' religious sentiments, denying that her request was meant to separate those whom God had joined, but rather was to prohibit man from joining those whom God had not.

Tristan was clearly influenced by those who advocated a new freedom in love relationships, but she did not go to such extremes as had either Enfantin or Fourier. She sounded more like the Saint-Simonian women or the associationists of this same period (late 1830s, early 1840s). Although she was clearly unimpressed by the "virtue" of chastity or virginity, she apparently assumed that a freely chosen marriage based on equality of the partners could provide enduring happiness. Divorce was, in Tristan's view, intended to encourage traditional morality: "Without divorce, religion and morality are powerless to correct habits." Because marriages could not be terminated legally, some would choose never to marry and others would choose to end the marriage in the only ways possible, by desertion or even murder. The right to earn a decent living would permit women to enter freely into love relationships in freedom, rather than to sell themselves for security.

The ability to earn the same wage for the same work was, in Tristan's estimation, simple justice for women;[69] it was also seen as a necessity for male workers:

> [Men] workers, you have not foreseen the disastrous consequences for you that would result from a similar injustice that is to the prejudice of your mothers, sisters, wives, and daughters. What has happened? The manufacturers, seeing how women workers are working faster and at half the pay, discharge every day men workers from their shops and replace them with women workers—And men fold their arms and die of hunger on the street!—That is how the factory heads have proceeded in England— Once entered upon this path, women are discharged to be replaced by *twelve-year-old children.—Savings of half of the salary!* At last, only *seven-* or *eight-year-old* children are given jobs.—If you let one injustice go by then you may be sure that it will give birth to thousands of others.[70]

The same facts form the basis for Tristan's argument in favor of equality of the sexes, as presented in *L'Union ouvrière:* not only is the status of women a "flagrant injustice," but the consequences for men are disastrous.

Because Tristan's line of argumentation is designed to convince men that women's emancipation is in their best interests, we are often left with the feeling that Tristan does not like poor women. She uses harsh language to describe them: "Working-class women are generally speaking brutal, malicious, sometimes hardhearted." Yet Tristan also shows respect for these displays of "bad character" and labels them challenges to subordination. Working-class women's "protest," she declares, "has been unceasing since the beginning of time. But since the Declaration of the Rights of Man . . . their protest has taken on a violent character which proves that the slave's exasperation has reached its zenith." [71]

Tristan asserts clearly that women's ignorance, hostility toward their husbands, or brutality toward their children is not their fault but that of society: "Left to the mercy of a mother and a grandmother who themselves received no education:—one of them according to her disposition, will be brutal and mean, will beat her and mistreat her without cause;—the other will be weak, uncaring, and will let her have her own way. . . . The poor child will grow up in the midst of the most shocking contradictions." Unlike their brothers, who are sent off to school, girls are kept at home to take care of the household or attend to younger children. This unfair burden has its effect: "Nothing sours the character, hardens the heart, or makes the spirit mean like the continual suffering that a child endures due to unjust and brutal treatment.—First of all the injustice wounds us, imposes upon us, places us in despair; then, as it prolongs itself, it irritates us, exasperates us, and dreaming only of a way to take our revenge, we end up ourselves becoming hardhearted, unjust, mean." As soon as possible a woman marries, not for love, but to escape parental tyranny. Marriage only perpetuates her misfortune; her husband, better educated, better paid for similar work, legally the head of the family, treats her with disdain. And "add to all of that the constant irritation caused by four or five noisy children, boisterous, tiresome, who are whirling around the mother, and all of that in a small worker's lodgings, where there is no room to move. Oh! one would have to be an angel come down to earth not to get irritated, become brutal or mean in such a situation." [72]

Tristan's description of married life among the poor stands in stark contrast to her Romantic utopian vision of what could be. If women were treated as equals by their husbands, all sources of irritation would be removed: "What would then be the heart-felt satisfaction, the spiritual security, the happiness of the soul of the man, the husband, the worker who will possess such a wife! . . . The household, instead of being a cause of ruin for the worker, would on the contrary be a cause of well-being." [73] It is thus in the name of men's self-interest that Tristan calls for the equality of the sexes.[74] "The law that enslaves woman and deprives her of education," Tristan declares, "oppresses you, working man." She continues:

> I have just shown that the ignorance of working-class women has the most disastrous consequences. . . . —They arrest all progress. . . . The poor creatures, not seeing beyond the *end of their noses,* as one says, get furious with the husband because [he] spent *a few hours of his time,* occupying himself with *political and social ideas.*—"Why are you troubling yourself with things that are none of your business? " they exclaim. "Think about earning enough to eat and let the world turn as it will.[75]

Following this line of argument, Tristan asserts that men's interests will be best served if the charter ("VOTRE CHARTRE") of the Universal Union of Men and Women Workers states that women receive equally the benefits of the union.

counting on men to liberate women

Workers, in '91 your fathers proclaimed the immortal declaration of the RIGHTS OF MAN, and it is to this solemn declaration that you owe the fact that today you are free men and equal in rights before the law.— Glory to your fathers for this great work!—But, workingmen, it remains to you, men of 1843, to accomplish just as great a work.—Your turn has come; liberate the last slaves that remain in French society; proclaim the RIGHTS OF WOMAN, and in the same words as your fathers proclaimed yours, say: "We, French proletarians, after fifty-three years of experience, acknowledge being duly enlightened and convinced that the oversight and contempt of women's natural rights are the only causes for the misfortunes of the world, and we have resolved to state in a solemn declaration, set down in our handwriting, her sacred and inalienable rights. We want women to learn of our declaration so that they will no longer be oppressed and degraded by man's injustice and tyranny, and that men respect in women, their mothers, the freedom and equality which they themselves enjoy.

　　1. The purpose of society being the common happiness of man and woman, the WORKERS' UNION guarantees to man and woman the enjoyment of their rights.

　　2. Those rights are: equality of admission into the Palaces of the WORKERS' UNION, either as children, wounded, or elderly people.

　　3. Since for us woman is equal to man, it is understood that daughters shall receive an education, although varying, but just as rational, just as solid, just as extensive in moral and professional science as boys.

　　4. As for old people and injured people, treatment in all ways shall be the same for women as for men.

Workers be sure of this, if you possess enough fairness, enough justice, to inscribe in your charter these few lines that I have just traced, then *this declaration of the rights of woman* will soon pass into the manners and customs; you shall see inscribed at the head of the law book that will govern French society—ABSOLUTE EQUALITY *of man and woman.*

Then, my brothers, and only then, will the HUMAN UNITY be CONSTITUTED.

Sons of '89, here is the work that your fathers have bequeathed to you![76]

Paradoxically, the first socialist theorist to call for the emancipation of the working class by the working class itself was calling for the emancipation of women by men.

yeah, why?
Neither group had the power to vote

In this respect Tristan's plan stopped short of that of the women of the *Tribune des femmes* who had conceptualized the promise of collective female action. It would be unfair, though, to conclude that Tristan actually expected women to wait passively for males to emancipate them. She herself undertook a tour of France to spread her message. It is true that she denied that she sought the post of "Defender of the Working Class" for herself, "since women were not admitted to the Parliament." [77] But her missionary sense of herself as the political representative of the working class so imbues the words of *L'Union ouvrière* that this denial, I believe, should be read entirely in the context of day-to-day practical politics whereby (as in her petition on divorce) Tristan believed it necessary to deny her self-interest in order to gain credibility. The historian who reads her words must conclude that Flora Tristan believed herself the Woman Messiah who *alone*—how unlike Suzanne Voilquin—would emancipate workers and women alike.

Tristan's seeming disavowal of an autonomous women's movement relates in part, at least, to her personality. She had always kept herself aloof from established groups. She called herself "the pariah" to express her sense of isolation; in her political life, no less than in her personal life, she separated herself from others. She criticized the Saint-Simonians: Their "error . . . is that they do not move; they wait," she wrote in her diary. [78] She found fault with the Fourierists: association—unlike union—required that workers know each other, hold the same opinions, have the same character, and share the same tastes and was therefore impractical. [79] She also rejected working-class writers for focusing narrowly on one or another "petite réforme particulière." Her program, on the contrary, would attack the fundamental cause of working-class misfortune, *la misère,* by demanding the rights of the working class "to work, to instruction, and to political representation." [80]

It was not Tristan's style to acknowledge her debts to other thinkers. For example, she claimed the distinction of being the first socialist theorist to speak directly to workers: "At the rostrum of the Chamber of Delegates, at the Christian pulpit, in the assemblies of the world, in the theaters, and most of all in the courts of law, workers have often been talked about, but no one has yet tried to talk *to the workers.* It is a way that must be tried." To assure that her message would reach the intended audience, Tristan set for herself the task of going

> with my union project in my hand, from town to town, from one end of
> France to the other, to talk to the workers who do not know how to read
> and to those who do not have the time to read. . . . I will go find them

yikes!

in their workshops; in their garrets and even, if needed, in their taverns, and there, face to face with their poverty, I will compel them, *in spite of themselves*, to escape from this frightful poverty which is degrading and killing them.[81]

Salvation is brought to you by . . .

Yet Tristan's "tour de France" was not in reality so different from the "mission" that Suzanne Voilquin undertook in 1833–34 nor from the other Saint-Simonian "apostolic" missions. Only the consequences were different—tragically so. Tristan fell ill and died on this journey. During her last weeks, she was cared for by the Saint-Simonians Elisa and Charles Lemonnier at their home in Bordeaux.

The object of the feminists' search—a viable program of action—remained elusive. Tristan's project for a workers' union had depended too much on one person. Yet her strategy, to link women's emancipation to an organized working-class movement, did not completely fail the cause of women's emancipation. She had captured the attention of the French working class and won their esteem and love. Unlike the women of the *Tribune des femmes* and unlike Herbinot de Mauchamps, Flora Tristan was not forgotten because the working class continued to celebrate her ideas and her work. And among those workers who kept alive their memory of Tristan were those who sustained her ideal of sexual equality. These workers would be important feminist allies in the years just ahead.

Honoré-Victorin Daumier. From the series *Les Divorcées*. Le Chavivari, June 1848.

CLUB FÉMININ.

Nous demandons 1° Que le jupon soit remplacé par la culotte.
2° Que les maris s'occupent de l'intérieur au moins trois fois par semaine.
3° Enfin qu'il n'existe entre l'homme et la femme aucune autre distinction que celle qu'il a plu à la nature de leur accorder.

Artist unknown. *Club féminin* (Women's club). Lithograph de Gosselin [Editeur]. Courtesy Bibl. Nat. Paris

CLUB DES FEMMES LIBRES

(La Presidente) Citoyennes ! tout ce que je puis vous accorder, c'est de ne parler que vingt cinq à la fois
(1. Auditoir) Nous demandons la tête des maris, à moins pourtant, qu'on ne remette de suite, le divorce
en vigueur   (On pense que les maris accepteront le divorce)

Masson (signed on reverse). *Club des femmes libres* (Free women's club). 1848. Coll. de
Vinck 112, no. 14.156. Courtesy Bibl. Nat. Paris

Camille, je vais au Club,

— Soignez le pot-au-feu et couchez ma fille de bonne heure ...... si elle crie, vous lui donnerez
à téter — Avec quoi, Bobonne ?   — Avec le biberon, imbécile ! ....

(Signed by initials): A.D.C. *Camille, Je vais au club* (Camille, I go to the club). Coll.
de Vinck 112, no. 14.160. Courtesy Bibl. Nat. Paris

Artist unknown. *Le Bureau de parapluies au club des femmes* (The desk at the women's club). Lithograph. *Le Charivari,* June 17, 1848. Courtesy Bibl. Nat. Paris

Edouard de Beaumont. *Banquet fémino-socialist.* From the series *Actualité's.* Coll. de Vinck 112, no. 14.158. Courtesy Bibl. Nat. Paris

Edouard de Beaumont. From the series *Les Vesuviennes*. Originally printed chez Aubert; reprinted in *Le Charivari*, May 1, 1848. Coll. de Vinck 112, no. 14.136. Courtesy Bibl. Nat. Paris

LES VÉSUVIENNES.

— Comment pt'ite malhureuse, je te donne un état honorable, je te mets dans les chemises d'homme, et v'là que je te r'trouve dans les culottes d'une Vésuvienne . . . . . va, tu n'ès plus ma fille ! . . . . .

Edouard de Beaumont. From the series *Les Vésuviennes*. Originally printed chez Aubert; reprinted in *Le Charivari*, May 30, 1848. Coll. de Vinck 112, no. 14.141. Courtesy Bibl. Nat. Paris

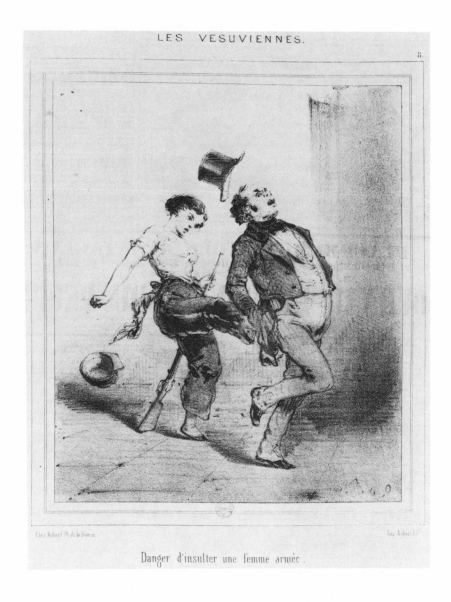

LES VESUVIENNES.

Danger d'insulter une femme armée.

Edouard de Beaumont. From the series *Les Vesuviennes*. Originally printed chez Aubert; reprinted in *Le Charivari,* June 1, 1848. Coll. de Vinck 112, no. 14.143. Courtesy Bibl. Nat. Paris

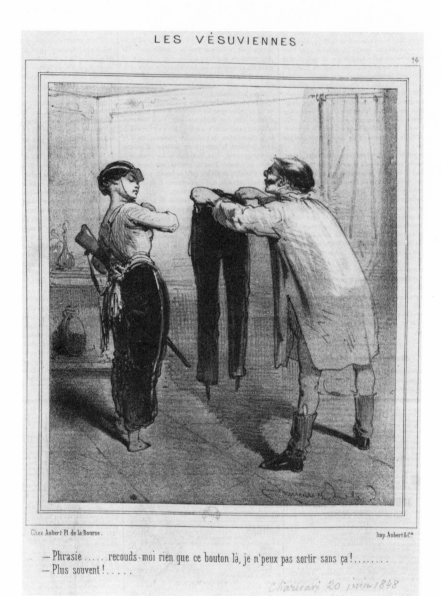

LES VÉSUVIENNES.

—Phrasie......recouds-moi rien que ce bouton là, je n'peux pas sortir sans ça!........
—Plus souvent!.....

Edouard de Beaumont. From the series *Les Vésuviennes*. Originally printed chez Aubert; reprinted in *Le Charivari*, June 20, 1848. Coll. de Vinck 112, no. 14.149. Courtesy Bibl. Nat. Paris

CHAPTER 6

Feminist Activism during the Revolutionary Upheavals of 1848–1851

O n February 24, 1848, following two days of demonstrations and street fighting, Louis-Philippe abdicated in favor of his grandson. This act, however, did not satisfy the demonstrators, who forced the Chamber of Deputies to yield control of the state to a group of moderate republicans and democratic socialists who formed a provisional government. The Republic was proclaimed.

The Republic was to be democratic. Earlier, the monarchy had refused to bend to demands to increase the size of the electorate and thus had sparked a campaign for electoral reform, which in turn had triggered the revolution. The most democratic of the reformers had won: one of the provisional government's first actions was to declare universal male suffrage and set an April date for national elections to a constitutional convention or "Constituent National Assembly."

A minority of the new government wanted the Republic to be "social" as well as democratic, that is, responsible to the needs of the poorer classes.[1] Economic crisis had undermined the legitimacy of the constitutional monarchy and prepared the way for revolution. The worst years of the depression were 1846 and 1847, but even though the economy was improving in 1848, unemployment was still high. Working-class demands that the government solve the unemployment problem had gained backers in the provisional government. In deference to the democratic socialists among them, the government reduced daily working hours, proclaimed the right to work, and established a commission to study the unemployment problem. This Luxembourg Commission, so named because it met at the Luxembourg Palace, was under the presidency of Louis Blanc, a democratic socialist known to be committed to the concept of producers' associations or "national workshops." Workers had good reason to expect that the Luxembourg Commission would recommend that the government provide credit for these producers' associations.

Feminists were heartened also, in the initial phase of the revolution, even though they had less reason than male workers to cheer. The Republic, however democratic or social, was certainly not feminist. But many sympathetic friends and allies had been catapulted into positions of power and influence. Feminists expected that their claims would find receptive ears in the new government.

The lifting of all restrictions on the press and assembly allowed feminists to regroup and renew their propaganda. From March until June their activities kept pace with the generally stepped-up rate of mass political involvement. (In Paris alone, 171 new newspapers and some 200 to 450 political clubs came into existence between March and mid-June.[2]) On March 19, Eugénie Niboyet began to publish the *Voix des femmes,* a "socialist and political journal, organ of the interests of all women." It was the French feminists' first daily political newspaper. Niboyet was immediately joined by feminists who had earlier been active in Saint-Simonism or Fourierism or had written for the *Gazette des femmes:* Jeanne Deroin, Désirée Gay (formerly Veret), Suzanne Voilquin, Elisa Lemonnier, and Anaïs Ségalas. Among the signers of articles are popular writers Gabrielle Soumet, Amelie Praï, and Adèle Esquiros. Unlike the *Tribune des femmes,* the *Voix des femmes* did not exclude men. Articles were written by Victor Hugo, Jean Macé, and Paulin Niboyet (Eugénie Niboyet's son). But the concept of feminist autonomy, if not female separatism, was retained. The first issue noted, "It is a mistake to believe that by improving the lot of men, that by that fact alone, the lot of women is improved."[3]

The *Voix des femmes* group formed a club, too, which after its first meeting took the name Société de la *Voix des femmes.* This close relationship between a journal and a political club was commonplace in the spring of 1848, according to Peter Amann, who has studied the 1848 political club movement.[4] There were also other clubs that focused on women's rights: the short-lived Club de l'Emancipation des Femmes (founded by a former Fourierist, Dr. Malatier, along with Adèle Esquiros and Jeanne Deroin), the Union des Femmes and the Collège Medical des Femmes (both founded by Malatier), the Comité des Droits de la Femme (Mme Bourgeois Allix), the Association Fraternelle des Démocrates de Deux Sexes, and the Société Mutuelle D'Education des Femmes (Deroin). The most radical of all were

F. Sorrieu. *Le Club des femmes* (The women's club). June 1848. Coll. de Vinck 112, no. 14.157. Courtesy Bibl. Nat. Paris

the Vesuvians, who explained their choice of title thus: "It represents our idea marvelously. Like lava, so long held back, that must at last pour out around us, [our idea] is in no way incendiary but in all ways regenerating." According to an article on the Vesuvians in the *Voix des femmes,* they were young (fifteen to thirty years old), unmarried, poorly paid workers. Their constitution went beyond the mere statement of equality ("The Republic recognizes neither masters nor slaves; it sees only children who are equally free.") to demand female military service and even that men and women dress the same. Apparently they wore a bloomer costume resembling that of the more radical American feminists. (Many of the political cartoons mocking feminists that were printed in 1848–49 depict young girls dressed in bloomers, although only Vesuvians actually did dress that way.) They demanded equality in marriage: "Husbands and wives are like associates, friends united by interests and affection. Neither should be a master." Going beyond the call for legal equality, they specified that husbands must share household chores and indeed threatened men with the punishment of perpetual military service for "delinquency." The more cautious editors of the *Voix des femmes* disapproved of their choice of a name for their group, as well as their attention-getting tactics, which included not only the bloomer costume but also frequent street demonstrations.[5]

Feminists were active, too, in democratic socialist clubs. Specifically, the Club des Amis Fraternels, the Club de la Montagne, the Club Lyonnais, the the Club de l'Emancipation des Peuples permitted women to express their opinions. At the Club Lyonnais, "a simple proletarian woman . . . demanded . . . that women no longer be the slaves of men, that they be admitted to take part in National Assembly debates to discuss their own rights, that they be permitted to direct their own business affairs, and that their work be sufficiently compensated so that they can live and by this means prevent liaisons that have the sole purpose of escaping from misery."[6] Etienne Cabet's Société Central permitted women to attend meetings, but only as *auditrices.* Similarly, the Club des Républicaines-Socialistes, presided over by a Fourierist, perhaps even Victor Considérant,[7] did not allow women to speak at meetings. The Fourierist journal, the *Démocratie pacifique,* frequently published feminists' articles. And even the virulently antifeminist socialist Pierre-Joseph Proudhon opened up his journal, *Le Représentant du peuple,* to feminist opinions; after November 1848 Pauline Roland published a regular column there.

Gavarni. *Poor dear! What have you done to your sex?* Undated. The author's collection.

Feminist Ideology

The language of these 1848 feminists was a blend of old and new. From utopian socialist feminism of the prior decades came the faith in the progressive development of society to a higher level[8] at which women's equality is possible:

> The reign of brute force is past; the one of morality and intelligence is beginning. The reasons that led our fathers to exclude women from all participation in government no longer have any value today. At a time when everything was decided by the sword, it was natural to believe that women, who could not take part in combat, should not have a seat in the assembly of the warriors. The question at that time was to destroy and to conquer by the power of the sword; today the question is to edify, to organize. Women must be called upon to participate in the great work of social regeneration that is preparing itself.[9]

Utopian "pacifism" as a *method* similarly remained intact: "The women . . . should cause no more loud riots. But every time that something shall turn against them, their devotion should not fail." Désirée Gay pledged that "the workers of the second arrondissement will not revolt violently; they know that women get their strength from their calm and their persevering will." And the 1848 feminists also accepted the Saint-Simonian male/female dualism, with its synthesizing "association": "According to us, the social individual, the complete being, is a man and a woman; therefore to each according to his capabilities; to each capability according to its works." They, too, believed that the "nature" of women differed from men's: "The head and the arm of humanity, that is man; the heart of humanity, that is woman." [10]

Although the 1848 feminists retained the faith that a new world order required the "association" of these two different capacities, their description of woman's unique nature no longer saw her as the Saint-Simonians' ethereal being who incarnated love and sentiment. Instead, she was a very real and concrete being, one that was recognizable to all 1848 audiences— a mother: "Woman has received a double power of creation: one physical, one moral—*childbirth* [my emphasis] and regeneration." It was woman as mother who would transform the world: "A great social reform is necessary, inevitable, but this reform, in order to be complete [and] durable cannot emanate from man alone. Man only knows how to establish order through despotism, woman only knows how to organize by the strength of her *motherly* love [my emphasis]. Both together they will know how to gain order and freedom." [11]

Defining woman as mother was not, of course, a new idea. In the eighteenth century, Rousseau's writings suggested this image. In the nineteenth century, it was embellished by female educational writers Claire de Rémusat, Pauline Guizot, and Albertine Necker de Saussure to buttress their arguments that women should be better educated. Exalting women's role as mother was not even new to feminists. Suzanne Voilquin had written in 1834: "Maternity! . . . . our most beautiful attribute; it is woman in her full flowering. In the religion of the future it will no longer be a virginal madonna, as a feminine model, that we will present for the adoration of the Believers: it will be the mother." [12] And also in 1834, Pauline Roland, in a letter to Charles Lambert, had referred to her "mission" as "la maternité sacerdotale." [13]

Now, however, the image of woman as mother became the linchpin of the feminist rationale for sexual equality. In much the same way as Enfantin had earlier borrowed the patriarchalist concept of woman as Eve (woman defined primarily by her sexual aspect), but then turned it upside down and used it to justify woman's superiority, 1848 feminists transformed the concept of motherhood. Woman's unique role as mother would no longer explain her confinement to domestic life; it would justify her participation in the public sphere.

That 1848 feminists had rejected the Saint-Simonian love-priestess image is not surprising; it was too closely tied to Enfantin's system of sexual morality. Feminists feared, with good reason, that the public would connect feminism to "immorality," and they hastened to reassure their audience. Not that they were covering up their real feelings: by 1848, there were no sexual radicals among them. When feminists discussed sexual issues, they talked only about women's vulnerability to men's exploitation, never of women's potential sexual pleasure. Even the Vesuvians, shockingly radical in some ways, were sexual conservatives; their constitution required that all women marry by age twenty-one and all men by age twenty-six.[14] Similarly, Pauline Roland, who had been among the sexual radicals in 1834, now wrote: "The mistakes of youth call for a difficult atonement in mature life. . . . Starting out twenty years ago under the influence of the false theory that woman alone is the family . . . I find myself [now] condemned to live that life that I confusedly foresaw . . . in all its rigor." She continued: "Marriage must be founded on fidelity." [15] Elsewhere she wrote that even divorce, the legitimacy of which she recognized, had become for her a recognition of a failure for which the state should punish the guilty by taking away their children to be raised by a blameless couple.[16]

We have already examined how and why feminists had earlier rejected sexual liberation and "love without marriage"; in the fifteen-year period since the collapse of Saint-Simonism, little had changed that would lead them to reconsider their position. On the contrary, in 1848, feminists were even less able to contemplate a life of self-sufficiency for women. Female employment opportunities had worsened. Rapes—at least those reported to the Paris police—were increasing at a dramatic rate.[17] Illegitimacy rates, although no longer rising, remained high. And socialist cooperative ventures that had once promised emotional and financial support in place of traditional families had collapsed. Few ideologues remained who championed such once-promising dreams as the Saint-Simonian family, the Fourierist phalanstery, or Tristan's workers' union.

Unlike Enfantin's image of woman as love-priestess, the motherhood image was "passionless."[18] It had other advantages over the Enfantinian image as well. For one, it was more concrete and therefore more appealing in 1848, as feminists moved toward down-to-earth politics and away from utopian mysticism. In fact, motherhood was the real-life situation of most 1848 feminists. The women of the *Tribune des femmes* had been young, unmarried, and generally living independently. Fifteen years later, most of these same women were mothers. Jeanne Deroin had married her friend Desroches in the mid-1830s; by 1848 she had three children. Pauline Roland had had four children, three of whom survived. Suzanne Voilquin, whose only child had died at two and a half weeks, was raising her niece, who had been orphaned in infancy. And mothers were highly respected now among the general public. French image-makers since Rousseau had popularized a rehabilitated image of women as mothers. In the 1830s and 1840s the mother had become a teacher—intelligent, purposeful, and moral—unlike Enfantin's love-priestess image, which could be used to prove that men had a monopoly over intellectual capacities. True, feminists sometimes still used imagery akin to Enfantin's—"She [woman] is like a ray of sunlight and love to enliven man's intelligence"—but they denied that women's intelligence was inferior to men's. In the first issue of the *Voix des femmes,* the editors asked: "What do we want? We want our total and complete emancipation, that is . . . to be recognized as equal to men in things that pertain to intelligence." The demand for an improved education, women's oldest demand, never lost its importance to feminists. Now, even as in the seventeenth century, they maintained that women were oppressed by ignorance ("Woman lacks power only because she is ignorant"), and they claimed the right to an equal education: "We do not claim to attack public education; it is particularly appropriate to the fraternity that leans toward universality. That which we are pointing out is . . . its insufficiency with regard to the instruction of young girls and women." [19]

Enfantin's dualism—sentimental women and rational men—was dangerously close to traditional patriarchalism, and feminists were justifiably wary. Now they even publicly adjured their former leader: "But when Enfantin attempted to proclaim free woman, when he designated her as the priestess of the future, the indolent odalisque, ignorant and sensual woman, he denied his master and broke off with the first disciple, Rodrigues, who wanted to lead men to the saintly equality of fraternity." Because Enfantin's priestess could so easily be twisted into an "ignorant and sensual woman," the maternal image appeared a much more useful alternative image to buttress the demand for emancipation. In their words, "The mothers of your sons cannot be slaves." [20] And: "The mother of future generations, she from whom will be born the glorious citizens of a world reborn, must not be a slave. She would be unworthy to carry them in her womb and to prepare them from childhood for the great destinies that await them." [21]

The equality of women/mothers was not merely "just": it was "necessary." With the same sense of religious mission with which Pauline Roland earlier took her first steps into sexual liberation, mothers now asked for equality so as better to serve humanity: "It is in the name of the holy obligations of the family, in the name of the tender servitude of the mother, that we come to say to you: Yes, we have the right as you do to serve our country in proportion to our strength. We have as you do the right to dedicate ourselves to the world." And later: "Why would you want to limit our dedication to a single being and to deny us the right to sacrifice ourselves to all of humanity?" [22] Age-old feminist demands were reshaped. The responsibilities of motherhood required that women be well-educated: "We must be able to instruct our children." Maternal responsibilities required that women be allowed to represent the state in civil acts (to witness, to be guardians, to notarize) and to vote: "It is above all this holy function of motherhood, . . . which requires that women watch over the futures of their children and gives women the right to intervene not only in all acts of civil life, but also in all acts of political life." [23]

How different these ideas were from the view of Claire Démar, who had connected women's lonely responsibility for childbearing to their oppression. But most other nineteenth-century feminists were unconcerned with breaking the bonds of motherhood; their concern was autonomy from men, not children. This was true of Suzanne Voilquin, Pauline Roland, Jeanne Deroin, and Désirée Gay, both in the early 1830s and again in

1848. As in 1833–34, feminists in 1848 questioned not women's responsibilities and roles within the home but the split between the domestic sphere and the public sphere and women's confinement to one—the domestic.

Left Support for Feminists

Feminists could apparently count on some support from the democratic socialists in the provisional government. The Republic's first minister of public instruction, former Saint-Simonian Hippolyte Carnot, arranged to have Ernest Legouvé teach a course at the Collège de France on the moral history of women. Legouvé's roots are clearly Saint-Simonian:

> God created the human species double; we utilize but half of it. Nature says two; we say one. We must agree with Nature. . . . The feminine spirit is stifled, but not dead. . . . We cannot annihilate at our pleasure a force created by God, or extinguish a torch lighted by his hand. . . . Let us then open wide the gates of the world to this new element; we have need of it.[24]

Feminists considered Legouvé their friend. In 1849, the course he offered at the Collège de France was published in book form and became popular. A reading of that book makes evident Legouvé's concern for the welfare of women. His lengthy list of wrongs French women are subjected to could have appeared in any feminist treatise:

> No history presents, we believe, more iniquitous prejudices to combat, more secret wounds to heal. . . . As daughters, no public education for them, no professional instruction, no possible life without marriage, no marriage without a dowry. Wives . . . do not legally possess their property. Mothers . . . have not the legal right to direct the education of their children; they can neither marry them, nor prevent them from marrying, nor banish them from the paternal house nor retain them there. . . . They can be neither the guardians of children other than their own sons or grandsons; nor [can they] take part in a family council nor witness a will; they have not even the right to testify to the birth of a child! Among the working class, what group is most wretched? Women. Who are they that earn from 16 to 18 sous for twelve hours of labor? Women. Upon whom falls all the expense of illegitimate children? Upon women. Who bear all the disgrace of faults committed through passion? Women. . . . Can such dominion endure? Obviously no. It will inevitably fail before the principal

of natural equity, and the moment has come to claim for women their share of rights.[25]

Legouvé was especially concerned with the right of women to an adequate education. To those who contended that to give a solid education to woman would be to corrupt her and to injure the family he answered that it "is in the name of the family . . . in the name of maternity, of marriage, of the household, that a solid and earnest education must be demanded for girls. . . . Without knowledge, no mother is completely a mother; without knowledge, no wife is truly a wife." Then he exclaimed indignantly:

> The state maintains a university for men, a polytechnic school for men, academies of art and trades for men, agricultural schools for men—for women, what has it established? Primary schools! And even these were not founded by the state, but by municipalities. No inequality could be more humiliating. There are courts and prisons for women, there should be public education for women; you have no right to punish those whom you do not instruct![26]

Legouvé also recognized the lack of protection given to women in the legal system, which was a paramount concern of feminists: "Our code, profoundly immoral, does not punish seduction, and punishes corruption only derisively and rape insufficiently. To declare void the promise of marriage is fearful immorality; to permit no investigation of paternity and to admit that of maternity, is as cruel as it is immoral." He described how "manufacturers seduce their workwomen, foremen of workshops discharge young girls who will not yield to them; masters corrupt their servant maids . . . clerks, merchants, officers, students deprave poor country girls and bring them to Paris, where they abandon them, and prostitution gathers them up." And he demanded:

> Punish the guilty woman if you will, but punish the man! She is already punished, punished by abandonment, punished by dishonor, punished by remorse, punished by nine months of suffering, punished by the burden of raising a child: let him then be smitten in turn; or else it is not public decency that you are protecting, as you say. It is masculine sovereignty, in its vilest form: seigniorial right [*le droit de seigneur*]!

Legouvé maintained that "impunity assured to men doubles the number of illegitimate children. . . . Impunity fosters prostitution; prostitution destroys public health and makes a profession of . . . license. Impunity, finally, surrenders half the human race as a prey to the vices of the other half." [27]

Attacking the subordination of woman in marriage, Legouvé was especially critical of the community property laws that made such subordination possible, "which permits the husband to dispose of the property of his partner, to sell the household furniture, to take possession of his wife's very jewels to adorn his mistress." As an alternative to community property, Legouvé suggested that the property of the partners should be divided into three shares: one for the wife, to be placed at her disposal five years after marriage; one for the husband; and one-third common to both, to be administered by the husband under the direction of a family council. Further, this council would have the provisional right to take away the management from the husband and entrust it to the wife, in case of his "incapacity or waste." [28] Legouvé also demanded that husbands, like wives, must be criminally liable for adultery.

It is clear why feminists liked Legouvé: he was on their side. But there was a limit to his vision, and that limit was the patriarchal family. He could not conceive of a family that did not rest ultimate power in one person; and he was convinced that that person must be the husband. The family council should limit the husband's power over the wife and temper his right to punish her (and his children), but could not deny it. Although husbands should be criminally liable for adultery, they would not be punished as harshly as adulterous wives.[29]

The circumscribed and always subordinate role that Legouvé envisioned for the adult woman also limited his education program:

> The question is not, in revealing to the feminine intellect the laws of nature, to make all our girls astronomers or physicians; do we see all men become Latinists by spending ten years of their life in the study of Latin? The purpose is to strengthen their minds by acquaintance with science, and to prepare them to participate in all the thoughts of their husbands, all the studies of their children.[30]

Legouvé believed in the "career of hidden utility and of modest devotion" for women. In the family, the task of the wife should be the management of domestic affairs, the children's education, and the comfort of the husband, to whom she should be an inspiration. In civil life, there were several fields of occupation which women might enter with success: art, literature, instruction, administration, and medicine. Indeed, Legouvé devoted an entire chapter to the remarkable administrative capacity of women and suggested that they should be responsible for the superintendence of prisons for women, hospitals, charitable institutions, and the legal guardianship of foundlings. But he concluded that women must be refused participation in all political acts and in all that concerns the government, because in these matters they have no aptitudes.[31]

The *Voix des femmes* group was grateful for Legouvé's friendship and endorsed his candidacy for a seat in the Constituent Assembly in the April elections. But they were not influenced by him to tame their more radical feminist position. They insisted on equality in marriages ("the most beautiful thing in the world is a man and a woman united in the name of liberty, of equality, and of fraternity") and on female autonomy ("woman is a free person. . . . She must build her life by means of her own work, her own love, her own intelligence").[32] They demanded woman's right to work: "The freedom that wealth gives is illusory; the freedom that work gives is the only real one." And they asserted that "the [woman] worker is right to revolt. What she wants is no longer organized charity, but justly distributed work." [33] They insisted, too, on the right to participate fully in political activities, arguing that "to exclude women from clubs . . . is to surrender the clubs to fanatics or to the censure of the agents of power." [34] And most significantly, they demanded their right to vote in the April elections.

For the utopians among them, this position on suffrage represented a significant departure from their earlier antipolitical stance. Jeanne Deroin, however, had been a republican in the early 1830s, even before converting to Saint-Simonism. Perhaps she had always harbored the republican belief that political rights, specifically the vote, could be a useful tool for social transformation. Eugénie Niboyet may also have been a suffragist by 1836, when the *Gazette des femmes* submitted its first petition demanding voting rights for women. In 1848, these two led the feminists' suffrage campaign. By this time, other former utopian socialist feminists such as Pauline Roland and Désirée Gay may also have been won over to republicanism and become convinced of the significance of suffrage—as had most socialists, male and female, feminist and antifeminist, by 1848.

For feminists, the extension of voting rights to all men forced the women's suffrage issue. In early March, Roland tried to vote in the mayoral elections in Boussac, where she was then living, but was turned away.[35] On March 16, Antonine Andrée de Saint-Gilles and some women "artists, workers, writers, [and] teachers" presented the first petition demanding that women be permitted to enjoy political and social rights and be recognized as the equals of men in all functions excepting those exclusively related to physical strength. The language of the petition is unmistakably Saint-Simonian:

> The couple is the social unit. The sovereign people therefore is you and we. . . . From the solidarity of the new and natural bonds that you will establish between man and woman will result, have no doubt, the marriage par excellence, the social marriage, a material, intellectual and moral trinity in work: marriage, at last, as regenerator of the world.[36]

On March 22, a delegation of the Comité des Droits de la Femme was received by Marrast, a member of the provisional government, to whom the delegates stated:

> In the name of the principle that has been proved by the experience of all times, that the men who make the laws do so to their own benefit, and therefore to the detriment of those deprived of that sacred right, you proclaim: "The election for all without exception." We come here to ask you if women are included in this grand generality as they are in the rights concerning workers. We are all the more justified in asking you this question since you have not designated them in the categories to be excluded! [37]

Marrast, responding for the provisional government, avoided the issue by concluding that this question should be answered by the National Assembly rather than the provisional government. He asserted that since the right of women to vote had never before been recognized, the provisional government did not have the authority to make such a radical decision. His response seems to have satisfied the women delegates. It also appeared to be acceptable, initially, to the *Voix des femmes* group. Niboyet wrote on March 26, "If we have held no demonstration before the members of the provisional government it is because, as you have stated, only the National Assembly has the power to establish our rights by decree." [38]

The *Voix des femmes* women did not hesitate, however, to demand the right of women to run for office. On April 6, Niboyet called for the election of George Sand to the Constituent Assembly. "The representative who unites our sympathies, is by type masculine and feminine, male by virtue of virility, female by divine intuition, poetry: we have nominated Sand." [39] Sand, however, dissociated herself entirely from this candidacy, not even paying the editors of the *Voix des femmes* the respect of responding directly to their journal. Instead she addressed a letter to the editors of the *Réforme:*

Sir, a paper edited by some ladies has proclaimed my candidacy to the National Assembly. If this joke only wounded my self-respect by attributing to me a ridiculous pretension, then I would let it pass like all of those jokes of which any of us can become the object. But my silence might engender the belief that I adhere to the principles for which this newspaper would like to become the organ. I therefore pray that you receive and make well known the following declaration: (1) I hope that no elector shall wish to lose his vote by succumbing to the whim of writing my name on his ballot; (2) I do not have the honor of knowing a single one of the ladies who form clubs and edit newspapers.[40]

Niboyet responded quickly and angrily: "Don't think we wished to shelter our cause under your glory, for our cause is good enough, just enough, to 'march with head held high and to defend itself.' " [41]

Two weeks later, the editors of the *Voix des femmes* resurrected their demand that *some* women—widows and single women, at least—be permitted to vote in the upcoming election. Despite Niboyet's earlier seeming acceptance of the idea that only the National Assembly could grant women the vote, the editors sent a petition to the provisional government demanding suffrage and at the same time civil rights for married women. They made clear that this was just a first step toward full equality,

that once the first civil rights are conceded, logic, along with common sense and equity, compels the other sex to concede integral emancipation, which alone will have the power to give meaning to the republican formula: Liberty, Equality, Fraternity; that history demonstrates, besides, that when women undergo an appropriate education they are capable of exercising all political and social functions.[42]

It appears that the provisional government did not take the trouble to acknowledge the petition.

Women did not vote in the April elections to the Constituent Assembly, nor could feminists have been pleased by the election results. Their allies, the democratic socialists, and even the moderate republicans, fared poorly. Of the almost 900 newly elected delegates (some were elected to more than one seat), half were monarchists. Indeed, only 285 delegates had been known as republicans before February. Only 55 were Left republicans or socialists. The Executive Commission, which now replaced the provisional government, no longer included the socialists Louis Blanc or Albert (Alexandre Martin). Still, feminists were optimistic, particularly after the new Executive Commission proposed a law to reestablish divorce and, then again, after Victor Considérant—now an elected delegate to the Constituent

Assembly—proposed that the new constitution grant women the right to vote. But the proposal on divorce was withdrawn, and Considérant's proposal on women's suffrage was voted down 899 to 1. Hippolyte Carnot remained the minister of public instruction, but his credibility with the assembly had been eroded because he had used his public office to attempt to influence the outcome of the election. Although he proposed a program of educational reform with an equal number of girls' and boys' schools, the assembly refused to consider it.

Silencing Feminists

The more conservative political climate following the April 1848 elections encouraged antifeminists, inside and outside of the government. Meetings of the Club de la *Voix des femmes* were invaded by ruffians. The first time this happened, May 11, the leadership decided to exclude men from future meetings; the second time, June 4, they agreed to permit men to attend meetings but only if they paid a doubled entry fee. But police authorities had a different plan to restore order; they shut down the women's club.

A split was developing among the feminists over how to cope with the continuing resistance to their claims. Their fears of increasing repression were exacerbated by the stepped-up pace of government repression against Left clubs in general. But whereas Eugénie Niboyet counseled caution in the face of government reaction, Jeanne Deroin was more feisty: she left, or was pushed out of, the *Voix des femmes* and soon after founded the *Politique des femmes*. The *Voix des femmes* folded in June, and Niboyet withdrew from the fray. Years later she was to write that 1848 was the unhappiest year of her life. She claimed that she had continued to support the constitutional monarchists and had never favored the republicans. Niboyet then stated that she had only reluctantly accepted the presidency of the *Voix des femmes* and that her primary concern had always remained the fate of women workers.[43] This reminiscence, however, contradicts her words and actions during the spring of 1848. Then, she concentrated primarily on the political question. Deroin's *Politique des femmes* group was focusing more on organizing women workers, but Niboyet would not join with them.

Deroin's choice of title for the new daily was to make clear her intention to continue the fight for women's political rights. Désirée Gay and Suzanne Voilquin joined with her, as did other women identified only as "workers." They were all more concerned with the social issue than Niboyet had been, and the balance of republicanism and socialism that characterized feminism in 1848 shifted, in the first issue of the *Politique des femmes* (June 18–24), slightly toward socialism. One senses particularly the increasing antagonism between women of different classes evident in the following felicitous dialogue between a "Lady" and a working-class woman ("A Voice"):

> *The Lady:* My dear friends, here is one of your own who speaks wisely. I like that kind of worker, and I am ready to join the workers in order to explain morality to those who are less enlightened.
> *A Voice:* We do not need any lessons in morality.
> *The Lady:* Also several of my friends and I would like to devote ourselves to the workers and organize them.
> *The Socialist:* Well then, help us to organize according to our tastes and our ideas, instead of trying to organize us according to yours.[44]

Désirée Gay had participated in the government's national workshop program, and her hardening class position may have reflected her experiences there. The Luxembourg Commission (under the presidency of Louis Blanc) had been created to solve the unemployment problem; "organize work" was the language of 1848. On the commission's recommendation, municipally funded and administered national workshops were established in Paris, but these employed men only. Women workers protested this exclusion, and in response, the municipal government agreed to organize female workers into workshops. The unemployed working women were granted the right to elect their own representatives to the municipal authorities who would administer the distribution of government work contracts. Désirée Gay was elected from the second arrondissement. It was a limited experiment, applying only to the luxury clothing industry. Worse yet, the pay levels designated by the authorities were too low even to permit the workers' subsistence. "The women workers are dying of hunger. The work they are given in the shop is a trap; the organization of women's work is despotism under a new name and the nomination of women is a hoax that men have perpetrated on women in order to get rid of them." [45]

As one solution Gay demanded that "women delegates . . . be seated at the Luxembourg Commission among the delegates of men." She continued:

> If men enter into an association to produce riches and to defend liberty, then women must join with them to regulate and save the riches and to

put equality and fraternity into practice. Thus they must ask the government to be in favor of special meetings between women, and then to permit them to go to men's general meetings, so that men and women can enlighten one another and agree on common interests, and most of all so that it cannot be said that the association that we hope for will give birth to two separate camps, men in one and women in the other.

Gay also insisted on more worker autonomy, reflecting the growing conflict between women of different classes. She criticized not only the all-male Luxembourg Commission but also the proposal to place a bourgeois female management over the women workers. According to Gay, female (bourgeois) advisers to the commission took money needed for subsistence salaries from underpaid workers. Bourgeois women knew little of the reality of working conditions; they senselessly required useless ornaments on clothing and simultaneously required that work be paid by the piece.[46]

Gay used her official position to argue for other meaningful demands: national restaurants, libraries, and meeting rooms where women could gather, as well as public washrooms and laundries. Here her purpose was not only to lighten women's work load but also to blur the distinction between public and domestic spheres, between women's "place" and men's. But her proposals were not welcomed by a government increasingly resistant to workers' demands. She was removed from her position as workshop director; the notice of her firing warned that the workshop itself would be closed if the workers protested the government action against her. Only a few days later, on June 22, this threat became moot when the government decreed the closing of all of the national workshops, halting even this limited assistance.

The closing of the national workshops sparked six days of bitter street fighting, the "bloody June Days." The plight of the poor had not improved during the spring of 1848 but had actually worsened. Disorder relating to property owners' fears of social revolution had halted the tentative economic recovery; yet still more unemployed crowded into Paris hoping to find work there that was not available in the countryside. The national workshops did little to reverse the crisis. They were a travesty of Blanc's vision: those limited number who were enrolled were given little productive work to do, and thus the workshops served more as charity than as true employment. Yet even this small attempt to provide work for the un-employed was viewed as social anarchy by the conservative government elected in April. In mid-May, rioting in Paris seemed to confirm the conservatives' worst fears. In June, they moved against the unemployed, but the response in the working-class quarters of Paris was immediate in defense of their fading dream of a social and democratic republic.

The government quickly put down the revolt; fifteen thousand people were arrested, four thousand deported. Many Left leaders, Louis Blanc included, were forced into exile. All political clubs were placed under police supervision, and new press laws were introduced reimposing a "caution" payment (against possible future offenses) from those who wished to publish newspapers. Written attacks against the government became indictable offenses.

The general repression fell upon women with particular severity. On June 28, they were forbidden to participate in political clubs. The *Politique des femmes* was doubly struck. First, Deroin had difficulty raising the "caution" money and could publish only one other issue (August) during all of 1848. Then when she finally secured adequate financial backing— Hortense Wild and the former Saint-Simonian Olinde Rodrigues came to her aid—the government required her to change the journal's name to *Opinion des femmes*. "La Politique" was denied to women.

Deroin was undaunted. The Constituent Assembly had prepared its constitution calling for a president and a single-chamber legislature. In December, Louis-Napoleon Bonaparte, nephew of the former emperor, was elected president. Elections to the Legislative Assembly were set for May. Deroin took up the cause of women's political rights once again: "The time has come for women to take part in the social movement, in the work of regeneration that is in preparation; incessant political convulsions are the sign of the suffering of societies and prove that man alone cannot organize them and indicate the coming of a new era." [47] Indeed, she had grown more daring over the past months. This time, Deroin decided that she should herself run for office and attempted to secure a place on one of the Seine "lists" for the assembly election. She placarded the city walls with her statement of candidacy:

> To the Voters of the Department of the Seine, Citizens:
> I come to seek your votes, by devotion to the dedication of a great principle: civil and political equality of both sexes.
> It is in the name of justice that I call upon the sovereign people against the negation of the great principles that are the foundation of our social future. If, using your right [to vote], you call to women to take part in the work of the legislative assembly, you will consecrate in all their integrity our republican dogmas: Liberty, Equality, Fraternity for all women as for all men.
> A Legislative Assembly, made up strictly of men, is as incapable of making laws as would be an assembly that was entirely composed of

privileged persons to discuss the interests of the workers, or an assembly of capitalists to uphold the honor of the country.

Jeanne Deroin, Candidate[48]

She looked for support, if not for herself personally, at least for the concept of sexual equality, particularly from democratic socialists. She addressed the following letter to the electoral committee of the Club des Démocrates-Socialistes:

Citizens,

You are Democratic-Socialists; you want the abolition of the exploitation of man by man and of woman by man; you want the complete, radical abolition of all privileges of sex, race, birth, caste, and wealth; you sincerely want all of the consequences of our great principles: Liberty, Equality, Fraternity.

It is in the name of these principles that do not allow any unjust exclusion that I present myself as a candidate to the Legislative Assembly, and that I come and ask for your support, if not to be admitted on the list of twenty-eight that will be presented to the vote of the electors, then at least that your sense of justice will not permit me to be kept off this list in the name of a privilege of sex that is in violation of the principles of fraternity and equality.[49]

Fifteen delegates to the central electoral committee responded positively and cast their votes for Deroin's inclusion on their list.[50]

For several weeks in April 1849, Deroin attended public or club meetings to present her ideas and her candidacy. Often she was not permitted to speak; frequently she was ridiculed or shouted down. Only at the Salle des Acacias in the Saint-Antoine quarter, among democratic socialists, were her ideas accorded respect. But although she succeeded that evening in obtaining a unanimous vote in favor of the principle of sexual equality, the group decided that to support her candidacy would be to throw away their votes because female candidacies were unconstitutional. This was a defeat for Deroin because she had asked them to demonstrate their belief that female candidacies were indeed constitutional by supporting hers.[51]

Feminists had reached a dead end. Their hopes to achieve social transformation through political means were unrealized. The government had denied them the vote, shut down their political clubs, and—theoretically at least—denied their right to participate in any political activity. Now Flora Tristan's strategy reemerged. Feminists proposed to regain lost ground by building voluntary associations of workers.

Already in 1848, workers had used the relaxation of antiassociation laws to form workers' cooperatives or mutual aid societies which, seemingly less threatening than producers' associations or national workshops, outlived the June repression. Some female workers' groups organized similarly. The *Voix des femmes* group formed an Association of Wage-earning Women to assist unemployed servants. Elisa Lemonnier and Désirée Gay organized the Club Fraternal des Lingères (linen seamstresses), which later became the Association Fraternelle des Ouvriers Lingères, the purpose of which was to provide retirement income and disability insurance. Suzanne Voilquin organized the United Midwives, who demanded an equivalent training to male obstetricians and asked that the state reimburse them directly for their work. The midwives explained that they often assisted at childbirths in families too poor to pay them. Their work should not, however, be viewed as female "service"; they performed a public function and demanded recognition of this fact in the form of remuneration by the state.[52] In December 1848, Pauline Roland left Boussac to return to Paris; there she founded the Fraternal Association of Socialist Male and Female Teachers and Professors.

In the summer of 1849, feminists undertook their most ambitious project, a federation of workers' associations. Jeanne Deroin initiated the project and, in the August *Opinion des femmes,* outlined an organizational plan for this Association Solidaire et Fraternelle de Toutes les Associations Réunies. The *Opinion des femmes* was fined five thousand francs as a "warning" after publishing the plan. Jeanne Deroin, unable to pay the sum, was forced to cease publication.[53]

During the months of August 1849 to May 1850, activity focused on organizing, recruiting groups, and defining the association's structure. Jeanne Deroin and Pauline Roland were particularly active in this work. Deroin was one of the five members of the organizing committee, and later she was elected to the Central Committee. By May, four hundred fraternal associations had joined. But then, on May 29, 1850, the police arrested all members attending a meeting at Deroin's home. (The discussion concerned the purchase of a building still owned by the former minister of the interior Ledru-Rollin, who was in exile.) Nine women were among those arrested, but six of them were released. Deroin, Roland, and Nicaud (director of the Laundresses' Association) were held for trial, along with twenty-seven men. The charge against the thirty, most of whom were pacifists, was conspiracy to overthrow the government by violence. Feminist principles were supposedly not on trial, but there can be no doubt that Deroin's and Roland's feminist activities and beliefs horrified the judges. The arrest order for Roland read: "For many years she has been pro-

mulgating communist-socialist opinions. An unmarried mother, she is the
enemy of marriage, maintaining that subjecting the woman to the control
of the husband sanctifies inequality." [54] And about Deroin, the following
"evidence" was entered into the records: "The lady Desroches, as some
kind of protest against marriage, has abandoned the name of her husband
to bear her maiden name." [55]

At first, the two accused feminists made no concessions to masculine
prejudice.

> *The Attorney-General:* What are your last names and your first names?
> *Jeanne Deroin:* Before answering, I must protest against the law by which
> you want to judge me. It is a law made by men; I do not recognize it.[56]

When the attorney-general addressed Roland, he asked, "What is your
opinion on the legitimacy of children and on marriage? " The defense
lawyer advised Roland not to answer. But she replied, "Yes, I shall answer.
I protest against marriage because, in the way that it is organized, it
maintains the inferiority of the wife vis-à-vis the husband." [57] Ultimately
one concession was made. Jeanne Deroin was implored by the defense
lawyer to deny her role as originator of the idea of the association. Her
male codefenders understood it would help their case if a man, in this
instance Delbrouk, took this responsibility. Jeanne Deroin gave in.

> I had been urgently begged, in the name of the association, not to
> acknowledge that I was the author of the project or of the act of Union
> of the associations.
> The prejudice that still prevailed in the associations was exacerbated by
> the preeminent role that a woman, devoted to the cause of women's rights,
> had taken in this work. Not wanting, in the presence of our adversaries,
> to start a debate among socialists on the socialist outlook, I contented
> myself to answer the question that was put to me: No, I have nothing
> to say for the associations.[58]

Deroin and Roland nonetheless received prison terms of six months
each. After their release, Deroin went into exile; Roland remained in Paris.
In the general gathering up of persons "dangerous to the state" that
accompanied Louis Napoleon's coup d'état in December of 1851, Roland
was reincarcerated and deported to a penal colony in Algeria. Although
influential friends eventually obtained her release, she died on the trip
back to Paris.

The effectiveness of the government repression of the 1848 feminists cannot be overexaggerated. It would be almost twenty years before feminists would regroup. After 1852, all their leaders were either scattered—Suzanne Voilquin to the United States, Jeanne Deroin to London, Eugénie Niboyet to Geneva, Désirée Gay to Belgium—or dead.

In London, Deroin published an *Almanach des femmes* in both French and English. She published Roland's last letters from prison in Paris and from Algeria, as well as an analysis of Saint-Simonian feminism written by Maria Talon. Deroin also covered developments in America and in England that would be of interest to feminists everywhere. In spite of the breadth of this coverage, she could reach only a very limited audience and had to cease publication in 1854.

Among leftists in exile there were frequent expressions of sympathy for the cause of women. In Jersey, Victor Hugo delivered a eulogy at the tomb of Louise Julien: "Friends, in future times, in that beautiful and peaceful fraternal and social Republic of the future, the role of women will be great. . . . The eighteenth century proclaimed the rights of man; the nineteenth century will proclaim the rights of woman." And in London, the committee of exiles affirmed: "The past has known only the woman oppressed, minor, [and] subjugated by man. The modern revolution will create a woman conscious and responsible, companion and not subject, the free woman who is equal to man." [59]

But in France, feminists were silenced, with devastating effects. In 1848–49, the French feminist movement was the most advanced and the most experienced of all Western feminist movements. Yet for the next twenty years, feminists would be unable to move forward. They would have to contend with attacks from the Left as well as the Right. And the only weapons that they would be able to employ would be their pens.

CHAPTER 7

La Querelle des Femmes
of the Second Empire

Conservative reaction

T he imperial government of Napoleon III maintained an elaborate system of both direct and indirect censorship of the press and prohibited open discussion of political issues in public meetings for most of the years (December 1851–71) of the Second Empire. These controls on the press and on assembly precluded feminist propaganda, organization, or agitation and limited the influence of those feminist sympathizers who had escaped the general proscription that had sent so many of the 1848–49 activists into exile. The woman question did not disappear, but for a time at least, the loudest voices in the by-now centuries-old "querelle des femmes" were antifeminist or outright misogynist.

During the 1850s and 1860s, antifeminism consolidated even on the Left, in significant contrast to the 1830s and 1840s, when patriarchal arguments had been voiced primarily by conservative right-wing theorists. Then, left-wing theorists had rarely battled feminists, even when they disagreed with their objectives. The favorable climate for feminists within leftist groups began to change in the 1840s. Both Auguste Comte and Etienne Cabet, for example, denied that women should have any political rights or public role, but in 1848, their positions were still flexible. Cabet permitted women to attend his club's meetings and, in April, he even promised to consider seriously supporting women's suffrage. The socialist Pierre-Joseph Proudhon and the republican Jules Michelet were more determinedly antifeminist than either Comte or Cabet. But even though their first writings on the woman question predate the 1848 Revolution, it was not until after 1851, when the state fully repressed feminists and their allies, that their antifeminist positions came to predominate among

151

leftists. The most influential republican theorist of the 1850s and 1860s, Jules Michelet, resurrected the patriarchalism of Rousseau; the preeminent socialist theorist, Pierre-Joseph Proudhon, went even further, stripping Rousseauist patriarchalism of its chivalrous cloak to expose its inherent misogyny. Feminists' hopes that they would soon win over those whose basic sympathies were with social transformation—those who spoke out for human equality, for progress, and for change—were dashed.

Feminists were overwhelmed. Few of them remaining in France had the literary skills to counter Proudhon's or Michelet's attacks. Organizing and even lecturing were forbidden to them. Yet feminist views continued to circulate, particularly in some of the more liberal of the Paris salons. And in time, two young women who frequented these circles, Juliette Lamber (later, well known as Juliette Adam) and Jenny d'Héricourt, were encouraged to denounce Proudhon and Michelet. Their works were hardly as popular or widely read as their opponents', but they were significant nonetheless. The next generation of feminists was emerging. The "querelle des femmes" of the Second Empire—the debate pitting Proudhon and Michelet against Adam and Héricourt—was more than a literary debate; it became the next chapter in the political history of feminism.

(Because he's right-wing for the workers

Left-wing Patriarchalism

small-workshops to combat industrialism

Pierre-Joseph Proudhon's attitudes toward women seem to have grown out of his ideas about marriage and the family. He regarded marriage as both a biological and a social necessity, essential to assure reproduction of the species as well as "justice" in society. His socialism—mutualism, as it came to be called—was the socialism of small, independent producers. Proudhon assumed that their workshops would be family workshops, where wives would work under husbands' direction, and so he feared that women's emancipation would threaten this form of family production. Yet he did not believe that men and women had much in common, and so feared that if given the choice, women might not marry. In *Qu'est-ce que la propriété?* (What is property?), written in 1840, Proudhon declared: "Between woman and man there may exist love, passion, ties of custom, and the like; but there is no real society. Man and woman are not companions. The difference of the sexes places a barrier between them, like that placed between animals, by a difference of race. Consequently, far from advocating what is now called the emancipation of woman, I should incline, rather if there were no other alternative, to exclude her from society." [1]

In 1846, Proudhon began his crusade to wrest socialism from the ideological control of those who would encourage extrafamilial social structures, in a chapter of *Système des contradictions économiques ou philosophie de la misère* (System of economic contradictions or philosophy of poverty), entitled "La Communauté est incompatible avec la famille." He criticized the Saint-Simonians and the Fourierists for their attacks on the traditional monogamous family.[2] According to Proudhon, "either community or family," but it was not possible to have both. For Proudhon, there was no choice. It was from the family that a man's personality took on its definitive characteristics, and it was from the family that men acquired their energy. For women, too, "community" would be an undesirable experience, as women "only aspire to get married in order to become sovereigns of a small state that they call their household. . . . The community is antipathetic to the mother of a family." [3]

In May–June 1848, Proudhon ran for office in the by-election to the Constituent Assembly. He incorporated his traditionalist position on the family and women into his platform, which he nonetheless labeled a "revolutionary program":

> The family is one of the advancements of humanity, like industry, art, science, morality, philosophy. . . . The family and property move along together, one leaning on the other. . . . With property, the role of woman begins. The household, this ideal institution that one tries in vain to ridicule, the household is the kingdom of woman. . . . Take away the household and you take away the foundation stone of the family . . . there are no more families. See, in the big towns, the working classes, falling little by little, because of the instability of the home, the poverty of the household and the lack of property, into concubinage and debauchery.
>
> The revolution of 1848 therefore does not attack the family, cannot attack it. All of its influence in that regard consists in obtaining the ideal of the family by reforming the economic base on which it rests.[4]

Proudhon was elected a delegate from the Seine; during the next year he was considered to represent extreme leftist opinion in the assembly. His insistence that women's options be severely limited so as to shore up the family signaled a shift in leftist politics which, in the recent past at least, had generally supported the expansion of opportunities for women. Now, Proudhon led a left-wing attack on Carnot's plan to give young girls an education equivalent to that available to boys:

> It is in treating education that one will have to decide the role of woman in society. Until she is married, woman is the apprentice, at the most

assistant-mistress; at the workshop, as in the family, she remains a minor and is not a part of the citizenship. Woman is not, as it is vulgarly said, the half nor the equal of man, but the sympathetic and living complement of man that makes him a whole person: this is the principle of the family and the law of monogamy.[5]

Many on the Left clearly supported Proudhon's position, and cartoons by Daumier and Gavarni, among others, in leftist publications exploited this new antifeminism. Feminists faced a backlash that was testimony, in no small measure, to their success in marshaling unexpected numbers to their cause.

During the 1850s and 1860s, Proudhon stepped up his attacks on feminism and on women. The most complete expression of his socialism, *De la justice dans la Révolution et dans l'eglise* (On justice in the Revolution and in the church), was published in 1858 and included two chapters on women and the family. His final work, *La Pornocratie ou les femmes dans les temps moderne* (Pornocracy or women in modern times), which was not published until after his death, was devoted exclusively to combating feminism. Clearly, Proudhon became increasingly obsessed with this battle. The working class did not disapprove: during the 1850s and the 1860s Proudhon became the predominant influence in the French working-class movement and in revolutionary circles. According to labor historian Jules Puech, the French delegates to the Geneva Congress of 1866 (the most numerous and influential of the various national delegations), were "tous proudhoniens."[6] And according to most historians, Proudhon (although he died in 1865) was still the predominant influence among participants of the Commune of 1871.[7] His popularity among workers during this period related to their fears of social and economic changes that were out of their control. The pace of industrialization increased enormously in the 1850s, and more and more women began to work outside the home. The family workshop began its long-term decline. Husbands who had been heads of small workshops with wives, children, and servants working under their supervision saw their limited power threatened. In *De la justice,* Proudhon overstated his case against women with illogical arguments to the point that some admirers were embarrassed by his conclusions.[8] The physical inferiority of woman, Proudhon proclaimed, was uncontested. Proudhon stated emphatically that physical force is a result of male sexuality because, he maintained, boys become stronger than girls after puberty. As additional supporting evidence, Proudhon observed that men are weaker after sexual intercourse. Having thus "proved" that the variation in physical force, for men, is the result of variations in virility rather than differences

in height or weight, he was satisfied that he had proved the relationship
between physical superiority and masculinity. "Woman is a diminutive of
man in whom one organ is missing that would permit her to become
[adult]." And later, woman is "a sort of middle ground between him
[man] and the rest of the animal kingdom." [9]

Proudhon next astonishes his readers with an extraordinary mathematical
formulation—"man's physical strength is to woman's as three is to two."
And since everyone, "either in the family or in the workshop functions
and works according to the strength that he possesses, the effect that is
yielded will be in the same proportion, three to two." He continues: "This
is what Justice demands . . . in short, the preponderance is acquired by
the stronger sex in the proportion of three to two, which means that man
will be the master and that woman will obey. *Dura lex, sed lex.*" [10]

Proudhon recognized that if it could be proved that woman's innate
intellectual capacity were the same or greater than man's her physical
inferiority would be compensated for. But, alas, here, too, he found the
female inferior. He disagreed with those who believed better education
could erase intellectual inequality. The intellectual inferiority of the female
was innate because "genius is . . . virility of the spirit, its power of
abstraction, of generalization, of invention, of conceptualization, which the
child, the eunuch, and woman are equally lacking." [11] Man's intellectual
ability rated a three; woman's a two.

Next, Proudhon set out to prove that woman was morally inferior as
well, building his argument in a similar fashion: *la force,* equated with
masculine sexuality, is "the starting point of virtue." The woman is an
immoral being, susceptible to prostitution: "Why is it that, independent
of economic and political causes that attach themselves to it, prostitution
is incomparably greater in women than in men . . . if it is not that her
self [ego] is weaker than ours." She is susceptible, also, to vanity—"That
which she dreams of being, if only for a day, an hour, a lady, princess,
queen, or fairy." He maintained, further, that justice meant nothing to
women and that they disdained equality, as evidenced by their need for
distinctions and preferential treatment: "Go to the theater, to a public
ceremony. What is it that flatters women most? the performance itself?
No, a reserved seat." [12]

After "proving" women's inferiority in three key areas, Proudhon com-
puted the mathematical results, concluding that concerning "the total value
of man and woman, their relationship and consequently their share of
influence will be as 3 by 3 by 3 is to 2 by 2 by 2, or 27 to 8." [13]

What significance did all of this ranting have in Proudhon's schema?
In the introduction to the two chapters "Amour et Mariage" and "Amour

et Mariage: Suite," Proudhon admitted that he hesitated in declaring his position on these issues. He had already had a few encounters with feminists (he mentions Daniel Stern and George Sand),[14] and he claimed he sought no others. "In the interest of common dignity and domestic tranquillity," he would have preferred to keep his opinions to himself. But others— "so-called emancipators"—had already stated their position, which he found abominable (he mentioned specifically Ernest Legouvé), and he therefore had to take issue with their opinions.[15]

Equality, to Proudhon, was not to be shared by all but only by all men, and even more specifically, all heads of household. Proudhon was in this respect less the revolutionary, more the *bon paysan* from the Franche Comté.[16] In fact, few French men of the time would have disagreed with Proudhon's statement that "the care of the household, the education of children, [and] the responsibility of public charity" should be the role of women.[17] And few of his French contemporaries would have found fault with this further clarification:

So still
alienating
her

> As for outside interests, I have not and do not want [these] for woman; for the same reasons, I do not want [for her] war; for it does not become beauty any more than does slavery.
>   I do not want politics [for her], because politics is war.
>   I do not want judicial, police, or governmental functions [for her], because that is still war.[18]

Concerning the division of responsibilities of the marriage between husband and wife, too, Proudhon reflected a common view:

> Once the household is established, man is charged with work, production, exterior relations; woman is charged with the administration of the interior. The division is determined by the respective qualities of the spouses. To the strongest, activity, battle, movement; to her who shines and who loves, but who should shine only for her husband, love only him, domestic cares, peace, and the modesty of the hearth. Both are responsible and free in their duties; however the husband will have the right of control over the wife, whereas the wife only has that of helping, advising, and informing her husband.[19]

But his revolutionary friends were disappointed that Proudhon, a true revolutionary in so many other ways, should uphold the status quo concerning women. Alexander Herzen, for example, his friend who had financed *Le Représentant du peuple* for Proudhon in 1848 and 1849, reacted to the publication of *De la justice* in a generally favorable way, but the chapters on love and marriage struck him as old-fashioned.

> Proudhon had his sensitive spot that had been bruised before, and there he was incorrigible; there the limit of his character was reached and, as is always the case, beyond it he was a conservative and a follower of tradition. I am speaking of his views of family life and of the significance of woman in general.
>
> "How lucky is our friend N.!" Proudhon would say jestingly. "His wife is not so stupid that she can't make a good *pot-au-feu*, and not clever enough to discuss his articles. That's all that is necessary for domestic happiness."
>
> In this jest Proudhon laughingly expressed the essential basis of his view of woman. His conceptions of family relationships were coarse and reactionary, but they expressed not the bourgeois element of the townsman, but rather the stubborn feeling of the rustic *paterfamilias,* haughtily regarding woman as a subordinate worker and himself as the autocratic head of family.[20]

Worse yet, whereas sometimes Proudhon merely appeared ordinarily traditional concerning women, at other times he was thoroughly reactionary and even shocked other traditionalists. His writing style never showed the gallantry associated with patriarchal Romanticism. Most traditionalist writers of the time tried to suggest that their views of women were at least fair, that women were "equal" partners: though not as intelligent or strong as men, they were morally superior. Proudhon, of course, recognized no moral qualities to compensate for inferiorities. He furthermore rejected any "taint" of Romanticism. In answer to the question he himself posed, "What part should love play in contracting a marriage?" Proudhon responded, "the smallest part possible. When two people show up to be married, love has supposedly accomplished its end. . . . That is why a marriage born only of love is so close to shame that a father who gives it his consent deserves reproach."[21]

At one point, Proudhon seems to have even embarrassed himself by the severity of his judgment and then reconsidered. In *De la justice,* he assigns woman twenty-seven points to man's eight in the area of "beauty." But his growing feud with leading feminists of his day, rather than converting him to their point of view, pushed him even further into a corner. Proudhon's very last written words, found in his unedited notes kept for the completion of *La Pornocratie,* read: "Oh, I have spoken too well of woman! I regret it." The note concludes: "Be sure to condemn what I have written about the beauty of women."[22]

The increased harshness of Proudhon's views, as expressed in *La Pornocratie,* is likely a result of the intensity of the debate in which he was involved. After the publication of *De la justice,* with its famous mathematics, a lively debate began with a number of feminist and women writers, who refuted Proudhon's formula in newspapers, brochures, and books. Proudhon kept a dossier of their arguments and especially of the writings of Jenny d'Héricourt and Juliette Lamber (Adam). As Jerome Langlois, his close friend, who introduced the posthumous publication of *La Pornocratie,* writes, "Proudhon was dreaming of an offensive turnabout. What was his life, after all, if not a long series of battles! He was gathering his materials and polishing his weapons." [23] Clearly, Proudhon considered himself at war. And reasoned argument has never been the hallmark of the propagandist in times of war.

Jules Michelet's audience was more bourgeois than Proudhon's and included the intellectual establishment as well as the portion of the general reading public that identified with liberalism and/or republicanism. He was certainly the most influential writer to concern himself with the subject of women during this period. By 1850, he was already a leader in French intellectual life. His reputation had been established in 1827 with the publication of the *Précis d'histoire moderne,* a work which was, until 1850, the basis of historical instruction in French schools.[24] The first six volumes of his celebrated *Histoire de France* were published between 1833 and 1843. As Edmund Wilson has written:

> He was the man who, above all others, had supplied the French of his time with a past. He was read with enthusiasm by writers as different as Lamartine, Montalembert, Victor Hugo, Heine, Herzen, Proudhon, Béranger, Renan, Taine, the Goncourts and Flaubert. He was an artist as well as a thinker, and so penetrated to parts of the intellectual world widely remote from one another and influenced a variety of writers in a curious variety of ways.[25]

Following the failure of the republican forces during 1848 and 1849, Michelet became depressed and pessimistic about what he considered a moral degeneration among the French. The Second Republic had been overthrown and the Empire was well entrenched. Everywhere individual liberty was overcome by *"industrialisme, machinisme, militarisme,* and the victim of this triumph everywhere was man." [26] Michelet believed that the French race itself was in jeopardy. He cited official statistics from 1856 to justify his concern. The number of "young men unqualified for military service, dwarfs, hunchbacks, the lame, during the seven years from 1831 to 1837 was only 460,000, but after only seven years it had increased by 31,000. The number of marriages was diminishing—in 1851 nine thousand less than the preceding year, in 1852, seven thousand less than in 1851!'' [27] He feared that if it were not for the French inheritance laws that made women rich, "no one would marry anymore, at least not in the large cities." In *La Femme,* Michelet relates having overheard the following advice given by an older man to a youth in the provinces: "If you are to stay here, you must get married, but if you live in Paris, it is not worth it. It is too easy to do otherwise." [28] Michelet linked the renaissance of French republicanism—which he fervently desired—to "moral regeneration," which for him meant the reconstruction of traditional family life. Like Proudhon before him, he opposed the utopian socialists, who had also linked political issues to "moral" issues but who had proposed family reorganization and female emancipation instead.

To explicate his views Michelet published *L'Amour* in 1858 and in 1860, *La Femme.* Both were written *about* women *for* men. Although women were reading, and indeed were to read and criticize Michelet, Michelet was oblivious to women—as readers, that is—as he makes clear in the preface: "To tell the truth, among men (but let us not say anything about it to women)." [29]

L'Amour begins with the by-now familiar statement that women are totally different beings from men.

> The love object, woman, is a being apart from others, more different from man than it seems at first glance.
>
> She does not do anything like us. She thinks, talks, and acts differently. Her tastes differ from ours. Her blood does not have the same flow as ours; sometimes it rushes forward like a shower from a storm. She does not breathe like us. In expectation of pregnancy and the consequent uplifting of the interior organs, nature has caused her to breathe principally in the area of the four upper ribs. From this necessity derives woman's greatest beauty, the soft undulation of the breast, that expresses all of her feeling in silent eloquence.
>
> She does not eat like us, not as much nor the same foods. Why? Mostly because she does not digest as we do. Her digestion is constantly disturbed by one thing: she loves from the bottom of her entrails. This deep cup of love (that is called the basin) is a sea of variable emotions that works against the regularity of digestive functions.
>
> The interior differences show up on the outside by an even more striking difference. Woman has a language apart.
>
> Insects and fish remain silent. The bird sings. Man has a distinct language, clear and enlightening word, the clearness of the verb. But

woman, beyond man's verb and the bird's song, has a magical language
that she intersperses into the verb or the song: the sigh, passionate breathing.
Incalculable power. She hardly makes her presence known and the heart
is moved. Her breast rises, falls, and rises again; she cannot speak and we
are persuaded in advance, won over to what she desires. What argument
of man could act like the silence of a woman? [30]

But to Michelet, what is of greatest significance is not that women are in
all ways different from men (an idea that in no way distinguishes Michelet
even from feminists), but that women are sick, constant invalids. First,
there is the "week of crisis." And "the week preceding that one is already
troubled." And in the eight or ten days that follow "this painful week,
a languor continues, a weakness. . . . In such a way that in reality, fifteen
or twenty days out of twenty-eight (one could say almost the entire time)
woman is not only sick but also wounded." [31]

The result of the female physical condition was, of course, an inability
to do productive work. "In reality, woman cannot work for long either
standing or sitting. If she is always sitting the blood rises, the chest is
irritated, the stomach obstructed, the head heavy. If she is kept standing
for a long time, as is a laundress or one who sets type at a printer's, she
has other blood-related accidents. She can work a lot, but changing positions,
as she does in her household, coming and going." [32] A husband must
alone work to support the household: "That is the paradise of marriage,
that man works for woman, that he alone provides, that he has the joy
to toil . . . for her." The wife's role? According to Michelet, the perfect
wife would say to her husband, "My friend, I am not strong. I am not
good for much except to love you and take care of you. I do not have
your strong arms, and if I spend too long at a complicated task, blood
rises to my head. . . . I could hardly invent anything. I have no initiative.
I am always waiting for you and I don't look beyond you." When the
husband returns, tired, from work, though, and finds "an infinite amount
of goodness and serenity," all is worth it. "This is the mission of women:
to refresh man's heart." [33]

Michelet gives detailed instructions for the creation of a happy home.
Women should be about eighteen years old when they marry; men should
be twenty-eight to thirty. Michelet next stresses the necessity for solitude.
The home should be in the countryside, away from all relatives:[34] "Two
people living together and not three, that is the essential axiom to keep
peace in a household." (But "a country girl who helps out and does not
interrupt private conversations" may live with them.) Why this solitude?
And why the necessity for the disparity in ages? In order for the husband

to have full power over his wife, indeed to mold her as a person: "You must create woman." [35]

> Take your wife away. Without breaking her family ties, live with her apart [from them]. The farther away her family is, the more your wife will belong to you. The more you will have the duty, the happiness to be everything to her. You may not neglect her. You are her father, and day by day you should enrich her spirit. You are her brother to sustain her with friendly conversation and gentle comradeship. You are her mother to care for her in her little womanly needs, to caress her, to spoil her, to put her to bed. . . . It is a little hard, but true. . . . It is the law itself of marriage. [36]

Long chapters in *La Femme* describe the unhappy condition of working-class women in mid-nineteenth-century France, for whom the ideal life was unobtainable. Even compared with the poorest paid male worker, their lives were harsh: "It is meat, it is wine, that are lacking for him; for her it is bread itself. She cannot regress any more nor fall any lower; one step more and she dies." Michelet is outraged at this situation: "One blushes to be a man." No woman, weak as she naturally is, should be expected to support herself. "She must have a household; she must be married." [37]

Nor should a middle-class woman be expected to support herself: "The worst fate for woman is to live alone." His discussion of the educated woman is sympathetic ("one must have compassion"). Given the "unfortunate" reality of his time, when some women had to earn income, he approves of the various certificates that permit them to teach and even advises making such certificates easier to obtain—but this does not change his belief that "woman is not alive without man." [38]

Michelet's prose style differed significantly from Proudhon's. His writings on women were in the Romantic tradition: they were gallant and seemingly sympathetic. But the differences were in style, not substance. Both writers considered monogamous family life as the means to "moral regeneration" and saw this regeneration as the necessary first step to the victory of their political ideals. Both stated that men and women were different and that their differences were hierarchical, women being inferior to men. Both believed that women should have no life outside the home. And both men were convinced that women's social inferiority was dictated by their physical inferiority. Feminists faced a formidable opposition.

Feminists Respond

Women committed to the feminist vision were not entirely absent from the literary debates that focused on women during these two decades of Napoleonic rule, but they worked alone and as a result lacked the strength that collective efforts had brought to the feminist struggle of earlier decades. Their primary concern was to defend women against the attacks of Proudhon and Michelet. Their success was in keeping alive the feminist tradition until new liberal laws would again permit that necessary ingredient for further advancement—organization.

Juliette Lamber (later Adam) was one of the first to pick up her pen as a weapon against Proudhon. She was an extraordinary individual and a worthy opponent of Proudhon. Her father, a doctor and a leader of the republican faction in his Picard town of Verberie, had overseen much of her education. His *Paradoxes d'un docteur allemand,* published in 1860, show him to have been decidedly feminist in his attitudes: "Women, conspire to be free. When you come into possession of your freedom, your autonomy, you will have a voice in matters, men will rely upon you and you will be of value in the balance of justice to the full weight of your heart." [39] Her maternal grandmother, who struggled with her father for the control of both Juliette's person and mind, was particularly ambitious for her granddaughter. Juliette would not disappoint them. Her salon would be the meeting place for all the luminaries of the Third Republic, and she would become directrice of the influential literary magazine *La Nouvelle revue.* The future Mme Adam would be called "La Grande Française" [40] by some and "la vieille doyenne des lettres françaises" [41] by others.

Adam made her literary debut in 1856 at the age of twenty, with publication of a letter to the editor of *Le Siècle,* Alphonse Karr, signed merely "Juliette." [42] She congratulated Karr on his criticism of contemporary female dress, giving her own opinions in a witty manner, and she managed to include some statements on the inequality of the sexes. Women's vanity and desire for luxury, she declared, led them to be dependent on those who could satisfy their needs.

Two years later, recently arrived in Paris and looking for the companionship which her unhappy marriage to Alexis La Messine did not provide, Adam met Jenny d'Héricourt through their mutual Saint-Simonian friends, Charles Fauvety, founder and editor of *La Revue philosophique,* and Charles Renouvier, one of that magazine's principal contributors. Outraged by the attitudes toward women expressed by Proudhon in *De la justice,* which had just appeared, Adam appealed to Héricourt to refute him. When Héricourt, the better known of the two, refused, Adam determined to take on the "Attila of Publicists" herself.[43]

Her *Idées anti-proudhoniennes sur l'amour, la femme et le mariage* was published in August 1858, only four months after the appearance of *De la justice*.[44] Adam began her refutation with a condemnation of Proudhon's general methodology, which she labeled a search for the "absolute" (in this case "justice"), the universal panacea for society's ills. "It was a certain narrow-mindedness that did not permit him to see the complexity of the social problem and made him believe that it could be solved by a simple formula." She then quickly dismissed his attitudes on love, that is, that the only purpose of love is reproduction. Such opinions, she stated, are "too old-fashioned, too out of keeping with universal thinking to have any power of proselytism on our contemporaries." Proudhon's mathematics, too, are dismissed as ridiculous ("coq-à l'âne").[45]

Adam held Proudhon's statements about women to be most dangerous, for they "express the universal feeling of men who, no matter what party they belong to . . . would be delighted if a way were found to reconcile both their selfishness and their conscience into a system that would permit them to preserve the benefits of exploitation based on strength, without fear of protests based on right." [46]

Proudhon, she said, thought he had proved women's physical inferiority, but he failed to note their compensating grace and beauty and their greater resilience. ("She bends and does not break. What Hercules would endure, without breaking, the stress of childbirth.") Furthermore, whatever physical superiority there might be in masculinity would be irrelevant in the industrial age. Finally, the notion that such greater force should result in greater benefits was not consistent with contemporary reality. The strongest men, she pointed out, are not the most powerful: "It is not true that those who produce the most are the most important to the government. I remember having heard a legislator of the old times say: 'While they work for us, we will legislate for them,' speaking thusly of those who produce material riches." [47]

Concerning Proudhon's assertion that women are intellectually inferior, Adam noted that in this case, too, his argument was based on the "right" of force. And she revealed the essential contradiction in his using certain female thinkers (Stern, Sand, and Staël) to buttress his arguments; they had intelligence enough, Adam notes, when their arguments were useful for Proudhon's purposes. In conclusion, she wrote:

M. Proudhon wishes to form the judicial instrument with the human couple. But in order to establish relations of justice between two beings, it is necessary not only that both beings be equal and have equivalent relations, as we have said, but it is necessary also for these two beings to be free. Man, M. Proudhon tells us, is *organized freedom;* very well, and I can readily conceive of two free and intelligent organisms concurring in the forming of a matter of conscience, generalizing it, making it the rule of their future actions, the law of their mutual relations. Here there is real justice, because there are two elements: knowledge and freedom; both parties know together and freely act together. But according to M. Proudhon, *woman does not know nor act on her own,* she receives her conscience from man; woman is not *organized freedom;* how could she establish relations of justice with a man? Does she know her own law if she is without conscience, and can she make her own law if she is only receptivity? And if she is incapable of determining her own law, how can she agree to a common law that would take her personality into account and would include in its totality the peculiar conditions of her being? Therefore, if this common law that is to rule the relations of man and woman is only the expression of the free being, of the male, it will only state half of the couple's relations. It will be completely to the benefit of the male.[48]

After refuting Proudhon, Adam elaborated her attitudes on women's issues. Her argument reveals the influence of her Saint-Simonian friends: "[Woman] supplies society with other elements than supplied by man, but that are no less indispensable. It is the agreement between feminine elements and masculine elements that provides social harmony, and it is their blending that determines humanity's progress." "Equivalence" became Juliette Adam's word to describe what she called "equality," which she distinguishes from "sameness" *(identité):* "Woman, being able to be declared superior to man in those duties proper to her sex, as man so could be in duties attributed to his own, there would only be between the two sexes a question of functional equality." [49]

Later she emphasized the importance of having distinct masculine and feminine duties:

I assert, then, that in a well-organized society there are male duties and female duties and I add that these last are no less numerous nor less important than others! . . .

As for that which pertains to professions, I see some that suit women as there are some that suit men. So those professions that demand strength should remain the lot of the stronger sex, and those that demand taste, tact, and dexterity should be as much as possible attributed to the weaker sex. The trades of mason, carpenter, joiner, locksmith, are obviously male trades, but those of sewing, retail trade, those of milliner and florist are certainly female professions, and there are a lot of others that one could, without inconvenience, add to these last ones as machines transform them and feminize them by equalizing them.[50]

Specifically, Adam demanded an equal place for women in education, medicine, and government administration, suggesting that a "mayoress" (*mairesse*) working alongside the mayor should oversee infant-care centers, insane asylums, and charitable institutions. Women must be well educated and indeed be given a *professional* education so that they could become productive:

> Work alone has emancipated man and work alone will emancipate woman. That woman could honestly earn the clothes that adorn her and beautify her, and instead of dragging her silk dresses and her lace shawls in the dust of the sidewalk, she will walk free and proud in the simplicity of an attire that will let her beauty show without tarnishing her virtue or pricing her honor. Since the education given to women is only good for making dolls of them does one have the right to be surprised that they end up, the poor creatures, by taking seriously the stupid role that they have been taught since childhood?[51]

Adam professed to place great value on woman's maternal role but asserted that this is not a universal or lifelong function:

> I maintain that it is not true that family life is adequate for the physical, moral, and intellectual activity of woman. The role of mother hen is doubtlessly very respectable but it does not suit everyone and is not as engrossing as it is said to be. Anyway, there are many women who do not marry, and also there are a great number who must add their daily work to the daily work of their husbands. Two providers in a household are better than one, and in a family where the father, who alone has work, must provide for the needs of his wife and three or four children, I wonder how one lives, if one lives, how one eats, if one eats, how one is clothed, lodged, and what education the children receive.
>   In any case work is edifying when it isn't excessive—then it is stupefying—and I do not see how the virtue of the wife needs to suffer from the labor of a workwoman. Who are the usual recruiting officers of prostitution, if it is not the impossibility of honest work, the insufficiency of the salaries, and lastly idleness, that everlasting ancestor of all vice? To open to women careers of free and decently paid work is to close the doors of the brothel.[52]

She demanded that women be valued as autonomous beings.

> *Question:* Is woman an autonomous person?
> *Answer:* Woman, considered by herself, is an individuality; she has her own laws which combine with natural laws; in one work, she is a being. She acquires the knowledge of the general laws to which she is subject and she takes hold of them by virtue of her intelligence; she is therefore an individual. Lastly, she is free in her conscience and makes her own moral law; she is therefore autonomous.[53]

And again:

> Woman, having been considered until now only from the point of view of the pleasure of the male or of the conservation of the species was only valued for her beauty or maternity. In a society that is formed by men and to their benefit, woman was only valued as a wife or a mother; but if woman is a free individual, an intellectual and moral individual, she will have her own value; she will make her own law. She will not take her conscience and her dignity from man any more than man receives his dignity and his conscience from some being outside himself.[54]

Finally, what catches our attention is Adam's gradual move away from Saint-Simonian dualism. She never disavows that view; on the contrary: "The two elements (male and female) whose combining forms the social being are not identical: if they were they would not form a new organism." But Adam sees this fact with such liberality that she effectively wipes out the significance of distinctions based on sex:

> Every human being has aptitudes that are his own. . . . Among these aptitudes, some have a masculine character and some have a feminine character. Nothing is simpler than to classify social occupations under one or the other label; but one must guard oneself against giving all the masculine qualities to all the men and all the feminine qualities to all the women. In application we find many exceptions. Thus muscular strength is predominant in man but there are many women who are more energetic than certain men. The exceptions are even more numerous in the intellectual domain. There are male intelligences among women and it isn't rare to encounter men who have qualities of delicacy, keen shrewdness, that are more often the endowments of the weaker sex. The same can be said of sentiment; it exhibits itself in some men as a feminine sensitivity, and there are some women who push the steadiness of their nerves to a point of stiffness, the strength of their hearts to the point of dryness, to the point of hardness.

If it is therefore useful, with respect to social organization, to be aware of the occupations that portray the feminine element and those that portray the masculine element, it would, however, be very dangerous to freedom to try to determine in advance the respective roles of men and women and to imprison either in occupations imposed by their respective sex.[55]

Adam also paid more attention to the necessity for divorce reform than did other women feminists (Flora Tristan excepted). Although her position did not diverge from that of the other feminists, we are instantly aware that she, like Tristan, had a personal stake in the matter. Marriage must be monogamous, she wrote, but it must also be dissoluble: "When life together is unbearable, life in common for the persons involved is the worst of slavery. . . . It is impossible to make two free beings keep for the rest of their lives a vow they made one day." Legal separation, which did not permit a new marriage, encouraged the worst behavior; divorce would improve morals. Adam also criticized the community property laws that then regulated most French marriages. She suggested instead that legally recognized contracts be drawn up that would "regulate the interests of the two parties and determine the conditions of their association." Each partner should have authority to "dispose of that which belongs to him and only that which belongs to him." [56] Ironically, the royalties from the sale of the *Idées anti-proudhoniennes* were "confiscated" by Adam's estranged husband, Alexis La Messine. The Civil Code gave him the right to do so.[57]

There is a blending of old and new ideas, old and new priorities, in *Idées anti-proudhoniennes.* Alongside Saint-Simonian arguments that honor womanly capacities and emphasize their value to society, Adam placed new arguments that were derived from a recognition of the rights of individuals. These arguments were, in fact, not new; they recalled feminism's French Revolutionary past. Their reemergence in mid-nineteenth century prepared the later alliance between feminism and republicanism.[58]

Juliette Adam's most immediate effect was to spur Jenny d'Héricourt to take up her pen again. In 1860, Héricourt published the two-volume *La Femme affranchie,* which would, in Héricourt's words, prove that "woman has the same rights as man" and "claim in consequence her emancipation." [59] During the previous decade, Héricourt had established herself as the principal feminist opponent of Proudhon, which is why Adam had expected her to refute *De la justice.* In December 1856, Héricourt had published an article in *La Revue philosophique* entitled "Proudhon and the Woman Question," which informed readers of that magazine that she and

Proudhon had already communicated on their differing opinions of women.[60] A later exchange of letters between them was reprinted in the February 1857 issue. In these letters to Proudhon, Héricourt set forth two arguments that are particularly significant. First, she rebutted Proudhon's statement that she was an exception to the generalization that men are more capable than women:

> I felt myself linked with my sex by too close a solidarity ever to be content to see myself abstracted from it by an illogical process. I am a woman— I glory in it; I rejoice if any value is set upon me, not for myself, indeed, but because this contributes to modify the opinion of men with respect to my sex. A woman who is happy upon hearing it said: *"You are a man,"* (sic), is, in my eyes, a simpleton, an unworthy creature, avowing the superiority of the masculine sex; and the men who think that they compliment her in this manner are vainglorious and impertinent boasters. If I acquire any honor, I thus pay honor to women. I reveal their aptitudes. I do not pass into the other sex any more than Proudhon abandons his own, because he is elevated by his intellect above the level of foolish and ignorant men; and if the ignorance of the mass of men prejudges nothing against their right, no more does the ignorance of the mass of women prejudge anything against theirs.[61]

And, second, she affirmed the justice of an autonomous feminist movement. Proudhon had warned against woman divorcing "her cause from that of man, and demanding for herself special legislation as though her chief tyrant and enemy were man." Héricourt responded, "You, sir, are the one who legislates especially for women; she herself desires nothing but the common law." [62]

Several chapters of *La Femme affranchie* explicate and/or criticize the works of Michelet, Proudhon, Comte, Legouvé, the Saint-Simonians, Cabetians, and Fourierists. Michelet came under the harshest fire:

> The book of Michelet and the two studies of Proudhon on woman are but two forms of the same thought. The sole difference that exists between these gentlemen is that the first is as sweet as honey and the second as bitter as absinthe. Nevertheless, I prefer the rude assailant to the poet; for insults and blows rouse us to rebel and to clamor for liberty, while compliments lull us to sleep and make us weakly endure our chains.[63]

Héricourt, of course, rejected Michelet's contention that women are sick beings, arguing that Michelet had erected "a physiological law into a morbid condition." [64] She had great sport poking holes in his more irrational arguments, ridiculing as fantasy, for example, a statement that any children conceived outside of marriage would resemble the husband rather than the lover.

And to Michelet's contention that woman could equal man in intellectual understanding but that nothing would be gained by granting her an education, Héricourt reminded Michelet that he had "no right to think and to wish in my place. I have, like you, an intelligence and a free will, to which you are bound, by your principles, to pay sovereign respect. Now I forbid you to speak for any woman; I forbid you in the name of what you call *the rights of the soul.*" In a style to rival the rhetoric of Michelet, she concluded:

> The misfortune, the irreparable misfortune, is that instead of climbing to the mountain top to look at every moving thing under the vast horizon, you have shut yourself up in a narrow valley, where, seeing nothing but pale violets, you have concluded that every flower must be also a pale violet; whereas nature has created a thousand other species, on the contrary, strong and vigorous, and which have, like you, right to earth, air, water, and sunshine.
>
> Whatever may be your love, your kindness, and your good intentions toward woman, your book is an immense danger to the cause of her liberty.[65]

Concerning Proudhon, Héricourt began by proclaiming, "Well, Mr. Proudhon, you have sought war with women! . . . War you shall have." She reminded Proudhon that women would not work for the revolution he so ardently desired without some hope of gain for themselves: "Woman is like the people: she wishes no more of your revolutions, which decimate us for the benefit of a few ambitious babblers. She will have liberty and equality for all men and women, or she will take care that no one shall have them." [66]

Of Legouvé, however, she wrote with respect:

> In every page of this book *[Histoire morale des femmes]*, we detect the impulse of an upright heart and lofty mind, indignant at injustice, oppression, and immorality. The author had served women well, and it is with pleasure that I take the opportunity to thank him in the name of those who are now struggling in various countries for the emancipation of half the human race.[67]

The second volume of *La Femme affranchie* was devoted to the exposition of Héricourt's own views on the nature and function of woman in love and marriage. She included some proposals for reforms which she believed should be made immediately. Again, as in Adam's earlier book, we recognize the gradual shift away from the Saint-Simonian dualism toward "Revolutionary" individualism.

According to Héricourt, it was "opponents" of sexual equality who maintained that there are different functions inherent to the different sexes. They might be right or wrong, Héricourt allowed, but "we shall never have a certain answer until we allow arbitrary restrictions to cease. . . . In *fact,* I know not, and you know no better than I, what are the true characteristics arising from the distinction of the sexes, and I believe that they can be revealed only by liberty in equality, parity of instruction and of education." For now,

> Let us leave each one to make her own autonomous law and to manifest herself in conformity with her nature, and take care only that rights shall be equal for all; that the strong shall not oppress the weak; that each function shall be entrusted to the one individual that is proved the best qualified to perform it. . . . Let us refrain then from all classification of faculties and functions according to sex. Besides being false, they will lead us to cruelty; for we shall oppress those, whether men or women who are neither yielding enough to submit to it nor hypocritical enough to appear to do so; and we shall do this without profit to human destiny, but, on the contrary, to its detriment.[68]

She moderated her radical position by temporizing: "As it is my principle that the function should fall to the functionary who proves his capacity, I say that at present, through the difference of education, men and women have distinct functions; and that we must give to the latter the place that in general she deserves." But she insisted nonetheless: "Let woman take the place therefore that is suited to her present development, but let her never cease to remember that this place is not a fixed point, and that she should continually strive to mount upwards until, her special nature revealing itself through equality of education, instruction, right and duty, she shall take her rightful place by the side of man and on a level with him." [69]

There can be no doubt that Héricourt recognized that she was removing the feminist structure from its Saint-Simonian base. "Let her [woman] laugh at all the utopian follies elaborated concerning her nature, her functions determined for eternity, and remember that she is not what nature, but what subjection, prejudice, ignorance have made her. Let her escape from all her chains, and no longer permit herself to be intimidated and debased." Enfantin is rejected. "The couple is a partnership formed by Love, an association of two distinct and equal beings, who would be unable to be absorbed by one another, to become a single being, an androgyne." And "Woman must not claim her rights as a woman, but only as a human person and a member of the social body." [70] Héricourt reintroduced the feminism of the French Revolution: "The two sexes, being of the same species, are before Justice and must be before the Law and Society, perfectly equal in Rights." [71]

In practical terms, however, Héricourt departed very little from the program of reform and even the tactics to achieve these reforms already worked out by earlier nineteenth-century feminists. Like the 1848 feminists, she insisted on moral purity: "Outside of chastity, there is nothing but degradation, injustice, impotence, slavery." She assented to divorce, but only to "strengthen" marriage. She suggested that divorce reform should require publicity of the reason for the marital rift. The parties would be free to marry again, "but what woman would be willing to unite herself to a man who . . . had treated his first companion badly? What man would consent to wed a woman in the same position? . . . Do you not think that the difficulty that would be experienced in contracting a new marriage [following adverse publicity] would be a brake on the inconstancy and bad conduct that lead to a rift?" [72]

Héricourt next discussed the Civil Code reforms she favored. Women should be permitted to sit on juries, should be members of boards of trade and chambers of commerce, and should be witnesses in all cases requiring the testimony of a citizen. Equal educational opportunities must be assured "because woman has a right, like man, to cultivate her intellect, and to acquire the knowledge bestowed by the state." [73] And all the professions should be opened up to women.[74]

Concerning marriage law reform, Héricourt proposed that the wife be permitted to be "mistress of her property, free to exercise any profession that suits her, and to be at liberty to sell, to buy, to give, to receive, and initiate lawsuits." [75] If community property should be the marital regime chosen by both partners in the marriage, then *both* partners must agree to the disposal of the common property, and in cases of differences of opinion, a family council would act as arbiter.

Héricourt concluded this list of by-now familiar reforms with a new demand, that "on the day of marriage each of the spouses should join his partner's name to his own; . . . the children should bear the double names of their parents until marriage, when the daughters should keep the mother's name, and the sons the father's; or else (if we wish to bring into the question the system of liberty) . . . it might be decreed that, on attaining majority, the child himself should choose which of the two names he would bear and transmit." [76]

Like feminists of earlier decades, Héricourt called on women to unite to struggle for female emancipation. Woman should

> establish a journal to maintain your claims; . . . found a Polytechnic Institute for women; . . . appoint an encyclopedic committee to draw up a series of treaties on the principal branches of human knowledge for the enlightenment of women. . . . You are to aid your sisters of the laboring classes to organize themselves in trade associations on economic principles more equitable than those of the present time. . . . And remember, remember above all things that *Union is strength.*[77]

But if Héricourt's ideas sometimes resembled those of earlier feminists (her list of reforms, for example, and her call for union), in some significant ways they differed. Héricourt agreed to postpone suffrage for uneducated women, even though uneducated men had the vote, not because she approved of the franchise of uneducated men but because this right, once granted, could not be withdrawn. "As to women, let them first acquire civil rights and obtain an education." It was not her willingness to show moderation that was new. In 1848, feminists had called first for suffrage for single women, postponing suffrage for married women for the time being. Héricourt also meant only to postpone: "It is important that men understand that you do not deny but that you simply postpone the political rights of your sex." [78] But now it was poor women who must wait. Thus a class bias emerged in Héricourt's work that was in sharp contrast with the commitment of the earlier feminists to association of women across class lines. The reemerging feminism of the Revolution, with its emphasis on individual rights and individual equality, was bourgeois and liberal in interest as well as ideology.

CHAPTER 8

The Reemergence of Feminist Activism

During the final years of the Second Empire, a series of liberal laws transformed the once repressive political scene and encouraged the reemergence of feminist activism. In 1868, a new press law permitted the establishment of newspapers without prior government authorization or the deposit of substantial "caution" money to guarantee payment of future fines; the new law also ended administrative censorship. Similarly, freedom of assembly was enlarged, and public lectures *(conférences)* to discuss political questions became an important element of political life of the late 1860s.[1] Feminists, like other advocates of reform, took advantage of the new liberty to present their case to the public.

Maria Deraismes, who would lead French feminists for the next several decades, made her public-speaking debut at this time. Louise Michel, Paule Mink, and André Léo addressed the particular problems of working-class women. Olympe Audouard spoke out for marriage reform. Beginning in 1866, a number of women's rights organizations were established, and, in 1870, the longest lasting of them, the Association pour le Droit des Femmes, was founded by Léon Richer, Maria Deraismes, Anna Féresse-Deraismes (Maria's sister), Louise Michel, Paule Mink, André Léo, and M. and Mme Jules Simon. This association was linked to the new feminist newspaper, *Le Droit des femmes,* which had been established in 1869. The publication was edited and written almost exclusively by Léon Richer, who devoted his limited funds and unlimited energies to its continuation.

The vitality of the movement, after nearly two decades of forced inactivity, was dazzling, but its progress for most of the next decade would be fitful. Feminists were still few in numbers and inexperienced. Also, war and the

173

French defeat by German armies, civil disorders, and the revolt of the Paris Commune deflected their activities after 1870. And then the first governments of the Third Republic, illiberal and even antirepublican, frustrated their renewed attempts to nurture their infant movement.

None of the new feminist leaders had participated in earlier struggles for women's emancipation. Of the prominent 1848 feminists, only Eugénie Niboyet had returned to France, but she was elderly now and had long since disavowed the more revolutionary aspects of her past. Neither Jenny d'Héricourt nor Juliette Adam joined the new feminist groups either, although the reason is not absolutely certain. Héricourt may have been in America in the 1860s;[2] by the mid-1870s she was again visible in feminist activities. Adam was in Paris throughout this period, but there were political differences between her and the majority group of feminists later, in the mid-1870s; perhaps already in the late 1860s tensions over issues unrelated to women's rights were separating them and explain her absence from feminist circles.

The new feminists were all republicans. Some were also connected to socialist groups and some to anticlerical associations, but in 1871, those feminists with links to revolutionary socialism—Louise Michel, André Léo, and Paule Mink—were exiled from France for taking part in the Paris Commune uprising. What remained of the recently organized feminist movement was restricted in both numbers and class politics. The ties between socialism and feminism had been cut. Whereas formerly the two had been united in opposition to the Napoleonic regime and, earlier, the constitutional monarchy, by the mid-1870s, republican feminists supported the regime which revolutionary socialists opposed.

Time and politics were both on the side of the liberal and bourgeois republican feminists. Already new educational and work opportunities were emerging, which promised to change the life circumstances of French women and ultimately to create the possibility—for the first time—of organizing extensively among women. Although these new opportunities began to appear in the 1860s, their effects would be felt in the 1870s and later.

The Falloux Law of 1850 had required that communes of more than eight hundred persons establish girls' primary schools, an improvement over earlier governments' neglect of girls' schooling. Then, in 1867, the freethinker Victor Duruy (minister of public instruction during the Empire's more liberal phase) required girls' primary schools in communes of five hundred persons. He established the first secondary level courses (not yet schools) for girls at this same time. It seemed, from the outpouring of books on the subject, that nearly everyone now favored a serious education for girls, or at least young girls. But opinion divided sharply over the role of the church. Before the passage of the Falloux Law, the church held a near monopoly on girls' education. The Falloux Law left the church's advantage over the state intact primarily by making it difficult for women other than nuns to obtain teaching positions. Although secular teachers were severely underpaid, nuns who did not have to meet the same certification requirements as secular instructors, could be paid even less. Duruy's secondary-level courses, taught by secular teachers, were viewed as a threat to the church's role in girls' schooling, and the church (led by Monseigneur Félix Dupanloup, the bishop of Orleans) opposed the courses primarily for this reason.[3]

The level of girls' education began to advance during these years. In the 1850s, the highest diploma that a girl could obtain was the *brevet supérieur* (at about the age of thirteen). The number who successfully achieved this degree increased from 356 in 1855 to 1,356 in 1875.[4] In the 1860s, the first women, all privately educated, entered the university. The Empress Eugénie, well known to have favored higher education for women, is considered responsible for authorizing women to enter the *facultés*. Emma Chenu was the first to earn a degree (in science); Madeleine Gibelin Brès, the daughter of a wheelwright, received the first medical degree, in 1870; and Julie Daubié was granted the first *license* in *lettres*, in 1871.

To enter the university, one had to pass the *baccalauréat* examination; yet there were no public *lycées* to prepare girls for this examination. Nor did private schools prepare them. The first *bachelières*, in the 1860s, were all privately tutored or self-taught. The case of Daubié is instructive.[5] She was not well-to-do—her father was a bookkeeper for a Vosges ironworks factory—and her formal schooling was minimal. She attended a girls' primary school, earned a *brevet elementaire*, and later learned Latin and Greek from her brother, who was a priest. She then became a governess and lived with a family of manufacturers. She evidently continued her studies on her own during this time. In 1858, she entered a competition sponsored by the Lyons Academy and won the first prize for her *La Femme pauvre au XIXe siècle*, a masterful and scholarly study of the causes of female poverty, which she traced to women's inability to support themselves. Daubié identified different forms of discrimination, which excluded women from all but a few jobs, and she related their low wages in these jobs to the sex segregation of the work force. She also examined the role of an inadequate education and sexual exploitation in buttressing the system of economic exploitation.

One of the Lyons Academy's judges was François-Barthélemy Arlès-Dufour, the former Saint-Simonian. He was impressed by Daubié's intellect[6] and encouraged her to sit for the *baccalauréat* examination. Daubié's request to Roulard, the minister of public instruction, to do so was denied in 1861, but in 1862, after much prodding from Arlès-Dufour and the intervention of the Empress Eugénie, she was permitted to take the examinations.

Women such as Julie Daubié, Madeleine Brès, and their contemporary, the scientist Clémence Royer, provided a new role model for younger women. They were truly exceptional women, but unlike most earlier "women worthies," they were committed feminists. Again, Daubié's life is exemplary. Her study of the causes of female poverty proposed feminist solutions, particularly that all jobs be opened to women at wages equal to men's and that women receive the same education as men and have access to traditionally male apprenticeships and other professional training programs. She proposed that the law be reformed in ways that would end women's sexual vulnerability, as, for example, permitting paternity suits, legal equality for "illegitimate" children, and freedom to marry for all of legal age. (At the time, soldiers were not allowed to marry.) In the mid-1860s, Daubié led the campaign to end government regulation of prostitution and called for penalties for participating men. In the early 1870s, just before her death, she organized a women's suffrage campaign. Daubié's, Brès's, and Royer's examples were followed in the 1870s, 1880s, and 1890s, when other "exceptional" women, such as Dr. Blanche Edwards and the first woman lawyer, Jeanne Chauvin, similarly linked their individual goals to the general cause of women's advancement.

But in 1868, improvements in women's education had not yet contributed to the development of a feminist movement. Feminist goals were incomprehensible to most French women and men. Women's economic independence in particular seemed a farfetched concept in the 1860s, when women were more than ever excluded from decently paying jobs. In the 1820s to 1840s, some women had held lower- and middle-level civil service jobs; for example, Pauline Roland's mother had been a postal clerk. Now these positions, and even the job of public hospital nurse, went to men as a result of the expansion of the political patronage system after the passage of universal male suffrage. Few teaching positions were available for women who were not nuns, so most daughters of the lower middle classes crowded into the fields of private instruction, teaching music, arts, foreign languages, and so forth. Only the new department stores—La Belle-Jardinière (1824), Le Bon Marché (1852), then Le Printemps, La

Samaritaine, and Les Galeries Lafayette—paid more than the better paying jobs in the garment trades or domestic service.

The situation for lower-class women was even worse. Illiteracy was the rule for them: in 1867, 41 percent of all marrying women could not sign their names. Most were employed in the agricultural sector, but supplemented their incomes with piecework from the clothing and textile industries. For example, of women employed in the cotton textile industry in the Nord, one-third worked at home.[7] The sewing machine was introduced into France at about this time and gave a further boost to the putting-out system. Nonetheless, more and more women, including married women, were working outside the home. In 1851, women were almost 40 percent of all factory-employed workers, although they were underrepresented in the better paying jobs. They were underrepresented also in the workers' mutual aid societies: in 1860, of almost a half million *sociétaires,* women numbered fewer than seventy thousand.[8]

Some feminists attempted to provide education for poor women. In 1862, Elisa Lemonnier founded the Société pour l'Enseignement Professionnelle des Femmes and with gifts from benefactors opened a school that would offer poor girls both a general education and some basic skills. The Société soon grew and opened other schools in the provinces.[9]

Adam, Héricourt, Daubié, and Lemonnier were not alone in recognizing the crisis proportions of women's precarious situation; but most reformers, socialists included, proposed as a solution raising *men's* wages to a level that would make it possible for wives to leave the work force. The reformers, of course, knew that not all women were married, but they seemed to believe that the single woman was merely a symptom of a disease brought on by the insufficiency of men's wages, which made marriage sometimes infeasible.

Fitting in with this ideology was a new emphasis on marital cooperation. Ernest Legouvé, Eugène Pelletan, Jules Simon, Alfred Naquet, and other men created a new role model for the 1870s and 1880s: now alongside the mother-teacher—whose popularity continued unabated—was the co-operative husband.[10] Edmond Adam, Juliette Adam's second husband, was an example of the new, supportive husband of an active (but not independent) wife. Married women were even encouraged to work with their husbands; only independence was discouraged. The most famous couple-as-working-partners were the Curies, Marie and Pierre.

Marital congeniality was the prescribed cure for women's sexual exploitation, too. Again, this goal seemed less threatening and more attainable than the feminists' aims to end sexual exploitation by promoting women's independence. In Paris, illegitimacy rates were already decreasing from their mid-century high, and the rates of fathers' recognition of their children from irregular unions were rising,[11] while the little public assistance once available for unmarried mothers was restricted. (In the 1850s, the imperial government virtually shut down the foundling homes' "tours"—revolving structures, located at the entrance to foundling homes, which had permitted women to leave infants there, unobserved.) Popular medical advice books— for examples, Gustave Droz's *Monsieur, madame et bébé* (1866) and August Debay's *Philosophie du marriage* (1849) and *Hygiène et physiologie du marriage* (1848)—now recognized the possibilities for women's sexual satisfaction (and even the significance of the clitoris) and urged men to take more time and show more understanding with their wives. But poets and novelists warned against sexual expression for women independent of men. The lesbian theme, which was introduced first in the 1830s with the publication of Balzac's *The Girl with the Golden Eyes* and Gautier's *Mademoiselle de Maupin,* was picked up in the 1860s and 1870s by Baudelaire *(Les Fleurs du mal),* Zola *(Nana),* and Daudet *(Sappho).* Their depictions of lesbian life identified the lesbian with vice and prostitution, physical unpleasantness, and evil—even murderous—instinct. Sexual expression was encouraged but, for women, only in marriage.[12] And husbands' gratification was still the more important. Debay encouraged wives who did not reach orgasm to pretend otherwise.[13]

In 1868, when feminists began to speak out again, the reformers' ideas were much in vogue. Indeed, the new feminists often sounded much like the more popular reformers. The line separating them was blurred particularly around family-related matters, and only over time would their differences—especially in regard to work-related issues—become clear.

The Public Lectures

Among the first women of this era to speak publicly in favor of women's rights was Olympe Audouard, who had already established a position in literary circles.[14] Born in Marseilles in 1830, she had married a notary public but separated from him in 1860, although a divorce decree could not be obtained until 1885. She traveled widely, in Egypt, Turkey, Russia, and America, supporting herself by writing descriptive travelogues: *Les Mystères du sérail* (1863); *Le Canal de Suez* (1864); *Les Mystères de l'Egypte dévoilés* (1865); *L'Orient et ses peuples* (1867); *A travers l'Amérique* (1869); *Les Nuits russes* (1876); and *Au Pays des boyards* (1881). In 1862 she founded the literary review *Le Papillon,* with the support of Alexandre Dumas (père), Tony Revillon, and the marquis de Pommereaux.

Audouard also attempted to publish a political review, *La Revue cosmopolite*, but because the imperial government considered her both antireligious and antigovernment, she was not permitted to do so. The official explanation, which was that a woman, not being a full citizen, was not allowed to publish a political review, led her to issue a scathing brochure, *Guerre aux hommes* (1866), and to petition the Corps Législatif to grant full political and civil rights to women.[15]

Audouard was well known when, in February 1870, she gave a lecture titled "Marriage, Separation, and Divorce" at a public debate between Catholics and socialists on marriage, divorce, and free union marriages. The police were there to keep order. Audouard described legalized marriage as a "marriage based on the despotic tyranny of man and on the subjugation, the total annihilation, of the will of woman." She derided legal separation for leaving a woman in tutelage, "which is never, however, protective" of her interests. She demanded the reestablishment of divorce "in order to guarantee family morality," quoting heavily from Louis-Napoleon's own *Idées napoléoniennes,* composed while he was a prisoner at Ham in 1830. The source for her "revolutionary" ideas seemed unknown to the police when they stopped the conference as she quoted Louis-Napoleon.[16]

Other women also spoke out during the closing years of the Empire. Conferences were held in Vaux-Hall to examine the rights of workers, and Paule Mink, André Léo, and Maria Deraismes all defended the rights of women workers there. Paule Mink, daughter of a Polish noble who had been in exile since 1830, had founded the Société Fraternelle de l'Ouvrière, which was both feminist and socialist in its orientation. André Léo[17] had already published two novels, *Un Divorce* (originally serialized in *Le Siècle*) and *Un Mariage scandaleux* in which she had favored equal rights within marriage and the reestablishment of divorce. In *Les Femmes and les moeurs,* she went further, demanding equal political rights for both sexes. Along with Maria Deraismes, she defended the principle that women should be paid the same as men for the same work, speaking primarily to working-class or leftist audiences.

Maria Deraismes was the most important of these public speakers. Born in 1828 into a wealthy bourgeois family, she was noted for her beauty, intelligence, and charm.[18] Her association with French feminism brought the movement prestige and respectability, as much because of her social status as her eloquence.

Her early education is described as Saint-Simonian.[19] Her father was a liberal republican and a deist; Deraismes was both to the end of her life. After her father's death, her older sister, Anna Féresse-Deraismes (widowed

Maria Deraismes. Courtesy Bibl. Marguerite Durand

at a very young age) took charge of Maria's education, which included training in Greek and Latin and a thorough study of foreign as well as French philosophers. Maria even learned Hindu and Chinese philosophies.[20] She was also well versed in the literature and theater of her day and wrote some comedies of her own; they were distinguished chiefly by their feminist tendencies.[21] She received further recognition from literary criticisms published in various newspapers.[22]

The journalist Léon Richer encouraged Deraismes to address the public at the Conférences Libre-penseuses à la Salle du Grand-Orient, of which he was one of the organizers. By her own account, Deraismes hesitated to undertake an activity that was still considered unseemly for a woman. But then she became so angered by an article in *Le Nain jaune,* in which Barbey d'Aurevilly violently attacked women writers as "les bas bleus" that she accepted the challenge.[23]

Deraismes was an immediate success, according to Siebecker, an editor of *La Liberté,* who reported on the conference for that paper.

I admit that I arrived at Maria Deraismes's feminist conference in a cheerful frame of mind. I expected to find a pedantic old spinster, affected and worthless.

I was greatly surprised to see a young woman 24 or 25 years old. She was slightly pale, with great refinement of shape and demeanor, of simple elegance, without ridiculous timidity or impudent self-assurance.

She won her listeners over from the outset. Her voice was of good timbre, her elocution easy, her language of great purity, her spiritual traits were shrewd without being spiteful, well cast. With all this a great deal of good sense and high erudition.

I was seduced along with the others.[24]

In 1867, she lectured only on literary or philosophical subjects. Over the next three years, aided by the new, more liberal laws, she spoke out forthrightly on the condition of women. A large number of the Parisian intelligentsia attended her lectures and were thus exposed to her ideas.[25] She believed that "the influence of the spoken word is superior to that of the written word" and that "the oratorical method has always been the most powerful ally to social transformation." [26] She later collected and published all her lectures from these years in a book entitled *Eve dans l'humanité,* a document of her feminism.[27]

Deraismes followed Héricourt and Adam in joining her defense of woman's rights to a defense of the family, which she perceived as a natural and positive social unit. "Free love" was condemned because it "is the annihilation of the family." The family is not a social invention; "it is natural—we find it in a rudimentary state, even among animals." In its ideal form, the family best serves the needs of individuals at all stages of life: "To the child, . . . dependent, more in need of being loved than of loving, it gives the unselfish tenderness of the father and mother." The young adult for whom "filial love" is not enough goes on to find satisfaction by forming a new family: "Marriage is the affective sentiment in its most intense and fruitful manifestation. To join one's life to the person that one cherishes most, to share with him pleasure, pain, interests, and duty, to give happiness while receiving it at the same time . . . is really the height of human happiness." [28]

For a while, Deraismes continues, the young married couple lives happily in a state of self-sufficiency, turned in on itself. But then children are born, and "the couple stops living for itself alone"; it is forced to concern itself with improving its position and fortune in a collective effort. "It is . . . marriage that offers the most security to the propagation of beings! Doubtless life can be transmitted outside of any rule, any contract, any public obligation; but then it has no guarantee of normal development;

it is given over to all the dangers of capricious abandonments." Such, for Deraismes, was the ideal, "the romance of the family; in other words, the family as it should be." [29]

In upholding the primacy of the family, Deraismes was in apparent agreement with a broad segment of French reform opinion. But like Héricourt and Adam, though unlike the popular reformers, she stressed that the relationship between wife and husband in the ideal family must be one of equality. She recognized that her ideal was not reality; in actuality marriage had been corrupted. "The inequality of the two sexes disrupts this harmonious plan." Thus "the family, which should be the best school for consciences, starts out by warping them because it depicts the perpetual violation of rights as legitimate. That is how the theory of the double standard gets taught in a setting where good morals and justice in relationships should instead be the law." [30]

Deraismes feared that the sexual license permitted men "diminished the urgency of marriage for them. For the young man, the first part of his youth, beginning even in adolescence, is the anticipation of marriage but with all the spice of variety and change. Why should he aspire to a definitive union when he can find such satisfactions without in the least giving up his independence?" In fact, the consequence of a "licentious" youth would be adultery for the married man: "He who has kept company with as many women as he could will never be able to content himself with only one woman. . . . The taste for variety, for whims, for unexpected feelings and the unhealthy curiosity that seeks to set up comparisons become habit." [31]

The effect of different sexual standards for men and women was far-reaching, according to Deraismes. Men had created a law limiting sexual experience to marriage and then exempted themselves from the law: "Men have established a law and then pass their lives breaking it." Thereby they created the necessity for two separate classes of women, one to live within the law, the other to satisfy men's "extralegal" desires. The first class of women, those who Deraismes said were often called "honnête" women, were largely from the middle class, for only they could count on a dowry to assure them of marriage, and only they could be kept at home, "under supervision and only going out when escorted." [32] These women would rarely experience passion because their marriages were based on rational calculation involving money rather than on emotional attraction.[33] Passion, then, plays no part in marriage. "All the . . . hours of happiness, of supreme joy, when the human soul vibrates on all its chords in complete blooming, these no longer exist in marriage. Under these conditions, the institution of marriage, foundation of the family, is . . . in real danger." [34]

It is interesting to note that among nineteenth-century French feminists, only Deraismes and Fourier—both unmarried and both likely celibate— wrote about sexual passion or fulfillment as a goal for women. But unlike Fourier, Deraismes, who was probably familiar with the recent medical advice literature on women's sexuality, would limit women's sexual expression to marriage. Deraismes denied the value of traditional premarital virginity if it was based on ignorance and submission but upheld its importance when based on intelligent reasoning: "Yes, of course purity is precious, virtue is touching and admirable; but to be valued, it must be the product of reason, of will, of independence, and not the product of ignorance and subordination." [35]

Although society, according to Deraismes, seems to admire the courtesan more than the "honest" woman, the courtesan is man's victim in the sense that men have created her to satisfy needs they cannot satisfy within the sterile marriages they themselves have created. The life of the courtesan exists entirely outside the laws of marriage and thus outside its protection. And indeed, the courtesan lives as a parasite on marriage, sucking from it all passion and joy and thereby destroying it. And yet, only she really commands men's respect: "The great sacrifices, the follies of passion pushed to the extreme of sacrificing honor and life are inspired by women who have lost it [virginity] long ago." [36] Eventually, this extralegal, immoral world would destroy family life.

Family life, thus segmented, must be reintegrated. All women should be permitted to experience the emotions of love, which should be the foundation of marriage and not achievable without equality of marriage. Further, the reintegration of family life requires improvements in women's education. Men are naturally drawn to their peers for adequate intellectual stimulation:

> The human person enjoys living with his peers, that is to say those who are like him in education, in knowledge. The difference in intellectual and scientific contribution between the marital partners disrupts the balance. Each feels uncomfortable, but particularly the husband: he is in spiritual isolation, in intellectual solitude. His wife knows nothing about most of the questions of interest to him. There is fellowship of concern, but no fellowship of ideas. [37]

To save the family, women must receive an education of similar quality to their husbands'. Without the communication made possible by similar education, a man will search outside the home in "le cabaret, le café, ou le cercle" for companionship unavailable at home. "This pressing need to look elsewhere for that which one does not believe it possible to find at home leads to gambling, debauchery, and drunkenness, which are the elements of family instability." [38] Thus, to restore stability to the family, certain elements now found only outside the home must be restored to the family circle: passion and educated reasoning.

For Deraismes, the family based on equality and enlightened rationalism was the foundation of a just society:

> When children attain the age of reason they will have witnessed an organization based on justice. Before any elementary instruction, by virtue of the example before their eyes, they understand the healthy notion of equality and right. Nothing shocks their young conscience; arbitrariness does not exist for them.
>
> Whereas under present conditions what can the education of boys be like? At a very early age they grow proud of being male and become furious when they are mistaken for girls; they insult their mothers instinctively. When they have barely reached adolescence, her virtues no longer serve as an example for them; their mothers seem servile. And wanting to display the independence of the male, they hurry to make mistakes even before passion pushes them to it.
>
> This miniature society—the family—prepares for the larger one. It contains all the seeds of society: justice, equality, right, freedom, solidarity. Here we have a ready-made school: a strong nation will come from it.[39]

Strong and stable families were no less important to Deraismes than to Michelet or Proudhon. All believed that a stable family unit fostered justice and equality in society. But Deraismes, unlike Michelet and Proudhon, insisted that the strength of the family depended on justice and equality in marriage. This opinion would predominate among feminists for the rest of the nineteenth century.

Organizing

In the last years of the Empire, feminists began to organize clubs that met regularly. Hubertine Auclert, in *Le Vote des femmes,* tells that a committee formed in 1866 held regular meetings at the home of Jules Favre. Its goal was to reform all marriage laws, substituting for "paternal authority" only the words "husbands and wives mutually owe each other fidelity, support, assistance." She lists as participants Emile Acollas, Jules

Simon, Charles Vacherot, Frédéric Morin, Joseph Garnier, Courcelles-Seneuil, Charles Lemonnier, André Cochut, Herold Clamageran, Paul Jozon, Jules Ferry, Floquet, Paul Boiteau, Henri Brisson, and Dr. Claudel.[40]

Sometime thereafter,[41] a group of men and women met at the home of André Léo to draw up the Charter for the Société de Revendication des Droits de la Femme, "whose goal was to establish schools for girls and thus hasten the legal recognition of the rights of women." [42] Auclert lists the following as founders: Mlle Caroline Demars, M. and Mme Leval, M. Antide Martin, Mme André Léo, M. Colfavru, M. and Mme Verdure, Mlle Toussaint, M. and Mme Elie Réclus, M. Ernest Hendle, M. G. Francolin, and Mlle Marie David. Regular participants at these meetings were Maria Deraismes, Paule Mink, Mme Jules Simon, and Louise Michel, a young teacher recently arrived in Paris. The exact activity of the Société is unknown, however, and historians usually confuse this group with the later Association pour le Droit des Femmes, perhaps because the people involved and the aims were similar.[43]

In April 1869, Léon Richer launched *Le Droit des femmes,* a weekly newspaper devoted to feminist issues. Richer's memory of the reaction to his paper was that its initial appearance had provoked laughter: "The big newspapers got involved in it: stupid jokes, spiteful insinuations rained down, dense as hail, on the little newborn paper." [44] The first edition carried a lead article by Ernest Legouvé, who presented the feminist program as he then understood it:

> Here are, as I see it, the two principal advancements that should be claimed: first, [the recognition of equal adult rights] for woman that would initiate her little by little into the governing of her own affairs and of the community property; second, the creation of a family council in which the woman would have the right to appeal against incapacity, tyranny, brutality, and sometimes the greed of a husband or father.

Maria Deraismes wrote the next article, "Ce que veulent les femmes":

> They want that which the oppressed and the subjugated have wanted since the beginning of time: their fair share of rights and freedom.
>
> What women want is for men to stop basing their greatness on the systematic debasement of women.
>
> What women want is not to be brought up, educated, molded according to some conventional image; an image conceived in the brain of poets, novelists, or artists and therefore unreal.

What women want, in short, is that you renounce this arbitrary, fictitious distribution of human faculties that affirms that man represents reason and woman represents emotion.

Therefore what women want is the development of their reasoning powers so they may fulfill their responsibilities and exercise legitimate power.[45]

The program advocated by *Le Droit des femmes* was specific rather than theoretical. Its demands represented the common ground between the positions of Legouvé and Deraismes: to improve the educational program in the girls' schools; to increase women workers' wages to fight prostitution; to work toward revising the Civil Code; to spread the idea of a single moral standard; to give women free access to the liberal professions; to gain application of the formula "à produit égal, salaire égal"; and to obtain freedom for women to dispose of their own wealth.[46]

Richer's newspaper was to last twenty-three years, under different titles and with different periodicity. In September 1871, it became *L'Avenir des femmes,* but in 1879, it resumed its original title. The journal was a weekly until 1876 when it became a monthly review; it was published biweekly after 1885. Throughout its entire existence, it had financial difficulties. Originally financed by Arlès-Dufour, it got through its first year thanks to the editor and administrator, a M. Pains, who subsidized all the publication costs until it became the property of shareholders, who formed a private company with capital of twenty thousand francs, a large sum for the time. In spite of promotion efforts, the paper never had many subscribers.[47] There were also difficulties in getting advertising, especially small classified advertisements, because the paper did not appear daily or weekly. After 1885, it was supported by a six-hundred franc per annum grant from the Ligue des Droits de la Femme.

Most of those connected with feminism wrote articles or letters for *Le Droit des femmes:* Marie Deraismes, André Léo, Amélie Bosquet, Julie Daubié, and, in later years, Eugénie Pierre, Hubertine Auclert, and Léonie Rouzade. Letters from Suzanne Voilquin, Eugénie Niboyet, and Jeanne Deroin show that even feminists of the earlier decades followed the events of these years through the pages of *Le Droit des femmes.*[48] Among the men who contributed, in addition to Ernest Legouvé, were Emile de Girardin, Frédéric Passy, Adolphe Guéroult,[49] and Edouard Laboulaye. In 1872, Louis Blanc wrote two articles titled "De l'émancipation civile des femmes" and "La Question des femmes." In 1885, René Viviani began his frequent collaboration. John Stuart Mill, a supporter of feminism in England, contributed a letter of appreciation, as did Jacob Bright.[50]

The newspaper included articles on general political issues. In the May 8, 1869, edition, it called for the election of liberal and democratic candidates who supported (1) disarmament and abolition of conscription; (2) lower taxes; (3) separation of church and state; and (4) free and compulsory instruction for everyone. In 1881, the newspaper took a strong stand against Gambetta's imperialistic moves. Throughout its years of publication it was anticlerical. But usually it confined its attention to feminist issues, hammering away on the same subjects, edition after edition, sometimes to the point of boredom: education, *puissance maritale,* divorce, *recherche de la paternité,* prostitution, *police des moeurs,* the social condition of the woman, workers' wages, and always, the financial problems of the journal itself.

Léon Richer searched for political tactics that would involve greater numbers of potential sympathizers in the feminist struggle. First, he organized a "banquet" (July 11, 1869) to introduce liberal legislators to feminist ideas. Adolphe Guéroult, who was then the publisher of *L'Opinion nationale,* agreed to sponsor it, "donating" his prestige as well as money to the cause. But the democratic party of the Corps Législatif proved insensitive to feminist appeals. The Manifesto of the Left Deputies (November 1869) ignored the women's issue, dissappointing Richer. Later, however, Richer convinced a few deputies to submit a bill to the Chamber to begin modification of the Civil Code according to feminist principles. The bill was prepared by Richer himself. But the actual deposition of the proposition was postponed more than once, until the war in 1870 finally made it a dead issue.

Richer next created an organization that would remain closely linked to the journal; its main purpose would be to search out funds and to organize other propaganda events. The Association pour le Droit des Femmes was founded in April 1870. Its original charter (published in *Le Droit des femmes,* April 24, 1870) read:

> The important question of the emancipation of women is making considerable and rapid progress all around us.
>
> In America, in England, in Germany, in Switzerland, in Italy, in Holland—but particularly in England and America—the most renowned thinkers are declaring themselves in favor of women's rights and powerful associations are forming on all sides to support this end.
>
> France, which has been until now indifferent and quiet, cannot remain behind the times any longer.

It is therefore urgent that all those who, in our country, recognize the principle of the equality of the two sexes before the law, join together and combine their efforts.

Consequently, the undersigned propose to form an Association whose object will be to organize legal demonstrations and to undertake an active propaganda to prepare the minds, both masculine and feminine, to understand the legitimacy of the progressive demand for the rights that are due each human person, but from which our laws and customs have disinherited women. Let us bring into realization this great thought of Pascal: "Not being able to make that which is strong, just, let us at least make that which is just, strong."

The Association is founded on the following premises:

Woman, as a human person, should be free and autonomous.

She must be free, since she is responsible.

She must be autonomous, since she is recognized to have a conscience and an intellect.

No responsibility without freedom.

No dignity without autonomy.

Woman must be considered, if not as identical to man, at least as his equal in humanity; that is equality in dissimilarity.

Do not man and woman belong to the same family, the same world? Do they not occupy the same position in the hierarchy of beings?

The duties of both sexes in society and in the family may be distinct, according to each one's aptitudes or vocation, but one would not presume them to be superior or inferior one to the other. Those that fall particularly to woman are just as useful, just as noble, just as elevated as those that a man ordinarily fulfills:—It is equality in diversity.

Moral duties should be the same for man as they are for woman. There are not two moral codes: one for woman and one for man. Only prejudice has been able to create such distinctions.

In this reference also man and woman are equal: It is equality in morality.

Therefore there is good reason to proclaim loudly the equality of the sexes before the law and with reference to morality.

The undersigned intend to do so and invite to join them all those persons of goodwill who wish to second their efforts.

The articles of incorporation indicate that the primary object of the organization was to popularize feminist goals (article 11) and that it viewed Richer's newspaper as its organ of propaganda (article 11, no. 1; and article 29).[51] The founders understood the enormity of the task ahead of them, just to gain adherents. Thus they created three categories of membership: "full" membership; a second category permitting a member to remain anonymous if she or he desired; and another anonymous category created to solicit membership from those who did not agree with all of the association's goals or tactics but were sympathetic to increased opportunites for woman. The original signatories were Léon Richer, Mme Léon Richer, Maria Deraismes, Veuve Féresse-Deraismes (Deraismes's sister), Amélie Bosquet, Emile Garcin, Nelly Lieutier, Camille Périer, Anaïs Tiranty, Louise Audebert, and the comtesse de Guyon. Richer was the only male signatory of the original group, a fact that bothered him, but he assured everyone that other men would soon join.

The Commune

Although there were not yet a large number of people who identified themselves with the fledgling movement, feminists' energy in 1868–70 was high: they seemed to be everywhere, doing everything. And although the government did not respond to their demands by voting changes in patriarchal laws,[52] there was obviously enough official sympathy toward feminists to guarantee their right to continue propagandizing their point of view. The future of feminism appeared bright.

Then, in July 1870, war broke out between France and Prussia. On September 2, Napoleon III and his army were taken prisoner at Sedan. On September 4, Paris mobs forced the Corps Législatif to proclaim the Republic. The new provisional Government of National Defense was drawn from among the republican deputies of the Seine (the Paris region), who had been elected to the Corps Législatif in the 1869 elections. The political experience of 1848 seemed to be repeating itself. Censorship of the press, assembly, and speech was lifted; the atomosphere was heady with revolutionary ideas. But again revolution was more popular in Paris than elsewhere. When national legislative elections were held in February 1871, a monarchist majority was returned to power. The newly proclaimed Republic began its life shakily.

The time was hardly the best for political experimentation. The war continued, and Paris was under siege from the end of September through January. Indeed, the differing experiences of those who were in the fray of battle from those in the more secure parts of France were background to the events of the spring. Many who could afford to do so had left Paris during the fall of 1870; those who remained were the working middle classes (artisans and tradespeople) and the working class. During the siege, the provisional government moved to Tours. After the February elections, the legislature established itself in Bordeaux; after the armistice it chose to return to Versailles rather than to Paris. The elected leadership of the National Guard (the "Fédérés") stationed in Paris became a parallel government to the national government even before the outbreak of civil war.

On March 18, the distrust between the conservative national government and the more radical Parisians reached the breaking point: Thiers (head of the executive power) ordered all government authorities, including the police, to evacuate the city; the Central Committee of the Republican Federation of the National Guard stepped in to fill the vacuum. Elections to the Commune—or municipal council—returned a majority of leftist Jacobin republicans and a significant minority of Proudhonian socialists. The Commune directed the city's defense and took some steps to implement a program of social revolution, but after a mere two months, the "Versaillais" retook the city. The Commune drowned in a bloodbath in the last week of May. Its actual impact was fleeting, although the impact of its legend was far-reaching, particularly on the future of socialism.

It has been difficult for historians to assess the Commune's effect on women and on feminism. Throughout the two months of its brief life, self-preservation was its paramount preoccupation and took priority over all aspects of its social program. Women's concerns were never primary. Yet women were active in Commune defense and politics on a scale unprecedented in earlier nineteenth-century French history.[53] Women had been active in the struggle against the Prussian troops; during the fall and winter months they had fought alongside their husbands and served as *ambulancières* (field nurses) and *cantinières* (water carriers). A Sophie Doctrinal had organized a "national workshop" in which seventy-two to eighty women workers sewed uniforms for the guard. Jules Allix had formed a committee of women to organize other such workshops. André Léo served on this committee, as did Elisabeth Dmitrieff, a twenty-year-old Russian émigré, friend of Marx, and member of the International.

Women had also been active in politics. What better evidence could there be of the increased acceptance of a new role for women than that, for the first time, they participated freely in revolutionary clubs, particularly the "clubs rouges"? Some of these clubs took on the added activity of assuring that men in their neighborhood did not desert from the army. The most renowned of these *vigilantes* was Louise Michel.

Not surprisingly, women such as Louise Michel now volunteered to defend the Commune from the Versaillais troops. The vigilantes once again took up their work of rounding up deserters and ferreting out traitors, and, again, some women fought as combatants. Louise Michel and Victorine Louvet fought with the 61st battalion under the command of General Eudes (Louvet's companion). Throughout the final "bloody week," the participation of women fighters was evidently unusually high. On Tuesday, May 22, several women (Elizabeth Retiffe, Josephine Marchais, Eugénie Suétens, Eulalie Papovoine, and Lucie Maris) were arrested along with the guardsmen of the 135th battalion who had been caught by the Versaillais troops in the act of burning the building of the Légion d'Honneur. One famous group of 120 women—Michel, Dmitrieff, and Nathalie Lemel among them—held off the Versaillais troops for four hours at the Place Blanche.[54] When the fighting was finally over, 1,051 women were arrested and brought before the War Council for sentencing.[55]

Eyewitness reports mention activities perhaps less exciting but no less important than combat. The journalist Maxime Vuillaume, for example, described a cooperative workshop where five to six hundred women met to assemble ammunition.[56] Hippolyte Lissagaray, also a contemporary of the Commune, reported on another such cooperative workshop where fifteen hundred women sewed sandbags for the barricades.[57]

About 130 women belonged to the Union des Femmes pour la Défense de Paris et les Soins aux Blessés. Dmitrieff was its head; Nathalie Lemel, Aline Jacquier, Marie Leloup, Blanche LeFebvre, and Aglaé Jarry were all members of the Central Committee. From mid-April to mid-May they held twenty-four public meetings at which they exhorted sizable audiences to fight off the Versaillais. In addition, members attended daily strategy sessions; one was to be present in each local office twenty-four hours a day. They concerned themselves not only with the defense of Paris and care of the wounded but also with the issues of women's work and education.[58]

Louise Michel was among the most active of the communardes.[59] She was forty years old in 1871 and had been active in Parisian leftist groups, including the new feminist groups, for years. She had come from the provinces, Audeloncourt in the Haute-Marne, in the late 1850s. Her mother was a servant; her father was probably the son of her mother's employers, although this is not certain. Michel was raised in the chateau where her mother continued to work and was educated by her mother's employers, whom she called *grandmère* and *grandpère*. After their death, she was on her own. She got a teaching certificate and taught in the village but then left for Paris. She could not teach in the public schools because she refused to swear the required oath of allegiance to the Empire. She opened her own private day school and taught classes in Elisa Lemonnier's school.

Perhaps because she was so well known and therefore highly trusted by the Commune and guard leadership, Michel was permitted to participate in all Commune activities at a level exceptional for a woman: she was a field nurse, a *cantinière,* a member of both the women's and men's vigilance committees of Montmartre, and a combatant with the 61st battalion. Later, while imprisoned in Nouvelle Calédonie for these deeds, Michel wrote her memoirs and a history of the Commune. Generous with her praises for the Commune's attitude toward women, she wrote that "people didn't worry about which sex they were before they did their duty. That stupid question was settled." [60]

André Léo disagreed. She was one of the founders, editors, and a frequent contributor to the radical newspaper *La Sociale,* in which her writings chronicled not only women's activities but also their troubles with the deeply entrenched male biases of the Commune and the guard leadership. On April 12, for example, she wrote that women wanted to serve the Commune but lacked organization to facilitate doing so. She called on the guard to enlist women "under these titles: Armed Action, Posts of Aid to the Wounded, and Mobile Kitchens." About five hundred women showed up at the Hotel-de-Ville the day after her article appeared, but they were rebuffed. And in the May 6 edition of *La Sociale,* Léo reported on nine ambulance nurses—officially commissioned by their municipal officers of the seventeenth arrondissement—who went from battalion to battalion offering to serve; they were rejected each time. Only Michel's intervention on their behalf finally won them a post, "but you couldn't believe how many obstacles, how many insults, how much hostility." [61]

Although the Commune had little time to make sweeping reforms, it did pass certain measures that made clear its desire for social change. Some of these acts directly concerned the status of women: free, compulsory, and lay education was decreed in principle and, it was announced, male and female teachers and school inspectors would be paid the same. For the first time, a woman, Marguerite Tinayre, was named a school inspector (for the twelfth arrondissement). Hospitals were also laicized, and laywomen were recruited to replace nuns as hospital workers. Pensions were voted for the widows and children of fallen guardsmen, and women and children of free unions were recognized as "legitimate."

Feminists applauded these measures but argued for more. They were particularly concerned about high unemployment rates—largely caused by the exodus of the wealthier classes including many businessmen and factory owners—that affected single women most. Unemployed men were drafted into the city's defense and paid a daily wage. Their wives were also paid directly by the Commune. But single women were bereft of income if unemployed. Dmitrieff pressed her friend Léo Frankel, a delegate to the Commune and chair of its Labor Commission, to take up the cause of unemployed women. He proposed a plan for cooperative workshops, but it was rejected by the Commune. He next suggested raising the price the government paid for uniforms in order to increase workers' income; a decision was also postponed. Finally, he got the Commune to pass a resolution favoring a minimum daily wage as well as an eight-hour day for women.

Although the Commune could have done more for women, one can understand why, in retrospect, Left feminists praised it. Its reforms gave women more than they had received from other French governments. In addition, the Commune's leaders were not misogynist. They were known to be increasingly "Proudhonian" in their politics but did not appear to hold such attitudes about women, even when they were not feminist. The leaders ignored many feminist claims but did not take advantage of their power to reverse the progress women had made in the past decade, as surely Proudhon, were he alive, would have done. On the woman question, male communards were not very different from the 1848 democratic socialists: they were sometimes sympathetic but most often uninterested in matters they considered tangential to the "really important," that is "male," concerns. Although familiar, this was not the antifeminism of Proudhon.

The defeat of the Commune hurt women and feminism more than its success would likely have helped. Once again, feminists were silenced— exiled or deported. Louise Michel and Nathalie Lemel were sent off to the penal island of New Caledonia. Paule Mink, André Léo, and Marguerite Tinayre all escaped, but they were condemned in absentia and could not return to France until after the general amnesty in 1880. The leadership of the still-young feminist movement was halved and—significantly— deprived of the leaders trusted by working-class and socialist groups. Partly by default, the feminist movement after 1871 would be bourgeois and liberal, for a time at least.

The way would not be easy for liberal feminists remaining behind in Paris. Much ground had been lost since 1870. There was less tolerance for feminism. Conservative monarchists and liberal republicans could agree on little, but both rejected the easygoing morals associated with the imperial court. Measures favoring an improved status for women—like Duruy's secondary-level courses—were confounded with the court's immorality, perhaps because the empress had identified with the cause of women's education. And there was the heightened fear that women who were not controlled were dangerous; the legacy of the Commune for women was the image of the *pétroleuse* (woman incendiary). France yearned for stability after the shocks of war and civil disorders, and women's emancipation was viewed as a threat to that stability.

Feminists resumed their work cautiously. In September 1871, Richer changed the title of his newspaper to *L'Avenir des femmes* to avoid alienating the conservative government.[62] The Association pour le Droit des Femmes was resurrected to organize other propaganda activities, understanding that the cause of feminism needed more friends before an activist politics could be contemplated. It raised money to subsidize Richer's newspaper directly and also began to fund the cost of free subscriptions for a large number of persons and for workers' groups and libraries.[63] In June 1872, the association organized a banquet for 150 people at the Palais-Royal (Restaurant Corazza), with Edouard Laboulaye of the Institut de France presiding. Victor Hugo sent his regrets for being unable to attend along with the following statement:

> I associate myself from the bottom of my heart with your useful manifestation. For forty years I have been arguing in behalf of the great social cause to which you are so nobly devoting yourselves.
>   It is painful to say: in the civilization of today there still remains slavery. Law has euphemisms: that which I call a slave it calls a minor. This minor according to the law, this slave according to reality, is woman. Man has unequally distributed the weight on the scales of the code, whose equilibrium is important to human conscience; man has put all the rights on his side and all the duties on the woman's side. From whence a deep disorder. From whence, the slavery of woman. In our legislation as it is, woman does not own, she has no existence in courts of justice, she does not vote, she does not count, she does not exist. There are male citizens, there are no female citizens. That is an extraordinary situation; it must cease.[64]

The entire July 8, 1872, edition of *L'Avenir des femmes* was devoted to a report on this banquet. Its major purpose seems to have been to make feminism a respectable political position. Richer appeared satisfied by the evening's results: "Who now can be afraid of being ridiculous when in the company with Victor Hugo, with Louis Blanc, with H. de Lacretelle, with Naquet, with Lemonnier, with the director of *Opinion Nationale,* Adolphe Guéroult, and with the director of *Siècle,* Louis Jourdan."

The Paris press gave broad coverage to the banquet, but it did not agree with Richer's assertion that feminism was not ridiculous. The newspaper *Le Français,* which published a long article on the banquet, concluded: "I vote, therefore I am. A woman is nothing unless she votes or is involved in politics. The Club speakers of 15 months ago and holy-mother Michel of the Commune have become models for the woman of the future." *Le Figaro* believed the emancipation movement was aimed at destroying the family. The *Courrier de France* agreed: "Wives and mothers, no more baby clothes; just a flag. No more *pots-au-feu;* just the ballot box: Woman the voter and soldier." Even Francisque Sarcey, who had already contributed some articles to *Le Droit des femmes,* wrote: "With reference to Victor Hugo's letter, we read it on an empty stomach. Perhaps one is more indulgent after a large dinner." [65]

In spite of the outpouring of ridicule from Parisian newspapers, the Association pour le Droit des Femmes determined to keep the issue in the public eye and to strengthen the bonds of those who had already committed themselves to its group. For this purpose it established monthly dinner meetings for association members. The first was held February 2, 1873, and was addressed by Jenny d'Héricourt. It was then, also, that Richer announced the association's intention to convene an international feminist congress during September of that year. But the political regime, uncertain during those years when no one knew whether a monarchy or a republic would emerge, took a still more conservative turn, which again struck at the already decimated grouping of feminists. It was recorded in the journal's March 24, 1873, issue that Olympe Audouard had been prevented from presenting a series of lectures in Paris on the subject "La Question des femmes." Minister of Interior Goulard claimed that "these conferences are nothing more than a pretext for a meeting of *overemancipated* women. The theories of Mme Olympe Audouard are subversive, dangerous, and immoral." Following the election of the monarchists' candidate, Marshal MacMahon, to the presidency of the Republic (May 1873), Richer conceded defeat, temporarily, and postponed the congress.[66] The Association pour le Droit des Femmes, which had changed its name to the Société pour l'Amélioration du Sort des Femmes in July 1874 in hopes of reassuring the government, was finally forced to dissolve in December 1875.

By 1875, the decade that had begun so promisingly offered little to feminists. Liberal measures passed in the final years of the Empire had allowed feminists to organize and propagandize again; but this liberalism was short-lived. Repression characterized the politics of the 1870s, and feminist organizing was halted. The possibilities for a feminist politics again were shown to be inextricably linked to the possibilities for free political expression.

CHAPTER 9

Republican Feminism

The Third Republic was a decade in the making. Monarchists controlled the Chamber of Deputies until 1877 and the Senate until 1879. Only the inability of Legitimists and Orleanists to resolve their conflicting ambitions prevented the Right from effecting a permanent restoration. Throughout the 1870s, republicans were cautious. They sensed that their chance to rule depended on creating the impression that they, not the monarchists, represented stability. The longer the Republic remained the regime—*faute de mieux*—the more likely it would come to be perceived as the regime of stability.

In 1878, feminists were all on the side of the Republic. They were certain its success would be their success. Already the republican victory in the 1877 Chamber of Deputies's election had worked for them: prohibitions against their public meetings had been lifted, and they were free to move ahead with their plans for an international congress. In 1879, the government gave its stamp of approval to their Société pour l'Amélioration du Sort des Femmes. Then, in 1881, after the republicans were firmly entrenched in power, the Ferry government passed a series of laws aimed at guaranteeing the fundamental liberties promised in the Declaration of the Rights of Man but only rarely permitted in the century since then: the law of June 30, 1881, guaranteed the freedom of assembly, and the law of July 29 guaranteed the freedom of the press. No longer would feminists have to obtain prior government approval for their meetings or public lectures, no matter the size of their expected audience. No longer would they have to secure large sums for "caution" money or obtain prior official approval for their journals. Finally, women were free to publish political newspapers.

One cannot overestimate the importance of these measures to the future of the French feminist movement. Before 1881, feminism had had a start-and-stop history. Arbitrary governments had the necessary apparatus to check energetic feminists whenever it was deemed that they had gone too far. Continuous censorship effectively limited the impact of the feminists' message. And from time to time, harsher forms of repression swept away feminists whose experience and leadership skills threatened the status quo. Historians who look for an explanation for the slowness with which feminist victories were achieved in modern France all too often overlook the obvious—the effectiveness of repressive governments in delaying the development of a mass movement.

The establishment of the Third Republic initiated a new phase in the history of the French feminist movement. For the first time, feminist groups survived beyond their infancy to reach maturity. Leaders who directed feminist efforts during these years did so for decades until retirement or death, not repression, removed them from the scene. They gained experience over the years and won more and more friends to their cause. Their organizations and their newspapers were institutionalized, and the next generation of leaders, theorists, and organizers were trained before the first retired.

Liberal Feminism

The feminist program during the 1870s and 1880s was the result of the collaboration of two dominant personalities: Maria Deraismes and Léon Richer. Deraismes was primarily active on the lecture circuit, and Richer ran the paper, Le Droit des femmes. Both were well known and respected by people who held power and could effect change.

Maria Deraismes was especially well known. Following her death, both Paris and Pontoise named streets after her. In Pontoise, where her country estate was located, she was the leader of the republican party. In 1881, she took over a daily political newspaper, Le Républicain de Seine-et-Oise, which successfully backed republicans for political office from this formerly monarchist stronghold. Deraismes was also active in the anticlerical movement. She was honorary president of the Fédération de Groupes de la Libre Pensée of Seine-et-Oise, and in 1881 she served as vice-president of the first national Anticlerical Congress. She successfully fought the exclusion of women from French Masonic lodges and became, in 1882, the first woman member of the lodge Les Libres Penseurs du Pecq. The lodge was soon dissolved as a result of this act of "impropriety," but in

1893, immediately before Deraismes's death, the Masons acceded to her efforts. With Georges Martin, she founded the first mixed lodge, La Grande Loge Symbolique Ecossaise de France Le Droit Humain.

Léon Richer, although more humbly born, was also well connected to the moderate republican leadership and, like Deraismes, his activities spanned the full range of republican concerns, including anticlericalism. He was a journalist who, during the 1860s, had written a weekly column, "Lettres d'un libre-penseur à un curé de village" for Adolphe Guéroult's *L'Opinion national*. From 1869, he was feminism's most tireless organizer, putting together both the 1872 banquet and the 1878 congress. Because *Le Droit des femmes* always had financial difficulties and could therefore never employ a sizable staff or pay outside contributors, the journal remained the personal expression of his ideas. He was, until his retirement in 1891, its principal writer (although often under the pseudonyms Georges Bath or Jeanne Mercoeur).

Deraismes worked out the tactics of feminism during these years—*la politique des brêches*. Borrowing the strategy of the dominant wing of the republican party (the "Opportunists"), Deraismes perceived that feminism could best advance by making small dents in the hard wall that patriarchy had constructed against women's claims. The feminist's task was to locate the loose brick and hammer against it. It was a realpolitik. She narrowed the scope of feminist demands to concentrate on changes that a socially conservative yet politically responsive legislature could be expected to pass into law. The primary focus of the feminist campaign thus became to convince influential public figures, particularly legislators, of the justice of their cause. Feminists presented the program of liberal republicanism, steering away from the radical or Jacobin program—universal suffrage— just as liberal male republicans had in 1791 steered away from universal suffrage. Their respect for the law was evident in their gradualist strategy, in their faith that a representative government could legislate equality, and in the value they placed on legal equality.

Richer left the most complete statement of the liberal feminist position on specific issues during this phase of republican feminism. In the 1870s and 1880s, he published four books on feminism: *Le Livre des femmes* (1872), *Le Divorce* (1873), *La Femme libre* (1877), and *Le Code des femmes* (1883). Although the first is an inconsequential collection of quotations and the second a brief plea for the reestablishment of divorce in the French Civil Code, *La Femme libre* and *Le Code des femmes* clearly illuminate his attitudes on women and his priorities among the issues.

Like almost all republican reformers, from antifeminists such as Michelet to feminists such as Deraismes, Richer was concerned about the health of

Léon Richer. Courtesy Bibl. Marguerite Durand

two social and political institutions—the family and the Republic. But unlike Michelet, though like Deraismes, Richer linked the emancipation of women to the welfare of the family and of the Republic. He blamed the restrictions society had placed on women's opportunities—especially on their intellectual development—as the single most important cause of disharmony within the family. He likened men and women raised so differently, educated so dissimilarly, to two different races, forced to cohabit but incapable of communication.

Since man alone was enfranchised he alone moved on. Woman, his daily companion, excluded from this benefit, stayed behind, and within the passing of half a century an enormous distance, an abyss, inexorably divided the two sexes.

Out of this division was soon born, within the heart of families, irreparable dissatisfactions, ruptures that one had not suspected.[1]

Richer specifically blamed the inferior education then accorded women for the disharmony that characterized French family life. Two separate systems of education, for girls based on religion and for boys based on science, had destroyed whatever harmony once existed in family life and resulted in "marriages that are no longer marriages, unions without name, cemented only by self-interest, in which man and woman, with different thoughts, different feelings, no longer know how to understand each other or to love each other. . . . Where man says *Yes,* woman says *No.* There is a complete separation, constant contradiction of ideas and feelings between man who is preparing the future and woman who is regretting the past."[2] Richer insisted that women's intellectual capacities were equal to men's.[3] It was the poverty of her education that destroyed harmonious family life; worse, it frustrated her mothering potential: "The mother is the first educator of the child. To teach, she must know; to instruct, she must understand."[4]

The emancipation of women was necessary not only to save the family, but also to safeguard the Republic: "It is time to think seriously about it: France will not rise again from the profound depression into which a sad succession of painful events have hurled and maintained it until a better directed and better educated woman can participate in the common task." Speaking to his republican colleagues who did not necessarily share his advanced views on the women's issue, Richer warned:

If we are to be a true nation, there can be no inconsistency between the political law that says *equality* and the civil law that says *authority.* . . . The habit of finding despotism in oneself ends up making despotism acceptable above oneself. It is an inevitable fact that tryanny in the family gives birth to tryanny in the state. . . . Why? Because it is impossible to be both monarchist and republican at the same time: monarchist at home and republican away from home.

But not only did Richer appeal to republicans' principles in the above high-minded manner; he also appealed to their self-interest with the utilitarian argument that "the Republic will never be consolidated in France if women remain opposed to it." Later he wrote, "I repeat it and I will continue to repeat it: we will only have a free society when women are free; for he who oppresses deserves to be oppressed. One domination calls into being another; the one which benefits us justifies the one that harms us." [5]

Richer's theory of sexual equality, like Adam's from which he likely borrowed, blended republican individualism with utopian socialist sex-class analysis. First, he made clear that by equality he did not mean what he, and Adam before him, termed *identité:* "Perhaps in order to avoid any misunderstanding, it would be better to say *equivalence.* For man and woman are not absolutely alike, neither in their tastes, nor in their needs, nor in their feelings. It is *equality* in difference; it is variety within the oneness of the species." He is not quite a Saint-Simonian here, but he is close. He continues, however, in a way that would have dismayed such Saint-Simonian women as Jeanne Deroin. Because women and men are not identical, they should have different activities: "We [men] are and will remain . . . in charge of outdoor work, and woman will remain, by her own preference, the guardian of the family, the diligent hostess of the domestic home." And further on he declared, "Yes, the family is her primary home for action, her preferred environment, her natural atmosphere; yes, this is primarily where her influence must be felt." Thus he answered the objections of those who feared that his proposed reforms would lead women to abandon their familial responsibilities: "By liberating woman, by asking that she be permitted to develop her intelligence . . . and to exercise those functions for which her natural faculties make her suitable, nobody intended by that to give her the absurd advice to abandon her sex. Nobody said that she should stop caring for her children or having her husband support them. . . . No, woman must remain woman; she can do nothing better." [6]

It is interesting that even in Richer's most basic demand—for equal education—his acceptance of a special role for women led him to the same compromise. Her education could be different—although not inferior: "The question is not to have both sexes always and ever follow an absolutely identical curriculum. No. Given the difference of occupations appropriate for men on the one hand and for women on the other, what we ask for women is an equivalent education to that which men receive. This instruction may be *different* if women themselves desire it but it cannot be inferior." [7] Just how a different education would overcome the disharmony he earlier attributed to separate education, he did not say, nor did he discuss at any further point how to assure that a "different" education would indeed be equal. Here, Richer does not even sound feminist; he sounds more like one of the "friendly" but not feminist reformers.

Yet Richer did agree that women's "circle of activity" might be enlarged:

> Women . . . do not live only within the family, they also live in society. . . . Everything that interests us touches them in some way. There is no political mistake, no social injustice of which they do not feel the repercussion and endure, along with us, the disastrous consequence.
>
> That is why, while recognizing that their place is at home, I do not systematically exclude them from certain jobs that until now have been reserved for men.[8]

And elsewhere, he was far more daring. For example, he wrote that women should not only be permitted to work, but should work: "If I were to treat the question of work purely from an economic point of view, I would strive to prove that it is a duty, just as much for woman as for man, to work. No one would have the right to consume more than he produces." Indeed, he declared, "France needs more, not fewer, workers in order to increase production." He recognized, too, that women have a right to work because "no one should be obliged to accept from another her daily subsistence." Even the married woman should be able to live from her own wages if that is her wish: "It is not suitable for all women to remain during their entire lives, at the mercy of a man. If the husband alone supports the marriage and maintains it, the wife falls into absolute dependence on him, made all the more painful because it is irreparable." Richer also made an astute observation about housework, one not normally associated with nineteenth-century ideas about work, but commonly expressed today: "I know of course that the housekeeping work that woman devotes herself to is not without value and that if it were compensated for in money, it would be equal to the pay for a worker's day. [But] one never makes this computation, and apparently the wife must remain the tributary of the husband." A wife should, Richer believed, have the right to demand that she "be supplied with the means to share joint expenses" and be permitted to exclaim, "I also contribute something to the household." [9]

Richer was more ambivalent, however, when he discussed employments that women could pursue. On the one hand, he declared that women's intellectual capacity is equal to men's, thus suggesting that there could be no justification for denying her access to the various jobs then closed to her. He analyzed the jobs outside the home which were open to women at that time and noted that they were mainly barred from the high-status professions: "When one is not afraid to bring woman out of the home to send her to work laboriously in stores or in workshops where her health is destroyed, her body loses its shape, and her morals are always in danger, how can one speak to me of her domestic duties as an absolute obstacle? " On the other hand, he accepted without question that women could not hold every job, for "undoubtedly there are some trades that no woman could practice." And later he concluded that "there are occupations suitable to each sex. . . . I recognize that this is so." [10]

Richer, like almost all feminists for the next fifty years or more, acknowledged that for working-class women, employment was a necessity; for other women, it was a right, if they wished to exercise it. The working-class husband or father was often incapable of supporting his wife or daughter. And even if the working-class male could support his family, women in this class must be prepared for "the contingencies that [always] threaten her" because male workers' jobs were precarious and sometimes dangerous. "When the family is stricken with the unexpected death of its provider, what will happen to the mother who is left alone with young children? She has no trade. If, when she was young, she had spent several years as an apprentice, all of that has long since been forgotten." For working-class women, "what must be done is to modify the actual working conditions of women, to moralize the workshop, and to search for a way to reconcile, better than has been done until now, the interests of the [female] worker with the respect that is owed to every woman and to motherhood." They should be paid equally for equal work.[11] For other women, "what must be done" was to open up all the professional and high-status jobs presently closed to them; Richer specified pharmacy and medicine.

The truly new, one could almost say "revolutionary," aspect of his argument, that women had a duty to work, was advanced only timidly and blunted by qualifiers such as "if she wishes it." It was contradicted by his conviction that women indeed did have a special role to fulfill in the home. When answering the argument that women should be at home taking care of children, he did not speak of "their duty to work" but instead noted that "there are women to whom this argument does not apply; those who do not wish to get married, widows, [and] the deserted ones." [12]

Richer's unquestioning acceptance of woman's special role as mother and homemaker was not unique; utopian socialists, too, had generally taken this stance, and it was the unanimous feminist position from 1848 on. But there were significant differences between Richer and the earlier feminists. First, he nowhere suggests the necessity of restructuring domestic work. It would be wrong to assume that he expected that wealthier women would be able to employ domestics to do their housewifely chores. This idea is not consistent with his eloquent words about women's maternal function; he expected women to do these chores for themselves and for their families. A better explanation is to note that when feminism became narrowly bourgeois—not in intent but certainly in the reality of its "personnel"—it became limited in its understanding of the real-life circumstances of working mothers. Earlier feminists, whose ties had been to the working class, recognized the oppression of the working woman who was solely responsible for housekeeping and childrearing in addition to her long work day outside the home. They offered a variety of solutions for this double burden: day care facilities (Roland); bureaucratic nurse-mothers (Démar); the communalization of housekeeping (Fourier); the creation of public restaurants and laundries (Gay). The difference between them and Richer likely related to their class difference. (Adam, Héricourt, and later bourgeois feminists also shared Richer's position.) Bourgeois feminism had ceased to learn from the experiences of working-class women. In this respect, it served even bourgeois women poorly.

Richer differed from earlier feminists in another way, which most likely related to his male perspective. The 1848 feminists used the language of woman/maternity and woman/morality to advance women's interests. Richer reversed ends and means. Thus female education no longer served women's emancipation. Rather, improved female education would enhance children's learning opportunities—particularly those of boys: "How many mothers today are in a position to bring up a daughter, and more importantly [sic] a son? Very few, if one takes into consideration the kind of education that is universally afforded them. . . . We need [women] to give us sons who are enlightened, stronghearted, steady-spirited, with well-developed intellects." [13]

Further, his writing was male-directed. (Although we assume this relates to his male perspective, we are reminded that Flora Tristan's writing was also male-directed.) His pronouns certainly make clear his assumption that he was writing to a male audience. This insensitivity to language contrasted starkly with his assertion that women had a right to interest themselves in public issues. His unstated assumption was that, in reality, they did not. At one point, indeed, Richer noted that women themselves were unaware of their oppressed situation.

Women for the most part do not worry about these matters! Try to turn their attention to these serious matters and most of them will laugh in your face. Are they interested in the manner in which acts of birth or acts of death are notarized? Do they have any desire to be witnesses in wills?

The code abuses them; the code dishonors them; the code inflicts outrage upon outrage on them; the code throws them back to the class of imbeciles and rougues; the code throws into suspicion their loyalty, their integrity, their morals; the code declares that it has no confidence in their testimony— and all of this does not move them! They remain indifferent in the face of this social inequity!

I am convinced that most of them are ignorant of the degrading position in which the law holds them. If they really knew to what degree they are humbled, their consciences would revolt and the feeling of their misjudged dignity would protest within them.[14]

His language was often tiresomely carping: he complained incessantly about women "who do not worry about these matters." One can only comment that the frustration of this man, fighting women's battles with little recognition from the beneficiaries of his endeavors, might excuse his occasional outbursts of exasperation that those whose struggle he waged were not fighting alongside him. Yet one wonders if his language and attitude did not indicate that he, in fact, excluded them a priori from their struggle.

Richer addressed himself to male legislators who could vote his proposals into effect. His program, in most respects, was a moderate version of the consensus position of liberal feminism after 1848. He focused on better, if not necessarily equal, female education and on improved status for women in the home. If women were to play properly their special role in the family, they must at least have equal rights there, which could be achieved by legal reform. Husbands alone currently had parental authority; it should be shared. Husbands alone had the authority to administer community property; it, too, should be a joint prerogative. To ensure that women were treated as equal partners in a family, they should not be classed with minors by the Civil Code and denied the right to testify in the courts, witness public acts, or sit on family councils.[15] Further, equality of the sexes required one single sexual standard of moral behavior, with sexual activity limited to marriage. Richer proposed two important changes in the code that would go far in creating that single standard: seduction of women over age fifteen should be considered a crime, and paternity, as well as maternity, should be established by the courts in cases in which the responsibilities of parenthood had not been freely recognized.[16]

Yet Richer was conservative only in comparison to other feminists. Few in France were willing to go as far as he would. Indeed, he may even have exaggerated the conservative elements of his position in these books because their purpose was to convince the as-yet unconvinced. Among themselves, feminists, including Richer, were more consistently daring, as was evident at the International Congrès du Droit des Femmes, which was finally held at the time of the 1878 Paris Exposition. Richer, along with Deraismes, dominated that congress, and he does not seem to have disapproved of any of the resolutions although some, such as the one on education, were more far-reaching than the positions he put forth in his books. A unanimous vote was obtained at the congress for the principle of "l'egalité absolu des deux sexes."

Eleven foreign countries and sixteen organizations were officially represented at the 1878 congress. Two hundred and nineteen people were signed up as official participants, among whom were nine deputies, two senators, and five Paris municipal council members.[17] Among the other celebrated names on the official roster were Julia Ward Howe, Theodore Stanton, and Albert Brisbane from the United States; and Aurelia Cimino Folliero, Anna-Maria Mozzoni, and Salvatore Morelli from Italy. For France, we see familiar names—Deraismes, Anna Féresse-Deraismes, Richer, Clémence Royer, and Eugénie Niboyet (then seventy-eight years old). We also see new names that became familiar after this congress: Hubertine Auclert, Caroline de Barrau, Léon Giraud, Virginie Griess-Traut, Nelly Lieutier, Eugénie Pierre, and Léonie Rouzade. In addition to the 219 "official" participants, more than 400 visitors heard the papers and speeches presented at the Grand-Orient Hall.

The resolutions of the four sections (Section Pédagogique; Section Economique; Section Morale; and Section Legislative) clearly present feminist priorities of the time. Political rights were not discussed. Education was still the primary concern: it should be the same for both sexes and indeed ("as in America") should be coeducational, as well as secular, free, and compulsory. Kindergartens should be estabished everywhere, and the curriculum should be based on the teachings of the liberal German educator Julius Froebel. Linked to their education demands is the insistence that mothers should nurse their own infants and that the state should support poor mothers for an eighteen-month period to make this possible. There is no explanation of why this point comes under education, but the decades-old understanding that mothers are the first educators and that the home as well as the school is a learning environment are emphasized by the unexplained association.[18]

The Economic Section called for absolute sexual equality in the work force: equal pay for equal work (both a matter of simple justice and necessity to end prostitution); the creation of apprentice schools and the admission of women to professional schools (the *Facultés* of the university);

the right for women, as well as men, to organize *chambres syndicales* and to belong to *conseils des prud'hommes* (the regulatory bodies for industry and commerce); and the suppression of all laws against "association" (that is, the right of workers, male and female, to organize unions). The congress called also for an elimination of the unfair competition from prison, convent, and orphanage production, which benefited from exemption from certain taxes, tariff charges, and child-labor laws. This section on economics concluded with a position statement that indicates that feminists never lost sight of the connection between women's economic independence and sexual equality but were struggling, too, to incorporate the concept of independence with the reality of women's work at home. "Taking into consideration that women's dignity and independence can only be safeguarded by work, that every woman whose means of living make her dependent on a man is not free, the congress demands for woman a freedom to work equal to man's, and recognizes the value and the merit of housework." [19]

The Morals Section demanded the end of prostitution, now legalized by the state's "Regulation System," public houses, and special health facilities for prostitutes: "By converting disorder into the exercising of a regular profession, the state sanctions the immoral prejudice that debauchery is a necessity for man." [20] Resolutions also supported *recherche de paternité*, punishment for the seduction of women over age fifteen (the law already punished seducers of those younger than fifteen), and an end to enforced celibacy in the army (which created "disorderly" relationships for soldiers and their lovers and high prostitution rates around army installations).

From the Legislative Section came resolutions for an overhaul of the Civil Code to equalize, "in all ways," the laws affecting husbands and wives; the reestablishment of divorce; the equalizing of criminal laws concerning adultery; the recognition of seduction as a crime: *recherche de paternité;* and a suppression of the *police des moeurs,* whose rights to round up prostitutes were limitless, leaving prostitutes bereft of protective liberties that common criminals took for granted.

The congress lasted three days and received a better reception from the Paris press than had the 1872 banquet. In response to an article in *Le Gaulois* which had ridiculed the congress ("At last we are going to laugh a little"),[21] Francisque Sarcey published an article in *XIXᵉ siècle* entitled "Il n'y a pas de quoi rire" in which he concluded: "We have the inveterate habit of believing that, in every conversation that includes women, one can only talk of frivolous and silly things; and if, by chance, the conversation should become serious and women express themselves, we only answer their good sense by addressing them in a low voice in terms of bluestockings or women philosophers, shrugging our shoulders, or letting go with some risqué story. [In so doing] we are only proud fools." [22]

Republican feminists had reason to be optimistic in the late 1870s and early 1880s. In 1879, liberal republicans took control of the Senate and the presidency: feminists' friends were now in power. The government soon authorized their Société pour l'Amélioration du Sort des Femmes. In 1880 and again in 1884, the feminist alliance with anticlericalism—a theoretical alliance as well as one of shared activities—bore fruit in two significant legislative victories: the creation of girls' secondary schools (the Camille Sée Law of 1880) and the reestablishment of divorce (the Naquet Law of 1884). Neither measure passed in exactly the form preferred by feminists, but liberals such as Richer and Deraismes hailed the compromise measures as victories nonetheless.

The Camille Sée Law was part of the extensive education legislation passed by the Ferry and Brisson governments between 1879 and 1886, which reformed the primary school system, making it free, obligatory, and secular, and modernized secondary and higher education. Schools to train instructors were created for every department, and two Ecoles Normales Supérieures to train primary school teachers were established, one at Saint-Cloud for men and another at Fontenay-aux-Roses for women. Members of the religious orders were prohibited from teaching in the public schools, in boys' schools after five years, and in girls' schools as nuns retired. The reform and modernization of secondary schools included the creation of day *lycées* for girls. Although a rigorous curriculum was adopted, the course of studies did not go so far as to include Latin and Greek, which were required for the *baccalauréat* examinations. The Ecole Normale Supérieure de Sevres was founded to train female secondary teachers.

The Naquet Law on divorce, like the Camille Sée Law, was passed as part of the liberal republican government's extensive anticlerical legislative program. The Senate, however, agreed to pass the measure only after it struck "mutual consent" from the list of allowable grounds. Adultery, grievous injury, and criminal conviction would be the only grounds for divorce, and separation agreements would continue to exist for those who would not or could not choose divorce. Although Richer had prepared the original proposition for Naquet, he claimed to be pleased with the final version because it included what he considered to be the most significant part of his draft, equality of treatment for both partners, particularly in the case of adultery.

During most of the years of the Third Republic, anticlericalism was the single most constant unifying factor for the entire Left and the single most important issue dividing Left from Right. The anticlericalism of republican feminism, although not simply pragmatic, certainly worked to the advantage of feminists during the final decades of the nineteenth century. Later, however, anticlerical arguments would be used against women, to justify withholding the vote from them. And there was another danger in the alliance between feminists and republicans around anticlericalism; it precluded the participation of practicing Catholic women in the feminist movement. It is easy, of course, to focus on the patriarchalism of the Catholic church and conclude that in these years at least, the church prevented the participation of Catholic women in the struggle for women's emancipation. But it must also be recognized that by identifying Catholic women with the enemy, feminists, too, made it impossible for them to participate. The gap between feminists and this large portion of the population would not be bridged.

For now, however, feminists were unconcerned with bridging the gap separating them from Catholic women. They were too busy fighting among themselves. No sooner had republican feminists begun to realize some of their program than they began to squabble. As a result of discord between Richer and Deraismes, Richer became inactive in the Societé pour l'Amélioration du Sort de la Femme. In November 1882, he formed a new group whose program was almost indistinguishable from that of the group surrounding Deraismes. But Richer's group, La Ligue Française pour le Droit des Femmes, had a masculine leadership under Richer and the "honorary" presidents.

Although we know from many sources that it was a falling-out between Richer and Deraismes that led to this break, no one explicitly tells the cause of the disagreement, and we are forced to surmise. A careful reading of Le Droit des femmes throws no light on the subject. Matters pertaining to Deraismes's group were reported in Le Droit des femmes although there are indications that her group was not very active after the 1878 Congress. Deraismes's various lectures, most often on literary subjects, were normally reprinted in Le Droit des femmes, and the journal always referred to Deraismes in excessively laudatory language. Any split between Richer and Deraismes was to be hidden not only from historians of the future but also from Richer's contemporaneous readership. All mention and announcement of Richer's decision to form a new organization in 1882 omits any reference to a need for a group different from the Société pour l'Amélioration du Sort de la Femme et la Revendication de ses Droits.[23]

Intuition suggests that the falling-out may have been more for personal than for political reasons. Certainly, the researcher studying Richer's writings cannot miss his enormous ego; nor was Deraismes noted for her modesty. One wonders whether there was enough room in one small group for these two leaders.[24] In retrospect, it seems that Richer was more important than Deraismes. He introduced her to the public in the first place, by having her speak at the Grand-Orient lecture series, which he had been organizing since 1865. He left the most complete exposition of the feminist ideology in book form. And most important, he kept the historical record of feminism of the time, *Le Droit des femmes*. But it was Deraismes, not Richer, who was feminism's celebrity. She was evidently a brilliant public speaker who could attract large crowds. She served as an example that the participation of women in public affairs could enhance political debate and republican values. Individuals who were drawn to support her personally would be drawn soon to support her claims for all women. Not an unimportant fact, her money financed many of feminism's activities, including the 1878 congress and another congress in 1889.[25]

But were there differences between Deraismes and Richer beyond their conflicting ambitions? One may presume that Deraismes and her supporters in the Société pour l'Amélioration du Sort de la Femme—all female— resented Richer's frequently condescending attitude toward women, both directly by his many outright attacks on "women who don't appreciate what I'm doing for them" and indirectly by the honorary tributes and positions he bestowed on men in the league. Richer seemed always to assume that the route to respectability was to increase male participation. Especially after he organized his own group in 1883, the honorary presidents were always men: Victor Hugo, then Victor Schoelcher, followed by René Viviani. A publication issued on the occasion of the league's fiftieth anniversary (1920), stated proudly:

> Founded by a man, the Ligue Française pour le Droit des Femmes has been since its inception, and has always remained, a mixed [integrated] association. Among the members who participated in our first election, in 1870, one finds MM. Louis Jourdan, director of *Siècle;* Eugène Pelletan and Gagneur, deputies; Charles Fauvety, director of *Solidarité.* Many deputies, senators and municipal councillors of Paris were constant members of the League; writers and scientists brought to it their concurrence, not hesitating to join. Let us cite among them: MM. Daniel Berthelot, Emile Deschanel, Alexandre Dumas, Yves Guyot, Jean Macé, Frédéric Passy, Auguste Vacquerie, Clovis Hugues, [and] Lucien Descaves.[26]

And, in the 1880s, it was Deraismes, not Richer, who responded most favorably to the challenge of radical feminism and its insistence that the feminist movement press for women's suffrage.

Radical Feminism

The issue of winning the vote had essentially lain dormant through the years of the Second Empire, when political liberties were meaningless even for the men who had them. With the collapse of the Empire, though, the issue once again became important. According to Richer, Julie Daubié had founded an Association pour le Suffrage des Femmes early in 1871.[27] The year before, she had published several brochures. The first contained the following manifesto:

> The extension of voting rights for men, the democratic form of governments, and the principles themselves of modern freedom, all call public attention to the question of the participation of women in the suffrage. . . .
>
> In free France of 1789, Condorcet and Sieyès energetically claimed the rights of citizenship for women, but then the first Empire and the oligarchical domination of limited suffrage stifled the liberal aspirations of progressive men.
>
> When the people acquired the right to vote in 1848, thinking people understood that the exclusion of half of humanity, classified a priori *imbecillus sexus* along with those forbidden for reasons of crime or misdemeanors, was a gratuitous insult for women, equal to men as French persons, equal before taxes both direct and indirect as well as before the penal code, and that it was ironic to call universal a suffrage that rejected women as minors lacking in judgment.

She concluded: "We regard suffrage as a right and a duty of the first order that we are not permitted to renounce. We shall claim it by the legal means that we already possess, with the firm hope of being supported by all progressive and forward-looking men.[28]

A few weeks later there appeared a brochure containing a copy of a letter dated September 20, 1870, written by Daubié in Paris to the mayor of her arrondissement:

> Mr. Mayor:
>
> The United States, England, etc., in order to admit women to voting rights, must reform laws that apply only to men. Thanks to civil equality, proclaimed in 1789, the text of our laws applies, without regard to sex, to all the French! . . .
>
> I have the honor therefore, Mr. Mayor, of declaring to you my intention of becoming enrolled in the electoral registers of your district, which is where I live, and to pray that you will favorably receive my declaration.
>
> In support of this initative, I am taking the liberty to remind you that even our last government made a liberal interpretation of the law about

diplomas of secondary education . . . even though there had been a long proscription against their rights. . . . Nor have women ever been excluded from the right of petition that all *French citizens* have acquired.

All the more reason then to hope that you will accede to our request. . . . [If, however, you do object], I beg you to tell me on what legislative text [your objection] is based and particularly from what authority it derives.''[29]

Daubié's intention was to have women, or at least unmarried women, in all twenty arrondissements write similar letters to their mayors. Daubié died soon thereafter, and both the association and action demanding the vote died also—stillborn.

The suffrage issue was next taken up by Hubertine Auclert. She is normally considered the founder of the modern French suffrage movement, but clearly she institutionalized the issue rather than introduced it. Auclert was born in 1848: "I have been a rebel against the crushing of women almost from birth. Man's brutality against woman, which terrified my childhood, prepared me early to claim independence and respect for my sex." Having read the newspaper accounts of the banquets organized by Richer in 1872, she decided to go to Paris. She was at that time orphaned and economically independent: "My life had been of little importance, everything was calm and perfectly simple: no accidents, no adventures, the existence of a recluse. But then, I became a crusader, not by choice but from duty. Since no one else would undertake that which I want to attempt, I overcame my excessive shyness and went to war like a medieval knight." [30]

In Paris, Auclert was made secretary to both the newspaper *L'Avenir des femmes* and the Association pour le Droit des Femmes. It was then that she studied the history of the feminist movement and determined that the program of 1848, which joined together political and civil rights (unlike the program of Richer and Deraismes) had to be revived. In 1876 she founded the group Le Droit des Femmes. This was right after the Association pour le Droit des Femmes had changed its name, so Auclert's choice of a name was viewed as a rebuke to the other's compromise. (In 1883, however, she renamed her group Suffrage des Femmes to avoid confusion with Richer's new Ligue Française pour le Droit des Femmes.) The motto of her organization was "No duties without rights; no rights without duties," and its goal was "perfect equality of the sexes before the law and before customs and morality." [31]

Auclert's group issued the following declaration or "Appeal to the Women of France" in 1876:

In spite of the benefits that came from our revolution of 1789, two kinds of individuals are still enslaved: proletarians and women. Women proletarians have an even more deplorable fate. . . .

We have no rights. As interested as we may be in the happiness of our country, we are pitilessly turned away from all meetings, whether elective or legislative. . . . We count for less than nothing in the state. A stupid and profoundly ignorant man counts for more in France than the best educated woman. He can name his legislators; woman cannot. She is a creature apart who is born with many duties and no rights.

What a strange anomaly! Woman is considered incompetent with regard to social or political life. She is likened to criminals and madmen, but when she breaks the law, she is just as severely punished as a man in full possession of his capacities. All liberal careers are closed to us; we must not interfere in any financial management; however, the public treasury finds us worthy for purposes of taxation! [32]

At the 1878 International Congress of the Rights of Woman, Auclert was not permitted to present her speech demanding political rights, "Léon Richer and Maria Deraismes, having found it too revolutionary." [33] She therefore had it printed with the subtitle: "Question qui n'est pas traitée au Congrès international des femmes." In this speech she made it clear that her goal was to demand total political equality for women:

In our claim for women's rights, it is important not to stray from the principle, it is important not to be evasive, [but] to aim straight for the mark. Would we be capable of helping women to free themselves if we, who have taken up their cause, should question part of their rights? It is to doubt a right when one does not dare affirm it. What would the oppressors think of women if those who want to free them from bondage concerned themselves particularly with not offending their oppressors and timidly asked in favor of women for a little more education, a little more bread, a little less humiliation in marriage, and fewer difficulties in life? [34]

The following year, 1879, she was a delegate to the Marseilles workers' congress, where she finally delivered her speech on the political rights of women. It appears that her words were well received:

The president of the session passed a vote of thanks to me, and the following day I was put in charge of directing the work of the Congress in the capacity of president. Named as [committee] reporter for the commission on the question of women, I was able to get a resolution passed in favor of the complete emancipation of woman. From now on this resolution will appear in the platform of socialist workers of France in the following form: Social and political equality of Woman. [35]

In 1881, Auclert founded the weekly newspaper *La Citoyenne*—along with Léon Giraud, author of *De la condition des femmes au point de vue de l'exercise des droits publics et politiques,* and Antonin Levrier, whom she married in 1888.[36]

> For this newspaper, whose only aim is to claim the equality of woman and man, we could not have found a better name than *La Citoyenne.* We ask for woman not only the civil rights of a French citizen but also the political rights of the citizen. In fact—and this may seem strange to some— our study of past events and our observation of present events has led us to place the political emancipation of woman ahead of her civil emancipation.

She went on to define "political emancipation" as the advent to woman of rights that confer the power to make laws—by oneself, if one is elected deputy; by delegation, if one is an elector. For Auclert, "Political rights are the keystone that . . . will guarantee all the other rights. As long as woman does not possess this weapon—the vote—she will be forced to submit to the system of patriarchy. All her efforts to conquer her civil and economic freedom will be in vain." She disagreed that either a political or a social and economic transformation of society would liberate woman if these did not specifically include equal rights for women. Only the "femme citoyenne" could guarantee equality:

> A change in the political condition of society would not help the destiny of women. . . . A change in the social and economic order would not free women; for even though every day the economic question may be resolved for a small number of women, their position would be the same the following day as it was the previous day. In France, women who are millionaires are subject to the same tyrannical laws as poor women.

Then follows an appeal for the unity of all women "of whatever opinion and whatever class they be, [for] all suffer or will suffer from the present legislation." [37]

Republican adversaries of feminism commonly presented two objections to women's political demands: that they were exempt from military service and that they were too heavily influenced by the church. Auclert responded: "It is ridiculous to object to women's vote on the basis of their exemption from military service since so many men vote without ever bearing arms. Furthermore, the maternity tax claims many more victims than the blood tax." Auclert did agree to the claim that the overwhelming majority of women were ardent champions of clericalism, but countered: "So that

woman need no longer go to church to appeal the tryanny of man to
God, she must be equal to man. So that woman no longer goes to pray,
she must vote." [38]

La Citoyenne remained the most important propaganda organ of the
suffragist point of view throughout the 1880s. In 1888 Auclert moved
to Algeria with her husband, leaving the direction of the paper to Maria
Martin. The paper began to change, losing its radical militant image and
increasingly confining itself to reporting news of women's or feminist clubs.
An argument between Martin and Auclert led to Martin's founding of *Le
Journal des femmes* and the demise of *La Citoyenne* in 1891.[39]

Auclert also published numerous statements of her feminist position in
book or pamphlet form. Besides the speech which she could not present
to the 1878 congress, she also wrote *L'Argent de la femme,* demanding
the "legal separation of wealth" (that is, an end to the community property
system); and *Le Nom de la femme,* to prove the advantages for women in
retaining their maiden names after marriage. But the two most noted of
her works were *Le Vote des femmes* and *Les Femmes au gouvernail. Le Vote
des femmes* (1908) records the history of the suffrage movement and justifies
its goals. Most of Auclert's speeches and petitions are reproduced here.
Les Femmes au gouvernail was published posthumously after World War
I, when the suffrage issue was less controversial. The main portion of the
text is a compilation of Auclert's previously published or spoken demands
for suffrage; it also includes a biographical essay on Auclert, by an unnamed
author.[40]

Auclert did not, however, limit herself to writing. She revived not only
the radical program but also radical activism. She attempted to register
for the vote in 1880 and when denied this right refused to pay her taxes.
She relented only after the authorities seized her household furnishings.
She also devoted enormous energy to drafting and presenting petitions to
the president of the Republic and to appropriate bureaucrats on the wide
variety of issues she supported, including the right of women to petition.
And in 1885 she conceived the idea of presenting female candidates for
the legislative elections. Her original intention was to back Maria Deraismes
alone, but the campaign grew to a slate of fifteen.[41] The better known
of the candidates were Deraismes, Louise Barberousse, Léonie Rouzade,
Madame Vincent, Lara Marcel (who wrote poetry under the pseudonym
René Marcil), and the widow Jeannot. Auclert maintained that if her
original plan of backing only one candidate had been adhered to, the
feminist "vote" would have fared better.

During the 1880s, the split between liberal feminists such as Richer
and Deraismes and radical feminists such as Auclert paralleled the split

Hubertine Auclert. Courtesy Bibl. Marguerite Durand

between Opportunists and Radicals among republicans in general. Dera-
isme's and Richer's "politique des brêches" had been fashioned before
the Republic was secure. Their gradualism was to assure stability, which
was valued because it was thought necessary to safeguard the Republic.

Deraismes and Richer ignored not only the issue of political rights but also economic positions that were seemingly so advanced that they would threaten the nation's fragile stability. Their first priorities were civil rights, which, if won, would provide women with that "equality of opportunity" which liberalism so valued. Women would then be free to engage in the political activity that Deraismes and Richer knew best, which was to bring influence to bear on a representative legislature. Their politics were male-directed because men sat in the legislature. And their politics were Paris-centered because legislators debated there. They compromised willingly because compromise was the style of legislative activity. Perhaps, too, they compromised willingly because such measures as the Sée and the Naquet laws, even in their truncated form, seemed like significant advances to those of their generation. (Richer and Deraismes were born in the 1820s, Auclert in 1848.)

Auclert labeled her tactics "assault" to contrast her radicalism with Deraismes's and Richer's opportunism. But she was not always unwilling to compromise. She drew up petition after petition, and as soon as one demanding suffrage for all women was denied, she would follow it with another insisting on votes for single women only. Hers was a specific form of radicalism: not an absolute unwillingness to compromise, but an insistence on the vote first. She cooperated with Deraismes and Richer to demand changes in the code and in education but pushed to reorder feminists' priorities away from the civil rights program of liberalism and toward the political rights program of radicalism.

If liberal feminism had been a response to the political reality of the 1870s, radical feminism was a response to the new France of the 1880s. Republican France was no longer so open to pressure from Paris-based groups as earlier regimes had been. Legislators responded more to their geographically dispersed constituencies. Until women were a constituency, feminists would lack the political clout necessary to translate their goals into law. And women, of course, could not be such a constituency unless they were voters.

In time, Auclert was able to convince some liberal feminists of both the justice of the suffrage movement and its pragmatic value. Deraismes responded first to Auclert's challenge; Richer lagged behind. Here the political differences between those two liberals is most clear. In his *La Femme libre,* Richer had devoted a chapter to "winning the vote." His position was to establish the right of women to vote but to state nonetheless that it was too soon to demand that right. In the first place, the public was still unprepared for the demand[42] and, second, until women were properly educated they might not use that vote "correctly" (the Republic first, then women). "Women have not yet laid claim to political rights. They know only too well—I speak of those who are in a position to understand—who would profit from this premature reform. Out of nine million women who have reached majority only several thousand would vote freely; the remainder would take their orders from the confessional." [43]

Richer dismissed compromise suggestions restricting suffrage to single women or educated women, and, indeed, the circumstance of universal male suffrage in France would have made these unlikely options. Richer was especially adamant that women should not be asked to pass an examination if men were not. His reason, however, was that no such literacy examination would indicate an individual's "political" intelligence:

> There is no assurance that a rich woman, who spends ten years in a convent school, who would be well informed on religious history, grammar, geography, drawing, piano, and other useful information, would vote any better than an honest woman worker, enlightened by her own pain about the real needs of the country. . . . All women must [have the right to vote] or none. If it is too early, let us wait; but let us not create special privileges, let us not establish classes.[44]

This statement, seemingly "democratic," indicates clearly that Richer believed that women should have the vote only when they were educated for it and that education was wholly in the political sphere. "Passing the examination" would, therefore, be agreement with Richer's views, rather than the views of the priest. Richer here seemed hardly more prepared than the church he railed against to grant women true autonomy. Auclert lamented: "On the question of women's rights, M. Richer, quite interested in the issue by virtue of being a man, is like a solicitor in a case, inclined to let things drag on over time in order to spare himself some work. We, on the contrary are like heirs who are anxious to enjoy that which we know belongs to us." [45]

Deraismes was more open to Auclert's points of view. In 1879, only one year after silencing Auclert at the first international congress, she spoke out publicly for the vote. She first distanced herself from Richer's position that Catholic women would undermine the Republic:

> One would be led to believe that clericalism was an invention of women. But who really introduced the priest into politics? Who made him an elector, a deputy, a senator, if it is not the Constitution that was drafted by men? Who permitted the priesthood to invade education if it was not by the law promulgated by men?
>
> What! Women in politics would spoil everything? Alas! It seems to me that in this regard things have already progressed quite far! [46]

Rather than suggest that voting women could undermine the Republic, she insisted that nonvoting women were the denial of it:

> The politics of universal suffrage are the cornerstone of all societies that care about progress. If it has not attained all the results that one had hoped for, it is because universal suffrage, divided in half, has only operated on one lame foot, without making use of a good part of its strength, by refusing to use woman as a helper. . . . Political life must be spread out into all ranks, to all the members of society, without discrimination on the basis of wealth, social position, or sex. [47]

In 1879, when Deraismes gave a speech on "universal suffrage," she did not mention women until twenty pages into the printed text. By 1882, however, she addressed the Masonic Lodge at Pecq specifically on the subject of women's political rights:

> We want to reclaim our revolutionary tradition, continue the work of enfranchisement. The eighteenth century stopped at men; it made them citizens. The nineteenth century must move on to women and proclaim their citizenship.
>
> At the present time, the involvement of women in matters of general and collective interest is a historical necessity. [48]

In 1885, Deraismes agreed to be included on Auclert's "slate" and thus became part of the nascent suffrage movement.

There were then distinctions between Richer's and Deraismes's politics that showed up most clearly in their differences over the suffrage issue. Both thought the time "too soon" to demand political rights for women. Both were responsible for silencing Auclert, who in 1878 wished to air her arguments in favor of suffrage at the international congress. But whereas Richer felt that women were not "ready" for the vote and feared that their Catholic sympathies would undermine the Republic, Deraismes felt that republican male politicians were not ready to grant the vote and that to demand it too soon would undermine the possibility of obtaining other victories for women. Still, one should not exaggerate the differences between these two feminists, nor even their differences from Auclert. The three disagreed on means alone, not on ends. All three stated repeatedly that women indeed had the capacity, right, and duty to vote. But Auclert's refinement was that the first victory should be the vote. Until women won that goal, the other goals, which Auclert strongly believed in— increased professional and educational opportunities and equality of civil rights—could never be achieved.

In 1889, it was evident that unity, or at least an alliance, between liberal and radical feminists was possible. In that year the government planned to celebrate the centennial of the Revolution with a universal exposition. Among the many conferences, congresses, exhibitions, and expositions which the state would subsidize would be a "woman's congress" celebrating the role of women in society, especially their charitable activities. Without a doubt, the republicans in power in 1889 had a quite different conception of women from that of their confrères of 1789. But although the government had improved its position on women, not surprisingly, it had not advanced as far as feminists would have liked. Because the leadership of the feminist movement felt that the government-inspired congress did not represent the aspirations of their movement, they determined to hold a separate woman's congress, truly and avowedly feminist in orientation.

It seems that the idea for an alternate congress came independently from both Richer and Deraismes, but they were quickly able to combine their efforts. Thus the Congrès Français et International du Droit des Femmes, held in Paris June 25 to 29, 1889, was under the sponsorship of both Deraismes's and Richer's groups. We notice also among the congress officers the name of Léon Giraud, the longtime associate of Auclert (who was then residing in Algeria and was absent from the struggles of feminism during this period). Thus one can say that liberal and radical feminism presented a united face to the French public in 1889.

The cause of the split between these feminists and the government-sponsored congress arose from the government's naming a president for that congress who, to feminists in 1889, was corrupted by his position on the issue of "protective legislation." This was Jules Simon, a participant in feminist groupings of the late 1860s but no longer acceptable in 1889, not having traveled the same path or arrived at the same point twenty years later.[49] Yet the two congresses were not enemies of each other. Eugénie Potonié-Pierre reported favorably on the "other congress" in *Le Droit des femmes*. Many people participated in both: Maria Martin of *La Citoyenne* was secretary of the government-sponsored congress; Mme Griess-Traut, vice-president of Deraismes's Société pour l'Amélioration du Sort de la Femme, was present at it, as was Richer. Organizers of the government Congress—Jeanne Schmahl, Isabelle Bogelot, and Emilie de Morsier—not only attended the feminist congress but also donated money to help organize it.

The format of the two congresses was different. That of the government one was to describe the role French women played in charity, education, arts, sciences, and literature. The feminist congress included similar information on its program: one of its four sections, Section Historique, was organized along these lines. But the other three were explicitly political. The Section Economique resolved that exploitive work conditions must be transformed by legal and constitutional reforms that would allow wives to control their own earnings (reform of the Civil Code) and permit all women to participate in the administration of industry and commerce. The implication was that special legislation that limited work hours for women but not men sidestepped without solving the real problems of working-class women. In addition, economic resolutions called for salaries for women teachers equal to those of male teachers; access to the liberal professions (the legal profession was specified); the right to work in certain specified bureaucratic fields (public assistance, wet nurse inspectors); and removal of apprenticeship programs from the factories to the trade schools. The Section de Moral called for the suppression of the *police des moeurs* and the demolition of the Saint-Lazare prison (for prostitutes). The Section Legislative demanded a code revision "in the direction of justice and absolute equality" and called for permitting paternity suits.[50]

Although the resolutions did not focus on political rights, the suffrage issue was not silenced, as it had been in 1878.[51] Léon Giraud specified that political rights were necessary for workers, and he managed to get a very toned-down version of this concept into the economic resolutions.[52] Jules Allix, speaking on morality, referred to the immorality of denying to women the right to vote.[53] Giraud, however, was not satisfied with a mere "airing" of the issue. In an August 18 letter to the editor of *Le Droit des femmes,* he declared that he was thwarted in his effort to get a resolution in favor of suffrage passed at the last day's plenary meeting and protested *Le Droit des femmes*'s lack of coverage of his efforts.

The success of the congress cannot be measured in numbers: official participants (176 individuals and 13 groups) were slightly fewer than in 1878, which can partially be accounted for by the cost of registration.[54] The meetings were not open to the nonpaying public, so it cannot be ascertained whether larger numbers would have liked to attend (as an estimated 400 had in 1878). Its significance lies more in who attended it and how it was viewed: women participants outnumbered men by almost three to one; and the congress received favorable mention in more than six hundred newspapers around the world.[55]

Republican feminism had, as Richer had hoped, become more respectable. But although it gained in this regard, it lost something that earlier feminists had valued—an ability to speak to women across class lines. This is not to say that republican feminists ignored women of the lower classes. In the 1889 Congress, as in the earlier 1878 one, resolutions that would have improved the situation of poor women were passed. Yet by 1889, none of the prominent republican feminists, neither Richer, nor Deraismes, nor Auclert, addressed the particular concerns of poor women as workers. As republicans and socialists moved further apart from each other, republican feminism—both its liberal and radical branches—came to represent best the interests of middle-class women.

The Growing Gap between Republican Feminists and Socialists

Although republicanism and socialism had been closely connected from the 1840s to 1870, that alliance unraveled once republicans came to power. The split between republican feminists on the one side and socialists and socialist feminists on the other occurred at the same time. Already in 1871, the experience of the Commune had pitted liberal republicans— including liberal republican feminists—against socialists. Neither Richer nor Deraismes had supported the Commune, although others of the original Association pour le Droit des Femmes—Louise Michel, Paule Mink, André Léo, and Noémie and Elie Reclus—threw themselves into the revolutionary activities. After 1871, when participants in the Commune were exiled or deported, republican feminism was represented by women and men whose perspective was more narrowly bourgeois. This became increasingly true in the 1880s.

Hubertine Auclert tried to keep the old alliance between republicanism and socialism alive. In 1879, she attended a workers' congress in Marseilles, where she presented her plea for suffrage—the speech that Deraismes and Richer had refused to place on the agenda of the International Congress of the Rights of Women the year before. Auclert was well received in Marseilles and got socialists to adopt resolutions, which she helped draw up, favoring complete civil and political equality and women's right to work: "The congress, considering that a role must depend on the choice of the individual who fills it, assigns no special role to women. They will take the roles and the places in society to which their vocations call

them." [56] After that congress, Auclert worked to organize the Paris section
of the newly founded Fédération du Parti des Travailleurs Socialistes de
France, but when, a year later, the party split between mutualists and
collectivists, Auclert sided with the losing mutualist faction and thereafter
became inactive in socialist politics. [57]

Léonie Rouzade had been introduced to socialism by Hubertine Auclert
but, having sided with the collectivists in the 1880 split, remained active
among them after Auclert withdrew. In 1880, she founded the Union
des Femmes along with Eugénie Pierre (after 1881, Eugenie Potonié-Pierre)
and Marguerite Tinayre, who had just returned to France following the
general amnesty of communards. The union's politics were more fully
socialist than Auclert's had been. Whereas Auclert had simply advocated
an alliance between radical feminism and socialism, Rouzade's goal was
to develop a collectivist theory of feminism. She was evidently familiar
with Fourierism and resurrected the demand that the traditional mother
role be collectivized. In the 1880s, however, even collectivists were horrified
by this notion. [58]

After 1879, the workers' party accepted the principle of sexual equality,
but it divided over a strategy for implementation. The party's head, the
Marxist Jules Guesdes, argued that sexual equality would follow from the
social revolution and that it would be wrong to work now, before the
revolution, to obtain civil and political rights—"bourgeois rights"—for
women. The Union des Femmes felt strongly that Guesdes's policy, a do-
nothing policy in the political context of the 1880s, was antifeminist. They
had friends enough in the party, particularly in the "gradualist" wing led
by Paul Brousse, to win acceptance of a compromise position. At the
1880 Le Havre party congress, a resolution was passed instructing the
party to work for women's civil and political rights, not necessarily because
these rights were significant by themselves but rather because they would
attract women to the party.

The Union des Femmes was short-lived, a victim, unfortunately, of the
infighting among opposing factions of the workers' party. In 1881, the
Union des Femmes proposed that the party back Rouzade for office for
a seat on the Paris Municipal Council. Although the Broussists worked
for her election, the Guesdists did not: this became the pretext for the
next significant split in French socialism. Rouzade was on Brousse's side,
of course, and, like Auclert before her, became inactive in socialism after
siding with the losing faction.

In the 1890s, Eugénie Potonié-Pierre was the most active among feminists
of all political standings. Deraismes and Richer had retired; Auclert was
living in Algeria; Rouzade had become less active after the defeat of the

Eugénie Potonié-Pierre. Courtesy Bibl. Marguerite Durand

gradualists. Potonié-Pierre organized two congresses, one in 1892 and another in 1896, that brought together a wide range of republican and socialist feminists. Her influence even brought Paule Mink back into the feminist fold. She also involved other former communardes, including Nathalie Lemel, now active in the trade union or syndicalist movement, and new, younger syndicalists such as Marie Bonnevial, one of the founders of the teacher's union. But Potonié-Pierre could not bridge the widening gap between bourgeois and working-class women. An alliance between socialism and republicanism was possible only in earlier decades, when both groups were associationist and the perceived enemy was the upper-classes (the "notables"). Now the republican middle classes were the establishment and governed in their class interest while the working class had adopted the ideology of class struggle. Feminism was helpless, for the present, to overcome this division in French politics.

The 1890s, following the retirement and death of so many experienced leaders (even the younger Potonié-Pierre died unexpectedly of a cerebral hemorrhage in 1898), was a time of floundering for feminist groups. Yet in this instance, the setback was momentary, a pause rather than a true arresting of feminist activism. The leaders of the twentieth-century movement were already emerging. They were present at the 1889, 1892, and 1896 congresses and were learning from the experience of the older generation. A momentum had been established.

By the century's end, feminists had a clear sense of direction. Their frequent congresses had allowed them to discuss, debate, and vote on a program that was widely endorsed among them. It was a step-by-step plan of action to translate vision into reality, to obtain political, economic, and sexual equality for women. Much of their program now concerned political rights: the suffrage issue had been legitimated. They sought, too, the civil rights of French citizenship, such as the right to witness and notarize official documents, to be guardians of children in addition to their own, and to sit on juries. They demanded the right to administer the conditions of work (to sit on the *conseils des prud'hommes* and the *tribunes de commerce*) and pressed for economic equality: a secondary education that would, like men's, prepare them for the *baccalauréat* examinations (key to entering France's professional schools); and their right to work at jobs of their own choosing, to be paid for their work at rates equal to men's, and to control their own earnings. Sexual equality would be obtained by liberating both wives and prostitutes from arbitrary male domination: wives, by revamping the Civil Code to create a true partnership in marriage, and prostitutes, by holding men financially responsible for the support of their illegitimate offspring *(recherche de paternité)* and by abolishing the *police des moeurs* and the Saint-Lazare prison, thus assuring prostitutes their basic civil rights.

Some of the feminist program was realized by century's end: in 1897, women secured the right to witness public acts (although this applied to single women only) and, in 1898, the right to vote for judges of the *tribunes de commerce* (although not the right to sit as judges themselves). In 1885, women had gained the right to practice medicine in the public hospitals and, in 1900, they won the right to practice law. For feminists, the nineteenth century ended on an optimistic note.

Conclusion

An overview of feminist development in nineteenth-century France reveals a history that is discontinuous, tied in important ways to the political fluctuations of French history, to a variety of traditions that contradict one another (Enlightenment individualism versus utopian socialism, for example), and to a set of particular experiences in definable epochs. This discontinuity contrasts dramatically with the largely continuous history of American and English feminism and explains the comparatively slower pace of success.

In France in the nineteenth century, when politics divided the country sharply in two, the fate of feminism was always linked to the fate of the political Left. Illiberal regimes feared the revolutionary potential of the Left and repressed leftist propaganda and organizing. This explains nineteenth-century French feminism's recurring start-and-stop cycles and the frequency with which an entire generation of experienced leaders was silenced, as happened in 1793, in 1834, in 1850, and in 1871. The effect of the 1850 repression was particularly devastating. Previously, French feminism was the most advanced and energetic feminist movement in the Western world, but by 1850 its leaders were all in jail or in exile.

Only after the liberal republicans secured their power in 1879 did the political climate for feminism change. Only then did it become less dangerous to propagandize and organize. As the century drew to a close, feminists were hopeful of success. They scored many legislative victories; most important were the creation of girls' secondary schools and the reestablishment of divorce. This momentum continued into the twentieth century. At the moment when sheer frustration at their lack of success was driving English and then American feminists into increasing militancy, French feminists were confident that the government was on their side and that success was near.[1] In 1907, they won for mothers the right to equal authority with the father over minor children; the right of the mother alone, in the case of illegitimate children, to exercise the "paternal" authority; and the right of married women to control their own earnings. In 1912, they established women's rights to initiate a paternity suit. A truly universal suffrage bill passed the Chamber of Deputies in 1919, but the political climate changed dramatically at that point and the bill was held up by the Senate until 1944.

This chronicling of the fate of nineteenth-century French feminism challenges historian Theodore Zeldin's contention that "feminism failed in France [because] it came early, . . . burned itself out, and produced a conservative reaction among women already in 1914." [2] It is now clear that feminism, which indeed came early in France, was frustrated at the start and that its progress was slowed—not because it "burned itself out" but because repressive governments repeatedly burned feminism. The pattern of feminism's failures and successes is actually the reverse of that which Zeldin noted. Although feminists continued to face reaction among women and men alike in the early years of the twentieth century, their movement was stronger then than ever.

The politics, as well as the fate, of French feminists was tied to their leftist allies. French feminism in the nineteenth century was both republican and socialist, and the differing programs feminists offered over the course of the century reflect these differing and sometimes contradictory traditions. In nineteenth-century France, feminism emerged among the Saint-Simonian socialists, a self-styled religious group. Suzanne Voilquin used religious terminology to describe her conversion to feminism. "I experienced a kind of dazzlement . . . God had spoken to me and truly brought me back to life." [3] The Saint-Simonian feminists had a vision that encompassed every area of human activity—private relationships between men and women and public activities in the economic and political sphere. They imagined a new social relationship of the sexes, one that would liberate women from arbitrary male domination. The vision was revolutionary, but the problem became how to implement it.

Saint-Simonians translated their vision into an attack on the patriarchal family. First, they called for free-love unions but then discovered that women's lives were unbalanced at the least, shattered at the worst, by their inability to provide support for themselves and their children. The Fourierists offered an alternative program of replacing the conjugal family by communal living and working units. They could not, however, implement their plan, for lack of money and lack of interest. The creation of an effective program of action necessitated compromise; it also promised some measure of success.[4] By 1834, feminists had switched their focus and reordered their priorities. They determined that economic independence must precede any further attack on the family. Their revised program rejected the *patriarchal* family, but no longer the family. If women could "freely" choose husbands (that is, marry for love rather than financial considerations) and be permitted to divorce husbands to rectify youthful mistakes, that was free enough union for the time being. Marriage should be equalized rather than destroyed.

The first vision also included sexual liberation. But here, too, experience transformed feminism, moving the program away from a single liberating standard of sexual morals toward a different but still single standard that extolled the old-fashioned virtues. This shift in feminist opinion was a logical response to the reality of women's experience in the nineteenth century. The women among the first nineteenth-century French feminists recognized that Enfantin's sexual liberation was not theirs. Their recognition came not simply because such liberation threatened unbearable financial burdens but also because nineteenth-century sexual relations were unlikely to be liberating, more likely to be unsatisfying if not actually life-endangering for women. Of all nineteenth-century French feminists, only Fourier and, later, Deraismes demanded women's rights to sexual feelings or fulfillment. Only Suzanne Voilquin referred to any aspect of her own sexual experience, but she wrote only of venereal disease, repeated miscarriages, and finally several years of mutually agreed-upon abstinence. The single standard of sexual morals that we call "Victorian" was propagated by women to serve women's needs.[5] Feminists agreed.

Saint-Simonians believed that women's character was inherently different from men's, but, in their view, this belief did not conflict with their goal that women "have the means to live independently."[6] Although Romantic patriarchalists had used arguments stressing women's uniqueness to limit women's public role, Saint-Simonian feminists argued that women's "inherent" pacifist and maternal traits necessitated their participation in the public sphere—by which they meant not only the rights and duties of citizenship but also access to jobs and professions on equal terms with men. Yet feminists who advocated women's equal participation in the public sphere never called for men's equal participation in the domestic sphere. Pauline Roland reconciled the demand for independence and the acceptance of sole domestic responsibility by claiming "woman alone is the family."[7] Claire Démar also insisted on independence from men but assumed that women alone would tend to children's daily needs. Although she wanted government employees to take on childrearing responsibilities and thus free women for other, nonmaternal jobs, these government employees would be women. Fourierists took the same position. In contrast to the Saint-Simonians, they did not teach that the nature of women differed in some innate way from men's; in this respect they followed the tradition of Enlightenment individualism. But they still assumed that women should manage domestic life. Fourier's radicalism was in his advocacy of the destruction of the isolated household and its replacement by phalansteries where housekeeping and childrearing functions would be shared, but even he assumed that these functions would be performed mostly by women.

By 1848, the Saint-Simonian view of women as endowed with special virtues had merged into the Romantic cult of motherhood. Feminists once again were responding to the reality of women's experience. The contemporary ideology of motherhood extolled female virtues, while other aspects of the nineteenth-century concept of womanhood denigrated women by viewing them as being limited in intelligence and naturally submissive. Feminists built on the respect accorded women as mothers to demand their better treatment. In the historically specific circumstances of mid-nineteenth-century France, then, the cult of motherhood actually served feminism's purpose.

The fact that nineteenth-century French feminists used the concept of motherhood to demand equal rights for women may help explain why they never advocated birth control.[8] The practice was widespread in France throughout this period, and feminists, who had small families, themselves probably practiced some method of family limitation. But condemnation of birth control was at least as widespread as its actual practice. Among right-wing politicians, allied with the Catholic church, approval for birth control was unthinkable; but even among socialists the practice was condemned. Socialists were reacting to the antipoor bias of the early birth control advocates, whose arguments were still closely linked to Malthusian population control arguments.[9] Utopian socialist feminists were also put off by the Malthusian link to birth control. In 1848, Désirée Gay wrote: "As women . . . we protest the ideas of Malthus. We have witnessed with pain, these past few years, the activities of Miss Martineau and several other intelligent English women who have declared themselves in favor of this doctrine . . . [which is] immoral."[10]

It may also have been difficult for feminists to advocate birth control without seeming to advocate sexual liberation, which, by the late 1830s, they had ceased to do. The language of birth control advocates would of necessity focus attention on women's sexuality, and this would have been perceived as dangerous. Not only might the very discussion of sexual matters provoke the wrath of the government, but also feminists would likely feel threatened in a more personal, psychic way by advocating something that would liberate them sexually when they did not believe this to be in their best interests. In the United States, feminists had the same attitude toward sexuality; but there they did not ignore the birth control issue but rather resolved their ambivalence by demanding "voluntary motherhood" by planned abstinence rather than contraception.[11]

After 1870, republicans dominated the feminist movement. Their program differed in significant ways from the earlier socialist program. The political context had changed; the class base of the movement had changed; women's material reality had changed.

In 1879, republicans gained control of the National Assembly. Republican feminists championed the reforms that their socially conservative yet politically liberal friends could be influenced to pass into law. They concentrated their energies on winning over influential public figures to the justice of their cause.

This alliance with republicans in power worked to the feminists' advantage. The republican emphasis on individual equality and also the opportunity that a liberal regime finally provided to organize, to publish, and to speak out created the conditions for political change. But there can be no question that the legislative victories were testimony to the feminists' hard work. Whereas Richard Evans contends that new education and divorce laws resulted from republican anticlerical influence and concern,[12] we have seen that republican anticlericalism (recall Rousseau or Michelet) was not feminist until feminists convinced anticlericals of the logic of the alliance.[13] Feminists clarified and propagandized the demand for improved female education. Léon Richer actually wrote the divorce bill that Alfred Naquet introduced in the Chamber of Deputies. True, feminists convinced legislators of only a piece of their total demands. The divorce law, for example, did not permit divorce by mutual consent or allow a partner found guilty of adultery to remarry. The 1880 Camille Sée Law failed to include a course of study that prepared girls for the *baccalauréat* examination.[14] But even these limited reforms were significant to the experience of French women and to the future of feminism. The establishment of free and obligatory primary schooling and the possibilities for higher education threw into sharper relief the discrimination that still burdened women. Better educated women resented that they were not prepared for the *baccalauréat* exams. Although more women than ever could become schoolteachers, there were far too few positions for the many women who sought them. Other professional jobs needed to be opened to women. And the situation of the schoolteacher was not enviable. She was sent off into the provinces, spied upon by local authorities, restricted in her activities, and resented by right-wing sympathizers and by all Catholics because she represented the anticlerical state.[15] The next generation of feminists would be heavily represented by schoolteachers; the Ecole Normale Supérieure at Sèvres would be a particularly receptive recruiting place for feminist activists.

Although few of the feminists' reforms could be passed without the alliance with republicans, the limitations of these gains also reflected republican limitations. The lack of discussion of social and economic questions among the feminists' allies precluded structural changes that went beyond legal and constitutional reform.

Changes in ideology reflected also the changing class base of the movement. Working-class women were most concerned about women's sexual vulnerability, economic insecurity, and double burden when wage work was added to domestic work. In the first half of the century when working-class women shaped the movement's direction, their issues were paramount. Bourgeois feminists were most concerned about civil and political rights, married women's property rights, and access to the professions. When leadership in the movement passed to them, in the 1870s, feminist priorities shifted accordingly.

Nonetheless, for most of the century, feminists of both classes worked together. The number of feminist activists was not large; feminists knew each other well and met together frequently. There was a feeling of trust among them and agreement on a wide range of feminist concerns. Although they sometimes disagreed on priorities, for most of the century they did not allow their differences to interfere with their limited opportunities for action.

Toward the end of the century, however, disagreements between bourgeois and working-class feminists became more difficult to resolve. By this time, the movement was larger and more highly structured, and its leadership was more identified with the bourgeois political establishment. Feminism's class perspective narrowed and, on occasion, instances of prejudice erupted that marred the increasingly tenuous class alliance.[16] The split between working-class and bourgeois feminists related to the split between republicans and socialists. Only late in the century did the republicans come to power; socialists remained in opposition, only now they were in opposition to the republicans. At the same time the two political groups were becoming increasingly class-identified. Feminists, too, were dividing by class.

An examination of one century of feminism's much longer history reveals an ideology closely linked to women's material reality. Most obvious was the effect of changing work opportunities, which, for most of the nineteenth century, seemed to worsen. The evolution in feminist ideology reflected women's increased economic insecurity. Only late in the century did new opportunities arise, primarily in the public service sector. These jobs, however, were highly competitive and open to educated women only; not surprisingly, feminists then increased their pressure for higher education. Republican feminists also fought to open more professional jobs to women, a matter of particular concern to young and unmarried women of their class. They championed, too, the right of any woman—younger or older, single or married—to choose the fulfillment of a vocation for which she might believe herself particularly suited. The "right to choose" sense of their arguments was in the tradition of Enlightenment individualism; it is not certain that republican feminists really expected married women of their own class to work. More likely they assumed that autonomy for the married bourgeois woman would follow from her right to administer her own property and her share of the community. This belief corresponded to the values of most bourgeois French men who, unlike Saint-Simon and his followers in earlier decades, did not esteem highly productive labor activities but valued instead the aristocratic lifestyle of property management and political involvement.

Although the successes of nineteenth-century feminism date from the years of republican dominance of the movement, the role of earlier utopian socialist feminists should not be underestimated. Their influence was certainly larger than their numbers would suggest. Before 1850, several hundred women may have been connected to Saint-Simonism and the Fourierists in Paris and Lyons. Elsewhere in France, the numbers were even fewer. Suzanne Voilquin and Flora Tristan toured France, and both recorded that women rarely welcomed their ideas. Yet in spite of their limited numbers, utopian feminists were able to create a reservoir of good feeling and sympathy for women that was translated into an improved image of women in Romantic literature and greater attention to the worst abuses that had condemned poor women in particular to lives of misery. Later reforms, especially in education, could not have been achieved without the energetic activity of these utopians. That nineteenth-century France adopted a more favorable attitude toward women is not controversial. What has not been well enough understood, however, is the utopian feminist contribution to these new sentiments. The roots of Romantic thought extend back to Rousseau and therefore to a misogynist source. It was the utopians who transformed the Romantic attitude toward women. Popular writers such as George Sand and Victor Hugo credited these feminists with influencing their writings, although often the popular writers did not grasp or support the entire feminist message.[17]

The influence of French feminism extended beyond the borders of France. John Stuart Mill was a friend of the Saint-Simonian Gustave d'Eichthal. In his *Autobiography,* Mill traces his feminism to Saint-Simonian influences.[18] Fourier's dreams of associationist communities were never realized in France but fared better in the United States. Angelina Grimké Weld and her husband Theodore lived for several years in a community inspired by

Fourierist teaching. In later decades, communications between foreign and French feminists continued; only then, the American and English feminists became the inspiration to the French. Hubertine Auclert corresponded with Susan B. Anthony. Theodore Stanton resided in Paris and was closely associated with Auclert and Léon Giraud; he also knew Richer and Deraismes. Josephine Butler, the leader of the campaign against the English Contagious Diseases Act, traveled and spoke in France. She knew Maria Deraismes and Julie Daubié, some of whose work she translated into English. Before 1889, most French feminists were anticlericals of Catholic descent, but by 1900, a significant number of Protestants and Jews were among the feminist leadership. Their "conversion" to feminism owed much to their personal and familial ties to English and American feminists.

By 1900, French feminists had adopted a program and determined to implement it by using political tactics based on compromise. Seemingly conservative, the program nonetheless provided a plan of action that sustained feminism in later decades. In her pathbreaking 1966 article, "The Longest Revolution," Juliet Mitchell attempted to describe the complexity of change that feminism demands. She categorized women's experience into four "structures"—production, reproduction, sexuality, and socialization of children—and posited that the liberation of women can be achieved only if all four structures are transformed. She nonetheless recognized the possibility of piecemeal revolution: "A revolutionary movement must base its analysis on the uneven development of each structure and attack the weakest link in the combination. This may then become the point of departure for a general transformation." [19] This sounds like Deraismes's "politique des brèches." In fact, Deraismes's "error" may have been only that she misjudged the "weakest link." She hoped first to equalize marriage through reforms of the Civil Code, but the vote, not marriage, proved to be the weakest link. [20] Not Deraismes's marriage reform but Auclert's suffrage was the first "breach" after all.

During the nineteenth century, no feminist group attempted to organize women into a mass political movement. The Saint-Simonians had traveled widely to propagandize their point of view, but they did little actual organizing and, further, the organizing that they did do—in Paris and Lyons—was not for political work. Flora Tristan wanted to organize workers throughout France into unions that would be feminist as well as socialist, but she died before she had gotten very far. Other feminists throughout the century, however, functioned either as propagandists and/or organized small, local groups whose purpose was to pressure the Paris-based government to decree or legislate reforms. In this respect, they functioned like other nineteenth-century French political groups.

Yet gains in civil rights and professional opportunities, the result of feminist activities during the nineteenth century, would make possible the organizing of women into a mass movement in the twentieth century. When the socialist parties transformed the nature of French politics and created a new rank-and-file party, feminists were ready to follow suit. By placing nineteenth-century French feminism within its historical context, by understanding the framework in which it developed as well as what preceded and what followed it, it becomes clear that this movement was a significant chapter in the centuries-long struggle to emancipate women—a part of the longest revolution.

Notes

Notes to Chapter 1

1. Among the many studies that describe the patriarchal system, see especially Simone de Beauvoir, *The Second Sex,* trans. H. M. Parshley (New York: Bantam Books, 1961); Dorothy Dinnerstein, *The Mermaid and the Minotaur: Sexual Arrangements and Human Malaise* (New York: Harper & Row, 1977); Frederick Engels, *The Origin of the Family, Private Property, and the State,* trans. Robert Vernon (New York: Pathfinder Press, 1972); Eva Figes, *Patriarchal Attitudes* (Greenwich, Conn.: Fawcett, 1970); Margaret Mead, *Male and Female* (New York: William Morrow & Co., 1975); Margaret Mead, *Sex and Temperament* (New York: William Morrow & Co., 1963); Kate Millet, *Sexual Politics* (New York: Doubleday & Co., 1970); Juliet Mitchell, *Psychoanalysis and Feminism* (New York: Vintage Books, 1975); Adrienne Rich, *Of Woman Born: Motherhood as Experience and Institution* (New York: W. W. Norton, 1976); and Evelyne Sullerot, *Woman, Society, and Change,* trans. Margaret Scotford Archer (New York: McGraw-Hill World University Library, 1971).

Historians are unable either to pinpoint the origin of patriarchy or to provide an adequate explanation for its widespread acceptance. Anthropologists (see especially Mead, *Sex and Temperament*) and historians can uncover an endless variety of ways that different cultures may distinguish sex roles. Clearly, our modern Western understanding of "appropriate" sex roles is not universal. But some distinctions based on sex, and value systems in which the female role is viewed as inferior or subordinate, do in fact appear to be universal. In the nineteenth century, the social anthropologist Lewis Morgan wrote an influential study setting forth "evidence" that matriarchal civilizations had existed before patriarchal civilization. This evidence, however, is not convincing to many twentieth-century scholars (feminists included). Also in the nineteenth century, Engels argued that the origins of patriarchy coincided with the origins of private property. Today's scholars, however, attribute the "cause" of patriarchy to a complex of reasons including private property but also relating to the "institution" of motherhood (see especially Rich and Dinnerstein) and even sexual fears (see especially Claude Lévi-Strauss, *Structure Anthropology,* trans. Claire Jacobson and Brooke Grundtest Schoept [London: Penguin Press, 1968] on the incest taboo). In *Woman, Culture, and Society,* ed. Michelle Zimbalist Rosaldo and Louise Lamphere (Stanford: Stanford University Press, 1974), Rosaldo presents a useful private/public dichotomy to cope with the female/male dichotomy. She thus recognizes the universality of patriarchy but at the same time discusses historical and cultural variations. Her thesis is that when the public/private dichotomy is sharpest, women's status is lowest and vice versa.

2. In nineteenth-century France, the wife's adultery was no longer considered punishable by death, but several causes célèbres indicate that the husband who killed his unfaithful wife was considered to be "avenging his honor." He was usually punished only lightly, if at all.

3. In Greek, Roman, and Judaic law, a woman passed from the tutelage of her father to that of her husband, or upon widowhood to that of his male relative, or, finally, of her own son if he were the only remaining male in the family. She could be given a dowry, but that would not become *her* property.

4. 1 Timothy 2:12.

5. Ephesians 5:22–23.

6. Galatians 3:28.

7. 1 Corinthians 11:7–9.

8. de Beauvoir, *The Second Sex*, p. 93.

9. Héloise is the best-known such woman of this era.

10. This is the conclusion of David Herlihy. See "Land, Family, and Women in Continental Europe," *Traditio* 18 (1962): 89–120.

11. See especially Jacob B. Burkhardt, *The Civilization of the Renaissance in Italy* (New York: New American Library, 1961).

12. The same conclusion is made in pathbreaking studies by Joan Kelly-Gadol, who used, as example, the Italian Renaissance experience, and Hilda Smith, who focused on England in the sixteenth and seventeenth centuries. See Joan Kelly-Gadol, "Did Women have a Renaissance?" in Renate Bridenthal and Claudia Koonz, eds., *Becoming Visible: Women in European History,* (Boston: Houghton Mifflin, 1977), pp. 137–64; Joan Kelly-Gadol, "The Social Relation of the Sexes: Methodological Implications of Women's History," *Signs* 1 (Summer 1976): 809–23; and Hilda Smith, "Feminism and the Methodology of Women's History," in Berenice A. Carroll, ed., *Liberating Women's History* (Urbana: University of Illinois Press, 1976), pp. 369–84.

13. Originally universities had served to train clergy, an important but limited function. The exclusion of women from the university dates to its clerical (and thus male, celibate) past.

14. Philippe Ariès, *Centuries of Childhood: A Social History of Family Life,* trans. Robert Baldick (New York: Vintage Books, 1962), p. 58: "Boys were the first specialized children. They began going to school in large numbers as far back as the late sixteenth century and the early seventeenth century. The education of girls started in a small way only in the time of Fénelon and Mme. de Maintenon and developed slowly and tardily. Without a proper educational system, the girls were confused with the women at an early age, just as the boys had formerly been confused with the men, and nobody thought of giving visible form, by means of dress, to a distinction which was beginning to exist in reality for the boys but which still remained futile for the girls."

15. See Smith, "Feminism and Methodology of Women's History," pp. 380–82, for a critique of Ariès's equation of "boyhood" with "childhood": "What Ariès fails to grasp . . . is that the phenomenon he is witnessing comes more from a changing conception of manhood than from a developing view of childhood. . . . It is not so much that boys were confused with men in the medieval period but that the ideal of the adult male had not taken its form as yet. That ideal is intricately connected with all of those changes Ariès notes in his work—educational advancement, economic in-

dependence and a general emphasis on individual accomplishment. In practical terms this development led to an exclusion of women from the humanist brand of learning because of their limited vocation. Their domestic service did not require the training of the diplomat, or bureaucrat, or merchant."

16. Olwen Hufton, "Women and the Family Economy in Eighteenth-Century France," *French Historical Studies* 9 (Spring 1975): 11. Hufton makes clear that this new role for women remained unknown in the popular classes for several centuries after it became common for upper-class women.

17. Carolyn C. Lougee, *Le Paradis des femmes: Women, Salons, and Social Stratification in Seventeenth-Century France* (Princeton: Princeton University Press, 1976), pp. 5, 53–54.

18. Evelyn Gordon Bodek, "Salonières and Bluestockings: Educated Obsolescence and Germinating Feminism," *Feminist Studies* 3 (Spring–Summer, 1976): 186. "The salon was really an informal university for women—a place where they could exchange ideas, avail themselves of some of the best minds of their time, receive and give criticism, read their own works and hear the works of others, and, in general, pursue in their own way some form of higher education" (ibid., p. 185).

19. Ibid., pp. 191–92.

20. Jean-Jacques Rousseau, *Politics and the Arts: Letter to M. D'Alembert on the Theatre,* trans. Allan Bloom (Glencoe, Ill.: Free Press, 1960), p. 105. See also Rousseau, *Emile,* trans. Barbara Foxley (New York: Dutton, 1933), pp. 371–72: "I would a thousand times rather have a homely girl, simply brought up, than a learned lady and a wit who would make a literary circle of my house and instal [sic] herself as its president. A female wit is a scourge to her husband, her children, her servants, to everybody. From the lofty height of her genius she scorns every womanly duty, and she is always trying to make a man of herself after the fashion of Mlle. de L'Enclos. Outside her home she always makes herself ridiculous and she is very rightly a butt for criticism, as we always are when we try to escape from our own position into one for which we are unfitted."

21. Lougee, *Le Paradis des femmes,* p. 41.

22. Rousseau, *Emile,* pp. 372, 350.

23. Ibid., p. 324–25, 322.

24. See the collection of essays by Theodore Zeldin, *Conflicts in French Morality* (London: George Allen & Unwin, 1970). His thesis is that on a wide variety of cultural and moral issues the concept of the "two Frances" was hardly true. He does not discuss the ideology of womanhood, but in this case, too, his thesis holds.

25. Quoted in Paule-Marie Duhet, *Les Femmes et la Révolution, 1789–1794* (Paris: Julliard, 1971), pp. 154–55, 206. According to Duhet, this anonymous passage appeared in the semiofficial *Feuille de salut public.*

26. Quoted in Raymond Deniel, *Une Image de la famille et de la société sous la restauration* (Paris: Les Editions Ouvrières, 1965), pp. 103, 191.

27. See Mary Daly, *Gyn/Ecology: The Metaethics of Radical Feminism* (Boston: Beacon Press, 1978), chap. 6; and Gunnar Heinsohn and Otto Steiger, "The Elimination of Medieval Birth Control and the Witch Trials of Modern Times," *International Journal of Women's Studies* (May–June 1982): 193–214.

28. The work of Christine de Pizan can be studied in Mathilde Laigle, *Le Livre des trois vertus de Christine de Pisan et son milieu historique et litteraire* (Paris: Honoré Champion, 1912). See also Susan Groag Bell, "Christine de Pizan (1364–1430): Humanism and the Problem of a Studious Woman," *Feminist Studies* 3 (Spring–Summer

1976): 173–84, which provides detailed biographical data including the correct spelling of the author's name; Lula McDowell Richardson, *The Forerunners of Feminism in French Literature of the Renaissance from Christine of Pisa to Marie de Gournay* (Baltimore: Johns Hopkins University Press, 1929); and Léon Abensour, *La Femme et le féminisme avant la Révolution* (Paris: Leroux, 1923). Richardson's appreciation of Christine de Pizan is far more restrained than Abensour's. Abensour finds in her works the first expression of feminism as we know it today; he bases all the feminist treatises of succeeding centuries upon the *Trésor des dames* and *La Cité des dames*. See Richardson, p. 34, and Abensour, pp. v–vi. The focus of Bell's study shifts from the origins of feminism to the life situation of a particular class of women ("studious" women) during the Renaissance. Bell thus highly "appreciated" Christine de Pizan without claiming for her the invention of feminism.

There is now an English translation of Christine de Pizan's *The Book of the City of Ladies* by Earl Jeffrey Richards (New York: Persea Books, 1982).

29. Mademoiselle de Gournay's *L'Egalité des hommes et des femmes* and her *Grief des dames* are collected by Maria Schiff in *La Fille d'alliance de Montaigne, Marie de Gournay* (Paris: Honoré Champion, 1910).

30. Poullain's works include *Egalité des deux sexes* (Paris: Sean du Puis, 1673), *La Liberté des dames* (Paris: Christophe Rémy, 1685), and *Education des dames* [publication information unknown]. These works are discussed in Henri Grappin, "Notes sur un feministe oublié: Le cartesian Poullain de la Barre," *Revue d'histoire litteraire de la France* (1913): 852–67; G. Lefèvre, "Poullain de la Barre et le féminisme au XVIIᵉ siècle," *Revue pédagogique* 64 (February 1914): 101–13; Lougee, *Le Paradis des femmes;* and Marie Louise Stock, "Poullain de la Barre: A Seventeenth-Century Feminist" (Ph.D. dissertation, Columbia University, 1961). According to Abensour, *La Femme et le féminisme avant la Révolution,* p. 154: "When feminism will have triumphed, his works will be celebrated as classics like *De l'esprit des lois* and the *Social Contract* in a democracy."

31. Poullain, cited in Stock, "Poullain de la Barre," p. 113.

32. See Fénelon, *De l'Education des filles* (Lyons: Rusand, 1809), and *Madame de Maintenon, institutrice* (Paris: H. Oudin, 1885), a collection of her writings edited by Emile Faquet.

33. See the list of the forty-three works published between 1713 and 1787 that Maïté Albistur and Daniel Armogathe include in a section aptly titled "Rebondissement de la querelle des femmes" (*Histoire du feminisme français,* 2 vols. [Paris: Editions des femmes, 1977], 1:166–68).

34. According to Stock (see "Poullain de la Barre," p. 197), his works continued to be quoted throughout most of the eighteenth century, falling into oblivion only at the end of that century. They were rediscovered in the early part of the twentieth century by Henri Piéson and Ascoli.

35. François Marie Arouet Voltaire, *Oeuvres complètes,* vol. 5, *Prix de la justice et de l'humanité* (Paris: Firmin Didot Frères, 1854–58), p. 454.

36. Abby R. Kleinbaum, "Women in the Age of Light," in Bridenthal and Koonz, eds., *Becoming Visible,* p. 221.

37. Charles de Secondet Montesquieu, *De l'Esprit des lois* (Paris: Firmin Didot Frères, 1868), pp. 243–45.

38. Denis Diderot and Jean le Rond d'Alembert, *Encyclopédie ou dictionnaire raisonné des sciences, des arts, et des metiers,* 17 vols. (Paris: David Le Breton, Durand, 1756), 6:468–76.

39. Denis Diderot, *De l'education publique* (Amsterdam: N.p., 1762).

40. Kleinbaum, "Women in the Age of Light," p. 226.

41. Evelyne Sullerot, *Histoire de la presse féminine en France, des origines à 1848* (Paris: Armand Colin, 1966).

42. Duhet, *Les Femmes et la Révolution,* p. 34. This document and many more from the 1789 to 1795 period have been translated into English and published in Darline Gay Levy, Harriet Branson Applewhite, and Mary Durham Johnson, *Women in Revolutionary Paris, 1789–1795: Selected Documents Translated with Notes and Commentary* (Urbana: University of Illinois Press, 1979).

43. Duhet, *Les Femmes et la Révolution,* p. 37.

44. Ibid., p. 41.

45. Elizabeth Racz, "The Women's Rights Movement in the French Revolution," *Science and Society* 16 (1952): 153.

46. Edwin Randolph Hedman, "Early French Feminism from the Eighteenth Century to 1848" (Ph.D. dissertation, New York University, 1954), p. 47.

47. Duhet, *Les Femmes et la Révolution,* p. 25.

48. I have translated from the text that is reproduced in Hubertine Auclert, *Le Vote des femmes* (Paris: V. Giard & E. Brière, 1908), p.78. The Levy, Applewhite, and Johnson book includes the entire text in translation, pp. 87–96.

49. Freely translated: "We led our canons to Versailles with braggadocio; it should be known that, even though we're only women, our courage is not to be sneered at." Quoted in Jane Abray, "Feminisim in the French Revolution," *American Historical Review* 80 (February 1975): 49.

50. Sullerot, *Histoire de la presse féminine,* p. 48.

51. Before 1793, the ony Parisian women's club was Etta Palm's Cercle Patriotique des Amies de la Vérité.

52. Duhet, *Les Femmes et la Révolution,* pp. 114–21.

53. Ibid., p. 130.

54. Ibid., p. 138.

55. Abray, "Feminism in the French Revolution," p. 57.

56. Françoise d'Eaubonne, *Histoire et actualité du féminisme* (Paris: Alain Moreau, 1972), p. 109.

57. Quoted in Duhet, *Les Femmes et la Révolution,* p. 164.

58. Sullerot, *Histoire de la presse féminine,* pp. 115–23. Sullerot has also found a cartoon dating from 1808, ridiculing the *Athénée,* and she hypothesizes that this may indicate that the journal did last longer than two issues and did have some public readership.

Notes to Chapter 2

1. Nicole Bothorel and Marie-Françoise Laurent, "La Femme en France au XIXᵉ siècle," in Pierre Grimal, ed., *Histoire mondiale de la femme* (Paris: Nouvelle Librairie de France, 1967), 4:118–19.

2. Marie d'Agoûlt, *Nélida* (Brussels: Méline, Cans et Compagnie, 1846), p. 178.

3. *Code Napoléon,* Edition originale et seule officielle (Paris: Imprimerie impériale, 1807). The Civil Code is often referred to as the Napoleonic Code. Napoleon participated

in the discussions of the draft and reportedly influenced many of the decisions affecting women.

I have reproduced the pertinent articles of the code in their original French for the convenience of those who may wish to examine my interpretation.

Art. 37: "Les témoins produits aux actes de l'état civil ne pourront être que de sexe masculin. . . ." Art. 980: "Les témoins appelés pour être présents aux testaments devront être mâles, majeurs."

4. Ibid., art. 442: "Ne peuvent être tuteurs, ni membres des conseils de famille . . . les femmes, autres que la mère et les ascendantes. . . ." Art. 390: "Après la dissolution du mariage, arrivée par la mort naturelle ou civile de l'un des époux, la tutelle des enfants mineurs et non émancipées appartient de plein droit au survivant des père et mère."

Even in the case of her own children, the woman's guardianship was less than total, especially when she remarried: Art. 931: "Pourra néanmoins le père nommer à la mère survivante et tutrice, un conseil spécial, sans l'avis duquel elle ne pourra aucun acte rélatif à la tutelle. . . ." Art. 395: "Si la mère tutrice veut se remarier, elle devra, avant l'acte de mariage, convoquer le conseil de famille, que décidera si la tutelle doit lui être conservée. A défaut de cette convocation, elle perdra la tutelle de plein droit. . . ." Art. 399: "La mère remariée et non maintenue dans la tutelle des enfants de son premier mariage, ne peut leur choisir un tuteur. . . ." Art. 400: "Lorsque la mère remariée et maintenue dans la tutelle, aura fait choix d'un tuteur aux enfants de son premier mariage, ce choix ne sera valable qu'autant qu'il sera confirmé par le conseil de famille."

5. Ibid., arts. 217 and 1421: "Le mari administre seul les biens de la communauté. Il peut les vendre, aliéner, et hypothequer sans le concours de la femme. . . ." Art. 1422: "Il peut disposer des effets mobiliers à titre gratuit et particulier, au profit de toutes personnes, pourvu qu'il ne s'en réserve pas l'usufruit. . . ." Art. 1428: "Le mari a l'administration de tous les biens personnels de la femme. . . ." Art. 905: "Le femme mariée ne pourra donner entre-vifs sans l'assistance ou le consentement spécial de son mari, ou sans y être autorisée par la justice."

6. Ibid., art. 12: "L'étrangère qui aura épousé un Français, suivra la condition de son mari. . . ." Art. 19: "une femme française qui épousera un étranger, suivra la condition de son mari."

7. Ibid., art. 214: "La femme est obligée d'habiter avec le mari, et de le suivre partout, où il juge à propos de résider."

8. The proscription was based on article 217, which required the husband's approval and responsibility for any financial transaction the wife could undertake.

9. Ibid., art. 384: "Le père durant le mariage, et, après la dissolution du mariage, le survivant des père et mère, auront la jouissance des biens de leurs enfants jusqu'à l'âge de dix-huit ans accomplis, ou jusqu'à l'émancipation qui pourrait avoir lieu avant l'âge de dix-huit ans. . . ." Art. 389: "Le père seul, durant le mariage, administre des biens personnels de ses enfants mineurs."

10. Ibid., art. 374: "L'enfant ne peut quitter la maison personelle sans la permission de son père."

11. Ibid., art. 375: "Le père qui aura des sujets de mécontentement très-graves sur la conduite d'un enfant, aura les moyens de correction suivants. . . ." Art. 376: "Si l'enfant est âgé de moins de seize ans commencés, le père pourra le faire détenir pendant un temps qui ne pourra excéder un mois; et, à cet effet le président du tribunal d'arrondissement devra, sur sa demande, délivrer l'ordre d'arrestation. . . ." Art. 377:

"Depuis l'âge de seize ans commencés jusqu'à la majorité ou l'émancipation, le père pourra seulement réquérir la détention de son enfant pendant six mois au plus. . . ." Art. 378: "Il n'y aura, dans l'un et l'autre cas aucune écriture ni formalité judiciaire, si ce n'est l'ordre même d'arrestation, dans lequel les motifs n'en seront pas énoncés. . . ." Art. 379: "Le père est toujours maître d'abréger la durée de la détention par lui ordonnée ou réquise. Si après sa sortie l'enfant tombe dans de nouveaux écarts, la détention pourra être de nouveau ordonnée."

12. In 1807, the original code permitted divorce under these terms. In 1816, the code was amended: divorce was prohibited but the Napoleonic terms for divorce remained the terms for a legal separation. See art. 229: Le mari pourra demander la séparation de corps pour cause d'adultère de sa femme.

13. Ibid., art. 230: "La femme pourra demander la séparation de corps pour cause d'adultère de son mari, lorsqu'il aura tenu sa concubine dans la maison commune."

14. *Code des délits et des peines* (Paris: Garnery, 1810), art. 337: "La femme convaincue d'adultère subira la peine de l'emprisonnement pendant trois mois au moins et deux ans au plus. Le mari restera la maître d'arrêter." Louis Bridel, *La Femme et le droit* (Paris: Librairie F. Pichon, 1884), p. 98: "Le droit de grâce . . . a toujous été considéré comme unun du souveraine. Que deviendrait du reste la puissance maritale, si le mari n'avait toujours le droit de disposer de sa femme."

15. Ibid., art. 339: "Le mari qui aura entretenu une concubine dans la maison conjugale et qui aura été convaincue sur la plainte de sa femme, sera puni d'une amende de cent francs à deux mille francs."

16. *Code Napoléon*, art. 213: "Le mari doit protection à sa femme, la femme obéissance à son mari." According to Paule Nancel-Penard, *L'Evolution de la jurisprudence relativement à la femme depuis 1804* (Bordeaux: Thèse droit pour le doctorat, 1940), p. 85, the courts consistently interpreted this as giving the husband the right to read the wife's correspondence to get evidence for separation—after 1884, for divorce—and to approve the friends she saw at home or away. According to Bridel, *La Femme et le droit*, pp. 95–96, the courts also interpreted art. 213 to mean that "l'acte conforme à la fin du mariage" could never be indictable, even when the husband had used violence to consummate it, that is, there could be no such thing, according to the law, as rape committed by husband against wife.

17. Ibid., art. 1388: "Les époux ne peuvent déroger ni aux droits résultants de la puissance maritale sur la personne de la femme et des enfants, ou qui appartiennent au mari comme chef."

18. Ibid., art. 8: "Tout Francais jouira des droits civils."

19. According to Theodore Zeldin, *France, 1848–1945*, 2 vols. (Oxford: Clarendon Press, 1973–77), 1:199, "Thiers declared that the Civil Code was impossible to improve—at most he could suggest only a few stylistic changes."

20. Louis Henry, "The Population of France in the Eighteenth Century," in D. V. Glass and D.E.C. Eversley, eds., *Population in History* (Chicago: Aldine 1965), p. 450.

21. Pierre Goubert, "Recent Theories and Research in French Population between 1500 and 1700," trans. Margaret Hilton, in Glass and Eversley, eds., *Population in History*, p. 469. In a follow-up article Goubert qualifies this generalization, noting that new research indicates some variation in female fertility rates. Women in Brittany and in French Flanders gave birth more frequently, and in the southwestern provinces, where birth control may have been practiced, births were usually at three-year intervals.

See Pierre Goubert, "Historical Demography and the Reinterpretation of Early Modern French History: A Research Review," in Theodore Rabb and Robert Rotberg, eds., *The Family in History* (New York: Harper & Row, 1971), p. 21.

22. Jean Bourgeois-Pichat, "The General Development of the Population of France," trans. Peter Jimack, in Glass and Eversley, eds., *Population in History*, pp. 504–5: Before 1740, expectation of life at birth was thirty to thirty-five years; in 1805, thirty-five years for males, thirty-eight for females; in 1860, forth-one for males, forty-two years for females.

23. Ibid., p. 490.

24. Etienne Van de Walle qualifies this generalization in his department-by-department statistical breakdown, noting that some islands of high fertility—particularly in Brittany and the Massif Central—existed throughout the century. See *The Female Population of France in the Nineteenth Century* (Princeton: Princeton University Press, 1974), p. 10.

25. Both Bourgeois-Pichat and Van de Walle reconstruct female population: "The genesis of this project—the interest in fertility, best considered from the female angle—as well as the fact that the female population is less disturbed by migration and less exposed to exceptional mortality in times of war, and therefore can be reconstructed more easily, suggested this choice" (Van de Walle, *The Female Population*, p. viii).

26. Bourgeois-Pichat, "The General Development of the Population in France," pp. 475, 489. The exceptional pattern of the French demographic revolution explains why total population grew so much more slowly than that of other European countries. If France had maintained up to 1880 the fertility shown during the eighteenth century prior to 1770, it would have had, by 1880, a population of 88 million instead of 38 million (p. 490).

Van de Walle's reconstructed numbers differ from Bourgeois-Pichat's. Van de Walle believes that Bourgeois-Pichat overestimated the rate of fertility decline before 1800 and underestimated the speed of the decline in the early nineteenth century. He notes further that the mid-century reversal in the overall fertility decline resulted from a reversal in only some departments. In most departments the decline continued (*The Female Population*, pp. 9, 136–44).

27. See the collection of articles in Hélène Bergues et al., *La Prévention des naissances* (Paris: Presses Universitaires de France, 1960); and Orest Ranum and Patricia Ranum, eds., *Popular Attitudes towards Birth Control in Pre-Industrial France and England* (New York: Harper & Row, 1972).

28. Cited by Etienne Van de Walle in "Motivations and Technology in the Decline of French Fertility," in Robert Wheaton and Tamara K. Harevan, eds., *Family and Sexuality in French History* (Philadelphia: University of Pennsylvania Press, 1980), p. 141.

29. This is the theory of Marc Bloch, *Les Caractères originaux de l'histoire rurale française*, who first denied the argument set forth by Frédéric Le Play, *L'Organisation de la famille* (1871), that the Napoleonic Code caused changes in inheritance practices. See William Parish, Jr., and Moshe Schwartz, "Household Complexity in Nineteenth Century France," *American Sociological Review* 37 (April 1972): 154–73.

30. Philippe Ariès, "Interprétation pour une histoire des mentalités," in Bergues et al., *La Prévention des naissances*, pp. 314–23.

31. Alfred Sauvy, "Essai d'une vu d'ensemble," in Bergues et al., *La Prévention des naissances*, pp. 389–90.

32. Ariès, "Interprétation pour une histoire des mentalités," p. 316.

33. Angus McLaren "Abortion in France: Women and the Regulation of Family Size, 1800–1914," *French Historical Studies* 10 (Spring 1978): 461–85; and Van de Walle, "Motivations and Technology in the Decline of French Fertility," pp. 139–52.

34. John Hajnal, "European Marriage Patterns in Perspective," in Glass and Eversley, eds., *Population in History*, pp. 101–146.

35. See Etienne Gautier and Louis Henry, *La Population de Crulai, paroisse normande* (Paris: Institut National d'Etudes Demographiques, Travaux et Documents, 1958); and Pierre Goubert, *Beauvais et le beauvaisis de 1600 à 1730* (Paris: Ecole Pratique des Hautes Etudes, 1960). These two works establish the theory for France.

36. John Hajnal, "The Marriage Boom," *Population Index* 19 (April 1953): 84.

37. Hajnal, "European Marriage Patterns," p. 102, lists statistics for Austria, Belgium, Denmark, Finland, France, Germany, Great Britain, Holland, Iceland, Ireland, Italy, Norway, Portugal, Spain, Sweden, and Switzerland. In Germany, only 10 percent of women were still single at age forty-five to forty-nine; in Italy, 11 percent; in Spain, 10 percent; in France, 13 percent.

38. Ibid., p. 104.

39. Ghénia Avril de Sainte-Croix, *Le Féminisme* (Paris: V. Giard et E. Brière, 1907), p. 137: "The third sex—that's what they call old maids in England—hardly exists in France."

40. Hajnal, "Marriage Boom," p. 84.

41. Edward Shorter, "Illegitimacy, Sexual Revolution, and Social Change in Modern Europe," *Journal of Interdisciplinary History* 2 (1971): 265–67.

42. See Louise Tilly, Joan Scott, and Miriam Cohen, "Women's Work and European Fertility Patterns," *Journal of Interdisciplinary History* 6 (Winter 1976): 447–76; and George D. Sussman, "The Wet-Nursing Business in Nineteenth-Century France," *French Historical Studies* 9 (Fall 1975): 304–28.

43. Louis Chevalier, *Classes laborieuses et classes dangereuses à Paris pendant la première moîtié du XIXe siècle* (Paris: Plon, 1958).

44. Mary Lynn McDougall, "Working-Class Women during the Industrial Revolution," in Bridenthal and Koonz, eds., *Becoming Visible*, p. 267; and Patricia Branca, "A New Perspective on Women's Work: A Comparative Typology," *Journal of Social History* 9 (Winter 1975): 133.

45. Quoted in Evelyne Sullerot, *Histoire et sociologie du travail féminin* (Paris: Editions Gonthier, 1968), p. 99.

46. Madeleine Guilbert, *Les Femmes et l'organisation syndicale avant 1914* (Paris: Editions du Centre de la Recherche Scientifique, 1966), p. 44.

47. Louise A. Tilly and Joan W. Scott, *Women, Work, and Family* (New York: Holt Rinehart and Winston, 1978), p. 131.

48. Joan W. Scott, "Men and Women in the Parisian Garment Trades: Discussions of Family and Work in the 1830s and 1840s," forthcoming in Roderick Floud, Geoffrey Crossick, and Pat Thane, eds., *The Power of the Past: Essays in Honor of Eric Hobsbawn* (Cambridge: Cambridge University Press).

49. Quoted in Sullerot, *Histoire et sociologie du travail féminin*, pp. 91–92.

50. Ibid. Out of 112,000 working women in Paris in 1860, 60,000 were employed in needlework.

51. Sullerot, *Histoire et sociologie du travail féminin*, p. 103.

52. Quoted in Guilbert, *Les Femmes et l'organisation syndicale*, p. 46.

53. According to Julie Daubié, *La Femme pauvre au XIXᵉ siècle* (Paris: Guillaumin, 1866), p. 51, *La Statistique de l'industrie, 1850*, declared that women were excluded from composition work in the Paris printing industry. Daubié devoted an entire chapter to an industry-by-industry examination of restrictions tying women to lower-paying jobs. She also gives statistics for apprenticeship programs, for example, for printers, no female apprentices at all; for leather glove workers, 1 female, 25 males; for jewelers, 100 girls, 2,200 boys.

54. Ibid., pp. 70, 45.

55. Jules Simon, *L'Ouvrière* (Paris: Librairie Hachette, 1862), p. 286. According to Sullerot, the average female daily wage was 0.81 francs in 1840; 1.5–2 francs in 1860; and 2–2.5 francs in 1875 (*Histoire et sociologie du travail féminin*, p. 90). In the 1820s, Suzanne Voilquin earned 1.5 francs per day as an embroiderer in a small workshop; but when she could get only piecework she earned considerably less—0.58 francs a day. (See Voilquin, *Souvenirs d'une fille du peuple ou la Saint-Simonienne en Egypte* [1866; reprint, Paris: François Maspero, 1978], pp. 95, 98–99.)

56. Simon, *L'Ouvrière*, pp. 286–87.

57. Sullerot, *Histoire et sociologie du travail féminin*, p. 95.

58. Marilyn J. Boxer, "Women in Industrial Homework: The Flowermakers of Paris in the Belle Epoque," *French Historical Studies* 12 (Spring 1982): 408–9.

59. Chevalier, *Classes laborieuses et classes dangereuses*, p. 311.

60. Shorter, "Illegitimacy, Sexual Revolution, and Social Change," p. 260.

61. Daubié, *La Femme pauvre*, p. 2.

62. Louis Reybaud, *Etudes sur le régime des manufactures et conditions des ouvrières en soie* (Paris, 1859), p. 201.

63. Guilbert, *Les femmes et l'organisation syndicale*, p. 44.

64. Daubié, *La Femme pauvre*, p. 2.

65. Theresa McBride, *The Domestic Revolution: The Modernization of Household Service in England and France, 1820–1920* (New York: Holmes & Meier, 1976), pp. 57–69, 119–20. Few married women were employed in domestic work in the nineteenth century, when "day work" was still uncommon.

66. One-third did so, according to McBride, p. 98.

67. Daubié, *La Femme pauvre*, pp. 2, 400.

68. A.-J.-B. Parent-Duchâtelet, *De la prostitution dans la ville de Paris*, 2 vols. (Paris: Chez Baillière, 1836), 1:32.

69. Julie Daubié, "French Morality under the Regulation System," in Josephine Butler, ed., *The New Era: A Collection of Twenty-five Pamphlets Relating to the Contagious Diseases Acts of 1864, 1866, and 1869* (Liverpool: T. Brakell, 1872), pp. 12, 15.

70. Quoted in Léon Richer, *La Femme libre* (Paris: E. Dentu, 1877), pp. 201–4.

71. Edith Thomas, *The Women Incendiaries*, trans. James Atkinson and Starr Atkinson (New York: George Braziller, 1966), p. 15. Some of the schools were intended to be coeducational but in reality were not because few girls were permitted by their parents to attend.

72. Sandra Horvath, "Victor Duruy and the Controversy over Secondary Education for Girls," *French Historical Studies* 9 (Spring 1975): 83–104.

73. Karen Offen, "A Feminist Challenge to the Third Republic's Public Education for Girls: The Campaign for Equal Access to the Baccalauréat, 1880–1924" (Paper presented at the Annual Meeting of the American Historical Association, December 1973).

The situation was always better in cities than in small towns or villages because municipal governments often supplemented the funds made available by the central government. Among city-born girls, a primary level of education was common throughout the century. In rural areas, however, illiteracy was still widespread until the end of the century.

74. There was three of these by 1850.

75. Horvath, "Victor Duruy," p. 85.

76. Barbara Corrado Pope, "Angels in the Devil's Workshop: Leisured and Charitable Women in Nineteenth-Century England and France," in Bridenthal and Koonz, eds., *Becoming Visible,* p. 308.

77. Patriarchalists in late eighteenth- or nineteenth-century England and America more commonly handled the threat posed to male dominance by woman's autonomous sexuality by denying or disregarding the existence of that sexuality. Rousseau's Sophy or Flaubert's Emma Bovary, however, are sexual beings who require either increased solitude (Rousseau) or alternate useful activities (Flaubert) to protect male energies (Rousseau) or the social order (Flaubert).

78. Juliette Adam, "French Girls," *North American Review* 154 (April 1892): 449–50.

79. Shorter, "Illegitimacy, Sexual Revolution, and Social Change," pp. 256–57.

80. Daubié, *La Femme pauvre,* p. 20.

81. Marie d'Agoûlt, *Essai sur la liberté* (Paris: Librairie d'Amyot, 1847), p. 125.

82. Pope, "Angels in the Devil's Workshop," pp. 308–9.

83. Adam, "French Girls," p. 450.

84. According to McBride, *Domestic Revolution,* pp. 18–21, some French families which by the profession and education of the husband must be classified "bourgeois" did not employ even one servant. Approximately 50 percent of Parisian servants and 70 percent of Lyonnais servants worked alone. For a household to have more than two or three servants was unknown except among a very few extremely wealthy families. McBride notes that the number of servants per household in England, although more than in France, was fewer than commonly believed.

85. Jesse R. Pitts, "Continuity and Change in Bourgeois France," in Stanley Hoffman, ed., *In Search of France* (New York: Harper & Row, 1965), p. 255.

86. Sussman, "The Wet-Nursing Business in Nineteenth-Century France," pp. 304–28. The reverse was true among urban working-class women, who continued to send their children to the countryside to be nursed. The absolute numbers of children "put out" to be wet-nursed increased in the nineteenth century with the growth of the urban working class.

87. Barbara Corrado Pope, "Maternal Education in France" (Paper presented to the Western Society for French History, December 1975).

88. Jules Michelet, *La Femme,* 15th ed. (Paris; Calmann Lévy, 1885), pp. 37–38.

89. Adeline Daumard, *Les Bourgeois de Paris au XIXᵉ siècle* (Paris: Flammarion, 1970), p. 185.

90. According to John Shaffer, the increased numbers of schoolchildren in the last decades of the century created increased teaching opportunities for women. But the number of women qualified to become teachers and desiring access to virtually the only professional opportunity available for lay women (nuns monopolized the nursing profession) created a true crisis. In 1898, the Paris schools limited their recruiting to those who had applied before 1896, thereby cutting back to seven thousand the number of applicants for the two hundred openings that next academic year. (See Shaffer, "Family Class and

Young Women's Occupational Expectations in Nineteenth-Century Paris," in Wheaton and Hareven, eds., *Family and Sexuality in French History*, pp. 179–200.)

91. Thomas, *Women Incendiaries*, p. 17. Her statistics are from the 1860s.

92. Daubié, *La Femme pauvre*, pp. 128–73.

93. Daumard, *Les Bourgeois de Paris au XIXe siècle*, pp. 196–97.

94. Ibid., p. 187.

95. See below, chapter 6, for Sand's dissociation from the feminists in the 1848 Revolution.

96. Daumard, *Les Bourgeois de Paris au XIXe siècle*, pp. 191–96.

97. Pope, "Angels in the Devil's Workshop," p. 319.

98. Evelyne Sullerot, *La Presse féminine* (Paris: Armand Colin, 1966), pp. 19–23. The most important of these magazines were *Le Journal des femmes* (1832–35). *La Mère de famille* (1833–36), *La Mère-Institutrice* (1834–37), *Journal des mères et des jeunes filles* (1844–47), and during the Second Empire, *Le Conseiller des dames*.

Notes to Chapter 3

1. The publication of Charles Fourier's *Théorie des quatre mouvements* preceded the Saint-Simonian exposition of feminism by two decades, but Fourier's writings remained generally unknown until Victor Considérant undertook the task of "translating" them into a more comprehensible style, beginning only in 1832–34. Although I have therefore chosen to begin with the Saint-Simonians, an accurate chronology of feminism should note the likelihood that Enfantin had read Fourier and borrowed freely, although without acknowledgement, from him.

2. See G. Célestin Charles Alfred Bouglé, *Socialismes français* (Paris: Libraire Colin, 1946), pp. 372–73: "In the development of the Saint-Simonian doctrine the main character changed more than once. At first, it was the learned that [Saint-Simon] wanted to push to the foreground. At other times, bankers took the lead. Then the focus was on the proletarians. Finally—woman appears and monopolizes all attention; in her glory, one might say, the rest fades away. . . . [Then the problem of women's status] became the central problem for Saint-Simonism and the collective obsession of its followers."

3. The standard history of the Saint-Simonians remains Sébastien Charléty's *Essai sur l'histoire du Saint-Simonisme* (Paris: Hachette, 1896). I found it useful for detailing Saint-Simonism's socialist activities and theoretical development. But Charléty ignores completely the movement's feminism, the participation of women in the movement, or even the role that theoretical issues concerning women played in the internal history of the movement, such as in causing the many scissions. For these matters the best introduction is still Marguerite Thibert's *Le Féminisme dans le socialisme français de 1830 à 1850* (Paris: M. Giard, 1926).

The Saint-Simonians carefully documented both their activities and their theoretical work. Some of these materials they published themselves, others were collected, cataloged, sometimes even recopied, for what was intended to be their own library. It is these unpublished materials that make up the Fonds Enfantin (hereafter, FE) collection at the Bibliothèque de l'Arsenal. A superb bibliography of all writings relating to Saint-Simonism but particularly the unpublished materials, is Jean Walch, *Bibliographie de Saint-Simonisme* (Paris: J. Vrin, 1967).

4. In the Fonds Enfantin collection (FE 7861, no. 13), there is a clipping of an article by Eugène Pelletan from an unidentified newspaper, dated December 12, 1853. He makes a connection between Saint-Simonian practices and Ecole Polytechnique traditions. Although I am unaware of any other historian who has made this connection, I found it intriguing. "The Saint-Simonian doctrine was the Polytechnical School enlarged to the breadth of a society. Same principles for both: ranking by merit; same kind of lifestyle, regimented living conditions, the barracks, meals taken together. . . . In moving to Saint-Simonism, the artillery officer or the genius followed, under another form, the traditions of the school."

5. Both the *Globe* and *Feuilles populaires* were distributed free. The *Globe* had been a liberal journal in the 1820s, edited by Pierre Leroux; in November 1830 it (and Leroux) became Saint-Simonian. Michel Chevalier then became editor.

6. Charléty, *Histoire du Saint-Simonisme*, p. 104.

7. These figures are from ibid., pp. 102–22; Charléty notes that on some special occasions the audiences numbered in the thousands.

8. The workshops never got past the organizing stage and the workers' "rewards" for joining remained a "place in the [Saint-Simonian] hierarchy" (ibid., p. 117).

9. *The Doctrine of Saint-Simon: An Exposition, First Year, 1828–1829*, trans. Georg C. Iggers (New York: Schocken Books, 1972), p. 85. This work is credited to Bazard, Enfantin, Carnot, Rodrigues, Fournel, and Duveyrier.

10. [Emile] Barrault, "Les Femmes," in Prosper Enfantin and Henri, comte de Saint Simon, *Oeuvres de Saint Simon et d'Enfantin*, published by members of the committee set up by Enfantin for the execution of his last will, 47 vols. (Paris: E. Dentu; Ernest Leroux, 1865–78), 44:183–84.

11. I said God Father and Mother

Of all men and all women

Because these simple words

Comprise our RELIGIOUS FAITH

"Paroles du Pere à la cour d'Assises," April 8, 1833, in *Oeuvres*, 8:230. See below, note 16, for more about Enfantin's use of the word "androgyny."

12. Barbara Welter, "The Cult of True Womanhood: 1820–1860," *American Quarterly* 18 (Summer 1966): 151–74, reprinted in Jean E. Friedman and William G. Shade, eds., *Our American Sisters* (Boston: Allyn & Bacon, 1973), p. 96.

13. FE 7643, "Archives," 1:509–10. The table of contents dates this letter September 1829. The Archives of the Fonds Enfantin are volumes of letters and other documents that were recopied, by hand, during Enfantin's imprisonment. Many include Enfantin's comments in the margins.

Enfantin's response to Buchez is "Lettre Lᵉ," October 2, 1829, *Oeuvres*, 26:97–117.

14. Thibert (*Le Féminisme dans le socialisme français*, pp. 31–35) asserts that in the development of the new morality, Enfantin borrowed heavily—without acknowledgment—from Fourier. As proof, she quotes from Laurenz von Stein ("Enfantin had in his library the first work of Fourier, the *Théorie des quatre mouvements*") and from Gustave d'Eichtal ("The new revelation was to embrace, at the same time, politics and morality, but Saint-Simon only gave to the world a political lesson; the principle of the Equality of MAN AND OF WOMAN is, in his work, a simple political principle. It is from another source, from the writing of Ch. *Fourier;* that *our Father* must have drawn his *inspiration* for his moral revelation").

15. Enfantin to his mother, August 18, 1831, *Oeuvres*, 27:194.

16. Enfantin, "Enseignements fait par le Père Suprème," *Réunion générale de la famille: Séances des 19 et 21 novembre 1831* (Paris: Bureau du Globe, 1832).

Saint-Simon had borrowed the Catholic language and analytical framework of the trinity to describe human nature (humans have reasoning, emotional, and action qualities) and to categorize men (scientists, artists, and industrialists). Enfantin's analytical framework of constants, mobiles, and the synthesizing love of the couple-pope is not, however, a trinity of three distinct parts. In certain respects it is more like Hegel's dialectic, but again there are important differences. The constants and mobiles are not in conflict like the synthesis and antithesis; nor does Enfantin's "synthesis" represent process and change and a new stage that supersedes the prior thesis/antithesis. On the contrary, Enfantin's tripartite moral system was static. Thus I use the terms dualism and synthesis rather than either dialectic or trinity to discuss Enfantinian Saint-Simonian thought.

Similarly, Enfantin does not use the word "androgyny" (God Father and Mother or the couple-pope) as we have in the 1970s and 1980s. Male and female—for Enfantin's androgyny—are distinct parts within the whole. Today's androgyny is a dialectical synthesis, an entirely new being, neither male nor female.

17. Bazard, unlike Enfantin, uses a Hegelian dialectic method to argue that the new morality will move from monogamy to promiscuity. See [Saint-Amand Bazard], *Réligion Saint-Simonienne. Discussions morales, politiques et religieuses qui ont amenées la séparation qui s'est effectuée au mois de novembre, 1831, dans le sein de la société Saint-Simonienne* (Paris: Paulin, Delaunay and Heideloff, 1832).

18. Enfantin, *Réunion générale de la famille: Séances des 19 et 21 novembre*, p. 52: "I have told you that I was no assembly president, nor even a tutor, nor teacher; that I was not even a priest. I am the father of humanity! . . . If anyone protests here against the authority that I have assumed, let him now leave."

19. Thibert points out that Michel Chevalier, Edmund Talabot, and Euryale Cazeaux probably gave Enfantin the idea for his "expediant de conciliation." She reprints a letter of October 1831, in which they wrote: "To accomplish this task [the liberation of the woman] you transported yourself into a visionary future; and there, giving full vent to your imagination, you dreamed the life of this ideal woman. You deluded yourself to such a point as to proceed as though you were a woman who summed up in herself all women. . . . You thought that you knew yourself; but you deceived yourself, for you are not the woman, and the woman truly free from marriage and celibacy and from exploitation, she alone can say what she was, what she is, and what she will be" (Thibert, *Le Féminisme dans le socialisme français,* p. 44). The *compte rendu* of the November 19 meeting, however, suggests that Duveyrier first proposed this "temporizing strategy" (ibid., p. 40).

20. *Réligion Saint-Simonienne; Ceremonie du 27 novembre* (Paris: Guiraudet, 1831), p. 4.

21. Enfantin to Laurent, October 15, 1832, FE 7646, "Archives," 4:250.

22. The influence beyond Saint-Simonian circles to inspire a new understanding for the plight of prostitutes is evidenced in the works of Parent-Duchâtelet, *De la prostitution dans la ville de Paris* (1836); and L.-B. Villermé, *Tableau de l'etat physique et moral des ouvriers employés dans les manufactures de coton, de laine, et de soie,* 2 vols. (Paris: J. Renouard, 1840).

23. The pretext for the police action was that Saint-Simonians had violated article 291 of the Penal Code, which forbade meetings of more than twenty persons unless prior official authorization was obtained. The real purpose was likely to permit the police

to search through Saint-Simonian papers and carry off those that would best serve the government's purpose in the upcoming inquest. Although no one incident seems to have caused this harassment, the government likely viewed the Saint-Simonians' growing popularity among workers and their attacks on the inviolability of private property as potentially disruptive if not outright revolutionary.

24. d'Eichtal to Enfantin, November 9, 1832, *Oeuvres*, 8:146–48.

25. Ibid., 29:129.

26. Enfantin to Resseguier, December 1829, in ibid., 26:196: "Our ladies (Madame Bazard, her daughter, her niece, Madame Fournel, Madame Sarchi, and another sister of Rodrigues) have begun to meet and to work."

27. Claire Bazard to Enfantin, FE 7645, "Archives," 3:114. According to Suzanne Voilquin (*Souvenirs,* p. 112), "She knew how to talk to workers but not at all to women."

28. Enfantin to Fournel, October 26, 1830, FE 7644, "Archives," 2:313–14; and Claire Bazard to the Fathers Enfantin and Bazard, October 6, 1830, ibid., p. 309.

29. See Voilquin, *Souvenirs,* p. 113: "It was to Mme. Cécile Fournel that we were attracted; she welcomed us with perfect warmth and won us over by her gracious goodness."

30. *Oeuvres,* 5:223. But Charléty (*Histoire du Saint-Simonisme,* p. 161, citing the *Globe,* February 8, 1832) says that Fournel contributed 68,417 francs.

31. Ibid., 3:21.

32. For the number of women, see Enfantin to Fournel, October 26, 1830, FE 7644, "Archives," 2:33–34. Charléty (*Histoire du Saint-Simonisme,* p. 115) estimates that at this time Saint-Simonian audiences were usually between four hundred and five hundred persons.

33. Voilquin, *Souvenirs,* pp. 110–11.

34. In the autobiographical chapter that concludes Eugénie Niboyet's *Le Vrai livre des femmes* (Paris: E. Dentu, 1863), pp. 222–45, she does not mention her involvement with the Saint-Simonians. This information is from Thibert, *Le Féminisme dans le socialisme français,* pp. 202–3, n. 2.

35. Louise Crouzat to Démar, in Claire Démar, *Textes sur l'affranchissement des femmes,* followed by an explanation of Saint-Simonian symbolism and ideology by Valentin Pelosse (Paris: Payot, 1976), p. 136.

36. Charléty, *Histoire du Saint-Simonisme,* pp. 115–16, says that women comprised one-third of the total of 330 "faithful."

37. Voilquin, *Souvenirs,* p. 110.

38. It is not clear from Charléty, or any other source, if these projects were ever actually implemented. They were, however, organized, and participants were signed up.

39. "Correspondance du *Globe* (Dames)," FE 7608, 112 letters.

40. I draw the same conclusion from the tallies of numbers of women in Saint-Simonian audiences, which are frequently mentioned in Saint-Simonian correspondence. And, among other slogans, the *Globe's* masthead carried the phrase "Appel Aux Femmes."

41. FE 7777, "Correspondances diverses (147 lettres)," includes sixty-five letters from Pauline Roland, forty-two of which were to Aglaé Saint-Hilaire.

42. Thibert, *Le Féminisme dans le socialisme français,* pp. 198–99.

43. Voilquin, *Souvenirs,* p. 109.

44. Charléty, *Histoire du Saint-Simonisme,* p. 60.

45. Jeanne Deroin, "Profession de foi," FE 7608, no. 39, p. 17.

46. Voilquin, *Souvenirs,* p. 110.

47. Deroin, "Profession de foi," FE 7608, no. 39, p. 31.

48. Enfantin to Duveyrier, August 1829, *Oeuvres,* 26:19.

49. "Prédication: Le Prolétaire et la femme," ibid., 45:359.

50. Claire Bazard to the Fathers Enfantin and Bazard, October 6, 1830, FE 7644, "Archives," 2:309v.

51. "Allocution du Père Enfantin à la Famille," March 9, 1831, FE 7645, "Archives," 3:116–17. This source does not list Aglaé Saint-Hilaire as a member of the Collège. Suzanne Voilquin (*Souvenirs,* p. 112) remembered that she was a member and I have therefore included her, but she may have been in error.

52. In a letter to Claire Démar, May 18, 1833, Louise Crouzat wrote that she "preached": "You must know that I went yesterday to preach in a little town named Saint-Foy near Lyons. . . . I was the only Saint-Simonian woman, therefore the first from Lyons to preach to men."

Démar responded (end–May/June 1833): "You are the first and only woman, not only of Lyons, but also of Paris, who has preached to men!" (Démar, *Textes,* pp. 137–38, 50).

53. Claire Bazard to Resseguier, September 2, 1830, FE 7644, "Archives," 2:341.

54. Enfantin, *Réunion générale de la famille: Séances des 19 et 21 novembre,* pp. 55–56.

55. Voilquin, *Souvenirs,* p. 118.

56. Crouzat to Démar, May 18, 1833, in Démar, *Textes,* pp. 136–37.

57. Voilquin, *Souvenirs,* pp. 119, 113.

58. FE 7824, no. 22.

59. Frank Manuel, *The Prophets of Paris* (New York: Harper & Row, 1965), p. 191.

60. Jean-Baptiste Duroselle, "Michel Chevalier, Saint-Simonien," *Revue Historique* 82 (1956): 292–306.

61. *Oeuvres,* 27:155–56. For Pelosse's commentary, see Démar, *Textes,* pp. 169–226.

62. FE 7824, no. 22.

63. FE 7645, "Archives," 3:262.

64. *Tribune des femmes,* 1:107. Thibert has found similar evidence, quoting Cécile Fournel: "I only know one fault of Père Enfantin. It is in not taking into account the feelings of women; it seems that, with the exception of this divine being whose prototype is always in his imagination, there is nothing to be found in us" (*Le Féminisme dans le socialisme français,* p. 206).

Notes to Chapter 4

1. Enfantin, *Réunion générale de la famille: Séances des 19 et 21 novembre,* pp. 36–37. The *compte rendu* of that meeting records the responsive outcry of "many women: Yes! Yes!"

2. See FE 7646, "Archives," 4, for Fournel's letters written in 1832. Of particular interest are three letters to S. A. Bazard (April 12, April 30, and June 5); one to Claire Bazard (May 2); one to Enfantin (May 20); and one to Henry [sic] (June 4). Many of these letters are also in FE 7727, in her own handwriting, which is much easier to read. FE 7727 also includes her letters to Elisa Lemonnier.

3. Cécile Fournel to Elisa Lemonnier, June 15, 1832, FE 7727, no. 9.

4. Ibid.

5. Cécile Fournel to Enfantin, May 20, 1832, FE 7646, "Archives," 4:94v, 95v.

6. Cécile Fournel to Elisa Lemonnier, June 15, 1832.

7. Cécile Fournel to Henri Fournel, June 4, 1832, FE 7646, "Archives," 4:112, 112v.

8. See FE 7647, "Archives," 5:323–53, for the correspondence "du Père avec Cécile Fournel, 1832–33." Almost every letter between December 1832 and February 1833 refers to Cécile's illness.

9. See FE 7646, "Archives," 4:141v, for a letter from Aglaé Saint-Hilaire to Enfantin, dated December 7, 1832: "Yesterday, poor Cécile was completely demoralized." She quotes Cécile: "I cannot live this way. The doctrine is making me ill; it has changed my husband. . . . I must go away to die calmly in some other place."

10. Cécile Fournel to Enfantin, April 10, 1833, FE 7647, no. 345v. Also letters to Enfantin, June 21, 24, 1833, and August 1, 1833, and to Aglaé Saint-Hilaire, June 21, 1833, all in FE 7647, "Archives," 5.

11. Cécile Fournel to Enfantin, December 22, 1832, FE 7647, "Archives," 5:324; to Beranger, June 24, 1833, FE 7727.

12. Marie-Reine, *La Femme libre* (*Tribune des femmes* 1, no. 1), p. 8; repeated in the second, third, and fourth issues.

13. According to Hilda Smith, feminists in seventeenth-century England communicated with each other and read each others' works but did not join together for collective action or propaganda. See Hilda Smith, "Feminism in Seventeenth-Century England" (Paper presented at the Second Berkshire Conference in Women's History, Radcliffe College, Cambridge, Mass., October 1974).

In France, during the Revolution, there were many examples of individual feminist activity and also many examples of female group activities that were not feminist. The Société des Républicaines-Révolutionnaires was exceptional—a female group of feminist inspiration. But because the exigencies of war and inflation forced this short-lived group to postpone its feminist demands and to concentrate its efforts on sharing the "burden" of war and revolution, I have granted the honor of "first" to the *Tribune des femmes* collective.

14. The *Tribune des femmes* is published in two volumes of 280 and 184 pages. Most issues are undated, although the second issue is dated August 25, and the final issue April 1834; sometimes an individual article is dated. The first four issues are numbered pages 1–8. The fifth issue begins p. 33, and thereafter all issues are numbered consecutively to the end of each volume. After the first four issues, I have used the title *Tribune des femmes* for all references to minimize the confusion of the changing titles.

15. *Tribune des femmes*, 1:33. This issue is dated October 8, 1832.

16. Ibid., 2:1.

17. Jeanne-Désirée, ibid., 1:70.

18. In her *Souvenirs* (p. 124), written some thirty years later, Voilquin says that Veret and Guindorf withdrew from the *Tribune des femmes* quite early because they had become Fourierists. My differing explanation here is from the *Tribune des femmes*, 2:181, and also from a careful reading of the articles Guindorf wrote after resigning the directorship: these articles make clear her continuing commitment to the journal and her continuing identification with the Saint-Simonians even after her views came to reflect Fourierist ideas. Only later in the decade did she identify herself as a Fourierist.

19. *Tribune des femmes*, 1:36.

20. *Apostolat des femmes* (*Tribune des femmes* 1, no. 3), p. 2: "Our apostolic mission [thus labeling their journal] is composed primarily of proletarian women." See also Pauline Roland to Charles Lambert, January 1834, FE 7777.

21. See Voilquin, *Souvenirs*, pp. 93–99, for a description of her work. She writes both of her satisfying employment in a small *atelier* and of her much less fortunate experience working at home at "piecework," earning less than half her former income.

22. Pauline Roland to Aglaé Saint-Hilaire, November 1832, January 6, 1833, October 9, 1834, FE 7777.

23. *Tribune des femmes*, 1:36.

24. Both Reine Guindorf and Désirée Veret were unmarried in 1832–34. Suzanne lived alone after her separation (May 1833). Pauline Roland lived alone until the fall of 1834, when she entered a "free union" with Jean-François Aicard. Jeanne Deroin was single, also, during that time, although she later married her "good friend" Desroches. Only one author—Christine-Sophie—seems to have been a mother (*Tribune des femmes*, 1:45) in the early 1830s.

25. Enfantin wrote, "I neither inspired nor ordered the work of the women. I merely approved it" (FE 7670).

26. See Charles Lambert, "Journal de Voyage de Marseille à Alexandrie," October 14, FE 7803: "We should make a general *mea culpa* to the proletarian women, . . . Suzanne . . . [and] her journal that we in no way aided." See also Marie-Reine, who wrote in the *Tribune des femmes*, 1:36: " [We are] girls of the people with no . . . financial resources other than the product of our needlework." Later (*Tribune des femmes*, 2:181), Suzanne Voilquin wrote that Jeanne Désirée founded the journal "without any material means to begin that work."

27. This information is from Auffray's (the *Tribune des femmes* printer) official declaration, on file at the Archives Nationales, F^{18} II 22.

28. *Tribune des femmes*, 1:36.

29. Voilquin, *Souvenirs*, p. 138.

30. Ibid., p. 119.

31. *Tribune des femmes*, 1:73–74.

32. Marie-Reine, *La Femme libre* (*Tribune des femmes* 1, no. 1), p. 8.

33. *La Femme libre* (*Tribune des femmes* 1, no. 1), p. 7.

34. *Tribune des femmes*, 1:169–70.

35. Ibid., 1:69.

36. *La Femme libre* (*Tribune des femmes* 1, no. 1), p. 2.

37. *Tribune des femmes*, 1:36.

38. *La Femme libre* (*Tribune des femmes* 1, no. 1), p. 2.

39. Ibid., p. 6.

40. *Tribune des femmes*, 1:147.

41. Ibid., 2:167. The statement is extraordinary for using the feminine *travailleuse*. Although nineteenth-century social reformers, including feminists, wrote often about "women of the working-classes," "workers" were inevitably male.

42. Ibid., 1:95.

43. *Apostolat des femmes* (*Tribune des femmes* 1, no. 2), p. 2.

44. Ibid., (1, no. 4), p. 2.

45. Marie-Reine, *Tribune des femmes*, 1:199.

46. Josephine-Félicité, ibid., 1:45–46.

47. J. Désirée to Père, October 20, 1832, FE 7646, "Archives," 4:388v.

48. *Tribune des femmes,* 1:69.

49. Cécile Fournel to Enfantin, April 9, 1833, FE 7647, "Archives," 5:349; to Aglaé Saint-Hilaire, June 21, 1833, FE 7727, no. 28.

50. Clorinde Rogé to Aglaé Saint-Hilaire, February 15, 1833, FE 7624, no. 42.

51. Démar, *Textes,* pp. 139, 51.

52. Suzanne Voilquin, *Tribune des femmes,* 2:180.

53. Cécile Fournel to Aglaé Saint-Hilaire, undated, FE 7727, no. 40. I believe it was written in June 1834.

54. Voilquin, *Tribune des femmes,* 2:181.

55. Voilquin, *Souvenirs,* p. 127.

56. Voilquin to Enfantin, [February ?] 1838, FE 7627, no. 62. Voilquin was hurt to receive notice of the legal proceedings and particularly upset that she was criminally accused of desertion. She wrote that she could have halted the action merely by responding that she was willing to come to America as soon as her husband sent her the money, but "à quoi bon."

57. *Tribune des femmes,* 2:169–79.

58. Ibid., 2:173.

59. Voilquin, *Souvenirs,* p. 139.

60. Pauline Roland to Aglaé Saint-Hilaire, May 13, 1832, FE 7777.

61. Roland to Aglaé Saint-Hilaire, August 9, 1832, repeated in her next letter to Saint-Hilaire, August 23, 1832, FE 7777; Roland to Charles Lambert, September 9, 1833, FE 7777.

62. Roland to Charles Lambert, January 1834, FE 7777.

63. Adolphe Guéroult, quoted in Edith Thomas, *Pauline Roland: Socialisme et féminisme au XIX^c siècle* (Paris: Marcel Rivière et Cie, 1956), p. 67.

64. Démar, *Ma loi d'avenir,* in *Textes,* pp. 80, 87, 86, 72.

65. Ibid., pp. 72, 75, 86, 87. On page 86, she writes of the necessity for a "more or less lengthy cohabitation."

66. Voilquin, *Souvenirs,* pp. 127–28.

67. Démar, *Textes,* pp. 88, 93, 91. Démar does not clarify whether she merely opposes the nineteenth-century concept of legitimacy or assumes the child will know only the mother and not the father.

68. Ibid., p. 91.

69. Ibid., pp. 93–94.

70. Roland to Aglaé Saint-Hilaire, November 1833, FE 7777. The concept of "maternité sacerdotale, maternité sans père avoué" was not Roland's alone. About this same time the *Tribune des femmes* (1:71) reviewed a publication by James de Laurence, *Les Enfans [sic] de Dieu,* in which the author says that "the family should be based on the mother" and developed an argument similar to Roland's.

71. Roland to Aglaé Saint-Hilaire, June 24, 1834, FE 7777.

72. *Tribune des femmes,* 1:116; ibid., 2:181.

73. Clorinde Rogé to Enfantin, June 20, 1845, FE 7776, no. 52.

74. *Tribune des femmes,* 1:65–66.

75. Ibid., 1:63.

76. Ibid., 1:64.

77. Voilquin, *Souvenirs,* p. 139.

78. Claire Bazard to Gustave d'Eichthal, March 1831, FE 7645, "Archives," 3:124v.

79. Claire Bazard to Enfantin, May 1831, FE 7645, "Archives," 3:138. This volume of the "Archives" includes five letters from Claire Bazard to Enfantin. Their sequence leads the reader to connect Bazard's "confession" to her final break with Enfantin in November. Since it was Enfantin, however, who designed the "Archives," we cannot be certain if the link between the events was real or merely that which Enfantin wishes us to believe.

80. "Enseignement," December 1831, in *Oeuvres*, 16:131. Abel Transon also criticized the public confession. At the meeting of November 19, he gave this as cause for his leaving the movement (See Enfantin, *Réunion générale de la famille: Séances des 19 et 21 novembre*, p. 29).

81. "It seems that you write only for prostitutes. . . . Why should you base your ideas on that which is defective? Just because there are hunchbacks, must there be an order that all clothing have a place for a hump? It would be better to say to the hunchbacks: try to stand more erect, in the end you will straighten up, for you were born to be straight also" (quoted in Thibert, *Le Féminisme dans le socialisme française*, p. 50).

82. Voilquin, *Souvenirs*, p. 115.

83. Quoted in Thomas, *Pauline Roland*, p. 71.

84. Cécile Fournel to Aglaé Saint-Hilaire, postmarked "juin," FE 7727, no. 40.

85. Démar, *Textes*, p. 75.

86. Démar to Enfantin, January 1833, in ibid., p. 42. See also Démar to Louise Crouzat, May/June 1833: "I have not yet found a woman who has completely understood me, even though I have searched for one" (ibid., p. 54).

87. Roland to Aglaé Saint-Hilaire, November 27, 1832, FE 7777.

88. Suzanne Voilquin's preface is reprinted in Démar, *Textes*, pp. 162–63.

89. Voilquin, *Souvenirs*, p. 211. Even more emphatically than her rejection of Démar's moral views, Voilquin rejected Démar's views on motherhood: "But *maternity!* It is our most beautiful attribute. It encompasses all other feelings without excluding a one; it is woman in her full flowering. In the religion of the future it will no longer be a virginal madonna, as a feminine model that we will present for the adoration of Believers: it will be the mother!" (from the preface to *Ma loi d'avenir*. See Démar, *Textes*, p. 164).

90. Démar to Enfantin, January 1833, in Démar, *Textes*, p. 43.

91. Voilquin, *Souvenirs*, p. 392. "Papillon" was the term used by Fourierists for those who were "by nature" sexually attracted to many.

92. Eugénie Soudet, "Une Parole de femme!" FE 7627, no. 57.

93. Adrienne Baissac to Enfantin, FE 7626. (This letter is attached to a letter from Bazin to Enfantin, dated December 16, 1834. It is identified as a "Protestation from Adrienne Baissac" in the table of contents.)

94. See particularly two letters by Marie Talon to Cécile Fournel, February 28, 1834, and the second undated, FE 7785, nos. 104 and 105. In the Saint-Simonian manner it is explained that one is "intime," the other is "public." The letter of February 28 refers to what Fournel had written Talon in a letter that is now lost of "the orgie" in Egypt. Talon had just mailed the tenth issue of *Foi nouvelle: Livre des actes*, which carried a plea that women go to Egypt. She then wrote to Fournel that she hoped she was not delivering them up to a "harem."

95. Cécile Fournel to Aglaé Saint-Hilaire, September 31, 1833, FE 7727.

96. See especially the "Journals de Ch. Lambert en Egypte," FE 7744, 7745. Both Lydia Elhadad, in her introduction to Voilquin's *Souvenirs* (p. 38), and Valentin Pelosse,

in his commentaries to Démar's *Textes* (p. 160), say wrongly that Lambert was the father of Voilquin's child. Lambert's diary is clear on that point, although it seems that Voilquin was also having an affair with Lambert. See also Voilquin to Enfantin, (undated but likely February 1838), FE 7627, no. 62.

97. Voilquin, *Souvenirs,* p. 115.

98. Roland to Charles Lambert, January 1834; to Aglaé Saint-Hilaire, November 1833; to Aglaé Saint-Hilaire, October 9, 1834, all in FE 7777.

99. Voilquin, *Souvenirs,* pp. 137–38.

100. Voilquin, *Tribune des femmes,* 2:180.

101. Of particular interest is the "Profession de foi" of Madame Beranger in which she states her expectation that the Saint-Simonian family would take care of her children if they were orphaned (FE 7794).

102. Voilquin, *Souvenirs,* pp. 113–14, 124, 123.

103. Démar, *Textes,* pp. 42–43.

104. Roland to Audemar, April 29, 1847, quoted in Thomas, *Pauline Roland,* pp. 93–94.

105. Roland to Charles Lambert, September 21, 1847, FE 7777.

106. Guéroult to Charles Lambert, September 27, 1854, cited in Thomas, *Pauline Roland,* p. 171.

107. Voilquin to Enfantin, January 9, 1847; February 5, 1848, FE 7791.

108. See Daubié, *La Femme pauvre,* for an occupation-by-occupation discussion of all possible employments for women in the 1860s, none of which paid a wage that would permit independence. The class of women which Daubié calls "poor" are the two classes I have identified here, the lower levels of the urban middle class and the upper levels of the working class.

109. A useful illustration of the long-term upward mobility of many male workers is an 1872 inquiry cited in Georges Duveau, *La Vie ouvrière en France sous le Second Empire* (Paris: Gallimard, 1946), p. 415. This inquiry noted that 80 percent of employers were former workers and a further 15 percent were sons of workers.

110. For the American case see Linda Gordon, "Voluntary Motherhood: The Beginnings of Feminist Birth Control Ideas in the United States," *Feminist Studies* 1 (Winter–Spring 1973): 5–22; and Nancy F. Cott, "Passionlessness: An Interpretation of Victorian Sexual Ideology, 1790–1850," *Signs* 4 (Winter 1978): 219–36.

111. "Enseignements fait par le Père," p. 18.

112. *Tribune des femmes,* 1:91. Reine Guindorf uses the same words: ibid., 1:115.

113. Démar, *Textes,* pp. 93–94.

114. *Tribune des femmes,* 1:204; ibid., 1:113.

115. Ibid., 1:114.

116. Ibid., 1:146.

117. *Apostolat des femmes* (*Tribune des femmes* 1, no. 3), p. 3. See also *Tribune des femmes,* 1:215.

118. *La Femme libre* (*Tribune des femmes* 1, no. 1), p. 2.

119. *Tribune des femmes,* 1:125.

120. Josephine-Félicité, *Tribune des femmes,* 1:127. See also Marie Talon's 1853 reminiscence in Jeanne Deroin's *Almanach des femmes* (p. 86): "The Saint-Simonian man was still a man; he took advantage of this idea of liberty, . . . turned it to his own account. It was only in a few exceptional instances (and I certainly place M. Enfantin in the foremost rank of these exceptions) that the offer of enfranchisement was sincere."

121. *Tribune des femmes,* 1:93.

122. Voilquin, *Souvenirs,* pp, 94, 97–98, 82, 83, 112. Because Voilquin continued the relationship after the incident, one might wonder if she exaggerated the violence in her *Souvenirs* to protect her reputation, but this seems unlikely. Although her *Souvenirs* are generally honest, she does omit from them experiences she wished forgotten and could have chosen to do so in this case, too.

123. "Come the Great Council of Women": *Tribune des femmes,* 1:64.

124. In their documentary *Women, the Family, and Freedom* (Stanford: Stanford University Press, 1983), Karen Offen and Susan Groag Bell have reprinted "Appel aux femmes" by Jeanne-Victoire, translated by Anna Wheeler for the June 15, 1833, issue of *Crisis.*

125. See especially one letter to Hoart, February 11, 1834, FE 7791. It appears that he had hurt her feelings in some way. She writes: "I had believed that the line of demarcation which separated the privileged from proletarians was wiped out [among us].

126. Voilquin, *Souvenirs,* p. 112.

127. *Tribune des femmes,* 1:146.

128. Ibid., 2:182.

129. Ibid., 1:96–98.

130. Voilquin to Enfantin, [February 1838], FE 7627, no. 62.

131. Voilquin, *Souvenirs,* pp. 118–19.

132. *Tribune des femmes,* 2:153.

133. Voilquin, *Souvenirs,* p. 190.

Notes to Chapter 5

1. See *Tribune des femmes,* 2:180. Voilquin writes, "Other women will continue this work of theory, strong and devoted women also, but attached by their ties and affections to our cherished France."

2. Although Marguerite Thibert has identified the influence of Fourier on Enfantin's ideas on sexuality, the difference between the two thinkers is significant. Fourier is clearly the more radical. Whereas Fourier wished to encourage the fulfillment of all passions and therefore approved no social or legal constraints on sexual expression, Enfantin had invented an elaborate system of regulation.

3. Charles Fourier, *Théorie des quatre mouvements et des destinées générales: Prospectus et annonce de la découverte:* (1808; reprint, Paris: Jean-Jacques Pauvert, 1967), p. 147.

4. Ibid., p. 123.

5. Charles Fourier, *Traité de l'association domestique-agricole* (1822; reprint, Paris: Edition Anthropos, 1966–67), p. 334.

6. Charles Fourier, *Le Nouveau monde industriel et sociétaire* (1829; reprint, Paris: Flammarion, 1973), p. 236.

7. Fourier, *Théorie des quatre mouvements,* p. 119.

8. Ibid., p. 143: "I would argue from this treatise . . . a conclusion that has been expressed many times before: It is that there is nothing sinful in our tastes or characters; they [tastes and character] are portioned out with the variety and proportion in keeping with our future destiny. And there is nothing sinful on earth save civilized and incoherent

order, which can in no way bow to the systems of our passions. [Our tastes and character] are all adapted to the needs of the associationist order."

9. Fourier's associationist order incorporates "competitiveness," although he rails against *égoïsme*.

10. Fourier, *Théorie des quatre mouvements*, p. 135.

11. Ibid., p. 113.

12. Ibid., p. 141. Fourier does not do away with either private property or economic differences; the full development of all the passions, however, will create an equality of happiness. "In brief, if there is no perfect happiness for the human species except in the order of association, . . . it is that it will assure the full development of the twelve radical passions. . . . It follows that in this new social order the least fortunate individuals, man or woman, will be much happier than the greatest of kings is today; for real happiness comes only from satisfying all of one's passions" (ibid., p. 120).

13. Ibid., p. 144.

14. Ibid., p. 156.

15. Letter from Vidal to Considérant, Lyons, August 31, 1836: "Saint-Simonism was only a poetry and in no way a science. . . . For this reason it accomplished nothing."

Letter from Fanny Schmalzigang to Lechevalier, May 20, 1832: "I believe that Fourierism has been able to analyze and clearly resolve questions that Saint-Simonism could only raise but left us, so to speak, in suspense."

Both letters quoted in Thibert, *Le Féminisme dans le socialisme française*, p. 123.

16. Ibid., p. 124.

17. Vigoureux was Fourier's second disciple (after Just Muiron). She introduced Considérant to Fourierism; later Vigoureux's daughter married Considérant (ibid., pp. 130–33).

18. Zoé Charlotte Gatti de Gamond, *Fourier et son systme*, 5th ed. (Paris: Capelle, 1841–42), pp. 250–51.

19. *Tribune des femmes*, 1:38–39; ibid., 2:166.

20. Even the proposal to use the land located at Condé-sur-Vosges was severely limited in scope, calling for the construction of a boarding school for four hundred children. In 1848, Considérant ran for Constituent Assembly office as a "républicain socialiste." In his statement of candidacy he declared that he accepted Fourier's ideas "only partially" and rejected particularly "his ideas on marriage." See Hubert Bourgin, "Victor Considérant, son oeuvre," *La Révolution de 1848* 5 (1908):698.

21. From the front cover. *La Gazette des femmes* appeared monthly from July 1836 to May 1837 and again from December 1837 to April 1838. The issues until April 1837 were thirty-two pages but sixteen pages thereafter.

22. Alfred Cobban, *A History of Modern France*, vol. 2, *1799–1945* (Baltimore: Penguin Books, 1961), p. 97.

23. *Gazette des femmes*, 1, no. 1 (July 1836):36.

24. Marie-Louise Puech, "Une Supercherie litteraire: Le véritable rédacteur de la *Gazette des femmes* (1836–1838)," *La Révolution de 1848* 32 (June–August 1935): 303–12; and Evelyne Sullerot, *Histoire de la presse féminine*, pp. 195–209.

25. *Journal des femmes*, June 1835, quoted in Sullerot, *Histoire de la presse féminine*, p. 194.

26. Sullerot, *Histoire de la presse féminine*, pp. 195, 197, 193–94.

27. Puech, "Une Supercherie litteraire," p. 309.

28. Sullerot, *Histoire de la presse féminine*, p. 195.

29. *Gazette des femmes,* 2, no. 12 (December 1837): 2.

30. Ibid., front covers.

31. Ibid., 1, no. 1 (July 1836): 1.

32. Ibid., 1, no. 2 (August 1836), back cover.

33. Flora Tristan to Eugénie Niboyet, October 11, 1836, in Flora Tristan, *Lettres,* ed. Stéphane Michaud (Paris: Editions du Seuil, 1980), pp. 64–65.

34. *Gazette des femmes,* 3, no. 1 (January 1838): 11.

35. Hortense Allart de Meritens, *La Femme et la démocratie de nos Temps* (Paris: Delaunay, 1836).

36. *Gazette des femmes,* 1, no. 5 (November 1836): 153–54.

37. This was the Protestant reform group in which Eugénie Niboyet was active.

38. Poutret sometimes signed Mme Poutret de Mauchamps, other times Marie Poutret de Mauchamps, Madelaine Poutret de Mauchamps, or Marie-Madelaine Poutret de Mauchamps. In 1838, she signed herself Marie-*Magdaleine* Poutret de Mauchamps.

39. *Gazette des femmes,* 2, no. 3 (March 1837): 65–68, and repeated in 3, no. 2 (February 1838): 17–20. The petition requested the king to identify himself as "Roi des français et Roi des Françaises" instead of simply as "Roi des Français."

40. *Gazette des femmes,* 1, no. 1 (July 1836): 7.

41. Ibid., p. 1.

42. Ibid., 1, no. 6 (December 1836): 191.

43. Ibid., 1, no. 2 (August 1836): 33.

44. Ibid., 1, no. 6 (December 1836): 161.

45. Ibid., 2, no. 1 (January 1837): 1–6; ibid., 3, no. 1 (January 1838): 1–5; ibid., 1, no. 5 (November 1836): 129–41. The latter petition was also printed as a pamphlet and distributed separately.

46. Ibid., 2, no. 4 (April 1837): 81–85.

47. Ibid., 2, no. 5 (May 1837): 97–103.

48. Ibid., 2, no. 2 (February 1837): 33–39.

49. Ibid., 1, no. 4 (October 1836): 97–107.

50. Ibid., 1, no. 3 (September 1836): 65–71.

51. Eleanor Flexner, *Century of Struggle: The Women's Rights Movement in the United States* (1959; reprint, New York: Antheneum, 1968), pp. 50–52, 65.

52. *Gazette des femmes,* 3, no. 4 (April 1838): 47.

53. Ibid., 1, no. 2 (August 1836): 64.

54. Ibid. Herbinot, continuing to press on this issue, thereafter referred to the celebrated author as "Mme A. Dupin." See, for examples, vol. 1, no. 3 (September 1836): 84, 96.

55. These examples are from vol. 2, no. 3 (March 1837): 70 ff.

56. Quotes are from the transcription of the hearing, reprinted in vol. 2, no. 12 (December 1837): 3–5, from the *Journal des débats,* May 21, 1837.

57. *Gazette des femmes,* 3, no. 3 (March 1838): 44.

58. For one example: "A young Englishwoman disembarked from a steamer with her husband at one o'clock in the morning. Suddenly a customs official whisked her away, made her take off all of her clothes, and when she was entirely naked, searched her *everywhere.* The young woman was so frightened by this external and internal search that she caught a chill and has been bedridden for a month" (*Gazette des femmes,* 3, no. 2 [February 1838]: 78).

59. Before Poutret's second trial, she and Herbinot were baptised and married. They probably hoped to restore her respectability in the eyes of the tribunal; Herbinot was likely also motivated by a desire to assure that his wealth would provide for Poutret during his incarceration.

60. Stéphane Michaud, introduction to Flora Tristan, *Lettres*, pp. 31–32, 36.

61. Flora Tristan, *L'Union ouvrière* (3d ed., Paris, 1844; reprint, Paris: Editions d'Histoire Sociale, 1967), pp. 108, 5.

62. Ibid., p. 130.

63. Ibid., p. 101: "One must consult the works of Fourier . . . also, in Owen."

64. Ibid., p. 28: "The workers' union will enjoy a real power, that of money."

65. See Bernard H. Moss, *The Origins of the French Labor Movement, 1830–1914: The Socialism of Skilled Workers* (Berkeley and Los Angeles: University of California Press, 1976), chap. 2.

66. "Droit au travail" was a term whose "invention" is normally credited to Louis Blanc, but the concept was so popular, for example, the Saint-Simonian's "rehabilitation of manual labor," that it is difficult to credit Blanc with inventing more than a slogan.

67. Tristan, *L'Union ouvrière*, pp. 68, 60–61.

68. Flora Tristan, *Promenades dans Londres* (Paris: H.-L. Delloye, 1840), p. 110.

69. Tristan, *L'Union ouvrière*, p. 54: "It is to be noted that in all professions exercised by men and wmen, that the female workers' day is paid less than half that of the male worker, or, if she works by the piece her pay is even less. Being unable to understand such a flagrant injustice, the thought that strikes us first is this:—Due to his physical strength, man must do twice as much work as woman. Well, reader, it just happens that the opposite is true. . . . Women are paid half as much . . . because they work faster than men; they would earn too much money if they were paid at the same rate. Yes, they are paid, not with respect to the work that they perform, but with respect to the small amount of money that they spend, due to the deprivations they impose upon themselves."

70. Ibid.

71. Ibid., pp. 53, 63.

72. Ibid., pp. 52–53, 59.

73. Ibid., p. 65.

74. Ibid., pp. 68–69: "It is therefore not in the name *of the superiority of woman* (as I will no doubt be accused) that I tell you to claim rights for woman! . . . I rely on a stronger foundation.—It is in the name of *your own self-interest,* men, of your *own improvement,* men; lastly it is in the name of *universal well-being for all men and women* that I urge you to claim rights for woman, and in the meantime to *acknowledge* them for her at least in *principle.*"

75. Ibid., pp. 66, 68.

76. Ibid., pp. 69, 70–71.

77. Quoted in Jules Puech, *La Vie et l'oeuvre de Flora Tristan, 1803–1844* (Paris: Librairie Marcel Rivière et Cie, 1925), p. 308.

78. Ibid., p. 313.

79. Tristan, *L'Union ouvrière*, p. 6.

80. Ibid., p. 12.

81. Ibid., p. 10.

Notes to Chapter 6

1. See John M. Merriman, *The Agony of the Republic: The Repression of the Left in Revolutionary France, 1848–1851* (New Haven: Yale University Press, 1978), p. 51: "A placard on the barricade of the porte St. Marceau on June 23, 1848, defined the 'democratic and social republic' as 'democratic in that all citizens are electors . . . [and] social in that all citizens are permitted to form associations for work.' "

2. The figure for newspapers is from ibid., p. 26. For the political clubs, see Peter H. Amann, *Revolution and Mass Democracy: The Paris Club Movement in 1848* (Princeton: Princeton University Press, 1975). He identifies 203 clubs by mid-April, after which the club movement peaked (p. 33). Laure Adler, *A l'Aube du féminisme: Les premières journalistes (1830–1850)* (Paris: Payot, 1979), p. 125, says that the number reached 450 by June.

3. *Voix des femmes,* March 19, 1848.

4. Peter Amann, "The Paris Club Movement in 1848," in Roger Price, ed., *Revolution and Reaction: 1848 and the Second French Republic* (London: Croom Helm, 1975), pp. 120–21.

5. *Voix des femmes,* March 28, 1848.

6. Quoted in Edith Thomas, *Les Femmes de 1848* (Paris: Presses Universitaires de France, 1948), p. 47. She provides no source.

7. This is suggested by Louis Devance, in "Femme, famille, travail et morale sexuelle dans l'idéologie de 1848," *Romantisme,* nos. 13–14 (1976): 89.

8. Note this familiar Fourierist refrain: "The degree of liberty granted to women is the thermometer of the liberty and happiness of men" (*Voix des femmes,* April 27, 1848).

9. *Voix des femmes,* March 26, 1848.

10. Ibid., April 16, 20, March 31, 22, 1848.

11. Ibid., April 23, 19, 1848.

12. Voilquin, preface to *Ma Loi d'Avenir,* in Démar, *Textes.*

13. Roland to Charles Lambert, January 1834, FE 7777.

14. *Voix des femmes,* March 28, 1848.

15. Roland to G. Le Français, May 25, 1851, quoted in Thomas, *Pauline Roland,* p. 172.

16. Roland, article in *Le Représentant du peuple,* December 25, 1848, quoted in Thomas, *Pauline Roland,* p. 114.

17. According to Shorter, "Illegitimacy, Sexual Revolution, and Social Change," p. 237, rapes climbed 50 percent between 1830 and 1855.

18. Psychoanalytic theorists have postulated that the image of woman *as mother* is universally asexual. Feminist analysts Dorothy Dinnerstein and Nancy Chodorow relate this phenomenon to the universality of women-raised children, theorizing that humans, male and female alike, develop an ambivalence toward the first nurturer, woman. They desire her nurturing, which can make them feel secure and cared for, but fear her power, which can make them feel infantile and weak. Because sexuality is experienced as powerful, woman's sexuality must be denied if we are to feel free to experience her maternal warmth. See Dinnerstein, *The Mermaid and the Minotaur;* and Nancy Chodorow, *The Reproduction of Mothering: Pyschoanalysis and the Sociology of Gender* (Stanford: Stanford University Press, 1979). The term "passionless' is from Nancy F. Cott's article "Passionlessness."

19. *Voix des femmes,* April 23, 14, March 19, 1848.

20. Ibid., April 19, March 27, 1848.

21. Jeanne Deroin, letter to the editors of the *Liberté* (never printed there; "reprinted" in *Voix des femmes,* April 12, 1848).

22. *Voix des femmes,* April 5, 1848 (article by Niboyet reprinted from *Le Bulletin*); ibid., April 11, 1848.

23. *Opinion des femmes,* March 10, 1849.

24. Ernest Legouvé, *Histoire morale des femmes* (Paris: Gustave Sandré, 1849), pp. 12–13.

25. Ibid., pp. 2–3.

26. Ibid., pp. 66–67.

27. Ibid., pp. 68, 405–6, 80, 81–82.

28. Ibid., pp. 172, 174.

29. A decade later, feminist Jenny d'Héricourt wrote a sympathetic analysis of Legouvé's work. But on this point she exclaimed: "Ah, M. Legouvé, is this logic? " See d'Héricourt, *La Femme affranchie* . . . 2 vols. (Brussels: A. Lacroix, 1860), 1:147.

30. Legouvé, *Histoire morale des femmes,* pp. 64–65.

31. Ibid., pp. 413–14.

32. Pauline Roland, "Morale socialiste: Lettres d'une prisonière," first printed in the 1851 edition of *La Liberté de penser* and in 1852, reprinted in the *Almanach des femmes,* pp. 152–53. This article was dedicated to her son Jean.

33. *Voix des femmes,* April 23, 14, 1848.

34. *Politique des femmes,* August 1848.

35. Thibert, *Le Féminisme dans le socialisme français,* pp. 317–18.

36. Quoted in Thomas, *Les Femmes de 1848,* p. 34.

37. *Voix des femmes,* March 21, 1848.

38. Ibid., March 26, 1848.

39. Ibid., April 6, 1848.

40. Sand's letter to the editor of the *Réforme* is reprinted in the *Voix des femmes,* April 10, 1848.

41. Ibid.

42. Ibid., April 26, 1848.

43. Niboyet, *Le Vrai livre des femmes,* p. 234. Niboyet was then still in exile in Geneva and likely wished official approval to return to France, which explains the Bonapartist politics which she then claimed were always hers.

44. *Politique des femmes,* June 18–24, 1848.

45. *Voix des femmes,* April 18, 1848.

46. Ibid.

47. *Opinion des femmes,* April 10, 1849.

48. Ibid.

49. Ibid.

50. "Campagne électorale de la citoyenne Jeanne Deroin et Petition des femmes au peuple," Supplément à *Opinion,* May 1849. Deroin's fifteen votes compare to forty votes cast for George Sand, who proved that while the feminists had spent the year becoming even more daring—they now demanded the vote for all women with no exceptions—Sand had not changed: "It would be monstrous if she [woman] should cut out of her life and duties the care of the home and of the family. . . . Should women participate in political life? Yes, some day, I believe so, . . . *as you do.* But is the day near? No,

I do not think so; and for the condition of women to be transformed it would require a radical transformation in society. . . . As for you, women, who claim to begin by exercising political rights, permit me to tell you again that you are entertaining yourself with child's play. Your home is burning, your domestic house is in peril and you want to go expose yourself to ridicule and public insults when you should be defending your home?'' (quoted in Thomas, *Les Femmes de 1848*, pp. 67–78).

51. "Campagne électorale de la citoyenne Jeanne Deroin," Supplément à *Opinion*, May 1849.

52. *Politique des femmes*, August 1848.

53. Adrien Ranvier, "Une Féministe de 1848: Jeanne Deroin," *La Revolution de 1848* 4 (1907–8): 339.

54. Thomas, *Pauline Roland*, p. 152.

55. Ranvier, "Jeanne Deroin," p. 425.

56. Ibid., pp. 424–25.

57. Thomas, *Pauline Roland*, p. 155.

58. Ranvier, "Jeanne Deroin," p. 429, from a signed statement from among Deroin's personal papers given to Ranvier after Deroin's death.

59. Jean Rabaut, *Histoire des féminismes français* (Paris: Editions Stock, 1978), pp. 152–53.

Notes to Chapter 7

1. Pierre-Joseph Proudhon, *Qu'est-ce que la propriété?* (Paris: Garnier Flammarion, 1966), pp. 274–75.

2. Pierre-Joseph Proudhon, *Système des contradictions économiques ou philosophie de la misère* (1846; reprint, Paris: Ernest Flammarion, 1897), pp. 274–81. "Let us mention briefly the Saint-Simonians, Fourierists, and other prostitutes [sic] who make much of reconciling free love with modesty, refinement, and the purest spirituality. Sad illusion of abject socialism, last dream of a delirious debauched people" (p. 278).

3. Ibid., pp. 278–79.

4. Article by Proudhon in *Le Représentant du peuple*, May 31, 1848, reprinted in Edouard Dolléans, *Proudhon* (Paris: Gallimard, 1948), p. 167. At this point in the published program Proudhon repeated his famous "courtesan or housewife" formula, which had first appeared in the 1846 *Système des contradictions économiques:* "Either courtesan or housewife (I say housewife and not servant), [but] I see no middle ground: what then is humiliating about this alternative? In what way is the role of woman, in charge of the conduct of the household, of all that has to do with food and with thrift, inferior to the role of man, whose proper function is the control of the workshop, that is to say the governing of production and exchange?"

5. Pierre-Joseph Proudhon, *De la création de l'ordre dans l'humanité ou principes d'organisation politique* (1849; reprint, Paris: Libraire des Sciences Politiques et Sociales, 1927), pp. 442–43.

6. See Jules Puech, *Le Proudhonisme dans l'association internationale des travailleurs* (Paris: Félix Alcan, 1907), p. 98.

7. According to George Gurvitch, *Proudhon* (Paris: Presses Universitaires de France, 1965), pp. 65–66, "All of the administrative, economic, and political measures taken

by the Commune drew their inspiration from Proudhon; even the name, les *féderes,* that
the Communards took for themselves [is from Proudhon]." Marx, writing several years
after the fall of the Commune, demonstrated that the failure of the Commune resulted
from the failings of "proudhonism," thereby agreeing that Proudhon was the predominant
influence on the Commune. See Karl Marx, *The Civil War in France,* introduction by
Frederick Engels (New York: International Publishers, 1933).

8. Some of his biographers, too, seem embarrassed by Proudhon's misogyny. Gurvitch,
for example, who devotes great attention to *De la justice,* "where all his thought is
passed in review" (p. 10), never mentions Proudhon's ideas on women, never refers to
sections 10 and 11 ("Amour et Mariage") of the book, and never mentions Proudhon's
last work, *La Pornocratie.*

Other biographers, such as Daniel Halévy (*Le Mariage de Proudhon,* [Paris: Librairie
Stock, 1955]) and George Woodcock (*Pierre-Joseph Proudhon,* [London: Routledge &
Kegan Paul, 1956]), are not at all embarrassed. Halévy (p. 95) lists *La Pornocratie* as
one of Proudhon's "grandes oeuvres." Woodcock (p. 214) writes, "One cannot immediately
dismiss Proudhon's statements with the amused contempt which at first sight their odd
form seems to deserve. Women are certainly inferior in strength. . . . It is also true
that there has never been a woman philosopher and that women in general tend to base
their moral judgments on emotional rather than rational criteria."

9. Pierre-Joseph Proudhon, *De La justice dans la Révolution et dans l'eglise* (Brussels:
Office de Publicité, 1860), bk 10, pp. 5, 6.

10. Ibid., pp. 6–8.

11. Ibid., p. 20.

12. Ibid., pp. 36, 30.

13. Ibid., p. 39.

14. Daniel Halévy reprints the following from Proudhon's notes (*Carnets,* March 16,
1848): "That woman [George Sand] writes like she pisses." See Halévy, *Le Mariage de
Proudhon,* p. 165.

15. Ibid., pp. 2–3.

16. See Dennis W. Brogan, *Proudhon* (London: Hamish Hamilton Publisher, 1934),
p. 11: "The suburb outside of Besançon where Proudhon was born still had a rural
character in the 1820s and 1830s. Proudhon became deeply steeped in their ways of
thinking and his work clearly indicates his understanding of the peasants' land hunger,
their rigid views of right living, their deep conservatism, all combined with their passion
for equality, their class consciousness, and their savage resolution to be each master of
his own fields *and of his own household"* [my emphasis].

17. Proudhon, *De la justice,* p. 142.

18. Pierre-Joseph Proudhon, *La Pornocratie ou les femmes dans les temps modernes* (Paris:
A. Lacroix et Cie, 1875), p. 12. "Pornocratie" is a word created by Proudhon from the
two Greek words for "rule of" and "prostitute."

19. Ibid., p. 56.

20. Alexander Herzen, *My Past and Present,* trans. Constance Garnett, rev. ed., edited
by Humphrey Higgens, 2 vols. (New York: Alfred A. Knopf, 1968), 2:817. Originally
published in Russian, 1861–66. Herzen provides the following explanation of Proudhon's
belief system: "The family, the first cell of society, the first cradle of justice is doomed
to everlasting, inescapable toil; it must serve as the altar of purification from the personal;
in it the passions must be stamped out. The austere Roman family in the workshop of
today is Proudhon's ideal. Christianity has softened family life too much. It has preferred

Mary to Martha, the dreamer to the housewife: it has forgiven the sinner and held out a hand to the penitent, because she loves much; but in Proudhon's family, just what is needed is to love little. And that is not all: Christianity puts the individual far higher in his family relationships. It has said to the son: 'Forsake father and mother and follow me'—to the son who in the name of Proudhon's *incarnation of justice* must be shackled once more in the stocks of absolute paternal authority, who in his father's lifetime can have no freedom, least of all in the choice of a wife. He is to be tempered in slavery, to become in his turn a tyrant over the children who are born without love, from duty, for the continuation of the family. In this family, marriage will be indissoluble, but in return it will be as cold as ice. Marriage is properly a victory over love; the less love there is between the cook-wife and the workman-husband the better. And to think that I should meet these old, shabby bogeys from right-wing Hegelianism in the writings of Proudhon!'" (p. 821).

21. Proudhon, *De la justice*, p. 144. Proudhon wrote to a friend, Tissot (October 28, 1851), about his own marriage: "I have married, at age 41, a simple Parisian working woman, with no fortune, but of serious morals and a perfect devotion. As for education, she is a lace lacemaker; for the rest, she is as little a *bas bleu* [bluestocking] as a *cordon bleu* [gourmet cook]. . . . I have made this marriage with premeditation, without passion, in order to become . . . a father of a family" (quoted in Dolléans, *Proudhon*, pp. 168–69).

22. Proudhon, *La Pornocratie*, p. 269.

23. Jerome Langlois, introduction to ibid., p. iv

24. Fritz Stern, *The Varieties of History* (Cleveland: World, 1956), p. 108.

25. Edmund Wilson, *To the Finland Station* (New York: Doubleday, 1953), pp. 16–17.

26. Quoted in Jean Guehenno, *L'Evangile éternel* (Paris: Bernard Grasset, 1927), p. 166.

27. Jules Michelet, *L'Amour,* 3d ed. (Paris: Librairie de L. Hachette et Cie, 1859), pp. 385–86.

28. Jules Michelet, *La Femme,* pp. 9–10.

29. Michelet, *L'Amour,* pp. xxi–xxii.

30. Ibid., pp. 1–3.

31. Ibid., pp. 4, 8.

32. Michelet, *La Femme,* p. 34.

33. Michelet, *L'Amour,* pp. 17, 15.

34. Ibid., pp. 36, 56, 53–60. In the passage on the home's location, Michelet's naturalism is particularly evident. He quotes extensively from Rousseau and from Froebel. He uses his romantic flowery language to draw images filled with light, sun, and flowers. In this setting, the man would have "100 thoughts, 100 concerns. She, one only, her husband" (ibid., pp. 297–98).

35. Ibid., pp. 49, 36.

36. Michelet, *La Femme,* p. 284.

37. Ibid., pp. 25, 24, 34.

38. Ibid., pp. 37, 41–42, 53. The final quote is the title to chapter 4.

39. Quoted in Saad Morcos, *Juliette Adam* (Beirut: Dar Al-Maaref—Liban, 1962), p. 4.

40. Winifred Stephens, *Madame Adam Juliette Lamber, La Grande Française, from Louis-Philippe until 1917* (New York: E. P. Dutton & Co., 1917), p. v.

41. Morcos, *Juliette Adam,* p. ix.

42. Ibid., pp. 15, 324.

43. According to Stephens (*Madame Adam,* pp. 48–52), Adam heartily disliked Héricourt. Stephens cites from Adam's personal papers: "*La forte* Jenny was conceited, censorious, pedantic, and an inveterate scandalmonger." Stephens tells us that Adam particularly resented Proudhon's indictment of George Sand and Daniel Stern; but when Adam suggested that Héricourt should refute Proudhon, Héricourt responded, "George Sand and Daniel Stern have got what they deserve. I insist upon virtue and I practice it. Proudhon has not dared insult me. I am certain of it, although I have not yet read his book."

44. Morcos (*Juliette Adam,* p. 16) writes that the feminist issue was then ever-present in her mind and that she had been working on a study to be entitled "Besoins intellectuels et moraux de la femme au dix-neuvième siècle" for the past two years. This previous work, according to Morcos, explains how she could prepare her first book so rapidly.

45. Juliette Lamber [Mme Adam], *Idées anti-proudhoniennes sur l'amour, la femme et le mariage,* 2d ed. (Paris: E. Dentu, 1861), pp. 5, 41, 48.

46. Ibid., pp. 41–42.

47. Ibid., pp. 43–44, 50.

48. Ibid., pp. 54, 103–4.

49. Ibid., pp. 127–28, 69.

50. Ibid., p. 70.

51. Ibid., p. 77.

52. Ibid., p. 78.

53. Ibid., p. 128.

54. Ibid., p. 79.

55. Ibid., p. 132.

56. Ibid., pp. 148, 152.

57. The second edition was published under the not very well-disguised pseudonym "J. Lambert," to prevent La Messine from acquiring the royalties, but again his "marital power" prevailed.

58. Adam played no role in this latter alliance. During the first decades of the Third French Republic she was the leading "révanchiste" and for this reason was often in opposition to the feminists allied to Republican Opportunism.

59. Héricourt, *La Femme affranchie,* 1:5.

60. The entire article is reprinted in ibid. (1:126–42). In it, Héricourt writes that Proudhon had proposed a debate between them but insisted that she must first choose for herself a male "sponsor" because he could not possibly engage in a one-to-one debate with a woman, for to do so might be construed as accepting her as an equal.

61. Ibid., 1:133.

62. Ibid., 1:129, 136.

63. Ibid., 1:94.

64. Ibid., 1:96.

65. Ibid., 1:104–5.

66. Ibid., 1:162–63, 185.

67. Ibid., 1:56.

68. Ibid., 2:109.

69. Ibid., 2:125.

70. Ibid., 2:126. Also in contrast to Enfantin, Héricourt maintained: "That which some have named the emancipation of woman through Love is her slavery. . . . Woman, sadly emancipated in this way, far from being free, becomes the slave to her instincts and to the passions of man." But here, Héricourt is flogging a dead horse. There were none left "who named the emancipation of woman through Love."

71. Ibid., 2:209.

72. Ibid., 2:149, 155. She insisted that divorce reform must protect the interests and welfare of women and children. "No one can compel a man to live with a woman whom he has ceased to love, but he must be constrained to fulfill his duties with respect to the children born of this union, and to keep his business engagements; in wronging his companion, in escaping from the burdens of paternity, he takes advantage of his liberty to the detriment of others: Society has a right to prevent this."

73. Ibid., 2:179.

74. She hedged the radicalism of her demand, exactly as Adam had, with the caution that if there were professions to which woman's nature did not suit her, "competition would show the falsity of ill-founded pretense." As an example, she reminds us, "Women are not forbidden to be carpenters or tillers, yet they do not become such, because their nature opposes it. . . . There is no need to prohibit what is impossible" (2:181).

75. Ibid., 2:182.

76. Ibid., 2:183–84.

77. Ibid., 2:204.

78. Ibid., 2:100.

Notes to Chapter 8

1. Maria Deraismes, *Eve dans l'humanité* (Paris: Librairie Générale de L. Sauvraîte, 1891), p. i: "The Empire, in its decline, feeling threatened, had, for political reasons and to regain an appearance of popularity, relaxed somewhat the strictness of its rule. At that time, the country that had been silenced for so long was thirsting for speeches that were honest and devoid of any official stamp. And it responded with eagerness and enthusiasm to this attempt at a free tribune. This was really the grand era of conferences, for they answered a general need."

2. See Priscilla Robertson, *An Experience of Women: Pattern and Change in Nineteenth-Century Europe* (Philadelphia: Temple University Press, 1982), p. 299. Robertson suggests (p. 300) that Héricourt was dead by 1871; she was not.

3. See Félix Dupanloup, *M. Duruy et l'éducation des filles* (Paris: Douniol, 1867); *La Femme chrétienne et française: Dernière réponse à M. Duruy* (Paris: Douniol, 1868); *Controverse sur l'éducation des filles* (Paris: Plon, 1875).

4. Rabaut, *Histoire des féminismes française,* p. 151.

5. See Bibliothèque Marguerite Durand (BMD), Paris, dossier Julie Daubié, for a newspaper clipping signed P. Bascou-Bance. Also, H. Wild, "Nos Contemporaines: Jeanne Deroin et Julie Daubié," Speech presented at the Congrès Intenational des Oeuvres et Institutions Féminines and reprinted in *Actes du Congres . . .* (Paris: Bibliothèque des Annales Economiques, 1889), pp. 473–79.

6. Indeed, a century later her work remains among the most useful sources for studying the conditions of French women at mid-nineteenth century.

7. Paul Leroy-Beaulieu, *Le Travail des femmes au XIXe Siècle* (Paris: Charpentier, 1895), pp. 150, 64.

8. Albistur and Armogathe, *Histoire du féminisme français,* 2:469, 471.

9. See Charles Lemonnier, *Elisa Lemonnier, fondatrice de la Société pour l'Enseignement Professionel des Femmes* (Saint-Germain: L. Toinon, 1866).

10. See chapter 5 for a discussion of Legouvé's very popular *L'Histoire morale des femmes.* For Pelletan: *La Famille, la mère* (Paris: Librairie Internationale, 1865); for Simon: *L'Ouvrière* (1861; 2d ed., Paris: Librairie de L. Hachette, 1862); for Naquet: *Religion, propriété, famille* (1869; reprint, Brussels: H. Kistemaeckers, 1877).

11. Shorter, "Illegitimacy, Sexual Revolution, and Social Change," pp. 260–61.

12. Lillian Faderman, *Surpassing the Love of Men: Romantic Friendship and Love between Women from the Renaissance to the Present* (New York: William Morrow, 1981). See pt. 2, chaps. 3–4, for an examination of these works by French authors.

13. Robertson, *An Experience of Women,* p. 188.

14. Although Audouard was not the first woman in France to speak publicly in favor of women's rights, it is appropriate here to remind readers how unusual this still was. During earlier revolutions (1789, 1848), feminists claimed the right to speak at the political clubs—Jeanne Deroin spoke frequently in April 1849 for her own candidacy—but each time the government eventually prohibited the women from continuing their public speaking on political issues. Among the Saint-Simonians, only Louise Crouzat in Lyons "preached" publicly, although in this case it is not clear if the prohibition was Saint-Simonian prejudice or the government's. In the *conférences* of the 1860s, Deraismes was the "first" to speak. But the government's consent to the novelty was arbitrary and capricious. In April 1869, seven women including Elisa Lemonnier—all members of the Administrative Council of Professional Schools—were denied the right to speak in a gathering devoted to examining government educational policy. The government's pretext was that women were excluded by law from civil and political rights. See Richer, *Le Livre des femmes,* p. 85.

15. In *Guerre aux hommes* (Paris: E. Dentu, 1866), Audouard detailed the methods used by men to discourage women who show promise in the arts, science, or literature.

16. Olympe Audouard, *La Femme dans le mariage, la séparation et le divorce* (Paris: E. Dentu, 1870), pp. 109–10.

17. The pseudonym of Léodile Champseix, née Bréa, who created the name by joining together the names of her twin sons.

18. *Obsèques de Maria Deraismes: Discours prononcés sur sa tombe le 9 février 1894, par Annie Jackson-Daynes, Virginie Griess-Traut, Ernest Hamel, Mme Vincent, Eugénie Potonié-Pierre, M. Dide, Mme Bequèt de Vienne, Gustave Hubbard, Mme Pognon, M. Raqueni, Mme Valette, Paule Mink, Mme Rouzade, M. Schacre, M. Fringuet* (Paris: N.p., 1895). Of the fifteen speakers, eleven mentioned her wealth, charm, and/or beauty in the first or second sentence. Both Hamel (p. 8) and Pognon (p. 29) assure us that her "spinsterhood" was self-chosen because of her aversion to the servile condition imposed on a French married woman.

19. "Discours de Ernest Hamel," ibid., p. 4.

20. Li Dzeh-djen, *La Presse féministe en France de 1869 à 1914* (Paris: Librairie L. Rodstein, 1934), p. 24.

21. Maria Deraismes, *A bon chat, bon rat* (1861); *Retour à ma femme* (1862); *Le Père coupable* (1862), all published in a general collection entitled *Théâtre chez soi* (Paris: Amyot, 1863).

22. Li Dzeh-djen (*Presse féministe,* p. 25) mentions *Le Grand journal* and *L'Epoque;* the National Biography mentions, in addition, *Le Nain jaune.*

23. The d'Aurévilly article later became part of a book, published in 1876, in which he rails against female writers, twenty-six of whom are singled out for special attention. See Jules Barbey-D'Aurévilly, *Les Bas-bleus* (Paris: Société Générale de Librairie Catholique, 1876). See also Maria Deraismes, *Oeuvres complètes,* ed. Anna Féresse-Deraismes, 3 vols. (Paris: Félix Alcan, 1896), 3:i ("Avant-propos").

24. Quoted in Jean Bernard, "Notice" to *France et progrès,* p. xvii, in Deraismes, *Oeuvres complètes,* vol. 1.

25. Deraismes, *Eve dans l'humanité,* p. i: "Our success surpassed all expectations. The great size and attention of the audience, the applause, the talk that these conferences generated gave me reason to believe that the realization of the legislative reforms that I was demanding would be forthcoming in the near future."

26. Maria Deraismes, *Nos principes et nos moeurs,* p. 9, in *Oeuvres,* vol. 3.

27. Individual lecture titles are "La Femme et le droit"; "La Femme et les moeurs"; "La Femme dans la famille"; "La Femme dans la société"; "La Femme dans le théâtre"; "La Femme telle qu'elle est"; "La Femme devant les tribunaux"; "Les grandes femmes."

28. Deraismes, *Eve dans l'humanité,* pp. 42, 44.

29. Ibid., pp. 44, 49, 45.

30. Ibid., p. 45.

31. Ibid., pp. 49–51.

32. Ibid., pp. 51, 29–30.

33. Ibid., p. 50: "When a young man decides [to marry], he is not pushed into a decision by the urging of his feelings or heart, which he has used and abused, but by rational planning. . . . He acts coldly, after consideration. The need for money, ambition, for hygienic reasons . . . the sudden need for order, and distaste for hotel life and restaurant manners, the desire for furniture that is well cared for, for a neat household, for a tranquil and even existence . . . the paternal instinct . . . a certain self-love not to disappear some day, without leaving behind living proof of one's existence . . . [all these] are usually the reasons that convince him to marry. . . . As for the rest, you can easily understand that the young man, satiated, blasé, who has drawn happiness at every well, simply considers legal union as an act of reason that can only offer a lesser and duller repetition of the charms, the raptures that he has previously enjoyed."

34. Ibid., p. 49.

35. Ibid., p. 52.

36. Ibid.

37. Ibid., p. 53.

38. Ibid., p. 59.

39. Ibid., pp. 64–65.

40. Hubertine Auclert, *Le Vote des femmes* (Paris: V. Giard and E. Brière, 1908), pp. 100–101.

41. Li Dzeh-djen, *Presse féministe,* p. 29, says 1866; Edith Thomas, *Louise Michel ou la velléda de l'anarchie* (Paris: Gallimard, 1971), p. 60, says 1868; Auclert, *Le Vote des femmes,* p. 101, says 1869; a special publication celebrating the fiftieth anniversary of the Association pour le Droit des Femmes (1920) says: "The previous year [to the founding of the association], a feminist society had already been created, but it seems that it only operated for a few months and one finds no traces of it at the time of the Association pour le Droit des Femmes." This information would place the group's

formation in 1869. (See *Cinquante ans de féminisme* [Paris: Ligue Française pour le Droit des Femmes, 1921], p. 60.)

42. Auclert, *Le Vote des femmes,* p. 101. Edith Thomas reprints from Louise Michel's *Mémoires* Michel's theory of the purpose of this group: "equality of education for both sexes . . . [and] sufficient remuneration for the work of women so as to eliminate the *necessity* for prostitution."

43. In 1881 the younger Société pour l'Amélioration du Sort des Femmes, then headed by Maria Deraismes, merged with this Société de Revendication des Droits de la Femme and became the Société pour l'Amélioration du Sort de la Femme et la Revendication de ses Droits.

44. *Le Droit des femmes,* January 1, 1888, p. 1.

45. Ibid., April 10, 1869, p. 1.

46. Ibid., May 15, August 28, December 11, 1869; *L'Avenir des femmes,* July 7, 1872, April 4, 1875, January 2, 1876, April 1, 1877.

47. Li Dzeh-djen, *Presse féministe,* p. 55. See also in *Le Droit des femmes,* January 4, 1885: "Women who read the review, even though they may have agreed with its ideas, did not dare commit themselves for fear of what society would say."

48. In 1883, Jeanne Deroin (then living in England) and Richer carried on a debate by correspondence over Richer's support for *recherche de paternité*. Deroin opposed both that and *recherche de maternité* and favored the anonymous *tour* instead (*Le Droit des femmes,* August 5, September 2, October 7, 1883).

Le Droit des femmes regularly listed financial contributors, including from time to time a gift from the "Legs Veuve-Voilquin."

49. Guéroult was the father of Jean Roland.

50. Mill's letter: August 4, 1872; Bright's letter: September 1, 1872.

51. Art. 11: "Propaganda being, at this particular time, the most pressing matter of the Association, the funds acquired from the payments of members or donors will be used first: (1) to support the publication of the official organ of the Association; (2) to organize conferences on the subject of women, in Paris as well as in the provinces." See also art. 29, stating that the journal *Le Droit des femmes* shall be the official organ of the association until the Executive Council decides otherwise.

52. Rabaut, *Histoire des feminismes français,* p. 158, mentions a law passed that required the state to pay expenses for poor women suing for separation. Duruy's education program is also relevant here.

53. Thomas, *Women Incendiaries,* is the most complete source for women's activities during the war and the Commune. See also Eugène Schulkind, "Le Rôle des femmes dans la Commune de 1871," *1848, Revue des Révolutions Contemporaines* 42 (February 1950).

54. Thomas, *Women Incendiaries,* p. 156.

55. *Enquête parlementaire sur l'insurrection du 18 mars* (Paris: Wittersheim, 1872), p. 548.

56. Ibid., p. 79.

57. Hippolyte Lissagaray, *Les Huit journées de mai derrière les barricades* (Brussels: Bureau de Petit Journal, 1871), p. 292.

58. Thomas, *Women Incendiaries,* chap. 5.

59. Edith Thomas's excellent biography of Michel has recently been published in an English translation (by Penelope Williams) by Black Rose Books of Montréal, Canada (1981). Michel's memoirs, entitled *The Red Virgin: Memoirs of Louise Michel,* have also

appeared in an English-language edition (trans. Bullitt Lowry and Elizabeth Ellington Gunter), published by the University of Alabama Press (1981).

60. Michel, *Memoirs,* p. 58.

61. Quoted by André Léo in her account of the incident, *La Sociale,* May 6, 1871.

62. *L'Avenir des femmes,* September 24, 1871, p. 1.

63. *Le Droit des femmes,* June 6, 1880.

64. *L'Avenir des femmes,* July 7, 1872.

65. All the letters were reprinted in *Cinquante ans de féminisme,* p. 67.

66. *L'Avenir des femmes,* July 6, 1873: "We no longer know where we are heading nor under what form of government we shall be living by the month of September. . . . In this situation, we cannot make our distant friends undertake a costly and tiring trip to have to tell them—at the last minute—that the projected meeting has been found to be too dangerous by our governments.

"We are in a state of siege and will still be so in September."

"We must adjourn the Congress."

Notes to Chapter 9

1. Léon Richer, *La Femme libre,* p. 19.

2. Ibid., p. 336.

3. Since the arguments of the opposition were then commonly "scientific"—that female intellectual capacity was inferior to the male because her brain is smaller in size—he quoted from a scientist, Louis Buchner *(L'Homme selon la science)* to refute their arguments (ibid., pp. 29–31): "Scientists have set up physiological objections to the ability of woman to learn by claiming that the volume of the female brain is considerably less than man's brain. . . . If the facts they rely on are true, one must accept the consequences thereof . . . [but] this is not the case here.

"In the first place the smaller size and weaker development of muscles in woman carries with it a lesser thickening of the corresponding nervous mass in the nerve centers, and therefore a natural reduction of the total volume of the female brain without causing the development and the energy of the cerebral regions that govern intellectual functions to suffer. In the second place even if the special cerebral regions develop less in women, one could attribute this to a lack of exercise and culture just as easily as to an original inferiority; for, as one knows, every organ, including the brain, in order to attain its perfection must find opportunities to function. To determine the intellectual value of a brain, one has to take into account, not only its size or its circumference but as well if not more, its inmost texture, and the refinement of each of its parts. It is not contrary therefore to common sense to imply, in this regard, that the female brain is actually better than the male brain because of its greater finesse."

4. Ibid., p. 336.

5. Ibid., pp. 10, 142–43, 145, 232. Richer here repeats political gossip that blamed (credited?) women—friends and wives of monarchist politicians—for the intrigues that almost resulted in a Bourbon restoration the previous year (1876): "I cannot oppose this intrusion of women into political affairs; if I did I would be betraying myself and my principles. Order and disorder, peace and war, are as interesting to women as they are to us; they may, if they please, get mixed up in politics, give advice, act, in short, in

whatever way seems best to them. But if we do not want their involvement to be harmful, we must see to it that women can think, can judge, can advise." And later, "If for no other reason, our own self-interest compels us to inspire in women the taste for freedom. The best way to do this is to let them enjoy freedom" (pp. 234–36, 336).

6. Ibid., pp. 36, 194, 197, 93.

7. Ibid., pp. 336–37.

8. Ibid., p. 198.

9. Ibid., pp. 93, 90–91.

10. Ibid., pp. 226, 93, 107. Among the trades women could not practice he specifies roofer and carpenter, as had Adam and Héricourt before him. One is curious to know if everyone plagiarized Adam or if indeed roofers and carpenters epitomized the male professions in the minds of the nineteenth-century French.

11. Ibid., pp. 92, 90. His analysis of pay scale differences between men's and women's wages indicates a greater disparity in 1875 than in 1860. See ibid., p. 109.

12. Ibid., p. 88.

13. Ibid., p. 10.

14. Ibid., pp. 77–78.

15. Ibid., p. 333.

16. Ibid., p. 335. Seduction of girls under fifteen was already considered a crime.

17. The deputies were Boudeville, Casse, Codet, Deschanel, Gagneur, Godissart, Laisant, Tiersot, and Talandier; the senators were Eugène Pelletan and Victor Schoelcher; and the municipal council members were de Hérédia, Level, Antide Martin, Georges Martin, and Morin.

18. This was not a plea that babies be breastfed—that was a given—but that mothers, rather than wet nurses, do this. Feminists understood that wet-nursing babies caused high infant mortality rates: the "put out" children were endangered, and the children of wet nurses were also endangered by this "competition" for the mother's milk. The statistics verify the feminists' understanding. See Sussman, "The Wet-Nursing Business in Nineteenth-Century France."

19. *L'Avenir des femmes,* September 1, 1878.

20. Ibid.

21. *Cinquante ans de féminisme,* p. 71.

22. Ibid., pp. 71–72; reprinted in *L'Avenir des femmes,* September 1, 1878.

23. *Cinquante ans de féminisme,* published in 1921, symbolizes by its title that the league founded by Richer in 1882 came to see its origins in the association founded in 1870, which "legally" was Deraismes's group, not Richer's. The name change for Deraismes's group related to a merger of her group with the group founded at the home of André Léo sometime in the late 1860s. By 1881, both groups were controlled by Deraismes.

24. René Viviani's memories suggest this explanation: "Outside of our little circle [the league], another more lively and also richer one existed. It had as an apostle a noble woman, Mlle Maria Deraismes. . . . There was *in spite of natural rivalry* [my emphasis] between the two groups, a bond for common action and a perfect agreement of views" (*Cinquante ans de féminisme,* p. 7).

25. According to Patrick Bidelman, *Pariahs Stand Up! The Founding of the Liberal Feminist Movement in France, 1858–1889* (Westport, Conn.: Greenwood Press, 1982), p. 90, there was great disappointment among feminists who outlived Deraismes that

she had bequeathed her estate entirely to her sister. Evidently, there had been high
hopes that at least some of her fortune would be left to the feminist movement.

26. *Cinquante ans de féminisme*, p. 15.

27. Richer, *La Femme libre*, p. 255.

28. Ibid.

29. Ibid., p. 257.

30. Hubertine Auclert, *Les Femmes au gouvernail* (Paris: Marcel Giard, 1923), pp. 2,
5.

31. Ibid., p. 6.

32. Ibid., pp. 6–8.

33. Ibid., p. 8.

34. Hubertine Auclert, *Question qui n'est pas traitée au Congrès international des femmes*
(Paris: Imprimerie de L. Hugonis, 1878), p. 4.

35. Auclert, *Les Femmes au gouvernail*, p. 10.

36. *La Citoyenne* became a monthly in 1884.

37. *La Citoyenne*, February 13, 1881.

38. Ibid., March 20, 1881.

39. Li Dzeh-djen, *Presse féministe*, p. 79. *La Citoyenne*, no less than *Le Droit des
femmes*, was always under financial pressure and continued to exist as long as it did
primarily because of the financial support of M. de Gasté, a deputy to the Chamber of
Deputies with strong feminist convictions.

After her return to Paris, following the death of her husband, Auclert wrote a regular
column for *Le Radical* under the heading "Le Féminisme." This collaboration lasted
from 1896 to 1909.

40. Charles Sowerwine, *Sisters or Citizens? Women and Socialism in France since 1876*
(Cambridge: Cambridge University Press, 1982), p. 208, n. 8, identifies this author as
Marie Chaumont, Auclert's sister.

41. Twenty-seven were invited to join the slate, but twelve refused, including Paule
Mink, Louise Michel, and Juliette Adam.

42. Concerning the abortive attempt of Julie Daubié to vote in the 1870 Paris
municipal elections, Richer wrote (*La Femme libre*, p. 260): "This isolated attempt could
not succeed. One essential element was missing: the tacit agreement of public opinion.
No reform, no matter how legitimate, can succeed if it has not been prepared in advance
and does not have the support of public opinion."

43. Ibid., p. 238.

44. Ibid., p. 240.

45. *La Citoyenne*, May 1885.

46. Maria Deraismes, "Le Suffrage universel: Discourse prononcé à la Société des Amis
de la Paix et de la Liberté, 1879," in *Eve dans l'humanité*, p. 164.

47. Ibid., p. 165.

48. Maria Deraismes, "Discours prononcé au Pecq, le 14 juillet 1882, à l'occasion de
l'inauguration du Buste de la République des Communes de Jacques France," in ibid.,
p. 180.

49. Deraismes's welcoming remarks at the opening plenary session make this clear:
"Since the president we were supposed to agree to was protectionist, we rejected him
and preferred that our Congress be free [that is, not official]." See *Congrès Français et
International du Droit des Femmes* (Paris: E. Dentu, 1889), p. 3.

50. For the resolutions, see ibid., pp. 258–59.

51. See the promise by Richer (*Le Droit des femmes,* January 6, 1889) that "no question should go unanswered. . . . If unacceptable or premature proposals [Richer's term for suffrage] are put forth, the majority will reject them and it will end there. It is only right that all opinions be expressed."

52. *Congrès* (1889), p. 258: "The Congress, believing that the question of women's work . . . cannot be resolved by legal and constitutional reforms . . . asks for civil and political emancipation . . . of the woman."

53. Although Allix was not permitted to complete his speech, this was because of his choice of language rather than his demand that women vote. See *Congrès* (1889), p. 155: "After he uttered a remark insulting the Chamber of Deputies, the president [Deraismes] withdrew his right to speak and energetically protested . . . what had just been said."

54. *Congrès* (1889), pp. vii–x.

55. Li Dzeh-djeh, *Presse féministe,* p. 35.

56. Guilbert (*Les Femmes et l'organisation syndicale avant 1914,* pp. 156–57) reprints the resolutions in their entirety. See also Madeleine Rebérioux, Christiane Dufrancatel, and Beatrice Slama, "Hubertine Auclert et la question des femmes à 'l'immortel congrès' (1879)," *Romantisme* 13–14 (1976): 123–42.

57. The mutualists favored an industrial sector of independent, propertyowning artisans. The collectivists favored the public ownership of the means of production. Although it is ironic that feminists allied with the mutualists, whose socialism derived from the antifeminist Proudhon, and opposed the collectivists, whose socialism drew upon the feminists Marx and Engels, the mutualist (and later, the "gradualist") feminists were harkening back to their utopian roots. They particularly resisted the Guesdists' ideology of class struggle.

58. Sowerwine, *Sisters or Citizens?* pp. 33–34.

Notes to Conclusion

1. See Steven C. Hause and Anne R. Kenney, "The Limits of Suffragist Behavior: Legalism and Militancy in France, 1876–1922," *American Historical Review* 86 (October 1981): 781–806.

2. Zeldin, *France: 1848–1945,* 1:352.

3. See chapter 3, at n. 43. Twentieth-century American feminists have described their first feminist stirrings with similar religious terminology. See Rachel Blau DuPlessis, "Washing Blood," *Feminist Studies* 4 (June 1978): 6—"To make a new analysis involves conversion, a sudden reseeing, as material present but unstressed, as material not given value in another context suddenly is made visible." Compare also Joan Cassell, *A Group Called Women* (New York: David McKay Co., 1977), pp. 18–19: "A raised consciousness . . . refers to something close to a conversion experience. . . . Beliefs and behaviors that previously would have been inconceivable are now natural indeed inevitable. . . . The end point in a raised consciousness is a new and transformed world."

4. Compare with Jo Freeman's analysis of the 1970s movement. She identified a "Radical Paradox" about which she wrote: "This is the situation in which the New Left women frequently found themselves during the early days of the movement. They found repugnant the possibility of pursuing 'reformist' issues that might be achieved

without altering the basic nature of the system, and thus would, they felt, only strengthen the system. However, their search for a sufficiently radical action or issue came to naught and they found themselves unable to do anything out of fear that it might be counterrevolutionary. *Inactive revolutionaries are much more innocuous than active reformists* [my emphasis]." See Jo Freeman, "The Women's Liberation Movement: Its Origins, Structure, Impact, and Ideas," in Jo Freeman, ed., *Women: A Feminist Perspective,* (Palo Alto, Calif.: Mayfield Publishing Company, 1975), p. 459.

5. I acknowledge here the influence of Linda Gordon. See "Voluntary Motherhood," pp. 12–13: "Feminists' hostility and fear of it [sex] came from the fact that they were women, not that they were feminists. Women in the nineteenth century were, of course, trained to repress their own sexual feelings. . . . They also resented . . . intercourse dominated by and defined by the male in conformity with his desires and in disregard of what might bring pleasure to a woman. . . . Furthermore, sexual intercourse brought physical danger. Pregnancy, childbirth and abortions were risky . . . ; venereal diseases were frequently communicated to women by their husbands." See also Cott, "Passionlessness," pp. 219–36.

6. The words are Reine Guindorf's. See chapter 4, at n. 114.

7. Pauline Roland. See chapter 6, at n. 15.

8. In the years preceding World War I, French feminists did begin to advocate birth control, led by Caroline Rémy (better known by her literary pseudonym Sévérine) and Dr. Madeleine Pelletier.

9. Angus McLaren, "Sex and Socialism: The Opposition of the French Left to Birth Control in the Nineteenth Century," *Journal of the History of Ideas* 27 (1976): 475–92; "Some Secular Attitudes toward Sexual Behavior in France: 1760–1860," *French Historical Studies* 8 (Fall 1974): 604–25; and "Abortion in France: Women and the Regulation of Family Size, 1800–1914," *French Historical Studies* 10 (Spring 1978): 461–85.

10. *Opinion des femmes,* August 21, 1848. Later, republican feminists similarly condemned birth control. Hubertine Auclert offered this solution to the "problem": "Maternity will cease to terrify French women when, instead of dishonoring or reducing them to dependency, it honors them by payments for indispensable service to the state" (Auclert, *Les Femmes au gouvernail,* p. 309).

11. Gordon, "Voluntary Motherhood." For the English experience, see Constance Rover, *Love, Morals, and the Feminists* (London: Routledge & Kegan Paul, 1970). In all three countries, France, the United States, and England, birth control was practiced before a theory advocating birth control was developed. Also, in all three countries, feminists were *not* among the early proponents of birth control. In England and the United States, too, feminists connected arguments favoring birth control to antipoor arguments or arguments favoring sexual license.

12. Evans, *The Feminists,* p. 128.

13. At the first anticlerical congress (1881), Deraismes got the following resolution inserted into the anticlerical program: "The Congress sets forth its wish that men, and especially free-thinking men, make their wives their companions in their meetings . . . and work to make them legally their equals. It is understood that political rights are included in the formula " 'Equality.' " (See Jean Bernard, "Notice" to Maria Deraismes, *France et Progrès* (Paris: Librairie de la Société des gens des lettres, 1873), pp. xxvii–xxviii.)

14. A 1904 divorce reform law permitted the "guilty" partner to remarry; but divorce by mutual consent is still not permitted today. *Lycée* education for boys and girls was equalized only in 1924.

15. See Ida Berger, ed., *Lettres d'institutrices rurales d'autrefois, rédigées à la suite de l'enquête de Francisque Sarcey en 1897* (Paris: Association des Amis du Musée Pédogogique, 1961).

16. Sowerwine, *Sisters or Citizens,* pp. 76–80.

17. Both David Owen Evans (*Social Romanticism in France, 1830–1848* [New York: Octagon Books, 1969]) and Roger Picard (*Le Romantisme social* [New York: Brentano's, 1944]) document the direct influence of the utopians on Romantic literature, including their influence in changing the image of women in literature.

18. Evans, *Social Romanticism,* p. 22. See also Georges Weill, "Le Saint-Simonisme hors de France," *Revue d'histoire economique et sociale* 9 (1921): 110–11.

19. Juliet Mitchell, "The Longest Revolution," reprinted in *Liberation Now!* (New York: Dell Publishing Co., 1971), p. 267. This article became the basis of Mitchell's book, *Woman's Estate.*

20. In France, married women did not win equal civil rights with their husbands until 1965.

A thought-provoking article by Ellen DuBois on the American suffrage movement ("The Radicalism of the Woman Suffrage Movement: Notes toward the Reconstruction of Nineteenth-Century Feminism," *Feminist Studies* 3 [Fall 1975]: 63–71) argues that the vote was a far more "radical" victory than historians generally have recognized. Nineteenth-century institutions were more vulnerable to change imposed by elections, and the vote therefore was a more significant vehicle of political change than it is today (she gives convincing evidence from local American politics). Moreover, the recognition of women's political rights transformed a centuries-old understanding that the family, not the individual, was the basic political unit. By recognizing the equal political rights of every adult, instead of the "head of household's" right to represent a family unit, a significant challenge to the patriarchal family in fact occurred.

Bibliography

Primary Sources

Manuscript Sources

The Bibliothèque de l'Arsenal, in Paris, has an extraordinarily rich collection of materials on the Saint-Simonians. Upon the death of Enfantin, the Saint-Simonian archives—carefully collected, recopied, annotated, and cataloged by Enfantin, Fournel, Dufour, Laurent, and Guéroult—were donated to the Arsenal. This Fonds Enfantin includes many cartons of personal correspondence, sermons, and other propaganda such as the "enseignements" and all of their newspapers. Of particular interest are the letters of Claire Bazard, Claire Démar, Cécile Fournel, Clorinde Rogé, Pauline Roland (65), Aglaé Saint-Hilaire, Marie Talon, and Suzanne Voilquin. See also the carton "Correspondance du *Globe* (Dames)"—112 letters from women describing their conversion to Saint-Simonism—and the diaries of Charles Lambert from Egypt.

At the Archives Nationales, Paris, are many manuscripts of Fourier and Considérant and papers and correspondence of the associationists. (See Série AS—Archives sociétaires.) Also at the Archives Nationales is the Series F[18]—Archives de la censure. I found useful information in inventories nos. 665 (Inventaire de la presse parisienne) and 625 (Imprimerie et Libraire).

The Bibliothèque Marguerite Durand, also in Paris, has the most extensive documentation for the later years of the nineteenth century. There are dossiers for all of the congresses; for all of the feminist organizations beginning with the 1870 Association pour le Droit des Femmes; and for all of the leaders of this period: Auclert, Deraismes, and Richer, and also Audouard, Daubié, Pontonié-Pierre, Rouzade, Royer, and many more. There are some materials for the first half of the century, too. See dossiers for Jeanne Deroin, Eugénie Niboyet, Pauline Roland, and Suzanne Voilquin. The director of the Bibliothèque Marguerite Durand, Mme Léautey, is exceptionally helpful.

Pat Bidelman kindly made available to me photocopies, made years ago, of two manuscripts that have since disappeared from their depositories: Hubertine Auclert, "Diary," Bibliothèque historique de la ville de Paris; and Jane Misme, "La Vie et la mort du féminisme," Bibliothèque Marguerite Durand.

281

Public Documents

France. Asemblée Nationale. *Annuaire de législation française.* Paris: Librairie générale de droit et de jurisprudence, 1881–.

————. *Code des Délits et des Peines.* Paris: Garnery, 1810.

————. *Code Civil.* Paris: Au bureau d'administration du recueil général des lois et des arrêts, 1817.

  Includes the 1816 law on divorce.

————. *Code Napoléon.* Edition originale et seule officielle. Paris: Imprimerie imperiale, 1807.

————. *Enquête parlementaire sur l'insurrection du 18 mars.* Paris: Wittersheim, 1872.

————. Ministère de l'Instruction Publique. *La législation de l'instruction primaire en France depuis 1789 jusqu'à nos jours. Recueil des lois, décrets, ordonnances, arrêts, règlements, décisions, avis, projets de lois, suivé d'une table analytique et précédé d'une introduction historique par Octave Gréard.* Paris: C. de Mourgues frères, 1874.

————. Ministère de l'Instruction publique. *Plan d'études et programmes de l'enseignement secondaire des jeunes filles.* Paris: J. Delalain, 1883.

————. Statistique Générale de la France. *Résultats généraux du dénombrement de 1866.* Strasbourg: Imprimerie Administrative de Veuve Berger-Levrault, 1869.

  The first listing of employment statistics by professional category and sex.

————. Statistique Générale de la France. *Résultats statistiques du dénombrement de 1891.* Paris: Imprimerie National, 1894.

  Employment statistics for 1891 are not comparable with those of other census years.

————. Statistique Générale de la France. *Résultats statistiques du recensement des industries et professions, 1896.* Paris: Imprimerie Nationale, 1901.

————. Statistique Générale de la France. *Salaires et coût de l'existence à diverse epoques, jusqu'en 1910.* Imprimerie Nationale, 1911.

  Statistics for 1840–45, 1861–65, and 1891–93 with male/female comparisons. Does not include domestic (primarily female) production.

————. Statistique Générale de la France. *Statistique internationale du movement de la population d'après les régistres d'etat civil.* 2 vols. Paris: Imprimerie Nationale, 1907–13.

  Particularly useful is vol. 1, *Résumé retrospectif depuis l'origine des statisques de l'etat civil jusqu'en 1905.* French censuses were done every five years. Beginning in 1851, birth rates are obtainable.

Proceedings of Feminist Congresses

Congrès International du Droit des Femmes: Compte rendu des séances plénières. Paris: Auguste Chio, 1878.

Actes du Congrès International des Oeuvres et Institutions Féminines, 1889. Paris: Société d'Editons Scientifiques, 1890.

Congrès Français et International du Droit des Femmes. Paris: E. Dentu, 1889.

Deuxième Congrès International des Oeuvres et Institutions Féminines, tenu au Palais des Congrès de l'Exposition Universelle de 1900: Compte rendu des travaux par Madame Pegard. 4 vols. Paris: Charles Blot, 1902.

Newspapers

Tribune des femmes. 1832–34.

Thirty-one issues in 2 volumes of 280 and 184 pages. Most issues are undated; the second issue is dated August 25, 1832. The first four issues are paginated individually; others consecutively (33–280 for the first volume). Also titled *La Femme libre, La Femme d'avenir, La Femme nouvelle,* and *L'Apostolat des femmes.* Edited by Suzanne Voilquin for most of its existence.

The *Tribune des femmes* is in both the Arsenal and the Bibliothèque Nationale, but only the Bibliothèque Nationale has a complete collection.

Foi nouvelle: Livre des actes. 1883.

Edited first by Cécile Fournel, then by Marie Talon.

Gazette des femmes. 1836–38.

Published monthly from July 1836 to May 1837 and again from December 1837 to April 1838. Frédéric de Mauchamps was its publisher and editor.

Voix des femmes. March–June 1848.

A four-page daily, appearing six days each week. Edited by Eugénie Niboyet.

Politique des femmes. 1848.

Only two, two-page issues appeared: June 18–24 and August. Edited by Jeanne Deroin.

Opinion des femmes. 1848–49.

One issue in 1848 (August 21); six issues in 1849, when it became an eight-page monthly. Edited by Jeanne Deroin.

Almanach des femmes. 1852–54.

Published in London by Jeanne Deroin in both French and English.

Le Droit des femmes. 1860–70; 1879–91.

Published by Léon Richer.

L'Avenir des femmes. 1871–79.

Published by Léon Richer. Continuation of *Le Droit des femmes* (1869–70; 1879–91).

La Citoyenne. February 13, 1881–November 16, 1891.

Published by Hubertine Auclert until 1888, Maria Martin to 1891.

L'Harmonie sociale. 1892.

Short-lived socialist weekly. Published by Aline Valette.

Le Journal des femmes. 1891–1911.

Successor to *La Citoyenne.* published by Maria Martin.

La Fronde. 1897–1905.

Daily. Published by Marguerite Durand. The most important feminist journal of the period that immediately follows the period of this study. First issue sold 200,000 copies.

Articles and Books by Contemporary Writers

Adam, Juliette. "French Girls." *North American Review* 154 (April 1892):447–58.

―――. *Idées anti-proudhoniennes sur l'amour, la femme et le mariage*. 2d ed. Paris: E. Dentu, 1861.

    Published under the name Juliette Lambert.

―――. "Woman's Place in Modern Life." *Fortnightly Review* 51 (April 1, 1892):522–29.

Agoûlt, Marie d'. *Essai sur la liberté*. Paris: Librairie d'Amyot, 1847.

―――. *Mémoires: 1833–1854*. Paris: Calmann-Lévy, 1927.

    Useful introduction by Daniel Ollivier.

―――. *Mes Souvenirs: 1806–1833*. Paris: Calmann-Lévy, 1877.

―――. *Nélida*. Brussels: Méline, Cans et Compagnie, 1846.

Allart de Méritens, Hortense. *La Femme et la démocratie de nos temps*. Paris: Delaunay, 1836.

Almanach féministe 1899. Paris: Edouard Cornély, 1899.

Almanach féministe 1900. Paris: Edouard Cornély, 1900.

    The *Almanachs,* edited by Marya Cheliga of the Union Universelle des Femmes, were annual reports of current news and included background articles.

Assolant, Alfred. *Le Droit des femmes*. Paris: A. Anger, 1868.

Auclert, Hubertine. *L'Argent de la femme*. Paris: Pedone, 1904.

―――. *Le Droit politique des femmes: Question qui n'est pas traitée au Congrès International des Femmes*. Paris: L. Hugonis, 1878.

―――. *L'Egalité sociale et politique de l'homme et de la femme*. Marseilles: A. Thomas et Cie, 1879.

―――. *Les Femmes au gouvernail*. Paris: Marcel Giard, 1923.

    Includes a lengthy biography by Auclert's sister, Marie Chaumont.

―――. *Le Nom de la femme*. Paris: Société du livre à l'auteur, 1905.

―――. *Le Vote des femmes*. Paris: V. Giard & E. Brière, 1908.

    The fullest exposition of her thought is found here.

Audouard, Olympe. *La Femme dans le mariage, la séparation et le divorce*. Paris: E. Dentu, 1870.

―――. *Guerre aux hommes*. Paris: E. Dentu, 1886.

―――. *Lettre aux députés*. Paris: E. Dentu, 1867.

―――. *M. Barbey d'Aurévilly: Réponse à ses requisitoires contre les bas-bleus, conference du 11 avril*. Paris: E. Dentu, 1870.

Avril de Saint-Croix, Ghénia. *Le Féminisme*. Paris: V. Giard & E. Brière, 1907.

Barbey d'Aurévilly, Jules. *Les Bas-bleus*. Paris: Société Générale de Librairie Catholique, 1876.

Baudrillart, Henri. "L'Agitation pour l'émancipation des femmes." *Revue des deux mondes,* October 1872, pp. 651–77. Reviews of J. S. Mill's *On the Subjection of women,* Julie Daubié's *La Femme pauvre,* and Alexandre Duverger's *De la condition politique et civile des femmes.*

Bazard, P[almyre]. *Aux femmes sur leur mission religieuse dans la crise actuelle*. Rouen: Brière, n.d. [1831].

[Bazard, Saint-Amand]. *Religion Saint-Simonienne. Discussions morales, politiques, et religieuses qui ont amenées la separation qui s'est effectuée au mois de novembre 1831, dans le sein de la société Saint-Simonienne. Première partie. Relations des hommes et des femmes, mariage, divorce.* Paris: Paulin, Delaunay, and Heideloff, 1832.

Bois, Jules. *L'Eve nouvelle.* Paris: Ernest Flammarion, 1897.

———. "La Femme nouvelle." *La Revue encyclopédique* 6 (November 28, 1896):832–40.
A self-styled "spiritualist" feminist.

Bonald, Louis de. *Du divorce considéré au XIXe siècle relativement à l'etat domestique et à l'etat public de société.* Paris: Adrien le Clerc, 1847.

Bouët, H. "Le Féminisme au point de vue économique." *Journal des economistes,* May 1899, pp. 178–97.
Laissez-faire economist who favored feminist goals but criticized their requests for government intervention on women's behalf.

Bridel, Louis. *La Femme et le droit.* Paris: Librairie F. Pichon, 1884.
Discusses the civil and criminal codes and its interpretation by the courts.

Butler, Josephine, ed. *The New Era: A Collection of Twenty-five Pamphlets Relating to the Contagious Diseases Acts of 1864, 1866, and 1869.* Liverpool: T. Brakell, 1872.
Includes the only work of Julie Daubié translated into English, "French Morality under the Regulation System" (from *La Femme pauvre*).

Casaubon, E. A. *Le Nouveau contrat social ou place à la femme.* Paris: Dupuy, 1834.

Chauvin, Jeanne. *Des professions accessibles aux femmes en droit romain et en droit français: Evolution historique de la position économique de la femme dans la société.* Paris: A. Giard & E. Brière, 1892.
Thèse pour le doctorat, faculté de droit. The last half of the study is on "temps modernes," it ends with her brief to open up the legal profession to women. In 1900, a special legislative act recognized Chauvin's right to practice law.

Cheliga, Marya. "L'Evolution du féminisme." *La Revue encyclopédique* 6 (November 28, 1896):910–13.

———. "Les Hommes féministes." *La Revue encyclopédique* 6 (November 28, 1896):825–31.

Crawford, Virginia M. "Feminism in France." *Fortnightly Review,* April 1897, pp. 524–34.

Daubié, Julie-Victoire. "De l'enseignement sécondaire pour les femmes." *Journal des economistes,* June 1865, pp. 382–402; August 1865, pp. 384–403; December 1865, 408–27.

———. *La Femme pauvre au XIXe siècle.* Paris: Guillaumin, 1866.
By "poor" women, she means unpropertied women like herself who, if unmarried, must support themselves but cannot. From schoolteacher to servant, they were all "poor" women.

Démar, Claire. *Textes sur l'affranchissement des femmes.* Followed by an explanation of Saint-Simonian symbolism and ideology by Valentin Pelosse. Paris: Payot, 1976.
Reprints Démar's *Ma loi d'avenir, Appel d'une femme au peuple pour l'affranchissement de la femme,* and correspondence; also, Voilquin's preface to *Ma loi d'avenir* and Bazard's critique of Enfantin's new morality.

Deraismes, Maria. *Eve contre Monsieur Dumas fils.* Paris: E. Dentu, 1872.

———. *Eve dans l'humanité.* Paris: Librairie Générale de L. Sauvraîte, 1891.

———. *France et progrès.* Paris: Librairie de la Société des gens de lettres, 1873.

———. *Nos principes et nos moeurs.* Paris: Michel Lévy frères, 1868.

————. *Oeuvres complètes*. Edited by Anna Féresse-Deraismes. 3 vols. Paris: Félix Alcan, 1896.

————. Théâtre chez soi. Paris: Amyot, 1863.

Deroin, Jeanne-Victoire. *Aux femmes*. Paris: Auffray, n.d. [August 1832]. Reprinted from *La Femme libre* (*Tribune des femmes* 1, no. 2).

Dissard Clotilde. *Opinions feministes à propos du Congrès feministe de Paris*. Paris: Giard et Brière, 1896.

Doctrine de Saint-Simon: Exposition, première année, 1828–1829. Edited by C. Bouglé and E. Halévy. Paris: Rivière, 1924. Translation: *The Doctrine of Saint-Simon: An Exposition, First Year, 1828–1829*. Translated by Georg G. Iggers. New York: Schocken Books, 1972.

   This work is credited to Bazard, Enfantin, Carnot, Rodrigues, Fournel, and Duveyrier.

Dollfus, Charles. "Bibliographie française." *Revue germanique, française, et étrangère* 18 (November 15, 1861):129–35.

   Short reviews of Proudhon's *Guerre et paix* and Adam's [Lamber's] *Idées anti-proudhoniennes*.

Dumas, Alexandre, fils. "Les Droits de la femme." *La Revue encyclopédique*, December 15, 1895, pp. 157–59.

   Letter to Marya Cheliga, written right before his death: "I wish that civil and political rights for women be exactly the same as for men." A 180-degree turn from his position in 1872.

————. *Les Femmes qui tuent et les femmes qui votent*. Paris: Calmann-Lévy, 1880.

   First step in Dumas's conversion to feminism and, particularly, suffragism.

————. *L'Homme-femme: Réponse à M. Henri d'Ideville*. Paris: M. Levy, 1872.

   His position in 1872 was starkly antifeminist.

————. *La Recherche de la paternité: Lettre à M. Rivet, deputé*. Paris: Calmann-Lévy, 1883.

————. *Théâtre complet*. 6 vols. Paris: Lévy, 1884–86.

   Vol. 1 includes *La Dame aux camélias* and *Diane de Lys*.

Dupanloup, Félix. *Controverse sur l'éducation des filles*. Paris: Plon, 1875.

————. *La Femme chrétienne et française: Dernière réponse à M. Duruy*. Paris: Douniol, 1868.

————. *M. Duruy et l'éducation des filles*. Paris: Douniol, 1867.

Duverger, Alexandre. *De la condition politique et civile des femmes: Réponse à quelques critiques de nos lois; modifications admissibles; études de legislation*. Paris: A. Maresque, 1872.

   Twenty-six page extract from an article originally published in *La Revue pratique de droit français*. Reformist, nonfeminist.

Enfantin, Prosper, and Henri, comte de Saint-Simon. *Oeuvres de Saint-Simon et d'Enfantin*. Published by members of the committee set up by Enfantin for the execution of his last will. 47 vols. Paris: E. Dentu, Ernest Leroux, 1865–78.

   Pertinent volumes: 1–13, 14, 16–17, 24–36, 41–45, 47. Enfantin's record of Saint-Simonian events; his correspondence to others (but rarely their correspondence to him); the sermons; the transcripts of the two trials. Some of these materials have been published separately, for example, many of the "Enseignements" and the *Doctrine de Saint-Simon: Exposition, première année, 1829*.

————. *Réunion générale de la famille: Séances des 19 et 21 novembre 1831.* Paris: Bureau de Globe, 1832.

Engels, Frederick. *The Origin of the Family, Private Property, and the State.* Translated by Robert Vernon. New York: Pathfinder Press, 1972.

Etrivières, Jehan des. *Les Amazones du siècle.* Paris: Destenay, 1882.
  Unsympathetic biographies of Louise Michel, Léonie Rouzade, Hubertine Auclert, and Eugénie Pierre.

Fouillée. "La Psychologie des sexes." *Revue des deux mondes,* September 15, 1893.

Fourier, François Marie Charles. *Le Nouveau monde industriel et sociétaire, ou invention du procédé d'industrie attrayant et naturelle distribuée en séries passionnées.* Paris: Flammarion, 1973.
  The most readable of Fourier's works. Originally published at the urging of the nascent Ecole Sociétaire, in 1829, to make his ideas more accessible to the general public. In *Oeuvres complètes,* vol. 6.

————. *Oeuvres complètes.* 6 vols. Paris: Librairie sociétaire, 1843.

————. *Théorie des quatre mouvements et des destinées générales: Prospectus et annonce de la découverte.* Paris: Jean-Jacques Pauvert, 1967.
  Originally published in 1808. Reprinted in *Oeuvres complètes,* vol. 1, from an 1840 edition. This is Fourier's first work.

————. *Traité de l'association domestique-agricole.* Paris: Edition Anthropos, 1966–67.
  Originally published in 1822. Reprinted in 1834 under the title Théorie de l'unité universelle; also in *Oeuvres complètes,* vols. 2–4. This is the fullest exposition of Fourier's ideas.

Frank, Louis. "University Opportunities for Women." *Educational Review,* December 1894, pp. 471–84.

Gasparin, le comte Agenor de. *Les Réclamations des femmes.* Paris: Michel Lévy, 1872.
  Sympathetic to most feminist demands, including the vote, but not divorce.

Gatti de Gamond, Zoé Charlotte. *Fourier et son système.* 5th ed. Paris: Capelle, 1841–42.
  See especially the chapter entitled "Condition des femmes en Harmonie."

Gide, Paul. *Etude sur la condition privée de la femme dans le droit ancien et moderne.* Paris: Durand et Pedone-Lauriel, 1867.
  Reformist, nonfeminist.

Girardin, Emile de. *La Liberté dans le mariage, par l'égalité des enfants devant la mère.* Paris: Librairie Nouvelle, 1854.

Giraud, Léon. *Des droits de la femme mariée sous le régime de la communauté relativement à l'aliénation de l'un de ses biens faits par le mari sans son consentement.* Paris: A. Rousseau, 1887.

————. *Essai sur la condition des femmes en Europe et en Amerique.* Paris: A. Chio, 1882.

————. *La Femme et la nouvelle loi sur le divorce.* Paris: G. Pedone-Lauriel, 1885.

————. *Les Femmes et les libres-penseurs: Réponse à M. Benjamin Gastineau pour sa brochure "Les Femmes et les Prêtres."* Paris: Perinet, 1880.
  Written under the pseudonym "Draigu."

————. *Souvenirs du Congrès pour le Droit des Femmes, tenu à Paris en août 1878.* Paris: A. Chio, 1879.

Haussonville, le comte de. *Misères et remèdes.* Paris: Calmann-Lévy, 1892.
  Sympathetic, reformist treatise on working-class women. Relies on Jules Simon's statistics.

Héricourt, Jenny d'. *La Femme affranchie: Réponse a Mm. Michelet, Proudhon, E. de Girardin, A. Comte et aux autres novateurs modernes*. 2 vols. Brussels: A. Lacroix, 1860. Translation: *A Woman's Philosophy of Woman: An Answer to Michelet, Proudhon, Girardin, Legouvé, Comte, and Other Modern Innovators*. New York: Carleton, 1864.

> The translation is poor and incomplete.

Herzen, Alexander. *My Past and Present*. Translated by Constance Garnett. Rev. ed. Edited by Humphrey Higgens. 2 vols. New York: Alfred A. Knopf, 1968.

> First published in 1861–66 in Russian. Herzen was Proudhon's friend and financed *Le Peuple* for him. Useful for comments on Proudhon's attitude on women.

Jacobs, Aletta [Mme C. V. Gerritsen]. *La Femme et le féminisme*. Paris: V. Giard & E. Brière, 1900.

> The bibliography of her private collection, donated to the John Crerar Library, Chicago, in 1904, to the University of Kansas Library in 1954, and now available on microfilm.

Janet, Paul. "L'Education des femmes." *Revue des deux mondes*, September 1, 1883, pp. 48–85.

Krug, Charles. *Le Féminisme et le droit civil français*. Nancy: Thèse droit, 1899.

Laboulaye, Edouard de. *Recherches sur la condition civile et politique des femmes, depuis les Romains jusqu'à nos jours*. Paris: A. Durand, 1843.

> Reformist, nonfeminist.

Langlois, Jérome A. *L'Homme et la révolution: Huit études dédiées à. P. J. Proudhon*. 2 vols. Paris: Germer Baillière, 1867.

> The sixth study (vol. 2, pp. 106–208) is on women. Although a patriarchalist, he is not so misogynist as Proudhon.

Lebassu, Joséphine. *La Saint-simonienne*. Paris: L. Tenré, 1833.

Leduc, Lucien. *La Femme devant le parlement*. Paris: V. Giard & E. Brière, 1898.

Legouvé, Ernest. *Histoire morale des femmes*. Paris: Gustave Sandré, 1849.

> Originally a lecture series at the Academy.

Lejéal, Gustave. "La Femme devant la loi." *La Revue encyclopédique* 6 (November 28, 1896):903–5.

———. "Le Mouvement féministe." *La Revue encyclopédique* 15 (June 1893):585–96.

Lemonnier, Charles. *Elisa Lemmonier, fondatrice de la Société pour l'Enseignement Professionel des Femmes*. Saint-Germain: L. Toinon, 1866.

Léo, André [Léodile Champseix]. *Un divorce*. Paris: 1869.

> Feminist novel.

———. *Un mariage scandaleux*. Paris: Librairie A. Faure, 1863.

> Feminist novel.

Le Play, Frédéric. *L'Organisation de la famille selon le vrai modèle par l'histoire de toutes les races et de tous les temps*. 1871. Reprint. Paris: Téqui, 1874.

> Reactionary. Very influential on French sociology scholarship.

Leroy-Beaulieu, Paul. *Le Travail des femmes au XIXᵉ siècle*. Paris: Charpentier, 1895.

> Salary statistics; labor legislation; suggestions for reform. Protectionist.

Lissagaray, Hippolyte. *Les Huit journées de mai derrière les barricades*. Brussels: Bureau de Petit Journal, 1871.

Lourbet, Jacques. *La Femme devant la science contemporaine*. Paris: Félix Alcan, 1896.

> Scientific attitudes toward women.

Magallon, comtesse de. "Le Féminisme—Victoire Daubié." *La Nouvelle revue*, August 15, 1898, pp. 667–95.

Malon, Benoît. *Le Socialisme intégral*. 2 vols. 1890. Reprint. Paris: F. Alcan, 1894.
Vol. 2, chap. 7, is on women.

Marcil, René. *Les Femmes qui pensent et les femme qui écrivent*. Paris: E. Dentu, 1889.

Marion, Henri. *Psychologie de la femme*. Paris: A. Colin, 1900.
Sympathetic, nonfeminist.

Michel, Louise. *The Red Virgin: Memoirs of Louis Michel*. Edited and translated by Bullitt Lowry and Elizabeth Ellington Gunter. University, Ala.: University of Alabama Press, 1981.

Michelet, Jules. *L'Amour*. 1858. 3d ed. Paris: Librairie de L. Hachette et Cie, 1859.
By 1894, twenty-three editions had been published.

———. *La Femme*. 1860. 15th ed. Paris: Calmann-Lévy, 1885.
By 1889, seventeen editions had been published. Its popularity extended into the twentieth century: in 1921, the 52nd edition was published.

———. *Les Femmes de la Révolution*. Paris: Adolphe Delahays, 1854.
Valuable as a source to comprehend Michelet's thought rather than the role of women in the Revolution. Assigns a pivotal role to women's desertion of the Revolution as causing its failure. Michelet's "solution" was to propose better control over women's potentially destructive independence.

Milhaud, Caroline. *L'Ouvrière en France: Sa condition présente, les réformes nécessaires*. Paris: Alcan, 1907.
Useful statistics.

Mill, John Stuart. *The Subjection of Woman*. 1869. Reprint. Cambridge: MIT Press, 1970.
A French translation appeared in 1869.

Naquet, Alfred. *Le Divorce*. 1877. Reprint. Paris: E. Dentu, 1881.
Historical overview and proposals for reform.

———. *La Loi du divorce*. Paris: E. Fasquelle, 1903.
Includes material that duplicates his 1877 book on divorce plus information on the 1884 law.

———. *Religion, propriété, famille*. 1869. Reprint. Brussels: H. Kistemaeckers, 1877.
Naquet's Saint-Simonian origins shine through.

Niboyet, Eugénie. *Le Vrai livre des femmes*. Paris: E. Dentu, 1863.
Her memory of the 1848 events are blurred, probably purposely.

Obsèques de Maria Deraismes: Discours prononcés sur sa tombe le 9 février 1894 par Annie Jackson-Daynes, Virginie Griess-Traut, Ernest Hamel, Mme. Vincent, Eugénie Potonié-Pierre, M. Dide, Mme. Bequet de Vienne, Gustave Hubbard, Mme. Pognon, M. Raqueni, Mme. Valette, Paule Mink, Mme. Rouzade, M. Schacre, M. Frinquet. Paris: N. p., 1895.
Some useful biographical data.

Parent-Duchâtelet, A.-J.-B. *De la prostitution dans la ville de Paris*. 2 vols. Paris: Chez Baillière, 1836.
Very important in its day and still important in the field.

Pelletan, Eugène. *La Famille, la mère*. Paris: Librairie Internationale, 1865.

———. *La Femme au XIXe siècle*. Paris: Pagnerre, 1869.

Pelloutier, Fernand, and Maurice Pelloutier. "La Femme dans la société moderne." *La Revue socialiste*, September 15, 1894, pp. 285–311.

————. *La Vie ouvrière en France.* Paris: Schleicher, 1900.

    See especially chap. 3 for women workers.

Pissarjevsky, Lydié. *Socialisme et féminisme.* Paris: Imprimerie Cooperative Ouvrière, 1910.

    The author, secretary of the Congrès International Permanent Féministe, attempts to reconcile socialism and bourgeois feminism.

Pizan, Christine de. *The Book of the City of Ladies.* Translated by Earl Jeffrey Richards. New York, 1982.

Poullain de la Barre, François. *Egalité des deux sexes.* Paris: Sean du Puis, 1673.

    Among the first French feminists.

————. *La Liberté des dames.* Paris: Christophe Rémy, 1685.

Proudhon, Pierre-Joseph. *De la création de l'ordre dans l'humanité ou principes d'organisation politique.* Paris: Librairie des Sciences Politiques et Sociales, 1927.

————. *De la justice dans la Révolution et dans l'église.* 1858. Reprint. Brussels: Office de Publicité, 1860.

————. *Les Femmelins: Les grandes figures romantiques, J.-J. Rousseau, Beranger, Lamartine, Madame Roland, Mme. de Staël, Mme. Necker de Saussaure, George Sand.* Paris: Nouvelle Librairie Nationale, 1912.

    Proudhon disliked male Romantic writers as much as female.

————. *La Pornocratie ou les femmes dans les temps modernes.* Paris: A. Lacroix et Cie, 1875.

    Incomplete; published posthumously. Includes Proudhon's notes for completing the fragments.

————. *Qu'est-ce que la propriete?* Paris: Garnier Flammarion, 1966.

    Proudhon's first book, originally published in 1840, gives the scandalous answer, "C'est la vol."

————. *Système des contradictions économiques ou philosophie de la misère.* 1846. Reprint. Paris: Ernest Flammarion, 1897.

Religion Saint-Simonienne: Cérémonie du 27 novembre. Paris: Guiraudet, 1831.

Religion saint-simonienne: Morale . . . Paris: Everat, [April] 1832.

    Five "enseignements" preached by Enfantin.

Renaudot, Maurice. *Le Féminisme et les droit publics de la femme.* Rennes: Thèse de Droit, 1902.

Ribière, Alphonse. *Les Femmes dans la science.* Paris: Nony & Cie, 1897.

Richer, Léon. *Le Code des femmes.* Paris: E. Dentu, 1883.

————. *Le Divorce, projet de loi précédé d'un exposé des motifs et suivi des principaux documents officiels se rattachant à la question.* With a letter and preface by Louis Blanc. Paris: Le Chevalier, 1873.

————. *La Femme libre.* Paris: E. Dentu, 1877.

    This is the fullest exposition of Richer's thought.

————. *Le Livre des femmes.* Paris: E. Dentu, 1872.

Rochard, Jules. "L'Education des filles." *Revue des deux mondes,* 1 February 1888, pp. 644–80.

Rodriques, O[linde]. *Réunion générale de la famille . . . 19 et 20 nov. Note sur le mariage et la divorce.* Paris: N.p., 1831.

Rousseau, Jean-Jacques. *Emile.* Translated by Barbara Foxley. New York: Dutton, 1933.

————. *La Nouvelle Héloïse.* Translated by Judith H. McDowell. University Park: Pennsylvania State University Press, 1968.

Rousselot, Paul. *Histoire de l'éducation des femmes en France.* 1883. Reprint. New York: Burt Franklin, 1971.

    From the time of Mme de Maintenon to 1870.

Saint-Amand, A[dèle]. *Proclamation aux femmes.* Paris: H. Fournier, n.d.

Simon, Jules. *L'Ecole.* 12th ed., including a resumé of the last official census. Paris: Librairie Hachette, 1894.

———. *L'Ouvrière.* 1861. 2d ed. Paris: Librairie de L. Hachette, 1862.

    Most influential of all nineteenth-century books on the subject. His statistics were frequently used by other authors, frequently by politicians to argue against women working in industry.

———. "Le Salaire et le travail des femmes: Les femmes dans la fabrique lyonnaise." *Revue des deux mondes,* February 15, 1860, pp. 916–53.

Simon, Jules, and Gustave Simon. *La Femme de 20ᵐᵉ siècle.* 13th ed. Paris: Calmann-Lévy, 1892.

Stanton, Theodore, ed. *The Woman Question in Europe.* New York: G. P. Putnam's Sons, 1884.

    Stanton wrote the chapter on France himself; the section on the legal status of French women, however, is quoted from a letter to him by Léon Giraud.

Talmeyr, Maurice. "Les Femmes qui enseignent." *Revue des deux mondes,* 1 June 1897, pp. 633–54.

    The unemployment crisis in nineteenth-century education: too many women trained to teach and too few positions.

Tristan y Moscozo, Flore Célestine Thérèse Henriette [Flora Tristan]. *L'Emancipation de la femme ou le testament de la paria.* Completed after her notes and published by A. Constant. Paris: 1845.

    Posthumous. Extensively rewritten by Constant from Tristan's notes left in his possession.

———. *Lettres.* Edited by Stéphane Michaud. Paris: Editions du Seuil, 1980.

———. *Méphis.* 2 vols. Paris: Ladvocat, 1838.

    The author's only novel.

———. *Nécessité de faire un bon accueil aux femmes étrangères.* Paris: Delauney, 1836.

———. *Pérégrinations d'une paria: Dieu, franchise, liberté.* 2 vols. Paris: Arthur Bertrand, 1838.

    Autobiography.

———. *Promenades dans Londres.* Paris: H.-L. Delloye, 1840.

———. *L'Union ouvrière.* 1843. 3d edition. Paris, 1844. Reprinted by Editions d'Histoire Sociale, 1967.

———. *Le Tour de France: Journal inédit 1843–1844.* Preface by Michel Collinet, notes by Jules L. Puech. Paris: Editions Tête de Feuilles, 1973.

    Includes diary entries from her "tour"—beginning April 12, 1844, ending with her death from typhoid.

———. *Le Tour de France, journal 1843–1844.* 2d ed. 2 vols. Text and notes by Jules Puech, preface by Michel Collinet, and a new introduction by Stéphane Michaud. Paris: Maspero, 1980.

Turgeon, Charles. *Le Féminisme français.* 2 vols. Paris: Librairie de la Société de Recueil Générale des Lois et des Arrêts, 1902.

    Antifeminist but useful as an introduction to feminism at the turn of the century.

Valbert, G. "L'Emancipation des femmes." *Revue des deux mondes,* November 1, 1880, pp. 204–16.

Veret, Jeanne-Désirée. *Aux femmes privilégiées.* Paris: Auffray, n.d. [1832].
Reprinted from *La Femme libre* (*Tribune des femmes* 1, no. 1).

———. *Lettre au roi.* Paris: Auffray, n.d. [1832]. Reprinted from *La Femme libre* (*Tribune des femmes* 1, no. 1).

Villermé, L.-B. *Tableau de l'état physique et moral des ouvriers employés dans les manufactures de coton, de laine et de soie.* 2 vols. Paris: J. Renouard, 1840.
Valuable statistics on women as well as men workers.

Voilquin, Suzanne. *Mémoires d'une Saint-simonienne en Russie (1839–1846).* Edited by Maïté Albistur et Daniel Armogathe. Paris: Editions des femmes, 1977.
From an unpublished, signed manuscript found in the Bibliothèque Marguerite Durand.

———. *Souvenirs d'une fille du peuple ou la Saint-simonienne en Egypte.* Introduction by Lydia Elhadad. Paris: François Maspero, 1978.
Originally published in 1866, Voilquin's memories of events in the 1830s appear accurate. They can be cross-checked against her correspondence on file at the Bibliothèque de l'Arsenal.

Secondary Sources

Books, Articles, and Dissertations

Abensour, Léon. *Le Féminisme sous le règne de Louis Philippe et en 1848.* Paris: Plon-Nourrit et Cie, 1913.

———. *La Femme et le feminisme avant la Révolution.* Paris: Leroux, 1923.

———. *Histoire générale du feminisme.* Paris: Librairie Delagrave, 1921.

———. *Le Problème féministe.* Paris: Aux Editions Radot, 1927.

Abray, Jane. "Feminism in the French Revolution." *American Historical Review* 80 (February 1975):43–62.

Adler, Laure. *A l'Aube de féminisme: Les Premières journalistes (1830–1850).* Paris: Payot, 1979.

Albistur, Maïté, and Daniel Armogathe. *Le Grief des femmes.* 2 vols. Paris: Hier et demain, 1978.

———. *Histoire du féminisme français.* 2 vols. Paris: Editions des femmes, 1977.

Amann, Peter H. *Revolution and Mass Democracy: The Paris Club Movement in 1848.* Princeton: Princeton University Press, 1975.

Ansart, Pierre. *Sociologie de Proudhon.* Paris: Presses Universitaires de France, 1967.

Ariès, Philippe. *Centuries of Childhood: A Social History of Family Life.* Translated by Robert Baldick. New York: Vintge Books, 1962.

Baelen, Jean. *La Vie de Flora Tristan: Socialisme et feminisme au 19ᵉ siècle.* Paris: Editions du Seuil, 1972.

Bardèche, Maurice. *Histoire des femmes.* 2 vols. Paris: Stock, 1968.

Beauvoir, Simone de. *Le Deuxième sexe.* 2 vols. Paris: Gallimard, 1949. Translation: *The Second Sex.* Translated by H. M. Parshley. New York: Bantam Books, 1961.

The English translation first appeared in 1952. Although the Bantam Books edition carries the claim "complete and unabridged," all English-language editions are much abridged from the original French.

Bell, Susan Groag. "Christine de Pizan (1364–1430): Humanism and the Problem of a Studious Woman." *Feminist Studies* 3 (Spring–Summer 1976):173–84.

Bellanger, Claude, Jacques Godechot, Guiral Rerrer, and Terrou Fernand, eds. *Histoire générale de la presse française.* 4 vols. Paris: Presses Universitaires de France, 1969. Vol. 2: 1815–71; Vol. 3: 1871–1940.

Berger, Ida, ed. *Lettres d'institutrices rurales d'autrefois, rédigées à la suite de l'enquête de Francisque Sarcey en 1897.* Paris: Association des Amis de Musée Pedagogique, 1961.

Bergues, Hélène, et al. *Prévention des naissances dans la famille.* Paris: Preses Universitaires de France, 1960.

See particularly articles by Jean Sutter, "Diffusion des méthodes contraceptives"; Alfred Sauvy, "Essai d'une vue d'ensemble"; and Philippe Ariès, "Interpretation pour un histoire des mentalités."

Bidelman, Patrick. "The Feminist Movement in France: The Formative Years, 1858–1889." Ph.D. dissertation, Michigan State University, 1975.

———. "Maria Deraismes, Léon Richer, and the Founding of the French Feminist Movement, 1866–1878." *Third Republic/Troisième République,* nos. 3–4 (1977):20–73.

———. *Pariahs Stand Up! The Founding of the Liberal Feminist Movement in France, 1858–1889.* Westport, Conn.: Greenwood Press, 1982.

———. "The Politics of French Feminism: Léon Richer and the Ligue française pour le droit des femmes, 1882–1891." *Historical Reflections/Réflexions historiques* 3 (Summer 1976):93–120.

Bloch, Ruth. "American Feminine Ideals in Transition: The Rise of the Moral Mother, 1785–1815." *Feminist Studies* 4 (June 1978):101–26.

Bodek, Evelyn Gordon. "Salonières and Bluestockings: Educated Obsolescence and Germinating Feminism." *Feminist Studies* 3 (Spring–Summer 1976):185–99.

Bolster, Richard. *Stendhal, Balzac et le féminisme romantique.* Paris: Minard, 1970.

Bory, Jean-Louis. *La Révolution de juillet.* Paris: Gallimard, 1972.

Bouglé, G. Célestin Charles Alfred. "Le Féminisme saint-simonien." *La Revue de Paris* 25 (September 15, 1918):371–99.

———. *Socialismes français.* Paris: Librairie Colin, 1946.

Bourgin, Hubert. "Victor Considérant, son oeuvre." *La Révolution de 1848* 5 (1908):453–79, 553–88, 637–54, 695–729.

Boxer, Marilyn. "Socialism Faces Feminism in France, 1879–1913." Ph.D. dissertation, University of California, Riverside, 1975.

———. "Women in Industrial Homework: The Flowermakers of Paris in the Belle Epoque." *French Historical Studies* 12 (Spring 1982):401–23.

Boxer, Marilyn J., and Jean H. Quataert, eds. *Socialist Women: European Socialist Feminism in the Nineteenth and Early Twentieth Centuries.* New York: Elsevier, 1978.

Branca, Patricia. "A New Perspective on Women's Work: A Comparative Typology." *Journal of Social History* 9 (Winter 1975):129–53.

———. *Women in Europe since 1750.* New York: St. Martin's Press, 1978.

Brault, Eliane. *La Franc-Maçonnerie et l'émancipation des femmes.* Paris: Dervy, 1953.

————. "Maria Deraismes: Laïque et Républicaine, Fondatrice du 'Droit Humain.'" *Cahiers laïques* 70 (July–August 1962):73–104.

Bridenthal, Renate, and Claudia Koonz, eds. *Becoming Visible: Women in European History.* Boston: Houghton Mifflin, 1976.

> Pertinent articles: Mary Lynn McDougall, "Working-Class Women during the Industrial Revolution"; Theresa McBride, "The Long Road Home: Women's Work and Industrialization"; Barbara Corrado Pope, "Angels in the Devil's Workshop: Leisured and Charitable Women in Nineteenth-Century England and France."

Brogan, Denis W. *Proudhon.* London: Hamish Hamilton Publisher, 1934.

Burkhardt, Jacob B. *The Civilization of the Renaissance in Italy.* New York: New American Library, 1961.

Calo, Jeanne. *La Création de la femme chez Michelet.* Paris: Nizet, 1975.

Camp, Wesley Douglass. "Marriage and the Family in France since the Revolution." Ph.D. dissertation, Columbia University, 1957.

Carroll, Berenice A., ed. *Liberating Women's History.* Urbana: University of Illinois Press, 1976.

> See particularly Hilda Smith, "Feminism and the Methodology of Women's History."

Cerati, Marie. "Elisa Lemonnier." In *Femmes extraordinaires.* Paris: Editions de la Courtille, 1979. Pp. 34–85.

Charles-Roux, E., G. Ziegler, M. Cerati, J. Bruhat, M. Guilbert, and C. Gilles. *Les Femmes et le travail du moyen âge à nos jours.* Paris: La Courtille, 1975.

> Bruhat is the author of the chapter on the nineteenth century.

Charléty, Sebastien. *Essai sur l'histoire du Saint-simonisme.* Paris: Hachette, 1896.

Chevalier, Louis. *Classes laborieuses et classes dangereuses à Paris pendant la première moîtié du XIXᵉ siècle.* Paris: Plon, 1958.

Chodorow, Nancy. *The Reproduction of Mothering: Psychoanalysis and the Sociology of Gender.* Stanford: Stanford University Press, 1979.

Cinquante ans de féminisme. Paris: Ligue française pour le droit des femmes, 1921.

> Published on the fiftieth anniversary of the Ligue.

Cobb, Richard. *A Second Identity: Essays on France and French History.* London: Oxford University Press, 1969.

> See "The Women of the Commune," pp. 221–36. Reprinted from the *Times Literary Supplement,* 14 January 1965.

Collins, Irene. *The Government and the Newspaper Press in France, 1814–1881.* London: Oxford University Press, 1959.

Contenson, Ludovic. *Féminisme: Les syndicats professionels féminins.* Paris: Bloud & Cie, 1910.

Corbin, Alain. *Les Filles de noce: Misère sexuelle et prostitution (19ᵉ et 20ᵉ siècles).* Paris: Aubier Montaigne, 1978.

Cott, Nancy F. *The Bonds of Womanhood: "Woman's Sphere" in New England, 1780–1835.* New Haven: Yale University Press, 1977.

————. "Passionlessness: An Interpretation of Victorian Sexual Ideology, 1790–1850." *Signs* 4 (Winter 1978):219–36.

Daly, Mary. *Gyn/Ecology: The Metaethics of Radical Feminism.* Boston: Beacon Press, 1978.

Darrow, Margaret H. "French Noblewomen and the New Domesticity, 1750–1850." *Feminist Studies* 5 (Spring 1979):41–65.

Daumard, Adeline. *La Bourgeoisie parisienne de 1815 à 1848.* Paris: SEVPEN, 1963.

———. *Les Bourgeois de Paris au XIXe siècle.* Paris: Flammarion, 1970.

Davis, Natalie Zemon. " 'Women's History' in Transition: The European Case." *Feminist Studies* 3 (Spring–Summer 1976):83–103.

Decaux, Alain. *Histoire des françaises.* 2 vols. Paris: Librairie Academique Perrin, 1972.

Deniel, Raymond. *Une Image de la famille et de la société sous la restauration.* Paris: Les Editions Ouvrières, 1965.

Desanti, Dominique. *Flora Tristan: La femme révoltée.* Paris: Hachette, 1972.

Devance, Louis. "Femme, famille, travail et morale sexuelle dans l'idéologie de 1848." *Romantisme,* nos. 13–14 (1976):79–103.

Dinnerstein, Dorothy. *The Mermaid and the Minotaur: Sexual Arrangements and Human Malaise.* New York: Harper & Row, 1977.

Dolléans, Edouard. *Histoire du mouvement ouvrier.* 3 vols. Paris. Librairie Armand Colin, 1939.

   Particularly vol. 1, 1830–71, and vol. 2, 1871–1920.

———. *Proudhon.* Paris: Gallimard, 1948.

———. *George Sand: Féminisme et mouvement ouvrier.* Paris: Les Editions Ouvrières, 1951.

DuBois, Ellen. "The Radicalism of the Woman Suffrage Movement: Notes toward the Reconstruction of Nineteenth-Century Feminism." *Feminist Studies* 3 (Fall 1975):63–71.

Duhet, Paule-Marie. *Les Femmes et la Révolution, 1789–1794.* Paris: Julliard, 1971.

Dupeux, Georges. *La Société française, 1789–1970.* Paris: Armand Colin, 1972.

Duroselle, Jean-Baptiste. *Les Débuts du catholicisme social en France, 1822–1870.* Paris: Presses Universitaires de France, 1951.

Duveau, Georges. *1848: The Making of a Revolution.* Translated by Anne Carter. New York: Pantheon Books, 1967.

Eaubonne, Françoise, d'. *Histoire et actualité du féminisme.* Paris: Alain Moreau, 1972.

Evans, David Owen. *Social Romanticism in France, 1830–1848.* New York: Octagon Books, 1969.

Evans, Richard J. *The Feminists: Women's Emancipation Movements in Europe, America, and Australasia, 1840–1920.* New York: Harper & Row, 1977.

Faderman, Lillian. *Surpassing the Love of Men: Romantic Friendship and Love between Women from the Renaissance to the Present.* New York: William Morrow, 1981.

Figes, Eva. *Patriarchal Attitudes.* Greenwich, Conn.: Fawcett, 1970.

Flandrin, Jean-Louis. *Families in Former Times: Kinship, Household, and Sexuality.* Translated by Richard Southern. 1976. Reprint. Cambridge: Cambridge University Press, 1979.

Flexner, Eleanor. *Century of Struggle: The Women's Rights Movement in the United States.* 1959. Reprint. New York: Atheneum, 1968.

Foucault, Michel. *The History of Sexuality: An Introduction.* Translated by Robert Hurley. 1976. Reprint. New York: Pantheon Books, 1978.

Gattey, Charles Neilson. *Gauguin's Astonishing Grandmother: A Biography of Flora Tristan.* London: Femina Books, 1970.

Gaudefroy-Demombynes, Lorraine. *Le Femme dans l'oeuvre de Maupassant.* Paris: Mercure de France, 1943.

Gautier, Etienne, and Louis Henry. *La Population de Crulai, paroisse normande.* Paris: Institut National d'Etudes Demographiques, Travaux et Documents, 1958.

Gennari, Geneviève. *Le Dossier de la femme.* Paris: Librairie Academique Perrin, 1965.

Geyl, Pieter. *Debates with Historians.* Cleveland: World Publishing Co., 1958.
    See the chapter on Michelet.

Glass, D. V., and D.E.C. Eversley, eds. *Population in History.* Chicago: Aldine, 1965.
    See particularly J. Bourgeois-Pichat, "The General Development of the Population of France since the Eighteenth Century"; Louis Henry, "The Population of France in the Eighteenth Century"; J. Hajnal, "European Marriage Patterns in Perspective"; and Pierre Goubert, "Recent Theories and Research in French Population between 1500 and 1700."

Goliber, Sue Helder. "The Life and Times of Marguerite Durand." Ph.D. dissertation, Kent State University, 1975.

Gordon, Linda. "Voluntary Motherhood: The Beginnings of Feminist Birth Control Ideas in the United States." *Feminist Studies* 1 (Winter–Spring 1973):5–22.

Goubert, Pierre. *Beauvais et le beauvaisis de 1600 à 1730.* Paris: Ecole Pratique des Hautes Etudes, 1960.

———. "Historical Demography and the Reinterpretation of Early Modern French History: A Research Review." In *The Family in History,* edited by Theodore Rabb and Robert I. Rotberg, pp. 16–27. New York: Harper & Row, 1971.

Grinberg, Suzanne. *Historique du mouvement suffragiste.* Paris: Henry Goulet, 1927.

Guehenno, Jean. *L'Evangile éternel.* Paris: Bernard Graddet, 1927.
    Biography of Michelet.

Guilbert, Madeleine. "L'Evolution des effectives du travail féminin en France depuis 1866." *Revue française du travail,* September 1947, pp. 754–77.

———. *Les Femmes et l'organisation syndicale avant 1914.* Paris: Editions du Centre Nationale de la Recherche Scientifique, 1966.

———. *Les Fonctions des femmes dans l'industrie.* Paris: Mouton et Cie, 1966.

Guilbert, Madeleine, and Viviane Isambert-Jamati. *Travail féminin et travail à domicile: Enquête sur le travail à domicile de la confection féminine dans la région parisienne.* Paris: Centre National de la Recherche Scientifique, 1956.

Gurvitch, Georges. *Proudhon.* Paris: Presses Universitaires de France, 1965.

Grappin, Henri. "Notes sur un féministe oublié: Le cartesian Poullain de la Barre." *Revue d'histoire litteraire de la France* (1913):852–67.

Grimal, Pierre, ed. *Histoire mondiale de la femme.* 4 vols. Paris: Librairie de France, 1967.
    Chapter 2 of volume 4, "La Femme en France au XIXᵉ siècle," is written by Nicole Bothorel and Marie-Françoise Laurent.

Hajnal, J. "The Marriage Boom." *Population Index* 19 (April 1953):80–101.

Halévy, Daniel. *Le Mariage de Proudhon.* Paris: Librairie Stock, 1955.

Hartman, Mary S. *Victorian Murderesses: A True History of Thirteen Respectable French and English Women Accused of Unspeakable Crimes.* New York: Schocken Books, 1967.

Hause, Steven C., and Anne R. Kenney. "The Limits of Suffragist Behavior: Legalism and Militancy in France, 1876–1922." *American Historical Review* 86 (October 1981):781–806.

Havel, J. E. *La Condition de la femme.* Paris: Librairie Armand Colin, 1961.

Hedman, Edwin Randolph. "Early French Feminism: From the Eighteenth Century to 1848." Ph.d. dissertation, New York University, 1954.

Heinsohn, Gunnar, and Otto Steiger. "The Elimination of Medieval Birth Control and the Witch Trials of Modern Times," *International Journal of Women's Studies* 5 (May–June 1982):193–214.

Hellerstein, Erna Olafson. "Women, Social Order, and the City: Rules for French Ladies, 1830–1870." Ph.D. dissertation, University of California, Berkeley, 1980.

Hellerstein, Erna Olafson, Leslie Parker Hume, and Karen Offen, eds. *Victorian Women: A Documentary Acccount of Women's Lives in Nineteenth-Century England, France, and the United States.* Stanford: Stanford University Press, 1981.

Herlihy, David. "Land, Family, and Women in Continental Europe." *Traditio* 18 (1962):89–120.

Hoffman, Stanley, ed. *In Search of France.* New York: Harper & Row, 1965.
See Jesse R. Pitts, "Continuity and Change in Bourgeois France."

Horvath, Sandra. "Victor Duruy and the Controversy over Secondary Education for Girls." *French Historical Studies* 9 (Spring 1975):83–104.

Hufton, Olwen. "Women and the Family Economy in Eighteenth-Century France." *French Historical Studies* 9 (Spring 1975):1–22.

Hunt, Persis. "Feminism and Anticlericalism under the Commune." *Massachusetts Review* 12 (Summer 1971):418–31.

Kanipe, Esther Sue. "The Family, Private Property, and the State in France, 1870–1914." Ph.D. dissertation, University of Wisconsin, 1976.

Kelly-Gadol, Joan. "Did Women Have a Renaissance? " In *Becoming Visible: Women in European History.* Edited by Renate Bridenthal and Claudia Koonz. Boston: Houghton Mifflin, 1977. Pp. 137–64.

———. "The Social Relation of the Sexes: Methodological Implications of Women's History." *Signs* 1 (Summer 1976):809–23.

Kraditor, Aileen S. *The Ideas of the Woman Suffrage Movement, 1890–1920.* New York: Columbia University Press, 1965.

Lacour, Léopold. *Les Origines du féminisme contemporain: Trois femmes de la révolution: Olympe de Gouges, Théroigne de Méricourt, Rose Lacombe.* Paris: Honoré Champion, 1912.

Lebois, André. *Le Dossier "tue-la!"* Avignon: Edouard Aubanel, 1969.
Reprints of Alexandre Dumas fils's *L'Homme-femme, réponse à M. Henri d'Ideville* and Emile de Girardin's *La Réplique de Girardin: L'Homme et la femme.*

Lebrun, François. *La Vie conjugale sous l'ancien régime.* Paris: Armand Colin, 1975.

Lefèvre, G. "Poullain de la Barre et le féminisme au XVIIᵉ siècle." *Revue pédagogique* 64 (February 1914):101–13.

Léonard, Jacques. *La France médicale au XIXᵉ siècle.* Paris: Gallimard/Juillard, 1978.

Leroy, Maxime. *Histoire des idees sociales en France.* 3 vols. Paris: Gallimard, 1950.

Lévi-Strauss, Claude. *Structural Anthropology.* Translated by Claire Jacobson and Brooke Grundtest Schoept. London: Penguin Press, 1968.

Levy, Darline Gay, Harriet Branson Applewhite, and Mary Durham Johnson. *Women in Revolutionary Paris, 1789–1795: Selected Documents with Notes and Commentary.* Urbana: University of Illinois Press, 1979.

Li Dzeh-djen. *La Presse féministe en France de 1869 à 1914.* Paris: Librairie L. Rodstein, 1934.

Li Mon. *Le Divorce en France.* Paris: Les Editions Domat-Mont Chrestien, 1936.

Lichtheim, George. *The Origins of Socialism*. New York: Frederick A. Praeger, 1969.

Lloyd, Trevor. *Suffragettes International: The World-Wide Campaign for Women's Rights*. New York: American Heritage, 1971.

Lougee, Carolyn C. "Feminism and Social Stratification in France." Ph.D. dissertation, University of Michigan, 1972.

———. *Le Paradis des femmes: Women, Salons, and Social Stratification in Seventeenth-Century France*. Princeton: Princeton University Press, 1976.

Lytle, Scott H. "The Second Sex (September 1793)." *Journal of Modern History* 27 (March 1955):14–26.

McBride, Theresa. *The Domestic Revolution: The Modernization of Household Service in England and France, 1820–1920*. New York: Holmes & Meier, 1976.

———. "A Woman's World: Department Stores and the Evolution of Women's Employment." *French Historical Studies* 10 (Fall 1978):664–83.

McLaren, Angus. "Abortion in France: Women and the Regulation of Family Size, 1800–1914." *French Historical Studies* 10 (Spring 1978):461–85.

———. "Doctor in the House: Medicine and Private Morality in France, 1800–1850." *Feminist Studies* 2 (1975):39–45.

———. "Sex and Socialism: The Opposition of the French Left to Birth Control in the Nineteenth Century." *Journal of the History of Ideas* 27 (1976):475–92.

———. "Some Secular Attitudes toward Sexual Behavior in France: 1760–1860." *French Historical Studies* 8 (Fall 1974):604–25.

McMillan, James C. *Housewife or Harlot: The Place of Women in French Society, 1870–1940*. New York: St. Martin's Press, 1981.

Maitron, Jean, ed. *Dictionnaire biographique du mouvement ouvrier français*. 10 vols. Paris: Les Editions Ouvrières, 1968.

Manuel, Frank. *The Prophets of Paris*. New York: Harper & Row, 1965.

Marks, Elaine, and Isabelle de Courtivron, eds. *New French Feminisms: An Anthology*. Amherst: University of Massachusetts Press, 1980.

Mayeur, Françoise. *L'Education des filles en France au XIXᵉ siècle*. Paris: Hachette, 1979.

———. *L'Enseignement secondaire des jeunes filles sous la Troisième Republique*. Paris: A. Colin, 1977.

Mead, Margaret. *Male and Female*. New York: William Morrow & Co., 1975.

———. *Sex and Temperament*. New York: William Morrow & Co., 1963.

Merriman, John M. *The Agony of the Republic: The Repression of the Left in Revolutionary France, 1848–1851*. New Haven: Yale University Press, 1978.

———, ed., *1830 in France*. New York: Franklin Watts, 1975.

Millet, Kate. *Sexual Politics*. New York: Doubleday & Co., 1970.

Mitchell, Juliet. *Psychoanalysis and Feminism*. New York: Vintage Books, 1975.

———. *Woman's Estate*. 1971. Reprint. New York: Vintage Books, 1973.

Moon, S. Joan. "The Saint-Simoniennes and the Moral Revolution." *Proceedings of the Consortium on Revolutionary Europe* (1976):162–74.

———. "The Saint-Simonian Association of Working-Class Women, 1830–50." *Proceedings of the Fifth Annual Meeting of the Western Society for French History, Las Cruces, New Mexico*, pp. 274–81. Santa Barbara, Calif., 1978.

Morcos, Saad. *Juliette Adam*. Beirut: Dar al-Maaref-Liban, 1962.

Moses, Claire Goldberg. "The Evolution of Feminist Thought in France, 1829–1889." Ph.D. dissertation, George Washington University, 1978.

————. "Saint-Simonian Men/Saint-Simonian Women: The Transformation of Feminist Thought in 1830s' France." *Journal of Modern History* 54 (June 1982):240–67.

Moss, Bernard H. *The Origins of the French Labor Movement, 1830–1914: The Socialism of Skilled Workers.* Berkeley and Los Angeles: University of California Press, 1976.

Nancel-Pénard, Paule. *L'Evolution de la jurisprudence relativement à la femme depuis 1804.* Bordeaux: Thèse pour le doctorat, 1940.

Noland, Aaron. *The Founding of the French Socialist Party.* New York: Howard Fertig, 1970.

O'Faolain, Julia, and Lauro Martines, eds. *Not in God's Image.* New York: Harper & Row, 1973.
    A collection of documents. Includes Mme de Sévigné's letters to her daughter.

Offen, Karen. "A Feminist Challenge to the Third Republic's Public Education for Girls: The Campaign for Equal Access to the Baccalauréat, 1880–1924." Paper presented at the Annual Meeting of the American Historical Association, December 1973.

————. "Introduction: Aspects of the Woman Question during the Third Republic." *Third Republic/Troisième Republique,* nos. 3–4 (Spring–Fall 1977):1–19.

————. "The 'Woman Question' as a Social Issue in Nineteenth-Century France: A Bibliographical Essay." *Third Republic/Troisième Republique,* nos. 3–4 (Spring–Fall 1977):238–99.

————. "The 'Woman Question' as a Social Issue in Republican France before 1914." Unpublished manuscript, Woodside, Calif., 1973.

O'Neill, William. "Feminism as a Radical Ideology." In *Dissent: Explorations in the History of American Radicalism.* Edited by Alfred Young. DeKalb, Ill.: Northern Illinois University Press, 1968. Pp. 273–300.

Parish, William, Jr., and Moshe Schwartz. "Household Complexity in Nineteenth Century France." *American Sociological Review* 37 (April 1972):154–73.

Perrot, Michelle. "L'Eloge de la ménagère dans le discours des ouvriers français au XIXe siècle." *Romantisme,* nos. 13–14 (1976):105–21.

Picard, Roger. *Le Romantisme social.* New York: Brentano's, 1944.

Pich, Edgard. "Littérature et codes sociaux: L'antiféminisme sous le Second Empire." *Romantisme,* nos. 13–14 (1976):167–82.

Pinkney, David. *The French Revolution of 1830.* Princeton: Princeton University Press, 1972.

Ponteil, Félix. *Histoire de l'enseignement: 1789–1965.* Paris: Sirey, 1966.

Pope, Barbara Corrado. "Maternal Education in France." Paper presented to the Western Society for French History, December 1975.

Prost, Antoine. *L'Enseignement en France, 1800–1967.* Paris: A. Colin, 1968.

Puech, Jules. *Le Proudhonisme dans l'association internationale des travailleurs.* Paris: Félix Alcan, 1907.

————. *La Vie et l'oeuvre de Flora Tristan, 1803–1844.* Paris: Librairie Marcel Rivière et Cie, 1925.

Puech, Marie-Louise. "Une supercherie littéraire: Le véritable rédacteur de la *Gazette des Femmes* (1836–1838)." *La Révolution de 1848* 32 (June–August 1935):303–12.

Price, Roger, ed. *Revolution and Reaction: 1848 and the Second French Republic.* London: Croom Helm, 1975.

Rabaut, Jean. *Histoire des féminismes français.* Paris: Editions Stock, 1978.

Racz, Elizabeth. "The Women's Rights Movement in the French Revolution." *Science and Society* 16 (1952):151–74.

Ranum, Orest, and Patricia Ranum, eds. *Popular Attitudes towards Birth Control in Pre-industrial France and England.* New York: Harper & Row, 1972.
    See especially two essays by Aries, "On the Origins of Contraception in France" and "An Interpretation to be Used for a History of Mentalities"; and Riquet, "Christianity and Population."

Ranvier, Adrien. "Une féministe de 1848: Jeanne Deroin." *La Révolution de 1848* 4 (1907–8):317–55, 421–30, 480–98.

Ratcliffe, Barrie. "Saint-Simonism and Messianism: The Case of Gustave d'Eichthal." *French Historical Studies* 9 (Spring 1976):484–502.

Rebérioux, Madeleine, Christiane Dufrancatel, and Béatrice Slama. "Hubertine Auclert et la question des femmes à 'l'immortel congrès' (1879)." *Romantisme,* nos. 13–14 (1976):123–42.

Reclus, Maurice. *Emile de Girardin.* Paris: Librairie Hachette, 1934.

Riasanovsky, Nicholas. *The Teaching of Charles Fourier.* Berkeley and Los Angeles: University of California Press, 1969.

Rich, Adrienne. *Of Woman Born: Motherhood as Experience and Institution.* New York: W. W. Norton, 1976.

Richardson, Lula McDowell. *The Forerunners of Feminism in French Literature of the Renaissance from Christine of Pisa to Marie de Gournay.* Baltimore: Johns Hopkins University Press, 1929.

Robertson, Priscilla. *An Experience of Women: Pattern and Change in Nineteenth-Century Europe.* Philadelphia: Temple University Press, 1982.

Rosaldo, Michelle Zimbalist, and Louise Lamphere, eds. *Woman, Culture, and Society.* Stanford: Stanford University Press, 1974.

Roussey, le Docteur B. *Education domestique de la femme et rénovation sociale.* Paris: Librairie Delagrave, 1914.

Rover, Constance. *Love, Morals, and the Feminists.* London: Routledge & Kegan Paul, 1970.

Rowbotham, Sheila. *Women, Resistance, and Revolution.* New York: Vintage Books, 1972.

Schirmacher, Kaethe. *The Modern Woman's Rights Movement.* Translated by Conrad Eckhardt. New York: Macmillan, 1912.

Serbonnes, Mlle de. *Evolution de rôle social de la femme.* Paris: Thèse Sciences Politiques, 1939.

Schiff, Maria. *Le Fille d'alliance de Montaigne, Marie de Gournay.* Paris: Honoré Champion, 1910.

Scott, Joan W. "Men and Women in the Parisian Garment Trades: Discussions of Family and Work in the 1830s and 1840s." Forthcoming in Roderick Floud, Geoffrey Crossick, and Pat Thone, eds., *The Power of the Past: Essays in Honor of Eric Hobsbawn,* Cambridge: Cambridge University Press, 1984.

Scott, Joan, and Louise Tilly. "Women's Work and the Family in Nineteenth-Century Europe." *Comparative Studies in Society and History* 17 (1975):36–64.

Shorter, Edward. "Female Emancipation, Birth Control, and Fertility." *American Historical Review* 78 (1973):605–40.

———. "Illegitimacy, Sexual Revolution, and Social Change in Modern Europe." *Journal of Interdisciplinary History* 2 (1971):237–72.

———. *The Making of the Modern Family.* New York: Basic Books, 1975.

Smith, Bonnie G. *Ladies of the Leisure Class: The Bourgeoises of Northern France in the Nineteenth Century.* Princeton: Princeton University Press, 1981.